CW00666652

ROAD TRIPS
GERMANY

ROAD TRIPS
GERMANY

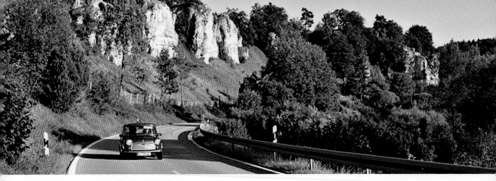

Above Driving along limestone cliffs, Altmuhl Valley, Bavaria

CONTENTS

Front cover: Sylvensteinspeicher in summer,
Sylvensteinsee, Bavaria

Above The Cathedral of Limburg overlooking the river Lahn in Limburg, Hesse

Above Colourful paintings on a shop's façade in Landshut, Bavaria

The rapid rate at which the world is changing is constantly keeping the DK Eyewitness team on our toes. While we've worked hard to ensure that this edition of Road Trips Germany is accurate and up-to-date, we know that opening hours alter, standards shift, prices fluctuate, places close and new ones pop up in their stead. So, if you notice we've got something wrong or left something out, we want to hear about it. Please get in touch at travelguides@dk.com

ABOUT THIS BOOK

Located in the heart of Europe, Germany offers its visitors a diverse experience. Historic monuments, evocative landscapes, scenic towns and romantic medieval cities await those driving through this fascinating country. From the green marshes and pristine sandy coasts of the north to the mountainous and wooded regions of the south, the 24 leisurely trips in this book take you on a trip through a hospitable country while showing charming, lesser-known places off the beaten track.

The delightful landscape ranges from the windy Baltic Coast to the remote valleys of the Black Forest and from rolling green pastures to dramatic mountain peaks. Travellers will discover reminders of Germany's riveting past, delve into the alluring multicultural life of its cities, enjoy fine traditional cuisine and marvel at the country's beautiful natural vistas. Expect delightful surprises around every bend, packed with the sights, sounds and flavours of the real Germany.

Getting Started
The front section of the guide provides all the practical information needed to plan and enjoy a driving holiday in Germany. It includes an overview of when to go and how to get there, advice on bringing your own vehicle or renting one and details of any documentation required. The motoring advice ranges from driving rules to road conditions, buying petrol to break-down or accident procedures – the kind of background knowledge that will help to make driving stress-free. There is information on money, opening hours, communications, health and safety and other practical matters, as well as advice on accom-modation and dining options, to ensure that you experience the very best of Germany's hospitality. A language section at the back lists essential words and phrases, including key driving-related vocabulary.

The Trips
The main touring section of the guide is divided into 24 scenic trips, ranging in duration from one to six days. All the tours can be undertaken in a standard vehicle, and no special driving skills are required. Each trip

begins with a list of highlights and a clearly mapped itinerary. There is useful advice on the best time of year to do the trip, road conditions, market days and major festival dates. The tour pages contain detailed descriptions of each stop on the route, linked by clear driving instructions. Side panels highlight information on the most authentic places to stay and eat. Tinted boxes feature background information and interesting anecdotes.

Each trip features at least one mapped town or countryside walking tour, designed to take a maximum of two hours at a gentle pace with stops along the way.

The tours are flexible: they can be linked to create a longer driving holiday; others can be shortened into day trips while based in a region.

Using the Sheet Map
A pull-out road map of the entire country is attached at the back of this guide. This map contains all the information you need to drive around Germany and to navigate between the tours. All motorways, major roads, airports – both domestic and international – plus ferry ports are clearly identified. This makes the pull-out map an excellent addition to the trip itinerary maps within the book. The pull-out map also has a comprehensive index for easy location of sights. The map is further supplemented by a clear distance chart so you can gauge the distances between the major cities.

Top left Outdoor café, Oberammergau, Bavaria **Top right** Imposing Burg Hohenzollern, Baden-Württemberg **Centre left** Lake Titisee, Baden-Württemberg **Centre right** Back road to Immenstadt, Bavaria **Below left** Half-timbered houses, Tangermünde, Saxony-Anhalt **Below right** Sandy beach, Sylt, Schleswig-Holstein

Above Roadside viewpoint looking towards the Willibaldsburg, Eichstätt, Bavaria

INTRODUCING GERMANY

Germany is a country of marked contrasts and this is nowhere more apparent than in its geographic diversity. Modern cities of glass and steel sit only a few minutes away from thickly wooded forests dotted with romantic castles. Germany's combination of multicultural cities, historic architecture and charming medieval villages set in breathtakingly beautiful country-side make it an ideal holiday destination. The country's main road network is extensive and well maintained, but it is the smaller roads that lead into the heart of the region. Here, through castles, villages and magnificent palaces, Germany's rich history is waiting to be discovered. Take a break to sample some exceptional wines – the most famous vineyards are in the western part of the country, especially the Pfalz and Rheinhessen regions – or take time to admire the natural landscape, from the stunning beauty of the German Alps to the myriad glacial lakes in the Müritz Nationalpark.

When to Go

The itinerary for each of the trips suggests the best times of the year to make the trip, based on the region. Visits to cities and historic buildings are best made in the spring or early autumn, as it can get very hot in summer. However, July and August are the ideal months for a vacation by the sea or one of the numerous lakes. Winter offers skiing in the Alps, southern Germany, the Black Forest or the Harz Mountains. The country also hosts numerous events throughout the year, which makes a visit worthwhile during any season. In autumn, visitors can participate in traditional folk-loric festivals such as Freimarkt in Bremen, which is held in mid-October. In December, festive Christmas markets are held all over the country. They are parti-cularly charming in southern German cities with historic town centres and are good places to pick up souvenirs and presents.

Times to Avoid

In late July and August, it can get rather hot, especially in the southwestern regions. The busiest period is during the school holidays, which see a great surge in traffic levels. These are set independently in each state and take place in early April (Easter holidays), July and August (summer holidays) and October (autumn holidays). Roads can get particularly busy around Easter and national public holidays. To enjoy a stress-free trip, it is best to avoid driving at these times of the year. A visit to northern and eastern Germany between November and late February can be unpleasant due to harsh winter winds and low temperatures. Ice, rain and sleet make it challenging to drive and sightseeing difficult.

Festivals

Nearly every town and village hosts a parade, street shows, concerts and fairs. These include folk festivals connected to local traditions, such as the asparagus or grape harvest. In April and May, the first spring fairs are held. It is also time for the solemn observance of Easter. In June, a number of classical music events take place and July is a popular month for lively wine and beer festivals. January and February are the Carnival season, while December is synonymous with Christmas celebrations.

National Public Holidays

New Year's Day (1 Jan)
Good Friday, Easter Sunday and Monday (Apr)
Labour Day (1 May)
Ascension Day (May)
Whit Monday (May/Jun)
German Unity Day (3 Oct)
Christmas (25/26 Dec)
Additional public holidays are held in most states.

Left Panoramic view of Berchtesgaden from Hochlenzer in the German Alps

Above Half-timbered buildings, Limburg an der Lahn, Hesse

GETTING TO GERMANY

A popular destination, Germany is well connected to the rest of the world. Every large city in the country has an airport, most of which offer international flights. The increase in the number of low-cost flights has made it much easier to travel to Germany from various European cities. Travellers from outside Europe may find it cheaper to fly via London to take advantage of the many budget flights available from the UK. All the major US airlines also operate regular flights to Germany. Car rental services are well established at all the big airports in the country.

Above The sleek Lufthansa Airbus airplane at Munich Airport

DIRECTORY

ARRIVING BY AIR

Air Canada
00800 669 922 22;
www.aircanada.com

British Airways
04215 57 57 58;
www.britishairways.com

Delta Airlines
069-299 937 71;
www.delta.com

EasyJet
www.easyjet.com

Eurowings
+49 221 599 882 22;
www.eurowings.com

Lufthansa
069 86 799 799;
www.lufthansa.com

Qantas
06929 957 14 21;
www.qantas.com

Ryanair
www.ryanair.com

United Airlines
06950 98 50 51;
www.united.com

Arriving by Air

Germany's most important airports are **Frankfurt am Main**, **Munich** and **Düsseldorf**, from where connecting flights can be made to other German cities. If coming from outside Europe, visitors are most likely to arrive at one of these major airports.

The largest German airports are Frankfurt am Main and Munich. The gigantic airport in Frankfurt comprises two huge terminals, which are connected by a fast overground railway. The airport in Munich is somewhat smaller, but still very popular. Among the rest, the busiest are Düsseldorf, Cologne-Bonn and Berlin. Most airports are 20–40 km (12–25 miles) outside the nearest city and connected to the centre by local transport or Autobahn. International hubs such as Frankfurt, Munich and Düsseldorf offer long-distance train connections.

Germany's national carrier is **Lufthansa**, which operates regular, scheduled flights to destinations all around the world. **British Airways** offers regular, scheduled flights from London (Heathrow and Gatwick) to major German destinations as well as from several regional airports in the UK. Germany and the US are well connected through direct flights from major US cities such as New York, Washington DC, Boston, Chicago, San Francisco and Los Angeles. **Air Canada** operates daily flights from Canadian hubs to Frankfurt and Munich in arrangement with Lufthansa. Other carriers that offer flights to Germany are **Delta Airlines**, **Qantas** and **United Airlines**. Travelling to Germany by air and then renting a pre-booked car is certainly the best option for tourists from North America, South Africa, New Zealand and Australia.

In addition to Lufthansa, budget airlines including **EasyJet**, **Ryanair** and **Eurowings** provide many links within and to Germany. These airlines offer cheaper fares than Lufthansa and use small airports as well as major ones.

Arriving by Sea

There are ferry ports in many coastal cities, including Kiel, Lübeck, Rostock, Travemunde and Sassnitz. The major operators are **DFDS Seaways**, **Scandlines**, **Stena Line** and **Color Line**. Visitors travelling to Germany by car from the UK will first have to decide which ferry crossing to use (unless using the Eurotunnel). The shortest crossings are from Dover to Ostende in Belgium, or to Calais, in France. However, these will also require a fairly lengthy road trip. The Holland route of Harwich to Hook is useful for those starting their trip in Germany's northern region. Travellers coming from Ireland should first connect with a ferry service from Dublin to England or France before taking one of the options mentioned above. The latest provision to make a journey from the UK to mainland Europe by car is by using the Eurotunnel from Folkestone to Calais. The car is carried by train in just 35 mintues.

Arriving by Rail

Long-distance trains called EuroCity (EC) or InterCity Express (ICE) trains connect all important German cities with major European destinations. There are also overnight trains (Nightjet) from various European cities such as Amsterdam, Brussels, Budapest, Paris, Rome, Venice and Vienna. **Eurostar's** high-speed passenger service also offers many options for travelling by train.

The **Deutsche Bahn**, Germany's national railway company, operates highly modern, high-speed trains, the InterCity Express (ICE). The long-distance ICE network connects all the major cities in Germany. However, ticket rates in the express trains can be expensive; book well in advance for lower prices. Seat reservations are recommended during the tourist season and public holidays.

Train tickets can be bought and reservations made through travel agents or at the railway station at the *Reisezentrum*, which also acts as an information centre. Tickets can also be reserved by telephone or through the Internet, where a detailed timetable can be viewed to plan an itinerary. **Eurail Passes**, such as the Eurail Global Pass, which allows unlimited travel in 33 countries, are also a good option.

Arriving by Coach

Travelling to Germany by coach is not a very enjoyable experience, as the distances are often long and fares not cheap when compared with low-cost airlines. **Flixbus** and **Eurolines** are the providers of international coach services to Germany.

Most towns have a bus station located in the town centre called ZOB (*Zentraler Omnibus Bahnhof*), where timetables can be obtained and tickets purchased. It is best to enquire at the tourist information centre for travel details.

Below far left Airport display board showing destinations and timings, Frankfurt **Below left** Ferry transporting vehicles, Konstanz **Below centre** The InterCity Express on the Mannheim-Stuttgart line **Below** Euroline ticket counter, Berlin

PRACTICAL INFORMATION

Germany is a country that is particularly well prepared to receive visitors. Public services operate smoothly and efficiently, and the health system is good. Every town, large and small, has a tourist information centre that can offer guidance on finding accommodation and information about local restaurants, attractions and activities. Germany is a safe country to travel in and its police are highly trained to deal with any emergency. Communication networks are good and almost all banks have ATMs.

Above Police patrol van

Passports and Visas

Citizens of EU member states, the UK, the US, Canada, Australia and New Zealand do not need a visa to visit Germany as long as their stay does not exceed three months. However, visitors from South Africa do need a visa. Nationals from most other countries require a Schengen Visa, named for the 1995 Schengen Agreement that abolished passport controls between 26 EU countries including Germany and all its neighbours. This visa is valid for stays of up to 90 days. Visitors should check with the German embassy or consulate in their own country prior to travelling or visit the **Federal Foreign Office** website and search for "visa agreements".

Most embassies, including those of the US and the UK, are located in Berlin but consulates can be found in other major cities.

Government Advice

Now more than ever, it is important to consult both your and the German government's advice before travelling. The **UK Foreign and Commonwealth Office**, **US State Department**, **Australian Department of Foreign Affairs** and the **Trade and the German**

Federal Foreign Office offer the latest information on security, health and local regulations.

Travel Insurance

All travellers are advised to take out travel insurance that offers cover for a broad range of possible emergencies. All foreign visitors need to have a medical insurance policy with sufficient protection.

In addition to medical insurance, a comprehensive policy will normally cover the holder for loss or theft of luggage and other belongings, such as passports and money, damage or injury to a third party, personal accidents and delayed or cancelled flights.

Health

Germany poses no serious health hazards for visitors and no specific inoculations are required before entering the country. For information regarding COVID-19 vaccination, follow government advice. Those who require prescribed medication should ensure that they take enough to cover their stay, as it may not be available locally.

Visitors are eligible for free emergency medical care in Germany provided they have a valid European Health Insurance

Card (EHIC) or UK Global Health Insurance Card (GHIC). Both GHIC and EHIC are a great help in emergencies, but do not cover all kinds of treatments and some may have to be paid for up front, leaving you to reclaim the money later. Non-EU travellers should have full medical cover in their travel insurance, and when necessary use public or private hospitals on a paying basis.

To call an **ambulance** in an emergency, dial 112. Pharmacies (*Apotheke*) can be identified by a sign bearing a large red "A". They are usually open from 8am to 6pm and also have a list of doctors in the area.

Personal Security

Germany is a very safe destination to visit, with low crime rates. As always, though, it's recommended that you stay alert to your surroundings and take the usual precautions with your belongings. Pickpockets are known to operate in busy tourist areas, particularly on public transport.

If you do have anything stolen, report the crime as soon as possible at the nearest police station. To telephone the **police** in an emergency, dial 110; for the **fire brigade**, dial 112. Get a copy of the crime report in order to make a claim on your

Above European Union passports **Above centre** Ambulance **Above right** Pharmacy building, Konstanz, Baden-Württemberg

insurance. Contact your embassy or consulate immediately if your passport is stolen or in the event of a serious crime or accident.

Germans are generally accepting of all people, regardless of their race, gender or sexuality. Although long celebrated as a liberal and tolerant country, homosexuality was only officially legalized in Germany in 1994. Despite all the freedoms that the LGBTQ+ community enjoy, acceptance is not always a given. If you do at any point feel unsafe, the **Safe Space Alliance** pinpoints your nearest place of refuge. In Berlin the **Maneo** emergency hotline run by **Mann-O-Meter** supports victims of homophobic behaviour, while **Lesbenberatung** is a lesbian-safe space that offers help and advice for women, girls and transgender people.

Travellers with Specific Requirements
Germany is well prepared to receive travellers with specific needs. Most public transport, tourist sights and accommodation facilities cater for those with mobility issues. Large museums and historic monuments have special ramps or lifts for people who are confined to wheelchairs. Offices and banks are also wheelchair-

friendly, and there are lifts at railway and underground stations. Many hotels, especially the higher grades, offer suitably equipped bedrooms. Contact **NatKo** for further information.

To make it easier for visitors with specific requirements, the **Tourism for All** project reviews and certifies places of tourist interest with accessibility. Many cities have guidance systems and walking indicators, while some museums offer tactile tours to assist the visually impaired. Audio induction loops are widely used in churches, concert halls and information centres to make venues and events accessible for visitors with hearing difficulties.

Language
German is the main language used in Germany, though many people also speak English, particularly in larger cities and in places frequented by tourists. Accents and dialects in Germany vary tremendously between regions and can at times be stronger in certain areas (Bavarian, Schwabian, Frisian and Saxon dialects are particularly challenging).

Below far left Pharmacy shop, Zwickau, Saxony **Below left** Cyclists in Baden-Württemberg **Below centre** Fire brigade, Berlin **Below** Tourist centre, Neustadt an der Weinstrasse, Rhineland-Palatinate

Mobile Phones, Wi-Fi and Postal Services

Postal and telecommunications services are very well developed in Germany. German phone numbers have area codes up to six digits long, beginning with 0 followed by a local number of five to nine digits, depending on the region. When dialling within the country, use the full area code.

Public telephones are serviced by Deutsche Telekom. Some accept coins, others require credit cards, or phonecards, which can be purchased at post offices. It is useful to have a mobile phone when travelling in Germany as public phones are increasingly scarce. Travellers should discuss their requirements with their domestic network provider beforehand. Many visitors travelling to Germany with EU tariffs will be able to use their devices without being affected by data roaming charges; instead they will be charged the same rates for data, SMS and voice calls as they pay at home. Visitors from outside the EU can buy a local SIM card that they can use in an inlocked mobile phone to avoid having to pay roaming charges.

Deutsche Post operates most postal services in Germany. Post offices are usually open Monday to Friday from 8am to 6pm and 8am to noon on Saturdays. Many hotels, restaurants and cafés provide Wi-Fi access to their customers.

Banks and Money

The Euro (€) has been Germany's currency since 2002. There are seven denominations of Euro banknote: the grey €5, the pink €10, the blue €20, the orange €50, the green €100, the yellow €200 and the purple €500. There are eight coins: €2 and €1, 50 cents, 20 cents, 10 cents, 5, 2 and 1 cents. The 2- and 1-Euro coins, are both silver and gold in colour. The 50-, 20- and 10-cent coins are gold. The 5-, 2- and 1-cent coins are bronze.

ATM machines can be found all over the country, but it is best to check with your bank or credit card company for fees. Travellers can change foreign currency at a bank or at exchange bureaus called *Wechselstuben*. There are no restrictions on the amount of foreign currency that can be brought into Germany. When changing cash, a commission may be charged for the transaction. It is best to check this before undertaking an exchange.

Most banks are open Monday to Friday from 9am to 3:30 pm with a lunch break from noon to 1pm. However, in larger cities they may keep longer opening hours. Exchange bureaus are located at airports and train stations as well as at many places that are frequented by tourists. It is advisable to take advantage of the services of the ReiseBank, which has branches at airports and railway stations. It is still possible to use travellers' cheques when travelling in Germany, even though taking money out at ATMs is more popular. One can cash cheques at banks and exchange bureaus.

Major credit, debit and prepaid currency cards are accepted in most shops and establishments.

Above Old clock face on half-timbered building, Limburg an der Lahn, Hesse

Contactless payments have become the norm since the COVID-19 pandemic, though they are not generally used on public transport. It is always worth carrying cash, as some smaller businesses don't accept cards.

Tourist Information

A very well-developed network of tourist information centres exists in Germany. These are usually run by the city or regional tourist authority and can be found all over the country. Tourist information centres have different names in Germany, such as *Touristeninformation*, *Fremdenverkehrsamt* or *Fremdenverkehrszentrale*. They provide information on opening hours of monuments and museums, accommodation, organized excursions and city tours. They also sell or give away useful material about city attractions, such as guidebooks, maps and postcards and may be able to find and book a hotel room. The website of **German National Tourist Office** is also a useful

Sign for Photography Museum, Deidesheim

Above Old-fashioned telephone booth **Above centre** Posters advertising events **Above right** Street vending machine for telephone cards

source of travel information. Many cities also sell a Welcome Card, which allows the user 2–5 days' free use of public transport and discounted access to museums.

Opening Hours

The opening hours of shops, offices and other businesses depend to a great extent on the size of the town. In larger cities, the usual office opening hours are Monday to Saturday from 9am to 6pm. Supermarkets and other shops often have longer opening hours (mostly until 8pm). In smaller towns, however, nothing tends to open until 10am. Shops everywhere are usually closed on Sundays. Museums and historic monuments are also usually open from 9am to 6pm. However, some places might be closed on a particular day, often Monday, so check opening hours before arranging a visit.

> **COVID-19** Increased rates of infection may result in temporary opening hours and/or closures. Always check ahead before visiting museums, attractions and hospitality venues.

Time

Germany uses Central European Time, which is GMT plus one hour. There is Daylight Saving Time between the end of March and the end of October, when the clocks move forward one hour on the last Sunday in March and back on the last Sunday in October.

Electricity

Germany's electrical system provides 220V, except in some hotel bathrooms, where a lower current is provided as a standard safety measure. UK 220V appliances can be plugged into German sockets with an adaptor. However, US 110V appliances will need a transformer.

Smoking in Public

Due to the federal system of government, the law on smoking in Germany varies from state to state. However, smoking is completely banned on public transport and in hospitals, airports, public and federal buildings, including the Parliament. However, there are differences between the German states when it comes to smoking in bars and restaurants. In some places, such as small pubs and bars, or during late hours, the ban is not observed at all.

DIRECTORY

MOBILE PHONES, WI-FI AND POSTAL SERVICES

International Access Codes
Australia: 0061

Ireland: 00353

UK: 0044

US and Canada: 001

TOURIST INFORMATION

German National Tourist Office
Beethovenstrasse 69, 60325 Frankfurt; 069 97 46 40; www.germany.travel

Below far left Information centre, Landshut, Bavaria **Below left** One of the many banks in Germany **Below centre** Notice board outside Rieskrater Museum, Nördlingen, Bavaria **Below centre right** Signpost along the road to Bad Harzburg, Lower Saxony **Below** Tourist information office in Würzburg, Bavaria

DRIVING IN GERMANY

Driving is one of the best ways to explore Germany. The road conditions are among the best in the world and a well-developed network of Autobahns (motorways) and major roads allows access to almost every corner of the country. However, it is the scenic drives away from the urban centres, through Germany's beautiful landscapes, that provide a unique experience. To make the most of your trip, it is best to know the basics of driving in Germany before setting off.

Above Driving along limestone cliffs, Altmuhl Valley, Bavaria

Insurance and Breakdown Cover

If you are travelling in your own vehicle, make sure that your insurance is valid in Germany, so that in the event of an accident any damage will be covered. When renting a car, insurance is usually included in the rate. However, you should check the details of the rental company's policy. Most UK motoring services such as the **Automobile Association (AA)** and **Royal Automobile Club (RAC)**, offer insurance for assistance, breakdown and recovery in Germany. European breakdown and repatriation cover is also available with the **Allgemeiner Deutscher Automobil Club (ADAC)**.

What to Take

In order to drive in Germany, EU drivers must hold a valid driving licence and carry the registration documents and insurance policy for the vehicle. Driving licences from America and Australia are recognized in Germany. However, citizens of some non-European countries should carry an International Driving Permit. Several agencies are authorized to issue the permit, including the automobile association of the driver's home country.

Seat belts are compulsory in Germany, and there must be a warning triangle and a high-visibility jacket in the car, in case of a breakdown. Also, every registered vehicle must carry a first-aid kit that includes disposable surgical gloves and a thermal blanket. If you rent a car, make sure that such a kit is provided with the car.

Road Systems

Germany is famous for the Autobahn – a well-developed network of toll-free motorways. The prefix "A" on a blue sign indicates the Autobahn. Besides the motorways, there are well-maintained major roads (*Bundesstrasse*), which can be distinguished by the prefix "B" on a yellow sign.

Speed Limits and Fines

There is no specific speed limit for driving on the Autobahn, although many sections have recommended speeds of 100–130 kph (62–81 mph). On major roads, the speed limit is 100 kph (62 mph), and inside a city and in built-up areas, it is 50 kph (31 mph). There are mobile speed cameras and radars (quite often at construction sites) and heavy fines may be imposed if you exceed these speed limits. As a rule, the most severe fines, including the possible revoking of a driving licence, begin at exceeding 20 kph (12 mph) over the speed limit. Fines can also be incurred for tailgating and parking in prohibited areas. In both cases, your car hire company will bill you for any ticket that is sent to them, along with an administration fee.

Do not drink and drive. The law is stringent and penalties high. The legal limit is 0.5 mg, but if you are stopped for another traffic offence, the limit drops to 0.3 mg. The police can impose a fine on the spot. It is also illegal to use a mobile phone while driving. This also applies if the car is standing but the engine is running. If caught, drivers will be fined €60. However, Bluetooth headsets are allowed.

Rules of the Road

Driving is on the right in Germany and seat belts must be worn at all times by the driver and all passengers, front seat and back. Knowing the general rules of the road is important. Be aware that overtaking other cars is only

Above Deer and cow crossing sign **Above centre** Motorway to Limburg an der Lahn, Hesse **Above right** Sign for the Romantic Road, Southern Germany

allowed in the left lane. Under no circumstances should you ever overtake on the right lane. If there is no sign indicating otherwise, there is a strict *rechts vor links* rule, meaning that a car or any other vehicle coming from a street on your right has the right of way.

Germans often drive very fast and quite aggressively. In the event of an accident on the motorway, or if a traffic jam necessitates an abrupt reduction in speed, drivers should turn on their flashing emergency lights to warn other drivers.

Distances are indicated in kilometres. Most road signs are internationally understood, though there are some signs which are specific to Germany. For example, on Autobahns, a yellow triangular warning sign with a row of cars indicates a possible traffic jam. On mountain roads, a sign showing a tyre wrapped in a chain, accompanied by the word *Schnee*, warns of difficult road conditions due to heavy snowfall requiring snow chains. A yellow sign with the word *Umleitung* indicates a diversion. A horizontal blue arrow with the word *Einbahnstrasse* refers to a one-way street. A special rule concerns the so-called Low Emission

Zones or Green Zones implemented in major cities throughout the country. One is only allowed to access such a zone if the vehicle carries an Emissions Badge *(Umweltplakette)*. If entering a Green Zone with a vehicle that does not display such a badge, you could be fined €100. Visitors can obtain a sticker permitting entry into environmental (pollution-controlled) zones from car dealers, repair centres and garages in Germany. It can also be ordered online at *www.umweltplakette.de*.

Buying Petrol

Germany has a good network of filling stations *(Tankstelle)*. Petrol *(Benzin)* and diesel are also widely available. The cost of fuel within Germany varies greatly; the lowest prices are at supermarkets; the highest are on the motorways. On smaller roads, and in more remote areas, it might sometimes take more time to find a petrol station, so make sure that you have enough fuel when travelling through less densely populated regions. Visit *www.gasoline-germany.com* for the latest updates on fuel prices in Germany.

DIRECTORY

INSURANCE AND BREAKDOWN COVER

Automobile Association (AA)
08000 88 77 66 (UK) or +33 825 09 88 76 (from abroad); www.theaa.com

Allgemeiner Deutscher Automobil Club (ADAC)
08005 10 11 12 (information); 08920 20 40 00 (breakdown service)

Royal Automobile Club (RAC)
+44 020 7930 2345 (from abroad); www.royalautomobileclub.co.uk

COMMON ROAD SIGNS

Anfang
Start

Ausfahrt
Exit

Gefahr
Danger

Halt
Stop

Steinschlag
Stone damage

Zentrum
Town centre

Below far left Speed limit sign
Below left Road along vineyards, Rhineland-Palatinate **Below centre** Sign to a guesthouse
Below centre right Road junction, Hesse
Below Road through Lower Saxony

Road Conditions

Most roads in Germany are well surfaced and usually well marked. However, the *Bundesstrassen*, or state roads, do vary in quality. In the north and west, and the touring areas of the Rhine Valley, Black Forest and Bavaria, the roads are well paved and in good condition.

The well-established network of motorways allows you to travel to most regions within a few hours. Regular maintenance work on the roads can generate problems, especially during the busy holiday season from July to mid-September. German-speaking drivers can listen to the radio for regular updates on the traffic situation or obtain information on traffic conditions by visiting the website *www.verkehrsinfo.de.*

Taking a Break

If you are feeling tired, or lost, it is a good idea to pull over and take a break. There are numerous sign-posted rest areas along motorways and major roads where you can park the car, stretch your legs and consult a map. Such places also often have clean public facilities. Motorways also have service stations at regular intervals, where you can stop for fuel and simple German food such as *Wiener Schnitzel* and *Currywurst*. On minor roads, and in remote areas, petrol stations may be few and far between.

The scenic landscape can sometimes be a distraction for drivers, so it is best to stop and admire the views. Parks and areas with nature trails also make good picnic stops.

Breakdown and Accident Procedures

If you have a problem on the Autobahn, you can use one of the yellow pillars with emergency buttons located along the road to call for help. In case of a break-down or accident, move the car safely off the road, turn on hazard lights and put out a warning triangle; it is compulsory to carry one and use it. Car hire companies will normally supply a number to call in case of an emergency or problems with the vehicle. Usually they use the assistance of the **ADAC** *(see p17)*; the motor-ing club will send a breakdown service. In case of an accident that involves another vehicle, you will need to exchange the insurance details, name, address and car registration details with the other parties involved, and if possible, jointly determine the cause of the accident.

In the case of a serious accident, the police are quick to arrive at the scene and provide support. For minor accidents, the police do not always appear, but you can call the emergency number 112 to ask for assistance if you have problems with the other party involved in the accident. Circumstances can be confusing at the time of an accident, so do not admit fault, accept liability or give money to any party, which is illegal in Germany. If possible, take down details from any inde-pendent witnesses. It is also wise to take photographs of any damage to the vehicle, as well as the scene of the accident.

Above Colourful Alpine walking map of Garmisch-Partenkirchen

Parking

Lack of parking space can be a problem in cities. Using one of the multi-storey car parks *(Parkhaus)* is a convenient option, although they can be expensive. A green or red sign in front of the car park will indicate whether there is an empty parking space. You pay for the number of hours that you park the car. Parking in city centres is often limited to 2 to 3 hours. Payment can be made with coins via apps such as *www.easypark.de*, or (rarely) credit card to an automatic parking-ticket machine, which will issue receipts that are placed on the inside of the windscreen. There are also parking meters with a timer that allow parking for up to 2 hours. In many large cities, there are "Park and Ride" areas outside the centre. It is possible to park your car here to take advantage of the well-developed public transport system.

It is never worth leaving your car in a prohibited area – a traffic warden will impose a fine and arrange for the vehicle to be towed away. Retrieving an impounded car is expensive and difficult.

Above Typical yellow road signs indicating route and distance **Above right** Slow-moving traffic in Pottenstein, Bavaria

Maps

Although mobile phones with Google Maps or free navigation apps such as MapsMe are useful, it is always helpful to have a map with you when driving through Germany. Free tourist maps are widely available but they are seldom useful for back-roads driving. The best option is to buy an up-to-date road atlas that provides detailed maps of all regions of Germany. You can usually purchase road maps at petrol stations, bookshops and tourist information centres.

Caravans, Camper Vans and Motorhomes

Camping in Germany is a great way to experience the country and enjoy its green landscapes. Caravans and motorhomes (RVs) are subject to the same rules of the road as other vehicles. There are many well-maintained campsites in the country that are ideal for a tour with a caravan, camper van or motorhome. These are generally open from April to September, although many are open year round.

Most campsites accept the Camping Card International (CCI), a document that can be used as a form of identity and is accepted by many campsites as security in lieu of a passport. Many campsites also offer discounts on presentation of the CCI.

When driving a caravan outside cities, do not exceed speeds of 70 kph (43 mph) and 100 kph (62 mph) on motorways. The traffic police are strict about speeding, so be aware that you might have to pay a heavy fine if caught driving too fast. The websites of the **German National Tourist Office** and **Eurocampings** offer up-to-date information about most campsites in Germany. They enable you to search for your desired camping location and give detailed information about sites.

Transporting Bicycles, Roof Racks and Caravans

Bicycle carriers, roof racks and caravans must be strongly attached to the car. You can either fix the bicycle behind the vehicle or on top of the car. If you are using a roof rack, make sure that the weight of the items you want to transport is evenly distributed on the rack. As far as caravans are concerned, make sure that the items inside are properly secured so that nothing moves around in case of braking or defensive driving action.

Below far left Driving through the town of Weilburg, Hesse **Below left** Transporting a bicycle on a car **Below centre** Camping sign near Pottenstein, Bavaria **Below centre right** Signpost to the walk around Blaubeuren, Baden-Württemberg **Below** Road patchwork on the isolated stretch to Havelberg, Saxony-Anhalt

Motorcycles

The drives presented in this guide are also ideal for a motorcycle trip. The well-maintained roads that crisscross Germany's countryside allow one to enjoy a feeling of freedom while discovering beautiful vistas. To rent a bike, get in touch with one of the major rental services well in advance, as rental stations do not always have them available. **AdMo Tours** is a national motorbike rental chain where motorcycles and dirt bikes can be booked for short periods. Several brands are available for hire, including BMW, Harley, Suzuki and many more. The **ADAC** has a useful website for motorbike rental in Germany.

It is mandatory for motorcyclists and passengers to wear protective helmets at all times. Drivers must have a valid driving licence to cover a motorcycle or moped, and an insurance policy.

The rules of the road are the same for motorcyclists as for other drivers, although you should take additional safety precautions. Go slow when filtering or driving between traffic lanes. Give other vehicles a wide berth when overtaking them, and be aware that they might not always see you. Motorcycles must have rear number plate lighting.

Driving with Children

Drivers must ensure that all passengers under the age of 12 wear seat belts or sit in an approved child restraint. Make sure that their seat belts are always fastened. This is obligatory by law, but also important for their safety. Babies must never be placed in a rear-facing child seat in the passenger seat if there is an active airbag fitted, as it can cause serious injury or death to the child in a crash. Children under the age of 12 have to be seated in a special child car seat. In this case, it does not matter if the child is seated on the back seat or on the front seat.

However, there is an exception to this rule for children who are shorter than 150 cm (93 inches). Children below this height have to sit in the back seat.

Remember to request any necessary child seats in advance when making your car hire booking.

Drivers with Disabilities

There are a number of parking concessions for disabled drivers in Germany. Visitors from non-EU countries who wish to apply for temporary parking permits should get in touch with the local council or the district authority. Germany's **Federal Ministry of Transport and Digital Infrastructure** can advise travellers on this matter. Applicants have to provide a disability ID and a passport-sized photograph. Medical documentation regarding their disabled status might also be required. Parking for disabled drivers can be found in all public areas, indicated with a sign displaying a wheelchair.

Car and Camper Van Hire

Most of the big international car hire companies, such as **Budget**, **Avis**, **Sixt** and **Hertz**, have offices at airports, railway stations and more expensive hotels, and offer a wide range of vehicles. The ADAC, Germany's and Europe's largest automobile club, offers rental services for tourists who do not want to bring their own vehicle to Germany. You can call the ADAC service number *(see p17)* to find out how to arrange the booking.

Above Motorcycles parked outside a café, Hollandische Viertel, Postdam, Brandenburg

To rent a vehicle, it is necessary to present a passport and a driving licence. Drivers must be over 18; however, check before you make your reservation regarding "age restrictions". It's recommended that you book in advance, especially during peak season – you will often get a better rate. Rental rates usually include unlimited mileage, but do double-check. Consider renting a smaller car than you may be used to at home, as they are much easier to handle on narrow country roads than big SUVs. If you need a child seat, it should be booked in advance as well.

Third-party insurance is compulsory and is included in the rate. Some rental agreements also include Collision Damage Waiver (CDW), which limits your liability for damages to the rental car, theft loss cover and personal injury insurance; others charge additional fees for these items. Be sure to read your agreement carefully so that you fully understand what your coverage and liabilities are. Some drivers may be able to use insurance from a personal credit card to claim CDW, but check carefully with your credit card company

Above Road gritter clearing snow from the road   **Above right** Taxis parked in the Odeonsplatz square, Munich

beforehand to make sure they will cover your trip abroad, and be prepared to show proof of cover.

Driving in Winter

If driving through Germany during the winter, you should buy or rent chains (if there is heavy snow) or at least the essential winter tyres. From December to March, roads in mountain areas can be coated with snow and ice. Motorways are kept clear, but minor roads may be closed completely, and access to other roads may only be permitted for vehicles fitted with snow chains.

When hiring a car, make sure you get winter tyres along with the car, even though many companies offer just regular summer tyres. Note that car hire companies usually charge extra for snow chains. Make sure that the tyres are in good condition. In case of an accident, if the car does not have adequate tyres, the insurance cover may not remain valid. The maximum speed possible with snow chains is 50 kph (30 mph). In Germany, winter tyres are not mandatory, but on-the-spot fines can be imposed if the vehicle is not equipped for winter weather conditions. In other words, fines

can be levied for not enough windshield cleansing fluid or use of the wrong sort of tyres. Bring plenty of warm clothes, a blanket, food and water during winter travel in case of major delays on the Autobahn, or if travelling under hazardous conditions in mountainous areas. Always reduce your speed in adverse conditions, as you will need a longer braking distance, and poor visibility gives less time to react.

In high-altitude regions and mountainous areas, you may encounter ice and snow in winter. Slow down, especially for curves and turns, and keep your actions steady and deliberate to avoid sliding out of control. If the car skids, take your foot off the accelerator – do not brake – and turn the wheel into the skid until the car corrects itself. Watch out for ice, especially on bridges and overpasses, which freeze up first. If you hit a patch, do not brake or turn the wheel, but keep as straight as possible and coast over it.

When conditions reduce light levels, dipped headlights should be used. Turn on fog lights whenever visibility is less than 50 m (164 ft).

DIRECTORY

MOTORCYCLES

ADAC
www.autovermietung.adac.de

AdMo Tours
www.admo-tours.com

DRIVERS WITH DISABILITIES

Federal Ministry of Transport and Digital Infrastructure
+ 49 (030) 18 300 3060

CAR HIRE

Avis
01805 21 77 02; www.avis.de

Budget
01805 21 77 11; www.budget.de

Hertz
01805 33 35 35; www.hertz.de

Sixt
01805 25 25 25; www.sixt.de

Below far left Camper van parked on the road between Wildsteig and Rottenbuch, Bavaria
Below left Snowy country road during winter
Below centre Bicycle secured to a motorhome
Below centre right Well-maintained road to Bad Harzburg, Lower Saxony **Below** Downtown shopping street in Neustadt an der Weinstrasse, Rhineland-Palatinate

WHERE TO STAY

Germany has numerous hotels, some even converted from palaces, castles and other historic buildings. The range of prices for a night's accommodation is wide, and depends on the services offered and the location of the establishment. Lodgings can be particularly expensive in the centres of larger cities. However, smaller towns located in the tourist areas often have rooms to rent at reasonable rates. Set amid country landscapes, charming, family-run hotels offering comfortable rooms and local specialities reflect the unique character of Germany's back roads.

Above Logo of Schloss Haigerloch, a luxurious three-star hotel, Baden-Württemberg, *see p232*

Hotels

Hotels in Germany are categorized according to the number of stars awarded for facilities, and not the standards of service. However, the star rating is no guide to the more subjective charms of a hotel, such as the style of decor or the kind of regional cuisine served. In larger cities, it is not difficult to find accommodation in deluxe hotels that are often part of an international chain. Away from the cities, high prices generally apply to rooms in comfortable hotels in beautiful locations or those provided within historic palaces or villas. There are many smaller hotels too, offering good, affordable lodgings. Often the name *Schlosshotel* indicates a hotel within a palace. Many of these hotels are featured on websites such as **Booking.com**, which can provide further information.

A hotel labelled *Garni* suggests that there is no restaurant on the premises, only a dining room where breakfast is served. *Apartmenthotels* offer suites with equipped kitchens or a kitchen annexe.

Guesthouses

Guesthouses *(Gasthof)* can be found throughout the country, usually located in private houses that function as traditional bed and breakfast places. Often labelled as *Pension* or *Hotel-pension*, the distinction between a small hotel, a pension and a private B&B varies from region to region. Quite popular, they offer good value for money. Located in smaller towns and villages, they are cheaper than hotels; however, the standards of service and facilities offered are also lower. The rooms are usually cosy and comfortable, and equipped with TV and a bathroom. Guests can also expect a large German breakfast in most guesthouses.

Youth Hostels

Youth hostels *(Jugendherberge)* represent the cheapest option for a stay and can be located in almost every town as well as major tourist areas in Germany. Some are housed in very attractive historic buildings. While they offer cheap lodging, the standards are still surprisingly good. Accommodation is usually provided

in double or triple rooms, as well as in dormitories. In order to stay at a youth hostel, guests must be members of the Youth Hostels Association (YHA) in their home country, or they can purchase an International Guest Card (€3.50 per night) on arrival. Prices vary between €12 and €25 per day, depending on the choice of room and the region where the hostel is located.

Camping

Summer is the best time for a camping trip to Germany, as most campsites close between November and March. These sites are well equipped, and usually have access to a shared kitchen, bathroom and laundry facilities, as well as refuse stations. Most offer power connections. Some also feature playgrounds and restaurants and organize sports activities. A lot of campsites also have additional cabins apart from pitches for tents, motorhomes or caravans. Visitors should reserve a spot well in advance if visiting during the busy summer season, especially at popular destinations.

Above Four-poster bed in Burghotel auf Schönburg, Rhineland-Palatinate, *see p151* **Above right** Oberhof resort close to Thuringian forest

Self-catering

Along the country roads, spectacular natural backdrops provide perfect settings for a picnic. Supermarkets are usually well stocked and offer all that travellers will need for an enjoyable outing, such as a great variety of food and camping crockery. Be sure to check the opening hours for supermarkets and convenience stores, as very few are open at night or on Sundays, and almost none for 24 hours. Outdoor markets, often held on Saturdays or Wednesdays, are also a good place to pick up fresh produce that is easily transported.

Booking

Reservations for accommodations can be made directly with the hotel through online booking or by telephone. Visitors can also contact the local tourist office and ask them to make the arrangements. The office can also provide information about rooms in private homes as well as advice on the availability of other accommodation options in the area. A written confirmation may be required to make a reservation, along with a credit card number. It is also best to inform the establishment concerned if arriving late or if delayed.

Facilities and Prices

With a wide range of accommodation on offer – from the basic to the luxurious – the facilities available generally reflect the price paid. Luxuries such as swimming pools and saunas are more often available in high-end hotels. For simple accommodation in beautiful surroundings, guesthouses are a good option. However, prices are also heavily influenced by other factors, such as the time of year.

In resort areas, prices are highest in summer, while in larger cities, spring and autumn are more expensive. Prices may also double if a city or region is hosting a special event. This is especially the case for commercial fairs and cultural festivals. In cities, hotels situated in the centre are particularly costly, as are establishments housed within historic palaces or charming villas. However, many hotels offer reductions at weekends.

Below far left Burg Stahleck alongside Rhine river, Bacharach, Rhineland-Palatinate, *see p152* **Below left** Campsite, Pottenstein, Bavaria **Below centre** Atlantic Hotel Sail City, Bremerhaven, Bremen, *see p36* **Below** Village guesthouse, Blaubeuren, Baden-Württemberg **Below right** Schloss Tangermünde, Saxony-Anhalt, *see p70*

DIRECTORY

ACCOMMODATION AND RESERVATIONS

Booking.com
www.booking.com

Deutsche Zentrale für Tourismus
*Beethovenstrasse 69, 60325 Frankfurt;
069 97 46 40; www.germany.travel*

Hotel Reservation Service (HRS)
*Breslauer Platz 4, 50668 Köln;
0221 207 76 00; www.hrs.com*

YOUTH HOSTELS

Deutsches Jugendherbergswerk DJH Service GmbH
Leonardo-da-Vinci-Weg 1, 32760 Detmold; 05231 740 10; www.jugendherberge.de

CAMPING

Deutscher Camping Club e.V.
*Mandlstrasse 28, 80802 Munich;
089 380 14 20; www.camping-club.de*

PRICE CATEGORIES

The following price bands are based on a standard double room in high season including tax and service:

Inexpensive – under €75
Moderate – €75–€160
Expensive – over €160

WHERE TO EAT

Each region of Germany can be distinguished by its cuisine. Menus increasingly feature local produce and there are markets where one can stock up on gourmet delights. Many establishments specialize in regional fare, which although heavy, is appetizing. In addition, traditional cuisine, notably Italian, Greek, Thai, Turkish, Chinese and Indian, is popular throughout the country and can be enjoyed even in smaller towns. Some fine restaurants run by master chefs serve European cuisine of the highest quality.

Above Local produce at the butcher's

Practical Information

Most restaurants are open from noon but sometimes close for a break between 3pm and 6pm, while cafés open from 9am. Many are closed for one day during the week. On Sundays, brunch is served in most places until 2pm. During the lunch period, between noon and 2pm, many establishments offer a fixed-price menu that is cheaper than in the evenings. Dinner is usually served from 7pm. Advance booking is recommended in popular city restaurants.

The cost of a meal depends on the location. While a three-course meal in some restaurants may cost €15, it will be more expensive in the downtown areas of larger cities. In more upscale restaurants, expect to pay up to €70. Alcoholic drinks can be quite costly, but beer, the national drink, is cheap. In general, the prices on a menu include service and tax, but it is common to leave a tip of around 10 per cent of the total bill. Many German restaurants still do not accept card payments; check before ordering. The logos of accepted cards may be displayed at the entrance.

In many good restaurants, the menu is written in German and English, and sometimes also in French. In cafés and less expensive restaurants, the menu may be handwritten in German, in which case the staff may help with a translation.

Restaurants

The term *Restaurant* is used to define both upmarket restaurants offering fine cuisine at steep prices and popular local establishments serving affordable food. For regional cuisine, visit one of the many *Ratskeller* found in the cellars of old town halls all across Germany, which serve *Sauerkraut* (fermented shredded cabbage) and regional specialities at affordable prices.

They usually have atmospheric interiors that are well adapted to the vaulted, dark spaces of the historic cellars. *Weinstuben* (wine bars) or *Bierstuben* (beer bars) also offer great local food, such as seasonal vegetables in a Hollandaise sauce or with dumplings, accompanied by local beverages. A *Gasthaus* refers to a rather simple restaurant serving good regional cuisine in a family atmosphere. Self-service venues offering snacks are known as *Imbiss*. These can vary from a stall serving baked sausages and cans of drink to kiosks with an extensive

choice of salads and fast food. In fact, in most large German towns, there are numerous kiosks serving Arabic, Turkish, Chinese and American food. For a sandwich or a healthy salad, visitors can also try the restaurants or cafeteria facilities in department stores, which are usually self-service.

Cafés and Bars

The term "café" has a number of connotations in Germany. Often, this is a place that offers good breakfast options in the morning and serves mostly international cuisine from noon onwards. Sometimes, a café will have a selection of cakes on display. In addition, at any time of the day and evening, customers can have coffee or ice cream. Many of these establishments turn into bars in the evening, when alcoholic drinks are served and live music is played.

A typical venue to have a drink in Germany is the *Kneipe*, which is best compared to an English pub in terms of its atmosphere. A wide range of alcoholic drinks is available here, and sometimes loud music is played. The most commonly served beer is Pils, a bottom-fermented pilsner lager. Brown ales are also popular.

Above Entrance to a restaurant near Schneider Brewery, Kelheim, Bavaria **Above right** Fish sandwich stall, Wieck harbour, Mecklenburg-Vorpommern

Schwarzbier, a top-fermented brown ale, is increasingly popular, as is Weizenbier, a bitter top-fermented beer. A small number of dishes such as *Strammer Max* (a slice of toast covered with ham and fried egg) are usually offered and customers can often enjoy indoor games such as pool, darts or table football.

Local Markets

Lively markets are held at designated locations in the centres of towns and villages all across the country. Shopping at these markets is the best way to sample local flavours. A good introduction to the specialities of the region, they have lively atmosphere and offer a great choice of fresh, high-quality food. Farmers come to these markets to sell their fresh produce.

Many farmers also have shops on their farm, where they sell their goods. When driving through regions known for their agricultural produce, keep an eye out for fresh fruit and vegetables, honey, wine or even sausages on sale. Each driving trip notes the location and days of the week for markets around the region. Other great places to visit are bakeries. A *Bäckerei*

specializes in bread and rolls, while a *Konditorei* mainly makes pastries, cakes and sometimes chocolates. Germans make excellent breads, often organic, from various grains. Bread in Germany is of two kinds: rolls *(Brötchen)* and loaves *(Brot)*. Delicatessens where one can find high-quality sausages, cheese, meat and fish are also worth a visit. Special deli counters can be also be found in major supermarkets. However, prices can be quite high here. All kinds of fresh meats and sausages can also be bought at butchers' shops *(Fleischern)*, easily found in any city or town.

Picnics and Outdoor BBQs

There are many nice locations especially designated for picnics in Germany. These are usually situated in pleasant green areas and equipped with outdoor tables and litter bins. Most towns have a shop or a delicatessen where one can grab picnic supplies such as cold cuts, sliced cheeses, breads and salads. Traditional German potato salad and pasta dishes are often sold in convenient deli-style plastic containers for easy carrying on a road trip.

DIRECTORY

PRICE BANDS

The following price bands are based on a three-course meal for one, including a half-bottle of house wine, cover charge, tax and service:

Inexpensive – under €25;
Moderate – €25–€45
Expensive – over €45

Below far left Atmospheric *Weinstube*, Würzburg, Bavaria **Below left** Cafés outside the Rathaus, Lübeck, Schleswig-Holstein **Below centre** Wine bar, Tüchersfeld, Bavaria **Below centre right** Roadside sausage stall, Rostock, Mecklenburg-Vorpommern **Below** Local market, Münsterplatz, Freiburg, Baden-Württemberg

THE FLAVOURS OF GERMANY

Germany is home to a variety of cuisines, with significant differences in culinary traditions between its regions. However, the country is unified by its love of meat, bread, sausages and beer. Though traditional meals can be high in calories, a new generation of chefs is improvising German classics to create "nouvelle" dishes. Fresh produce can be found at the many farmers' markets and charming stores across the country and homemade breads and cheeses and locally caught fish are usually of a high standard.

Above Pilsner, the popular bottom-fermented lager

Northern Coast
Northern German food is meant to sustain fishermen during long, cold days, and to this end is full of starches. The hardships of life in the northern coast are reflected in the hearty and filling cuisine of this region, much of which makes use of ocean fish such as halibut or plaice, or freshwater fish such as trout. The popularity of *Matjes*, salted herrings with cream and onions, served with baked potatoes, has spread from the northern cities to the rest of the country. Warming stews and soups, such as *Pichelsteiner Eintopf*, a one-pot dish with meat, potatoes and vegetables cooked in broth for the harsh winter months, are readily available, as is potato salad, which is served hot or cold with chopped pickle relish or onions. Potatoes, often cooked with bacon, are by far the most popular side dish in the region.

Rhineland and Southwestern Germany
This part of Germany, with its wine-growing regions along the rivers Rhine, Mosel and Neckar, is known for its superb, often French-influenced, gourmet feasts. Swabian food is rich,

traditional German cuisine. Pasta and bread feature largely in a Swabian meal including *Maultaschen*, large pasta parcels containing meat, cheese or vegetables served in soup or butter, or *Spätzle*, a type of pasta, which in Bavaria is made with beer instead of water. Swabian food is often referred to as "wet" food, since it is often drenched in sauce or melted butter. The Pfalz, a region of southwestern Germany, is famous for its *Pfälzer Saumagen*, sow's stomach filled with sausage, herbs and potatoes. The Franks, inhabitants of Franconia, part of Bavaria, produce perhaps the finest gingerbread in the country, as well as *Nürnberger Rostbratwürstchen* (small spicy roast sausages), and dishes using rare types of fish, such as sheatfish.

Saxony and Thuringia
Thüringer Bratwurst, a spicy roasted sausage served with mustard, originates from this east German region, as does *Sauerbraten*, roast beef marinated in vinegar. Meat is not the only option, however, as Thuringian food is heavily influenced by the wide variety of vegetables grown. Excellent asparagus, cabbage and cauliflower dishes are also served.

Saxony is widely known for its cakes, or *Stollen*; there are strict requirements which must be met for a cake to be considered an authentic *Dresdner Stollen*, including where it is made geographically. These cakes are usually served on or around Christmas. Another cake originating in Saxony is *Baumkuchen*, a multi-layered, pyramid-shaped cake covered in a chocolate glaze. Thuringia is more likely to offer *Bechkuchen* (sheet cakes), such as *Streusel-Kuchen*, a German crumb cake.

Bavaria
Much of southeastern Germany's cuisine is heavily influenced by Eastern Europe, as demonstrated by the goulash dishes and dumplings that regularly feature on the menu. *Knödel*, for example, are boiled dumplings made in a variety of ways with several types of filling, such as liver, onions, or egg; *Semmelknödel* are bread-based dumplings with onion and egg and *Leberknödel* are liver dumplings. Bavarian food, which the world identifies with Germany, is filling and hearty; beer and pretzels, white sausages,

Above Pretzels garnished with poppy seeds   **Above centre** Wine shop on Cremerstrasse, Wetzlar, Hesse   **Above right** *Spritzgebäck*, chocolate-dipped biscuits

Sauerkraut (dish made from fermented cabbage) and roast pork are fixtures of the traditional Bavarian menu. The *Weisswurst* (white sausage) has its origins in Munich, where several "rules" were made for its consumption, including not eating it after midnight.

Breads

Germany is home to an incredibly large variety of breads, including pretzels, *Laugenbrötchen* (salty sourdough rolls), *Semmel* (milk-dough rolls), *Berliner Landbrot* (mild rye breads), *Mehrkornbrötchen* (mixed grain rolls) and many more. Bakeries are ubiquitous, so freshly baked bread and rolls are always available, and in many regions, such as Swabia, there's no meal without bread. German breakfasts consist mainly of different types of bread and toppings such as jam or cheese.

Beer

Beer is more than the most popular beverage in Germany – it is a way of life, with many regional specialities and locally produced brews available throughout the country. Bavaria, a major brewing centre, is home to brands that are known the world over for quality and taste, such as Paulaner, Löwenbräu and Erdinger. Brown ales are popular, particularly in the south, but the most commonly drunk beer is Pilsner, a bottom-fermented lager.

Wine

Germany is renowned for its delicious white wines, particularly those made from the Riesling grape. Among the most highly prized are those from the Rheingau region. Lovers of red wine can try Assmannshausen Spätburgunder, produced from the Pinot Noir grape. German wines are largely categorized into three groups according to their quality: the lowest is *Tafelwein*, then *Qualitätswein* and the highest is *Qualitätswein mit Prädikat*. The term *Trocken* indicates a dry wine, *Halbtrocken*, semi-dry, and *Süss*, the sweet variety. Excellent sparkling wines known as *Sekt*, are also produced in Germany.

Below far left Tourist market, Lübbenau, Brandenburg **Below left** Traditional beer wagon, Ettal, Bavaria **Below centre** Allgau cheese factory, Immenstadt, Bavaria **Below** Grape vines, Reichenau, Baden-Württemberg **Below right** Typical German loaves, Bavaria

DIRECTORY

ON THE MENU

Backhendl
Roast chicken

Bratwurst
Grilled sausage

Currywurst
Sausage served with tomato ketchup and curry powder

Eis
Ice cream

Forelle
Trout

Eisbein
Boiled pigs' trotter

Käsekuchen
Cheesecake

Kuchen
Cake

Rindfleisch
Beef

Salat
Salad

Schinken
Ham

Suppe
Soup

Vorspeise
Starter

Wiener Schnitzel
Thin cutlet in breadcrumbs

Wurstsalat
Sausage salad

Road winding around Rossfeld mountain, Berchtesgaden

THE
ROAD TRIPS

TRIP 1

DRAMATIC NORTH SEA COAST

Lüneburg to East Frisia & the East Frisian Islands

HIGHLIGHTS

Architectural splendour

Take a walk in the once-rich Hanseatic city of Lüneburg,
with its charming churches and houses

Flowering orchards

Enjoy the scenic Altes Land, one of the most beautiful
fruit-growing regions in Europe, when the cherry
and apple trees are in full bloom

Lively medieval city

Visit the market square of Bremen, with its stunning
Renaissance town hall and the Roland statue, both
of which are UNESCO World Heritage Sites

Island adventures

Explore the remote and pristine landscape and
beaches of the East Frisian Islands

DRAMATIC NORTH SEA COAST

The sweeping, green marshy lowlands of northern Germany form the backdrop to this picturesque trip. Beginning at Lüneburg, the route traverses the state of Lower Saxony (Niedersachsen) to Germany's far northwest, East Frisia (Ostfriesland). It continues through scenic villages set in fields of heather and orchard blossoms in the Altes Land (Old Land) to reach some outstanding medieval city centres such as the one in the Hanseatic city of Bremen, whose grand Gothic and Renaissance landmarks are reminders of its remarkable former wealth. The trip also explores fascinating natural landscapes such as the North Sea tideland nature reserve and the East Frisian Islands (Ostfriesische Inseln).

ACTIVITIES

Take a traditional horse-drawn carriage ride through the moors and heathlands of the Lüneburger Heide

Go hiking on the many trails through the Lüneburger Heide

Enjoy a boat trip around the harbour of Bremerhaven

Cycle along the scenic route between the artist colonies of Worpswede and Fischerhude

Take a guided walk through the Nationalpark Niedersächsisches Wattenmeer nature reserve to learn about the area's unique ecosystem

| 0 kilometres | 20 |
| 0 miles | 20 |

KEY

Drive route

Above Tranquil landscape on the way to the East Frisian Islands, *see p39*

PLAN YOUR DRIVE

Start/finish: Lüneburg to East Frisia and the East Frisian Islands.

Number of days: 3–4 days, allowing half a day to explore Bremen.

Distance: 500 km (311 miles).

Road conditions: All roads along this trip are in very good condition.

When to go: For warm and dry weather, the best time to visit this region is between late May and mid-August. It is particularly lovely in late April, when cherry and apple orchards blossom.

Opening times: Most shops and attractions are open from 9am to 6pm, Monday to Friday.

Main market days: Lüneburg: Wed & Sat; Bremen: Mon–Sat; Verden an der Aller: Tue & Fri.

Shopping: Lüneburg's historic old town, an area with limited vehicular traffic, is ideal for shopping. Bremen's malls, such as the Lloyd Passagen and the Domshof Passagen, offer a good range of stores for shoppers.

Major festivals: Lüneburg: Lüneburger Sülfmeistertage (medieval festival), Sep/Oct; Bremen: Breminale (cultural festival), Jun/Jul; Freimarkt (general fair), Oct.

DAY TRIP OPTIONS

Spend a day on a family visit to the city of Lüneburg for a **walking tour** through the historic city centre or hike through the nearby Lüneburger Heide. Art enthusiasts can visit the **artist colonies** of Worpswede and Fischerhude, with their marvellous **art museums**, before visiting the Deutsches Schifffahrtsmuseum and the Deutsches Auswandererhaus in Bremerhaven. **Nature lovers** can experience a full day of **marsh walks** and **beach life** in the Nationalpark Niedersächsisches Wattenmeer on one of the lovely East Frisian Islands. For full details, *see p39.*

Above Apple orchard in Altes Land, *see p35*

Right Lush apple orchards in Jork, Altes Land
Below left Stately Rathaus on Am Markt,
Lüneburg **Below right** Outdoor cafés in Stade

VISITING LÜNEBURG

Parking
The most convenient car parks are at
the train station and the Rathaus.

Tourist Information
*Rathaus, Am Markt, 21335; 08002 20
50 05; www.lueneburg.info*

WHERE TO STAY

LÜNEBURG
Bergström *moderate*
This four-star hotel offers comfortable
rooms. Facilities include a pool and a
gym. Pets are allowed.
*Bei der Lüner Mühle, 21335; 03020 21 33
00; www.bergstroem.de*

Bremer Hof *moderate*
A perfect starting point for sightseeing,
this hotel has a restaurant that serves
traditional as well as innovative dishes
from northern Germany.
*Lüner Strasse 12–13, 21335; 04131
22 40; www.bremer-hof.de*

ALTES LAND
Altes Land *moderate*
The attractive Altes Land combines
village charm with modern comforts.
Its restaurant features regional cuisine.
*Schützenhofstrasse 16, 21635 Jork;
04162 914 60; www.hotel-altes-land.de*

STADE
Parkhotel Stader Hof *moderate*
Built in 1990, this well-known first-class
hotel has 100 rooms and 6 suites.
*Schiffertorsstrasse 8, 21682; 04141
49 90; www.parkhotel-staderhof.de*

Zur Hanse *moderate*
Surrounded by mansions, this private
hotel provides modern and
comfortable rooms.
*Am Burggraben 4, 21680; 04141 952 40;
www.hotel-zur-hanse.de*

① Lüneburg
Lower Saxony; 21335
This former salt-mining hub and
Hanseatic city was once one of the
richest in Germany. Lüneburg's past
wealth is evident in the splendid
gables that line the streets of its old
town. One of the city's three Gothic
churches, the **Johanniskirche**, has a
108-m (354-ft) high brick steeple that
leans more than 2 m (6 ft) from the
perpendicular. Built between 1300
and 1370 and restored in 1420, it
is considered a major example of
north German brick architecture.
   The city's most important
monument is the **Rathaus** *(closed
Mon)*, located in Am Markt. This
town hall, parts of which date back
to the 13th century, is one of the
most architecturally interesting town
halls in northern Germany. Its council
chamber features Renaissance woodwork by 16th-century artist Albert von
Soest, and the **Museum im Rathaus**
holds a remarkable collection of municipal silverware. To the left of the town
hall, the **Schroederstrasse** is lined with
good restaurants, cafés and bars. Stroll
on Ilmenaustrasse, which runs past
the old port on the Ilmenau river.
On Lüner Strasse stands the **Altes
Kaufhaus**, a former herring warehouse

with a superb Baroque façade. This
striking building was formerly used
to load salt on to ships. A walk across
the historic heart of the city leads to
Michaeliskirche, with its beautiful
basilica, consecrated in 1409.
   🚗 *From Lüneburg take the B209
towards Amelinghausen, then
follow the road to Soderstorf. Take
Schulstrasse towards Evendorf and
then Evendorf Dorfstrasse to Egestorf,
then get on to Schätzendorfer Strasse
in the direction of Hanstedt. In
Schätzendorf, turn left to Undeloh.*

② Lüneburger Heide
Lower Saxony; 21274
Situated south of Hamburg,
between the Elbe and Aller rivers,
the Lüneburger Heide is a remote,
enticing heathland and nature reserve.
The half-stepped terrain also serves
as grazing land for a special breed of
sheep, the Heidschnucken. Starting
at the pretty village of **Undeloh**, this
area can easily be explored on foot,
by bike or horse-drawn carriage
*(Mühlenstrasse 2, Bispingen; 05194 830;
www.erlebniswelt-lueneburger-heide.de)*.
The highlight is the traditional
village of **Wilsede**, whose tranquil
scenery and quaint houses set
among trees is a reminder of its

bucolic past. Not far from here is the **Wilseder Berg**, the highest point of the moraine region, which offers a panoramic view of the countryside.

🚗 *From Undeloh, head to Handeloh. Continue on Handeloher Strasse to Welle. Turn right on to the B3 and cross the A1. Continue on this road, at Ovelgönne turn left on to B73 and pass Neukloster Hedendorf. Turn right on Jorker Strasse to Jork.*

❸ Altes Land
Hamburg; 21635
The flat floodplains of the **Altes Land** along the banks of the lower Elbe teem with cherry and apple orchards. The area is particularly lovely between April and May, when the trees are in bloom and the whole country-side turns into an ocean of white and pink. In the midst of these natural surroundings, charming red-brick houses with thatched roofs and decorated gables await the visitor. There are a number of villages to be discovered, such as **Neuenfelde, Borstel, Steinkirchen, Hollern** and **Jork**, with many Baroque churches that are worth visiting. The unofficial capital of the Altes Land, Jork offers some delightful restau-rants. Neuenfelde attracts visitors with its pretty rose gardens; another draw is the historic windmill of Hollern-Twielenfleth.

🚗 *From Jork, continue driving towards Borstel, turning on Westerjork*

left to Grunendeich. Follow Mittelkirchen to Steinkirchen and carry on to Hollern. Follow the river on Hollernstrasse and take Altländer Strasse to Stade.

❹ Stade
Lower Saxony; 21680
A medieval Hanseatic town located to the west of Hamburg, Stade has retained most of its characteristic half-timbered buildings, the most attractive of which can be found along the old harbour, **Alter Hafen**. Located in a granary built during the time of the Swedish occupation in the 17th century, **Schwedenspeicher-Museum** *(closed Mon)* houses exhibits on the history of the town. Nearby, the Kunsthaus at Am Wasser West 7 displays the **Kaufmann Collection** *(closed Mon)*, comprising works of artists from Worpswede *(see p38)*. Other attractions are the **Bürgermeister-Hintze-Haus** at Am Wasser West 23 and the **Rathaus**, both of which date from the 17th century. Stade also has its share of grand churches such as the 14th-century Gothic **St Wilhadi** *(closed Sun)* and the 17th-century **St Cosmas und Damian** *(closed Sun)*.

🚗 *Take the B74 and continue past Elm. Turn right on to the B71 to Bremervörde passing Heerstedt to reach the A27. Cross the A27 to get on to Weserstrasse to reach Bremen's deep-water harbour, Bremerhaven.*

Baroque portal, Rathaus, Stade

Left Half-timbered houses along the Alter Hafen, Stade **Below** Moorlands covered in heather, Lüneburger Heide

EAT AND DRINK

LÜNEBURG

Elrado-House *moderate*
Situated in the heart of Lüneburg, off the market square, this homely steakhouse is the ideal place at which to dine after a walking tour. Enjoy good food in a friendly, rustic setting. *Am Markt 4, 21335; 04131 39 04 03; www.elrado-house.de*

Mama Rosa *moderate*
This Italian restaurant is both a trattoria and a gourmet food-and-wine store. Visitors can enjoy a light breakfast in the morning, lunch in the sun and drink a cappuccino in the afternoon or a glass of wine in the evening with Italian antipasto and a selection of homemade pasta dishes. *Bei der Abtsmühle 1, 21335; 04131 30 83 07; www.mama-rosa-lueneburg.de*

Röhms Deli *expensive*
The menu at this well-known gourmet bistro changes daily and is testament to the creative ideas of its Michelin-starred chef. *Heiligengeiststrasse 30, 21335; 04131 241 60; www.roehmsdeli.de; closed Sun & Mon*

ALTES LAND

Die Mühle Jork *expensive*
The chefs at this upmarket restaurant offer culinary twists, such as pork fillets with pear, and red wine and butter ice cream. The homemade cakes and pies are a treat. *Am Elbdeich 1, 21635 Jork; 04162 63 95; www.diemuehlejork.de; closed Mon, Tue & Jan*

STADE

Barbarossa *expensive*
This cosy restaurant in an old town house is located next to the harbour, so the seafood, such as freshly harvested oysters from Sylt Island, is delicious. The cuisine is excellent, as are the wines. *Salzstrasse 25, 21682; 04141 28 84; www.barbarossa-stade.de; closed Sun*

Knechthausen *expensive*
Savour homemade pasta, antipasto, meat and fish dishes and delightful desserts in the Knechthausen's peaceful ambience. It has a superb wine selection, too. *Bungenstrasse 20–22, 21682; 04141 529 63 60; www.restaurant-knechthausen.de; closed Sun*

⑤ Bremerhaven
Bremen; 27501

Bremen's harbour, Bremerhaven, is worth visiting for its museums. Designed by renowned architect Hans Scharoun, the **Deutsches Schiffahrtsmuseum** *(mid-Nov–mid-Mar: closed Mon; mid-Mar–mid-Nov: open daily)*, or the German Maritime Museum, includes an open-air museum and a harbour museum. This site features both originals and models of a wide range of ships. The most attractive exhibit here is the *Seute Deern*, the last great German sailing ship. The **Deutsches Auswandererhaus**, a museum, recounts the German emigrant experience of the 19th century with costumed models and replicas of the cabins and family histories written in the travellers' own words.

🚗 *Return to the B6, which meets the A27. Continue on the A27, then turn right on the B6 to reach Bremen.*

⑥ BREMEN
Bremen; 21895

A prosperous city on the Weser river with a colourful 1,200-year history, Bremen is Germany's oldest port still in use today. The magnificent town hall and the grand old statue of Roland, both on the market square, represent its main tourist attractions and are listed as UNESCO World Heritage Sites.

Above Statue of Roland in the Marktplatz, Bremen **Below right** Atlantic Hotel Sail City, Bremerhaven **Below far right** Fishing boat in Bremerhaven

VISITING BREMEN

Parking
Parking is available at Parkhaus Pressehaus on Langenstrasse.

Tourist Information
Böttcherstrasse 4 and in the Hauptbahnhof, 28195; 04213 08 00 10; www.bremen-tourismus.de

WHERE TO STAY

BREMERHAVEN

Atlantic Hotel Sail City *expensive*
Located on the waterfront, this hotel offers exceptional comfort and good service at fair prices.
Am Strom 1, 27568; 04713 099 05 55; www.atlantic-hotels.de

BREMEN

Ringhotel Munte am Stadtwald *moderate*
This traditional family hotel features a spacious spa and indoor pool. The hotel has two restaurants – Wels, which offers gourmet fish and game dishes, and Del Bosco serving Italian cuisine.
Parkallee 299, 28213; 04212 20 20; www.hotel-munte.de

Park Hotel Bremen *expensive*
The well-appointed Park Hotel offers high standards, with 177 individually styled rooms and suites, an extensive spa complex and a gourmet restaurant.
Im Bürgerpark, 28209; 04213 40 80; www.hommage-hotels.com

A two-hour walking tour

Exit the car park and continue on Langenstrasse, then turn left on Am Markt to the **Marktplatz** ①, the heart of the city. The town hall, the cathedral and the Roland statue dominate this impressive square. The statue of Roland, a knight of Charlemagne who is considered the city's protector, was erected in 1404. Roland's sword of justice symbolizes the judiciary's independence, and its engraved motto confirms the emperor's edict conferring town rights on Bremen. The second monument on the square is the statue of the Bremen Town Musicians, famous protagonists of a Grimm fairy tale.

Statue of the Bremen Town Musicians

Constructed in 1953, local legend has it that touching the front hooves of the donkey will make wishes come true. From here, turn right on to Am Dom to visit the Gothic town hall, the **Rathaus** ② *(daily guided tours)*. Built between 1405 and 1410, the edifice has a Renaissance façade that dates to the early 17th century. Inside the great hall, a lovely fresco from 1932 portrays Solomon's court. Walk along Am Dom to the 11th-century **Dom** ③ *(open daily)*, which stands nearby. The façade of this Romanesque cathedral features two spires. Inside are historic treasures such as the stone bas-reliefs dividing the western choir stalls. In the second eastern chapel, visitors can see the oldest Bremen sculpture of *Christ the Omnipotent*, dating back to 1050. Return along Am Dom and turn left on to Am Markt to the Mannerist **Schütting** ④, a former meeting place for merchants, with a Renaissance façade. Head south and walk along Am Markt, which becomes **Böttcherstrasse** ⑤. This lively street was transformed into a Gothic-cum-Art Nouveau fantasy in the 1920s by artists commissioned by the coffee magnate Ludwig Roselius. Don't miss the golden bas-relief at the entrance to the street. There are also attractions such as the Paula-Modersohn-Becker art museum. Return to the Rathaus and walk along Am Dom, turn right on to Balgebrückstrasse, left on to Dechanatstrasse and then turn right to reach the **Schnoorviertel** ⑥, located in the eastern quarter of the city centre. A historic area with many houses dating from between the 15th and 18th centuries, this district has a collection of art galleries and restaurants. Continue on this road,

which becomes Stavendamm, turn right on to Tiefer, which becomes Martinistrasse, to return to the car park.
🚗 *Cross the A27 and get on to Hauptstrasse, which becomes Falkenberger Landstrasse. Turn left on to Worphauser Landstrasse in the direction of Worphausen. Continue on this road, which becomes Ostendorfer Strasse. Turn left on Hemberg Strasse to Worpswede.*

Bremen Town Musicians

A famous fairy tale, the *Bremen Town Musicians* was written by the Brothers Grimm. In the story, a donkey, a dog, a cat and a rooster leave their farms when their owners decide to kill them. They meet by coincidence and decide to travel to Bremen, a town known for its free-spirited society, to make a living as musicians. On the way, they encounter some robbers in a cottage and frighten them away with their disharmonious music. The robbers abandon the cottage and the animals live there forever.

Above left Street musicians in the seaport city of Bremen **Above** The Bremen port by the Weser river

EAT AND DRINK IN BREMEN

Port Speicher XI *moderate*
The Speicher XI offers home-style cooking. Visitors can enjoy pizzas, pastas and a huge selection of drinks. The harbour museum is just next door.
Am Speicher XI, 28217; 04216 194 10; www.port-speicherxi.de; closed Mon–Tue

Meierei *expensive*
This restaurant serves mainly Mediterranean cuisine and offers a great selection of mostly Italian wines. In summer, visitors can dine on the terrace.
Im Bürgerpark 1, 28209; 04213 408 60; www.meierei-bremen.de; closed Mon–Tue

Restaurant Luv *expensive*
Traditional cooking is given a creative twist in this restaurant – the seafood is highly recommended. Diners can also sit outside by the promenade along the Weser river.
Schlachte 15–18, 28195; 04211 65 55 99; www.restaurant-luv.de

Above Village cottage with a thatched roof, Elisabethfehn **Above right** Verden an der Aller town centre **Below** Norderney, one of the many East Frisian Islands

CYCLING IN WORPSWEDE

Rent a bike *(Fahrradladen Worpswede; www.fahrrad-eyl.de)* and enjoy exploring the quaint village of Worpswede.

WHERE TO STAY IN EAST FRISIA AND THE EAST FRISIAN ISLANDS

Haus Norderney *moderate*
A modern B&B, offering ten individually decorated rooms.
Janusstrasse 6, 26548 Norderney; 04932 22 88; www.hotel-haus-norderney.de

Ostfriesenhof *moderate*
This first-class hotel has wonderful views of the East Frisian landscape.
Groninger Strasse 109, 26789 Leer; 04916 09 10; www.ostfriesen-hof.de

Parkhotel Wangerooge *moderate*
This four-star hotel in a villa offers single or double rooms and eight suites, all with extra-long beds.
Dorfplatz 16, 26486 Wangerooge; 04469 870 80; www.wangerooge-hotel.de

⑦ Worpswede
Lower Saxony; 27726
Situated northeast of Bremen, the small village of Worpswede is a must-see for art lovers. A number of famous painters, notably Fritz Mackensen, Otto Modersohn, Hans am Ende, Fritz Overbeck and Heinrich Vogeler, lived here from 1889 until the end of World War II. The greatest of them all was perhaps Paula Modersohn-Becker, one of the most important exponents of early Expressionism. The **Grosse Kunstschau** and the **Worpsweder Kunsthalle** *(closed Mon)*, where the work of the founding members of the colony is displayed, are worth a visit. Most of the paintings on display highlight the scenic beauty of northern Germany, showing moorland, birch trees and marshlands under wide open skies. Visiting poets such as Bohemian-Austrian Rainer Maria Rilke helped establish the legendary reputation of this hamlet. Even today, many painters live in Worpswede, and the village is proud of its cultural scene.

🚗 *Take the Kirchdamm to Grasberg and then the Speckmannstrasse to Fischerhude.*

⑧ Fischerhude
Lower Saxony; 27726
Another attraction for art lovers is nearby Fischerhude, which nestles in the Wümme river lowlands, surrounded by waterways and drainage canals that frame the captivating meadows and fertile fields. With its idyllic farmhouses, some of which are centuries old, this village leaves the visitor with a distinct impression of the region's lifestyle as it was hundreds of years ago. At the end of the 19th century, Fischerhude also became an important cultural colony, attracting artists such as Heinrich Breling, the landscape painter Otto Modersohn, the sculptor Clara Rilke-Westhoff and the author Diedrich Speckmann.

🚗 *Leave Fischerhude following signs to Sagehorn and then on to Oyten. Take the A1 towards Bremen, then the A27 southeastwards, and then Hamburger Strasse to Verden an der Aller.*

⑨ Verden an der Aller
Lower Saxony; 27238
The town of Verden an der Aller is known for its attractive churches, such as the **Johanniskirche**, the **Andreaskirche**, and the Lutheran cathedral, the **Dom**, all of which adorn the town centre. The cathedral's hall features a multi-sided presbytery and a passageway dating from between 1268 and 1311. The town's horse riding and racing tradition is honoured in the **Deutsches Pferdemuseum** *(closed Mon)*, which features a vast collection of equestrian artifacts. North of the cathedral, the Domherrenhaus

houses the **Historisches Museum**
(closed Mon), which displays exhibits
on the town's history.

🚗 *Take the minor road to Syke via
Thedinghausen. Follow signs to
Nordwohlde, turning right to
Harpstedt. Drive to Wildeshausen and
take the B213 to Cloppenburg. Follow
signs to the Museumsdorf.*

⑩ Cloppenburg
Lower Saxony; 49661
The market town of Cloppenburg
is famous for its interesting open-
air museum, **Museumsdorf**, a
re-creation of a medieval village.
Attractions include half-timbered
houses, windmills and a small 17th-
century church. Also worth a visit are
the megalithic graves of **Visbek** *(04445
89 00 35; www.visbek.de)* to the east of
Cloppenburg, which date from 3,500
to 1,800 BC. The main attraction is the
80-m (263-ft) grave known as Visbeker
Bräutigam (Visbek groom) and the
100-m (321-ft) Visbeker Braut (bride).

🚗 *Take the B72 and drive through
Aurich to join B210, then turn left,
taking B72 following signs to Norden.
Here, several ports serve as the
springboard to the Frisian Islands.*

⑪ East Frisia and the East Frisian Islands
Lower Saxony; 26506
With its unique landscape and lovely
beaches, East Frisia is a perfect place
to end a tour of northern Germany.
Meadows dotted with windmills char-
acterize the countryside. Along the
North Sea Coast extends the belt of
several East Frisian Islands: Norderney,
Baltrum, Langeoog, Spiekeroog and
Wangerooge. All around them is
the **Nationalpark Niedersächsisches
Wattenmeer**, listed as a UNESCO
World Heritage Site. A popular

excursion here is the "Watt Walk" to the
wetlands that are formed when mud
is deposited by tides. This tour by local
experts *(04919 196 96 60; Ledastrasse 10,
26789 Leer; www.ostfriesland-tourism.
com)* includes an introduction to the
unique ecosystem. Boat trips along
the rivers or coastline of East Frisia
are also a delightful way to explore
this nature reserve. The **Moor und
Fehnmuseum** *(mid-Mar–Oct: open
Tue–Sun)* in Elisabethfehn, southeast
of the town of Leer, is also worth
a visit. The museum is dedicated
to the extraction of peat and exhibits the world's largest plough.

Above Mudflats at low tide, East
Frisia **Below** Exhibits in the Grosse
Kunstschau, Worpswede

EAT AND DRINK

VERDEN AN DER ALLER
Pades *expensive*
Enjoy French, Italian and regional food
in an old town house or in its backyard.
*Grüne Strasse 15, 27283; 04231 30 60;
www.pades.de*

CLOPPENBURG
Margaux *expensive*
This pleasant restaurant in Hotel
Schäfer offers top-class German
cuisine in a relaxed ambience.
*Lange Strasse 66, 49661; 04471 24 84;
www.schaefers-hotel-cloppenburg.de;
closed Mon–Thu*

EAST FRISIA AND THE EAST FRISIAN ISLANDS
Kruse *inexpensive*
A congenial restaurant, Kruse offers a
great variety of high-quality local fish.
*Anna Strasse 15–17, 26486
Wangerooge; 04469 14 14; www.
fischrestaurant-kruse.de; closed Mon*

Weisse Düne *moderate*
The Weisse Düne serves typical island
specialities such as marinated crabs
with homemade dip and pickled
Matjes herring; *Wiener Schnitzel* (veal
coated in breadcrumbs) is also available.
*Weisse Düne 1, 26548 Norderney;
04932 93 57 17; www.weisseduene.com*

DAY TRIP OPTIONS
Bremen is a good base for day trips.

A day in Lüneburg
Visit historic Lüneburg ①, then hike
across the Lüneburger Heide ②.

*From Bremen take the A1 in the direc-
tion of Hamburg and then the A250 to
Lüneburg. Follow signs from Lüneburg.*

History beckons
Explore the art museums in
Worpswede ⑦ and Fischerhude ⑧
and enjoy exploring these scenic
villages. Next, tour the museums
in Bremerhaven ⑤.

*From Bremen take the A27 to
Ritterhude. Follow instructions
to Worpswede and Fischerhude.*

Bremerhaven can be reached via the A27.

Island life
Spend a day relaxing at the beaches
of the East Frisian Islands ⑪.

*From Bremen take the A28 and B72 to
Norden-Norddeich where the coastal
road leads to the different ports with
access to the East Frisian Islands.*

TRIP 2

WONDERS OF SCHLESWIG-HOLSTEIN
Wedel to Husum

HIGHLIGHTS

Ancient seaport city
Admire the unique red-brick Gothic architecture of
Lübeck, once home to German writer Thomas Mann

Little Switzerland
Explore the moraine hills of the Holsteinische Schweiz,
dotted with scenic lakes and quaint villages

Sailor's paradise
Visit the historic naval city of Kiel, which hosts the
Kieler Woche, the largest maritime festival
in northern Europe

Pristine beaches and spas
Enjoy the white sand beaches and superb spas
at Germany's popular resort-island, Sylt

WONDERS OF SCHLESWIG-HOLSTEIN

Situated between the Baltic and the North seas and bordered by the Elbe river and Denmark, Schleswig-Holstein is the northernmost state in Germany. A predominantly maritime region, it offers endless white-sand beaches and impressive lakes. The stops along this route include a visit to the historic old town of Lübeck, an architectural gem and a UNESCO World Heritage Site, and to the lovely lakes around Plön. The trip traverses pretty, tree-lined country roads through a largely agricultural region, where the pace of life is more relaxed, pausing at the charming towns of Holstein's Switzerland. The trip also weaves in a visit to the city of Kiel, which hosts the annual Kieler Woche, the biggest maritime festival in northern Europe.

ACTIVITIES

Watch ships entering and exiting the Elbe river at the Willkomm-Höft in Wedel

Take a bike tour through Fehmarn to enjoy the lovely scenery and fresh seaside air

Experience northern Europe's biggest sailing festival, the Kieler Woche at Kiel

Eat some of Kiel's famous smoked sprats or relax at one of the many stylish spas in Sylt

Above Glorious countryside of Holsteinische Schweiz, *see p46*

KEY

Drive route

PLAN YOUR DRIVE

Start/finish: Wedel to Husum.

Number of days: 3 days, allowing a day to explore Lübeck.

Distance: 524 km (326 miles).

Road conditions: The roads in this region are in good condition.

When to go: The trip is best enjoyed between May and September.

Opening times: Most shops and attractions are open from 9am to 6pm, Monday to Friday.

Main market days: Lübeck: Tue, Thu & Sat; **Kiel & Flensburg:** Wed & Sat.

Shopping: Marzipan, a popular sweet, is a must-buy from the Café Niederegger located in Lübeck's charming old town.

Major festivals: Kiel: Kieler Woche (Kiel week), Jun; Travemünder Woche (sailing race and cultural festival), Jul; **Sylt:** Kampener Literatur-und Musiksommer, (literature and music festival), Jul–Aug.

DAY TRIP OPTIONS

Those interested in **history** can head to Flensburg and then enjoy beach life at Sylt. Visit the town of Lübeck and stop at Fehmarn to admire its **scenic beauty**. For full details, *see p47*.

Below left Seventeenth-century Schloss in Eutin, Holsteinische Schweiz, *see p46* **Below** Scenic island of Fehmarn on the Baltic Sea, *see p45*

VISITING LÜBECK

Parking
Parkhaus Holstentor, near the Holstentor city gate, is the best spot for parking.

Tourist Information
Welcome Center; Holstentorplatz 1, 23552; 04518 89 97 00; www.luebeck-tourism.de; closed Jan–Easter & Nov: Sun

WHERE TO STAY

LÜBECK
Radisson Blu Hotel Lübeck *moderate*
The modern Radisson Blu has all the amenities of an upmarket business hotel. Its homely interior has a distinctive maritime touch. The hotel also offers an indoor pool and a fine German restaurant.
Willy-Brandt-Allee 6, 23554; 04511 420; www.radissonblu.com

Ringhotel Jensen *moderate*
One of the oldest hotels in the old town, this family-run place has individually designed rooms with modern facilities.
An der Obertrave 4–5, 23552; 04517 024 90; www.hotel-jensen.de

FEHMARN
Burg-Klause *moderate*
This family-run, four-star hotel has 37 well-appointed rooms and a restaurant.
Blieschendorfer Weg 1, 23769 Burg auf Fehmarn; 04371 500 20; www.burg-klause.de

IFA Fehmarn *moderate*
A three-star hotel with a beachfront complex and 422 apartments. It also offers wellness and spa services.
Burg, Südstrandpromenade 23769; 04371 890; www.ifa-fehmarn-hotel.com

Above Old mill beside a pond in the town of Ahrensburg **Below** Picturesque old town and canal in Lübeck

① Wedel
Schleswig-Holstein; 22880
Set on the Elbe river's right bank, Wedel was once an important cattle market. A reminder of this is the **Roland of Wedel** monument that stands in the Marktplatz. The main attraction is the **Willkomm-Höft** (welcome point) on the Elbe. Vessels arriving here have been traditionally greeted with flag signals since 1952, while the national anthem of the country of origin of the ship is played.
🚗 *Take Pinneberger Strasse to Pinneberg. Head to Schnellsen via Rellingen. Take the B432, then B433 to Hummelsbuttel. Get on to Poppenbutteler Weg. Take Saseler Damm/Saseler Chaussee to Ahrensburg.*

② Ahrensburg
Schleswig-Holstein; 22926
Located in the Tunneltal, Ahrensburg is part of the Hamburg metropolitan area. The town's highlight is the Renaissance **Schloss Ahrensburg** *(Mar–Oct: closed Mon & Fri; Nov–Feb: open Wed, Sat & Sun)*, which dates back to 1595. The building has four prominent corner towers and luxurious interiors.
🚗 *Head to the A1, cross it to reach Stubben then get on to Labenz. Take Klein Kinkrade then Hauptstrasse to Kastorf. Turn right onto B208 crossing Harmsdorf to Ratzeburg.*

③ Ratzeburg
Schleswig-Holstein; 23909
Ratzeburg is set on an island in the Grosser Ratzeburger See. In 1143, Heinrich der Löwe (Henry the Lion) became the ruler of the town and was responsible for the construction of the Romanesque **Dom** *(May–Sep: open daily; Oct–Apr: closed Mon)*. An early example of brick architecture, the cathedral features decorative elements in the southern vestibule.
🚗 *Return to Harmsdorf and continue on the B207 along Ratzeburger See to Lübeck.*

Statue in the town of Ratzeburg

---

④ LÜBECK
Schleswig-Holstein; 23552
By the end of the Middle Ages, Lübeck had become one of the richest and most powerful Hanseatic towns in Europe. Today, it is renowned for its unique *Backsteingotik* (north German Gothic brick architecture) and seven towers. The town was also home to Nobel Laureate Thomas Mann, one of the most famous figures in the German literary world.

A two-hour walking tour
Exiting the car park at the end of Wallstrasse, turn right on to Holstenstrasse to the **Holstentor** ①, or Holsten Gate. Based on Flemish designs, the gate was built by Hinrich Helmstede at the end of the 15th century. Continue on Holstenstrasse to the 14th-century **Petrikirche** ② *(closed Mon)*, or Church of St Peter, Lübeck's only five-naved church. Turn left into Schlusselbuden to visit **Marienkirche** ③ *(open daily)*, which houses great art treasures. From here, turn left into Mengstrasse to the **Schabbelhaus** ④, a charming patrician house with stepped gables. Return to Schlusselbuden and continue along Mengstrasse to

the Gothic **Buddenbrookhaus** ⑤ *(closed for renovation until 2023)*, once the home of Thomas Mann. It now houses a museum dedicated to the Mann family. Next, turn right on to Breite Strasse to the 13th-century **Rathaus** ⑥ *(open Mon–Sat, guided tours)*, Germany's most famous brick town hall. Return along Breite Strasse to the 15th-century **Jakobikirche** ⑦, a Baroque church on the right. Turn right into Koberg, then left into Grosse Burgstrasse to the **Burgtor** ⑧, an ancient gate that bears testimony to the town's historic fortifications. Return to Grosse Burgstrasse to the **Heiligen-Geist-Hospital** ⑨, a Gothic brick building, notorious for its spiky towers. Continue into Königstrasse, turn left on to Mühlenstrasse, then right on to Dankwartsgrube, and left again into Pferdemarkt for the **Herz-Jesu-Kirche** ⑩, on the right. This church houses a memorial to four clergymen who were executed during the Third Reich for resisting the Nazi regime. Across the parade square stands the **Dom** ⑪, built in the 12th and 13th century. Highlights include a triumphal cross sculpted from an oak tree. Get on to St Annen-Strasse to visit **Kunsthalle St-Annen** ⑫, or St Anne's Museum, which is housed in an Augustinian convent. Return to Kohlmarkt, turning left on Holstenstrasse for the car park.

🚗 *Take the A1 to Ratekau and then continuing further past Neustadt to take the B501 to Heiligenhafen. Then turn on to the B207 to Fehmarn.*

Thomas Mann

Thomas Mann, one of Germany's most influential writers, was awarded the Nobel Prize for literature for his works *Buddenbrooks* and *Der Zauberberg* (The Magic Mountain) in 1929. An anti-fascist, Mann emigrated to Switzerland in 1933 and to the US in 1938. Disowned by his country, he became the leading voice of *Exilliteratur*, the exiled German literature that was outlawed by the Nazi regime.

⑤ Fehmarn

Schleswig-Holstein; 23769

This Baltic Coast island is renowned for its serene beaches, pristine landscape and some 2,200 hours of sun per year. Explore Fehmarn on foot or a bike, relax at one of several wellness spas *(www.fehmare.de)* or play golf on one of the prettiest golf courses in Germany. The biggest village is **Burg auf Fehmarn**, home to the **St Nikolai Kirche**, or St Nikolai church. To the south-west of the island stands the 37-m (121-ft) tall lighthouse **Flügge** that offers panoramic views of the island.

🚗 *Retrace back on B207 then the A1 to Oldenburg. Turn on to the B202 to Lütjenburg then the B430 to the town of Plön, in Holsteinische Schweiz.*

Above left Tranquil shore of the island of Fehmarn **Above** Cycling on a narrow road in Fehmarn

BIKING IN FEHMARN

Bikes can be rented at **Conny's** *(Breite Strasse 46; 04371 13 03; www.fehmarn-fahrrad.de)*. Visitors can also get maps at the **tourist office** *(Sudstrand-Promenade 1; www.fehmarn.de)*.

EAT AND DRINK

RATZEBURG

Der Seehof *moderate*
This charming family-owned restaurant and hotel offers international and regional dishes.
Lüneburger Damm 1–3, 23909; 04541 86 01 01; www.der-seehof.de

LÜBECK

Schiffergesellschaft *moderate*
Located in a beautiful historic guild hall, this popular restaurant serves great beer and seafood. Book in advance.
Breitestrasse 2, 23552; 04517 67 76; www.schiffergesellschaft.com

Wullenwever *expensive*
One of the best restaurants in town, the Wullenwever serves local cuisine, with Mediterranean and maritime influences.
Beckergrube 71, 23552; 04517 043 33; www.wullenwever.de; closed Sun & Mon

FEHMARN

Aalkate Lemkenhafen *moderate*
Housed in a historic building from the 18th century, this restaurant offers eel specialities. These and other fish are smoked according to old local recipes and best enjoyed with a North German draught beer.
Königsstrasse 20, 23769; 04372 532; www.aalkate-original-fehmarn.de; closed Jan & Feb

Kajüte *moderate*
This simple restaurant serves regional seafood dishes as well as Polish specialities.
Breite Strasse 23, 23769 Burg auf Fehmarn; 04371 604 94 00; www. restaurant-kajüte-fehmarn.de

0 metres 300
0 yards 300

Hansahafen
Burgtor ⑧
AN DER UNTERTRAVE
KANALSTRASSE
KLINGENBERG
ENGELSGRUBE
KOBERG
GROSSE BURGSTRASSE
KLEINE GRÖPELGRUBE
LANGER LOHBERG
Jakobikirche ⑦
⑨ Heiligen-Geist-Hospital
FISCHERGRUBE
BREITE STR.
BECKERGRUBE
GLOCKENGIESSERSTR.
Schabbelhaus ④
MENGSTR.
Buddenbrookhaus ⑤
HUNDESTRASSE
③ Marienkirche
DR.-JULIUS-LEBER-STRASSE
ALFSTR.
Holstentor ①
Rathaus ⑥
HOLSTENSTR.
KOHLMARKT
FLEISCHHAUERSTRASSE
② Petrikirche
HUXSTR.
WAHMSTR.
GR. PETERSGRUBE
DEPENAU
KRÄHENSTR.
AEGIDIENSTR.
WEBERSTR.
MARLESGRUBE
DANKWARTSGRUBE
PFERDEMARKT
Herz-Jesu- ⑩ Kirche
HARTENGRUBE
⑫ Kunsthalle St-Annen
DOMKIRCHHOF
MÜNSTERSTR.
⑪ Dom
WILLY-BRANDT-ALLEE
Holstenhafen
POSSEHLSTR.
AN DER OBERTRAVE

WHERE TO STAY

AROUND HOLSTEINISCHE SCHWEIZ
Hotel Seeblick *moderate*
Set close to Plön's castle, this three-star hotel offers comfortable, clean rooms.
Rodomstorstrasse 70, 24306; 04522 39 93; ww.hotel-seeblick-ploen.de

KIEL
Hotel Kieler Yachtclub *expensive*
With views over the Kieler Förde, this hotel offers 21 rooms and suites.
Kiellinie 70, 24105; 0431 88 1 30; www.atlantic-hotels.de

SCHLESWIG
Hotel Strandhalle Schleswig *moderate*
A modern hotel with harbour views.
Strandweg 2, 24837; 04621 90 90; www.hotel-strandhalle.de

FLENSBURG
Hotel Flensburger Hof *moderate*
This hotel provides comfortable rooms.
Süderhofenden 38, 24937; 04617 07 16 70; www.hotel-flensburgerhof.de

SYLT
Dorint Söl'ring Hof *expensive*
Enjoy romantic views over the sea at this thatch-roofed resort.
Am Sandwall 1, 25980; 04651 83 62 00; www.soelring-hof.de

HUSUM
Romantik-Hotel Altes Gymnasium *expensive*
A country hotel with a wellness area.
Süderstrasse 2-10, 25813; 04841 83 30; www.altes-gymnasium.de

6 Holsteinische Schweiz
Schleswig-Holstein; 24301
The area's low moraine hills, which reach a height of 164 m (538 ft), and 140 lakes are the reasons why this area is known as Holstein's Switzerland. The best way to explore this region is on a bike tour. The main centre of this holiday area is **Plön** on the Grosser Plöner See or Lake Plön. **Preetz**, an old shoemakers' town and **Bosau**, home to a Romanesque church, are nearby. Visit the town of **Eutin**, referred to as the "Weimar of the North" because of its pretty buildings. Eutin's brick **Schloss** contains Rococo stuccowork and paintings by German artist Johann Heinrich Wilhelm Tischbein (1751–1828), which were inspired by the *Iliad* and the *Odyssey*, epic poems written by Homer.

 Take the B76 to Kiel. To reach the beach resort of Laboe, follow the B502 to the north.

7 Kiel
Schleswig-Holstein; 24103
Schleswig-Holstein's capital Kiel marks the beginning of the **Nord-Ostsee-Kanal**, or Kiel Canal, which was built at the end of the 19th century to connect the Baltic Sea and the North Sea. Germany's main submarine base during World War II, this town is now known for its beautiful coastline of tiny beaches and inlets. Every summer, the town attracts yachtsmen for the famous **Kieler Woche** or Kiel Week *(www.kieler-woche.de)*. A walk along the Schweden-Kai embankment leads to the **Nikolaikirche**, which has a Gothic altar, and to the **Rathaus** or town hall. About 6 km (4 miles) from the town is the **Freilichtmuseum Molfsee** *(closed Mon)*, an open-air museum with exhibits on German rural architecture. Around 18 km (11 miles) from Kiel is the beach resort of **Laboe**. Visit the **U-Boot Museum**, which tells the history of Germany's feared submarine fleet in World War II.

From Kiel, take the B76 to Eckernförde and on to Schleswig.

8 Schleswig
Schleswig-Holstein; 24837
A principal seat of the Vikings, Schleswig became a bishopric as early as 947. The town's main attraction is **Schloss Gottorf** *(closed Mon)*, which served as the residence of the dukes of Schleswig-Holstein from 1544 to 1713. This castle houses a regional museum, **Schleswig-Holsteinisches Landesmuseum**, and the **Archäologisches Landesmuseum**. Also visit the **Dom** *(open daily)*, which displays the Bordesholmer altar, a

masterpiece of Gothic carving. Stroll around the fishermen's district of **Holm** and visit the **Viking Museum Haithabu** *(Apr–Oct: open daily; open-air museum: closed in winter)*, which sheds light on the days when the Vikings used Schleswig as their headquarters.

🚗 *Take the B76, which becomes Bundesstrasse and then Schleswiger Strasse to Flensburg.*

9 Flensburg
Schleswig-Holstein; 24901
Germany's northernmost town, Flensburg was an important trading centre in the 16th century. The town's trademark northern gate, the **Nordertor**, dates from 1595. Visitors can explore the **Schiffahrtsmuseum** *(closed Mon)* or maritime museum. The town is home to four churches – the **Marienkirche** features a Renaissance altar; nearby **Heilig-Geist-Kirche**, or Church of the Holy Ghost, belongs to the town's Danish community; the **Nikolaikirche** houses a Renaissance organ and the **Johanniskirche** has a superb painted ceiling. About 9 km (6 miles) from the town centre stands the historic 16th-century **Schloss Glücksburg** *(May–Oct: open daily; Nov–Apr: open Sat & Sun)* with massive corner

towers. West of the town is **Seebüll**, where Expressionist painter Emil Nolde (1867–1956) lived and worked.
🚗 *Continue on the B199 to reach Klixbüll and at the T-junction turn left on B5 to Niebüll. At Niebüll take the car-train Niebüll-Westerland to reach the island of Sylt.*

10 Sylt
Schleswig-Holstein; 25980
The North Frisian Islands lie scattered in the North Sea 6 km (4 miles) off Schleswig-Holstein. Sylt, the largest island is 40 km (25 mile) long. Known for its posh villas, vibrant nightlife and Michelin-starred restaurants, its highlights include sandy beaches, red cliffs and the "Watt", the expanse of mudflats in **Nationalpark Schleswig-Holsteinisches Wattenmeer**. Relax at one of Sylt's many spas *(Arosa Sylt; www.a-rosa-resorts.de; Budersand; www.budersand.de)* before visiting **Westerland**, the main town. Stroll down Friedrichstrasse to a seafood restaurant, or take a detour to visit the neighbouring **Kampen**, an affluent resort. Also explore the nearby **Amrum** and **Helgoland**, Germany's only deep-sea islands.
🚗 *Retrace back on a car train from Westerland to Niebüll, then take the B5 to Husum.*

11 Husum
Schleswig-Holstein; 25813
A medieval seaport with a colourful North Sea harbour, Husum has a delightful old town. The town's central market square is filled with charming 17th- and 18th-century buildings. Husum was home to the German poet and writer Theodor Storm (1817–88), whose residence **Theodor Storm Haus** *(closed Mon)* now houses a small museum that displays exhibits related to the author's life.

EAT AND DRINK

AROUND HOLSTEINISCHE SCHWEIZ

Prinzeninsel *moderate*
This restaurant's menu features German cuisine in a stunning panoramic setting.
Große Insel 1, 24306 Plön; 04522 50 87 00; www.prinzeninsel.de; closed Mon–Tue

KIEL

Fischers Fritz Restaurant *expensive*
The smoked sprats here are delicious.
Martenshofweg 8, 24109; 04315 33 13 00; www.hotel-birke.de

SCHLESWIG

Restaurant Mühlenbach *moderate*
A range of grilled dishes is offered at this restaurant with an outdoor terrace.
Mönchenbrückstrasse 10, 24837; 04621 978 74 80; www.muehlen-bach.de; closed Mon

FLENSBURG

Restaurant Piet Henningsen *expensive*
This traditional restaurant serves local salty *Matjes* herring fillet.
Schiffbrücke 20, 24939; 04612 45 76; www.restaurant-piet-henningsen.de

SYLT

Sansibar *expensive*
A well-known watering hole, Sansibar offers excellent seafood.
Hörnumer Strasse 80, 25980 Rantum; 04651 96 46 46; www.sansibar.de

Above Red cliffs in Kampen, Sylt **Below** Sandy beach in Kampen, Sylt

DAY TRIP OPTIONS
A great range of day trips is possible along this route.

Museum and beaches
Head to Flensburg 9 to tour its maritime museum, then continue on to Sylt 10 to laze on its sandy

beaches before heading to one of the upmarket restaurants for dinner.

Continue on the B199 to Niebüll. Take the Niebüll-Westerland car-train to Sylt.

Culture and landscape
Visit Lübeck 4 to admire its

rich architectural heritage. Next, stop at Fehmarn 5 to enjoy the spectacular views of the coast before relaxing at one of the island's several wellness spas.

Take the A1 and then the B501 to Heiligenhafen and the B207 to Fehmarn.

TRIP 3

THE BALTIC COAST
Bad Doberan to Usedom

HIGHLIGHTS

Historic Gothic port
Explore Stralsund, a UNESCO World Heritage Site, where gorgeous medieval architecture forms a backdrop to everyday life

Leisurely beach life
Relax in a Strandkörb, a two-seater beach chair, found on powdery white-sand beaches throughout the region

Island playground
Escape to Rügen, a beautiful island that has belle époque villas, steam trains and chalk cliffs

Gourmet delights
Savour fresh fish at the harbour, served smoked straight from the boat, at Greifswald

White chalk cliffs at the Nationalpark Jasmund, Rügen

THE BALTIC COAST

Decorative Gothic brickwork in cosy old towns, beautiful beaches with their distinctive *Strandkörbe* (wicker chairs) and restaurants serving fresh fish are what make the Baltic Coast a popular holiday destination for Germans, even though it is yet to be discovered by foreign visitors. Going eastwards along the coastline and to the islands of Rügen and Usedom, this tour takes drivers through unspoiled scenery. The route starts inland in the spa town of Bad Doberan, then goes through Stralsund and Greifswald, ports of the medieval Hanseatic League. The tour also takes visitors to the belle époque resorts of the Kaisers on the islands of Rügen and Usedom and through former fishing villages on the Fischland peninsula, now transformed into fashionable resorts.

ACTIVITIES

Take a historic steam train to the seaside resort of Kühlungsborn from Bad Doberan

Browse for art in the ateliers of Ahrenshoop on the Fischland peninsula

Walk under the Baltic Sea through glass tunnels at the Ozeaneum in Stralsund

Take a boat trip along the north coast from Göhren to Sassnitz

Stroll along white chalk cliffs above a sparkling jade-coloured sea at the Königsstuhl on Rügen

See where the space race began in the Peenemünde Historical Technical Museum at Usedom

KEY

⬛ Drive route

0 kilometres 10

0 miles 10

Above Lighthouse along the coast, Rügen, *see pp54–5*

PLAN YOUR DRIVE

Start/finish: Bad Doberan to Usedom.

Number of days: 5–6 days, allowing one day to explore Rügen.

Distance: 456 km (283 miles).

Road conditions: There are excellent single-lane and dual-carriageway B-roads, except on Rügen, which has some short cobbled stretches.

When to go: The best time to visit for a beach holiday is between June and early September, though Rügen and Usedom can get busy between July and August. Christmas and New Year is also high season for visitors.

Opening times: Most shops are open from 9am to 5pm, Monday to Friday. Other attractions can be visited from 9am to 5pm, Tuesday to Sunday; they are generally closed on Mondays.

Main market days: Rostock: Mon–Sat; Stralsund: Tue & Fri; Greifswald: Tue & Thu–Fri.

Major festivals: Rostock: Hanse Sail (maritime festival), 1st or 2nd weekend of Aug; **Warnemünde:** Warnemünder Woche Regatta (boat races), 1st two weeks of Jul; **Stralsund:** Wallensteintage (folk festival), 3rd weekend of Jul; **Rügen:** Störtebeker Festspiele (theatre festival), Jun–Sep.

DAY TRIP OPTIONS

Culture lovers can stay in Bad Doberan to visit the graceful Münster. **Nature enthusiasts** can drive to Rostock and its **beach resort**, Warnemünde, a **chic art village** and a **bird-watcher's treat**. Families may prefer historic Stralsund, with its **fine beaches**, and a drive to the island of Rügen and the **charming town** of Greifswald. For full details, *see p57*.

Above Universitätplatz lined with colourful buildings, Rostock **Below left** Gothic Rathaus in Stralsund **Below right** Cistercian Gothic Münster in Bad Doberan

BAD DOBERAN TRAIN RIDE

The Mecklenburgische Bäderbahn Molli runs from Bad Doberan to the coastal resorts of Heiligendamm and Kuhlungsborn from late April to October as well as in winter. *03829 343 13 31; www.molli-bahn.de*

WHERE TO STAY

BAD DOBERAN

Hotel Friedrich-Franz-Palais *moderate*
The Duke of Mecklenburg's former guesthouse for aristocrat spa-goers offers pretty rooms. *August-Bebel-Strasse 2, 18209; 03820 377 92 90; www.hotel-friedrich-franz-palais.de*

FISCHLAND

Seezeichen *moderate*
The Seezeichen, a stylish spa hotel, has a terrace overlooking the sands. *Dorfstrasse 22, 18347 Ahrenshoop; 03822 067 83 00; www.seezeichen-hotel.de*

STRALSUND

Pension Peiss *moderate*
A friendly home-away-from-home, this pension has colourful modern rooms. *Tribseer Strasse 15, 18439; 03831 30 35 80; www.altstadt-pension-peiss.de*

① Bad Doberan
Mecklenburg-Lower Pomerania; 18209
Chinoiserie park pavilions, Neo-Classical buildings and a historic steam train *(daily)* to the seaside resort of Kühlungsborn, 6 km (4 miles) away from the town, are reminders of Bad Doberan's days as a fashionable health spa established in 1801 by the Duke of Mecklenburg, Friedrich Franz. Prior to this, the town's only claim to fame was its graceful Gothic **Münster** *(open daily)*. The church's rich medieval furnishings attest to the wealth of the Cistercian Order; the gilded high altar dating from 1300 is said to be the oldest wing altar in the world.

🚗 *Turn left out of the Münster car park to join the B105 to Rostock. Follow signs to Zentrum, then to "City" car park in Lange Strasse.*

② Rostock
Mecklenburg-Lower Pomerania; 18055
Industrialization after World War II turned Rostock into Germany's largest Baltic port and the biggest city in the state. However, it still has historic monuments and is a popular beach resort. One of the highlights of the city is the 15th-century **Marienkirche** *(open daily)* on Lange Strasse. Behind the church's altar is a contemporary

astronomical clock, whose clockwork apostles parade in front of Jesus when the clock strikes noon. Post-war rebuilding has returned some of the city's sights to their former glory. These include the **Neuer Markt** opposite the church, with its multicoloured gabled houses, the town hall and **Kröpeliner Strasse**, the shopping high street. To get to the beach, return down Lange Strasse to find the B103 to **Warnemünde**. The fish restaurants and boutiques of this seaside suburb are as much of a surprise as its powder-fine beach dotted with wicker chairs or *Strandkörbe*.

🚗 *Continue on the B103 for the ferry at Passagierkai across the Warnow to Hohe Düne. Drive to Niederhagen, turn right towards Rostock at Rövershagen, then take the B105 towards Ribnitz. After 10 km (6 miles), turn left to reach the Fischland peninsula.*

③ Fischland
Mecklenburg-Lower Pomerania; 18347
Artists acclaim the unspoiled rural landscapes of this peninsula, which extends parallel to the coast. In 1880, an artist's colony was founded in the fishing village of **Ahrenshoop**, which is now a chic seaside retreat. **Kunstkaten** *(closed Mon)* holds art exhibitions in a traditional house. Drive through the woods of Darss and beyond Prerow am Darss to **Zingst**, whose coastal marshes host middle Europe's largest crane roost in spring and autumn. Zingst also has the Heimatmuseum, which focuses on the peninsula's culture *(closed Tue)*.

🚗 *Take the main road to Barth, then follow signs to Löbnitz. Turn left to take the B105 to Stralsund. Turn towards the Altstadt on to the B96 and follow signs to the Ozeaneum car park.*

④ Stralsund

Mecklenburg-Lower Pomerania; 18439

An exquisite skyline hints at Stralsund's architectural wealth. Ringed by water, its Gothic core has impressed visitors for centuries, from the merchants who came to trade in one of the most powerful medieval ports in the Baltic to the UNESCO inspectors who awarded it World Heritage Site status in 2002.

A one-hour walking tour

From the car park, walk to the old harbour to see the windjammer **Gorch Fock** ① *(open daily)*, which is permanently moored here for tours. Among the 19th-century warehouses along the seafront is the **Ozeaneum** ②, where visitors can walk through the spectacular glass tunnels at the North and Baltic sea aquariums and explore the auditorium, which has life-size models of whales.

Behind it and across the Fährkanal, merchants' gabled houses line the **Fährstrasse** ③, which linked the hubs of medieval life in Stralsund: port and government. Carl Wilhelm Scheele, the 18th-century scientist who discovered the existence of oxygen, was born at No. 27–28, which now hosts exhibitions.

Continue down the street to **Alter Markt** ④ to see one of the finest ensembles of Gothic architecture in the Baltic – the 14th-century Rathaus (town hall) with its rosetted façade to let strong winter winds through; St Nikolaikirche *(open daily)*, whose Novgorod altar depicts fur traders hunting squirrels to sell to a Hanseatic League merchant; and Wulflam Haus, built for a wealthy patrician family. It is also possible to see reminders of the two centuries of Swedish rule that followed the Thirty Years' War – Commandantenhaus, the grey Baroque governor's residence with its Swedish coat of arms and, inside the town hall, a bust of the Swedish King Gustav Adolf. Walk south from Alter Markt, on to the high street, **Ossenreyerstrasse** ⑤; the bookshop at No. 14 is thought to be the town's oldest secular building, dating from 1258. Continue right, around the corner on to Apollonienmarkt, then turn right into Mönchstrasse to reach the 13th-century **Kloster**

Portal of the Nikolaikirche, Stralsund

St Katharinen ⑥. Now deconsecrated, it houses an aquarium *(open daily)* and a culture museum *(closed Mon)* with a muralled refectory. The museum ticket also provides access to the Gothic house of a merchant at No. 38 on Mönchstrasse and a museum of Mecklenburg folk culture at No. 23 on Böttcherstrasse. For an image of Stralsund in its prime, walk southwards down Mönchstrasse to **Marienkirche** ⑦ on Neuer Markt. The town's largest church has lovely stellar vaulting as well as views out to sea from its octagonal tower *(open daily)*. A ten-minute walk between the historic houses on Frankenstrasse off Neuer Markt leads back to the harbour and to the car park near the Ozeaneum.

🚗 *Return to the B96 and follow signs to Insel Rügen. Drive across the suspension bridge, then turn right towards Putbus. Parking is on the Markt.*

VISITING STRALSUND

Parking
Ample parking is available at the Ozeaneum car park on Hafenstrasse.

Tourist Information
Alter Markt 9, 18349; 03831 25 23 40; www.stralsundtourismus.de

EAT AND DRINK

ROSTOCK

Borwin *moderate*
Located by the harbour, Borwin has a beach-shack atmosphere that belies an excellent fresh fish menu.
Am Strande 2, 18055; 03831 490 75 25; www.borwin-hafenrestaurant.de

Zum Stromer *moderate*
This cosy restaurant serves regional and seafood dishes and offers great views from the terrace.
Am Strom 32, 18119 Warnemünde; 03818 57 97 87; www.restaurant-stromer.de; closed Tue & Sep–Jun: Mon & Tue

FISCHLAND

Ginger *expensive*
In the former home of artist Elisabeth von Eicken, this restaurant serves Mecklenburg and fine, modern dishes.
Dorfstrasse 39, 18347 Ahrenshoop; 03822 066 95 35; www.thiemegmbh-zingst.de

STRALSUND

Zur Kogge *moderate*
This 19th-century inn serves good-value Baltic fish.
Tribseer Strasse 26, 18439; 03831 28 58 50; closed Mon & Tue

Top Viewpoint on a cliff in the Nationalpark Jasmund, Rügen **Above** Neo-Classical hunting castle, Jagdschloss Granitz

BOAT TRIPS

Reederei Hiddensee *(www.reederei-hiddensee.de)*, **Adler Schiffe** *(www.adler-schiffe.de)* and **Weisse Flotte** *(www.weisse-flotte.de)* ferries ply along the north coast from May–Oct.

VISITING RÜGEN

Tourist Information
Heinrich-Heine-Strasse 7, 18509 Binz; 03839 314 81 48; www.binzer-bucht.de

WHERE TO STAY IN RÜGEN

Panorama Hotel Lohme *moderate*
This small hotel on a cliff has classic modern decor and great sea views.
An der Steilküste 8, 18551 Lohme (3.5 km/2 miles north of Königsstuhl car park); 03830 291 11 32; www.lohme.com

Cerês *expensive*
This five-star hotel brings metropolitan style to the traditional seafront.
Strandpromenade 24, 18509 Binz; 03839 36 66 70; www.ceres-hotel.de

⑤ Rügen

Mecklenburg-Lower Pomerania; 18556, 18546, 18609

Two centuries of tourism have not marred the appeal of Germany's largest island (926 sq km/357 sq miles). Whether exploring its rural villages, relaxing in beach resorts in belle époque villas, riding a vintage steam train or strolling along chalk cliffs, Rügen's appeal is timeless and simple.

① Putbus

Putbus's **Markt**, with its Neo-Classical theatre and smart Circus, would not look out of place in a city. In this large village, however, it appears almost aristocratic. Prince Wilhelm Malte I had hoped to create a Prussian St Tropez when he unsuccessfully planned the village as a health spa in 1809. Unfortunately, his castle was blown up with dynamite in the 1960s – the story goes that a local mayor wanted to impress East Germany's Communist rulers – although the orangery and park remain, as does the colonnaded **Badehaus**, or bathhouse, which lies 2 km (1 mile) away, near Lauterbach. From here, it is possible to take a boat trip to the Vilm Island Nature Reserve.
🚗 *Drive through Putbus towards the seaside town of Binz. Beyond Nistelitz village, turn left at the T-junction, then turn right to reach the Jagdschloss Granitz car park.*

② Jagdschloss Granitz

A Neo-Classical hunting castle of Prince Wilhelm Malte I, Jagdschloss Granitz *(May–Sep: open daily; Oct–Apr: closed Mon)* crowns the Tempelburg Hill, the highest point in east Rügen. Climb up the castle's 38-m (125-ft) high tower for a sweeping panorama of the Baltic Sea. An apocryphal tale explains this curiosity as the prince's ruse to settle a land dispute – Swedish rulers agreed he could own whatever he saw from his castle.

Spread along the coast beyond, **Binz**, Rügen's premier seaside resort, is renowned for its ornate villas and fine beach.
🚗 *Head through Binz to Sassnitz to take the B96 to the Nationalpark Jasmund and the Königsstuhl car park in Hagen village. Visitors can either take the bus*

The Rasender Roland

The Rasender Roland *(open daily; www.ruegensche-baederbahn.de)*, or Racing Roland, is a steam-powered narrow-gauge railway that plies on Rügen and provides an enjoyable change from travelling by car. The steam locomotives whistle out of Putbus station northward through the fields at 30 kph (19 mph), pause at Jagdschloss Granitz and Binz en route before terminating an hour later in Göhren in east Rügen.

to Königsstuhl, or opt for a pleasant 3-km (2-mile) stroll.

③ Königsstuhl

A road from Sassnitz cuts through the **Nationalpark Jasmund**, a landscape of spacious beech woods that cover white chalk sea cliffs. Romantic artist Caspar David Friedrich (1774–1840) immortalized the scenery in his etchings and oils, so popularizing the Königsstuhl that in 1865 Kasier Wilhelm I himself inspected the chalk bluff with his daughter Princess Viktoria. *Königsstuhl* literally means "king's chair", a name derived from the tradition that Rügen's early rulers followed to prove themselves worthy by climbing the 118-m (388-ft) high cliff. For a better view, walk 500 m (547 yards) south to the **Victoriasicht** viewpoint or to the beach via steep steps.

🚗 *Continue down the road to rejoin B96, then head towards Altenkirchen. Turn right to reach the car park at Putgarten. Tourist trains leave every 10 minutes for Kap Arkona and Vitt; otherwise it is a 2-km (1-mile) walk.*

Strolling the Stubbenkammer

The Königsstuhl is the most accessible of the Stubbenkammer cliffs that line Rügen's east coast. Marked by a blue stripe, the Hochuferweg path is a beautiful clifftop trail that leads south to Sassnitz. This 8-km (5-mile) long path, with beech woods on one side and a shifting emerald-jade sea on the other, passes the Kollicker Ort navigation light before proceeding through Ernst, Moritz, Arndt, Sicht and the Wissower Klinken viewpoints. Another hour's walk leads to Sassnitz, from where there are taxis or buses back to Königsstuhl.

④ **Kap Arkona**
Two lighthouses *(open daily)*, the smaller by the 19th-century Prussian architect Karl Friedrich Schinkel, afford a view over the rapefields that cover the cliffs of Kap Arkona, the wind-blown tip of Rügen. A 2-km (1-mile) path around the cape returns to the car park via the earthworks of the **Jaromarsburg**, a fortified temple of the Slavic tribes who occupied Rügen until the 12th century. Continue on the path to **Vitt**, an idyllic ancient fishing hamlet cupped in a dell behind the beach, where Slavic runes number some houses. Do not miss the folk mural in the village's 19th-century chapel.

🚗 *Return to Altenkirchen, then go to Wiek, and take the car ferry, Wittower Fähre. Drive to Gingst, then join the B96 at Samtens, and past Stralsund, join the B105 to Greifswald. Parking is available in the city centre, by the harbour and at the Markt.*

Above left Steam train on the narrow-gauge Rasender Roland **Above** Beautiful white-sand beach at Binz **Below** White chalk cliff at Kap Arkona, Rügen

EAT AND DRINK IN RÜGEN

Zum goldenen Anker *inexpensive*
Housed in a pretty, historic inn, this restaurant in Kap Arkona serves seasonal Baltic fish.
Vitt 2, 18556 Putgarten; 03839 11 21 34; www.gasthof-vitt.de

Strandhalle Binz *moderate*
Well-known for Mecklenburg dishes as interpreted by gourmet chef Toni Münsterteicher, this restaurant is housed in a vintage seaside hall in Binz and has an eclectic decor.
Strandpromenade 5, 18609; 03839 33 15 64; www.strandhalle-binz.de; closed early Jan–late-Mar

Right Visitors enjoying a walk on the pier in Ahlbeck, Usedom **Below** Ruins of the 13th-century Cistercian monastery, Greifswald **Below right** Alter Speicher – the half-timbered granary in Wolgast

WHERE TO STAY

GREIFSWALD

Kronprinz *moderate*
This old-fashioned four-star hotel near the cathedral has spacious but spartan rooms with reassuringly formal service.
Lange Strasse 22, 17489; 03834 79 00; www.hotelkronprinz.de

USEDOM

Das Ahlbeck Hotel & Spa *expensive*
Overlooking the beach and the pier, this four-star hotel features spacious rooms, a spa (with outdoor and indoor pools) and the excellent Düne 48 restaurant.
Dünenstrasse 48, 17419 Seebad Ahlbeck; 03837 84 99 40; www.das-ahlbeck.de

6 Greifswald

Mecklenburg-Lower Pomerania; 17489
This former Hanseatic town is situated 5 km (3 miles) from the Bay of Greifswald. Caspar David Friedrich (1774–1840), the Romantic painter, drew inspiration from the town's **Altstadt**, with its gabled houses and picturesque spires. Representations of the Gothic merchants' houses on the Markt and the cathedral with its striking twin-bulbed tower can be seen on his canvases in the excellent **Pommersches Landesmuseum** *(closed Mon)*, which also has displays on regional history. Drive 2 km (1 mile) east on Wolgaster Strasse to Wiek, a pretty harbour scented with the smell of smoking fish, then on to Eldena and the ruins of a 13th-century Cistercian monastery, another favourite subject of the artist.
🚗 *Continue past Eldena to Kemnitz, then to Pritzwald to reach the B111 to Wolgast. Parking is available on Platz der Jugend opposite St Petrikirche.*

7 Wolgast

Mecklenburg-Lower Pomerania; 17438
Now peaceful after being wrecked by war for centuries, the "Gateway to the island of Usedom" is an ideal stop on the drive. Visitors can walk behind the 14th-century parish church, **St Petrikirche**, which has part of an early Slavic temple next to the rear portal and a copy of 16th-century artist Hans Holbein's *Totentanz* frieze, into the cosy Altstadt. Rebuilt after being burnt down by Peter the Great of Russia in 1713, the old town clusters above a small harbour where grain ships docked in the 19th century.

Other highlights include the **Alter Speicher**, an 80-m (262-ft) long half-timbered granary, one of the largest buildings in the old town and the family home of Philipp Otto Runge (1777–1810), the famous Romantic painter.
🚗 *Continue on the B111 over the bridge on to Usedom. Turn left after 5 km (3 miles) to reach Peenemünde.*

⑧ Usedom

Mecklenburg-Lower Pomerania; 17424
The island, named after the village of Usedom and separated from the mainland by the Peenestrom Strait, is the second largest in Germany, covering an area of 445 sq km (172 sq miles). Renowned for its great natural beauty, Usedom has white beaches, forests, peat bogs and bays overgrown with rushes in the south. The island is linked to the mainland by two drawbridges near Anklam and Wolgast.

Historically, the most interesting spot on the island is the **Historisch-Technisches Museum** *(Apr–Oct: open daily; Nov–Mar: closed Mon)* at Peenemünde, located in military territory. On 3 October 1942, Luftwaffe scientists successfully launched a rocket here after seven years of testing. Originally intended for a jet plane,

Replica of a V-2 Vergeltungswaffen at Peenemünde

the technology was hijacked by the Nazis to develop the V-1 and V-2 *Vergeltungswaffen* (vengeance weapons) – flying bombs that were used to attack London in 1944. The museum documents this breakthrough in science and its post-war consequences.

Return to the B111 junction and then turn left to reach **Heringsdorf**. Park near the tourist office. The largest resort in Usedom spreads out behind a silvery sand beach with continental Europe's longest pier (508 m/555 yards). In the late 19th century, this was the playground of Prussia's elite, as is evident in the palatial summer residences on Delbrückstrasse promenade. Visitors can either walk or drive 2 km (1 mile) eastward to **Ahlbeck**, a smaller town and an elegant beach resort with villas, hotels and boarding houses gathered around a turreted pier.

Above left Marktplaz and Rathaus in Greifswald **Above** *Strandkörbe* on a beach in Usedom

EAT AND DRINK

GREIFSWALD
Fischer-Hütte *moderate*
Good-value fish is served straight off a boat or smoked in-house in this characterful place by the Wieck harbour.
An der Mühle 12, 17493; 03834 83 96 54; www.fischer-huette.de

USEDOM
Kulmeck *expensive*
Chef Tom Wickboldt lifts regional recipes to gourmet heights and embarks on culinary experiments, using herbs from the garden of this small, charming villa.
Kulmstrasse 17, 17424 Heringsdorf; 03837 848 80 40; www.kulmeck.de; open Wed–Sun dinner

---

DAY TRIP OPTIONS
Both Bad Doberan and Stralsund make good bases from which to explore the region.

Art, old and new
With Bad Doberan ① as a base, visit the Münster, its Gothic altars steeped in medieval mystery, then tour the Marienkirche in Rostock ② and the beach at Warnemünde. Drive to the art colony beach resort of Ahrenshoop on Fischland ③ for lunch and some window shopping.

Later, stroll on an unspoiled beach, then either admire the Darss-Museum Prerow or, in spring and autumn, go bird-watching at Zingst.

Take the B105 to Rostock and then the B103 to Warnemünde. Follow the driving instructions through Ahrenshoop to Zingst, then take the B105 back to Bad Doberan.

Culture and coast
In Stralsund ④ explore the Alter Markt's fine ensemble of Gothic buildings before driving to Rügen

Island ⑤ for a clifftop stroll at the Königsstuhl, the ideal way to work up an appetite for lunch on the beach at Binz. Leave the car at the car park in Jagdschloss Granitz, a Neo-Classical castle, and make the return trip to Putbus, Rügen's first resort, by vintage steam train. End the day relaxing at the beach resort of Binz, which is near the castle.

Take the B96 to Sassnitz, then follow driving instructions to Königsstühl and in reverse to Binz. Take the B196 to Bergen to rejoin the B96 for Stralsund.

TRIP 4

LAND OF A THOUSAND LAKES
Wismar to Neustrelitz

HIGHLIGHTS

Grand ducal palace
Marvel at the pomp of Schwerin's Schloss and visit
the orangery where Duke Paul Friedrich Franz II
tended his plants

Water wonderland
Enjoy cruising on the lakes, aboard a steam
launch from Waren or on a canoe in the
Müritz-Nationalpark

Abundant birdlife
Try to spot nesting ospreys and sea eagles
around the towns of Federow and Speck

LAND OF A THOUSAND LAKES

Numerous glacial lakes give the heart of Mecklenburg-Lower Pomerania (Mecklenburg-Vorpommern) its nickname, the "Land of a Thousand Lakes". This aquatic mosaic encompasses everything from small freshwater seas to myriad minor pools in the Müritz-Nationalpark, where astonishing birdlife is as much a part of the scenery as sweeping vistas. This tour takes drivers from coast to country: from the cobbled lanes of the medieval port of Wismar to Schwerin, the capital of the state, with its enchanting castle, then east into the state's rustic heart around Güstrow, finally ending at Neustrelitz, the former Residenzstadt of a duchy.

ACTIVITIES

Hunt for "Swedish Heads" in the medieval lanes of Wismar

See the work of Ernst Barlach, the Expressionist sculptor, in Güstrow

Board a vintage steamship for a cruise from Waren

Go canoeing in the Müritz-Nationalpark

Go bird-watching around Speck in the Müritz-Nationalpark

Above Buildings lining the Markt in Wismar, *see pp62–3* **Below left** Waters of Schweriner See, *see p63* **Below right** Steam tractor at the Agroneum museum in Alt Schwerin, near Müritzsee, *see p64*

PLAN YOUR DRIVE

Start/finish: Wismar to Neustrelitz.

Number of days: 2–3 days, allowing half a day to explore Wismar.

Distance: 250 km (155 miles).

Road conditions: Roads are good except in the Müritz-Nationalpark, where a section of paved track and unsurfaced road can be tricky in winter when it snows. Roads are well signposted outside the national park.

When to go: Late spring to autumn is a good time to visit the region. Visitors should not miss the spectacular annual crane migration in mid-October. Most facilities in the park close from November to April, and small lakes often freeze in winter.

Opening times: Most shops are open from 9am to 5pm, Monday to Friday. Attractions are open from 9am to 5pm, but are generally closed on Mondays.

Main market days: Wismar: Tue, Thu & Sat; Schwerin: Wed & Fri; Güstrow: Tue, Thu & Sat; **Waren:** Tue & Thu.

Major festivals: Wismar: Hafentage (harbour festival), 2nd weekend in Jun; Schwerin: Schlossfestspiele (music festival), Jun–Jul; Altstadtfest (old town festival), mid-Sep.

DAY TRIP OPTIONS

History and architecture lovers can visit Güstrow's **palace** and Wismar's **monuments**, while outdoor enthusiasts can stay in Waren in the Müritz-Nationalpark to enjoy a **lake cruise**, **walks** and **bird-watching** around Speck and then drive to nearby villages to go **canoeing**. For full details, *see p65*.

KEY

Drive route

Above Impressive Marienkirche in Wismar
Above right Schweriner See shore

VISITING WISMAR

Parking
There is public parking on Papenstrasse, between Grünestrasse and Bliedenstrasse. Parking is also available at the old port, Alter Hafen.

Tourist Information
Lübsche Strasse 23a, 23966; 03841 194 33; www.wismar.de; open daily

WHERE TO STAY

WISMAR

Townhouse Stadt Hamburg *moderate*
This classic hotel offers modern rooms and has one of the finest locations in town, on the Markt.
Am Markt 24, 23952; 03841 23 90; www.vagabondclub.com/wismar

SCHWERIN

Niederländischer Hof *moderate*
Subtle modern touches render sophistication to the old-world elegance of this splendid 19th-century hotel opposite Lake Pfaffenteich.
Alexandrinenstrasse 12–13, 19055; 03855 911 00; www.niederlaendischer-hof.de

Pension Am Theater *moderate*
Located a short distance from the Schloss, this hotel has cheerful, modern rooms.
Theaterstrasse 1–2, 19055; 03855 936 80; www.schwerin-pension.de

Speicher am Ziegelsee *moderate*
Housed in a former grain warehouse on the shore of Ziegelsee, this designer hotel has a spa and offers views over the lake. Summer evenings on the lakeside deck are a delight.
Speicherstrasse 11, 19055; 03855 00 30; www.speicher-hotel.com

① WISMAR

Mecklenburg-Lower Pomerania; 23952

A provincial town on the Baltic Sea, Wismar is worth a visit for its faded grandeur and historic charm. Renovation has repaired the damage wreaked by World War II to restore something of the looks of the town's golden ages. It was declared a World Heritage Site in 2002.

A 90-minute walking tour

Take Grünestrasse near the car park and turn left on to Dankwarstrasse to reach the cobbled **Markt** ①. A showpiece of restoration work, this is one of the largest market squares in north Germany. To the north of the square is the Neo-Classical Rathaus, which houses a museum *(open daily)* in its cellar with displays on the town's history. Cross the main shopping street, Hegede, behind the tourist office, to reach the town's Gothic quarter. Only an archdeacon's house on the corner of Sargmacherstrasse and the massive tower of **Marienkirche** ② remain from before the Allied bombing raids in 1945. Take a tour up the 80-m (262-ft) tower *(open daily)*, which has displays on medieval

Swedish Heads
Wismar's unofficial mascots, these brightly painted moustachioed figures have lions' heads for hats. One bust is in the Markt, two more are near the mouth of the old port, all replicas of two "Swedish Heads" that stood at the harbour mouth during the Swedish occupation. One theory behind the name suggests that the original busts came from an 18th-century Swedish merchant ship.

construction techniques. A little further, on Vor dem Fürstenhof, is the **Fürstenhof** ③. An Italian-style palace for the dukes of Mecklenburg, this Mannerist building has terracotta friezes that retell the stories of the Trojan Wars and the Prodigal Son.

Further down this road stands **St Georgen Kirche** ④, the largest church in Wismar. The Grosse Hohe Strasse leading northwards from the church portal threads down to the cobbled Lübsche Strasse, once a mercantile thoroughfare. On its junction with Neustadt is the **Heiligen-Geist-Kirche** ⑤ *(open daily)*, a fine example of a hospital church.

Take Neustadt from beside the church and continue down it to cross the Grube – Germany's first urban canal, dug in the mid-1200s – and to get to the ring road and the **Alter Hafen** ⑥. The port may look familiar to film buffs, as it was featured in the classic silent movie *Nosferatu* (1922). Opposite is the **Wassertor** ⑦, the last of the gateways in the town's medieval fortifications. Return to the Grube and follow it eastwards to the **Nikolaikirche** ⑧. This bulky late-Gothic basilica was once the church of medieval seafarers and, despite its size, managed to survive World War II's air raids. View glazed friezes on its façade before marvelling at the 37-m (121-ft) high interior with original frescoes. Continue alongside the Grube and then cross it on Schweinsbrücke or "pig bridge". Here stands the **Schabbellhaus** ⑨, a Dutch Renaissance mansion whose museum *(closed Mon)* contains one of the original "Swedish Heads" among many paintings and curios. Continue southwards on ABC-Strasse to reach the Markt, then take Dankwartstrasse and Grünestrasse back to the car park on Papenstrasse.

🚗 *Take Dr-Leber-Strasse, then join the B106 to Schwerin. Follow signs for Am Schloss car park opposite the palace.*

② Schwerin
Mecklenburg-Lower Pomerania; 19053
Situated amid several lakes, the state capital's main attraction is hard to miss. The ducal **Schloss**, bristling with towers and topped with a gilded turret like a crown, looks like something out of *Cinderella*. Duke Paul Friedrich Franz II's inspiration for the renovation of his dynastic residence came from the Loire's Chambord Chateau. The palace's showrooms *(closed Mon)* revel in ancestral pomp. Across the palace footbridge is the state museum, **Staatliches Museum** *(closed for renovations until 2024)*. Highlights include 17th-century Flemish art and works by Rembrandt. After the visit, enjoy a cruise (www.weisseflotteschwerin.de) on the Schweriner See.

🚗 *Drive around the lake to follow signs to Ludwigslust, then to the B321. In Zippendorf, park at Am Strand.*

③ Zippendorf and Muess
Mecklenburg-Lower Pomerania; 19063
About 3 km (2 miles) from Schwerin's city centre, the lakeside suburb of Zippendorf is a great place to relax on the beach or stroll around the lake. About 2 km (1 mile) from here lies another suburb, Muess. Its open-air museum, **Freilichtmuseum** *(mid-Apr–Oct: closed Mon)*, provides a glimpse of rustic Mecklenburg.

🚗 *Continue west on the B321 past Crivitz and turn left on B392 to Goldberg. Get on to the B192 to Dobbertin, turn right to Güstrow and follow signs to Zentrum. Turn left on to Wallenstein-strasse to park near the Schloss.*

Above Wismar's old town and canal
Below Ducal Schloss, on an island on Lake Schwerin

EAT AND DRINK

WISMAR
Reuterhaus *moderate*
This former Renaissance hall of a wine merchant is located behind the town hall and serves gutsy Mecklenburg dishes such as green kale and bacon or *Rippenbraten* (pork stuffed with fruit). *Am Markt 19, 23966; 03841 222 30; www.weinberg-wismar.de*

SCHWERIN
Orangerie *moderate*
Palm leaves and wicker seats highlight the interiors of Orangerie, which serves Mediterranean light lunches and sumptuous coffee and cake. *Schwerin Schloss, Lennéstrasse 1, 19053; 03855 25 29 15; www.schweriner-schloss-restaurant.de; closed Nov–Mar*

Weinhaus Wöhler *expensive*
Named after the wine trader who opened a cellar here in 1819, this place offers fish and meat dishes. The house speciality is *Sauerfleisch* (pickled meat). *Puschkinstrasse 26, 19055; 03855 58 30; www.weinhaus-woehler.de; closed Sun & Mon*

Right Dom in the town of Güstrow

VISITING MÜRITZ-NATIONALPARK

Tourist Information
Nationalpark Informationshaus, Damerower Strasse 6, 17192 Federow; 03991 66 88 49; www.nationalpark-service.de

Boat Rental
Charterpoint Müritz Grosse; Burgstrasse 1, 17192, Waren; 03991 16 55 59; www.charterpoint-mueritz.de

WHERE TO STAY

BURG SCHLITZ
Burg Schlitz *expensive*
Housed in Count Schlitz's Neo-Classical palace, this hotel has rooms decorated with Biedermeier furnishings.
Hohen Demzin, 17166; 03996 127 00; www.burg-schlitz.de

AROUND MÜRITZ-NATIONALPARK
Kleines Meer *moderate*
Situated near the waterfront, this friendly hotel is decorated in calm neutral colours.
Alter Markt 7, 17192 Waren (3 km/ 2 miles north of Müritz-Nationalpark); 03991 64 80; www.kleinesmeer.de

Below Back road to Waren **Below right** Baroque town church in Neustrelitz
Bottom Gently rolling countryside, Güstrow

④ Güstrow
Mecklenburg-Lower Pomerania; 18273
The old town in Güstrow is dominated by its 16th-century **Schloss** *(closed Mon)*, built by the Italian architect Franz Parr. Highlights include its banquet hall with striking stucco hunting scenes. Among its glass and antiques is the *Menagerie* series that Flemish artist Maerten de Vos (1532–1603) created at the height of the Age of Exploration. The nearby **Dom** contains the tombs of the palace's founder, Duke Ulrich, and his two wives. This early-Gothic basilica has a bronze angel by Ernst Barlach, Germany's finest Expressionist sculptor. His work can also be seen in **Gertrudenkapelle** (Gertrude Chapel) *(closed Mon)* and **Atelierhaus** *(closed Mon)*, 3 km (2 miles) east of Güstrow.
🚗 *From the car park, return to the main road and turn left on to Goldberger Strasse. Turn right on to Plauer Strasse for the B104. In Teterow, take the B108 to Burg Schlitz.*

⑤ Burg Schlitz
Mecklenburg-Lower Pomerania; 17166
Nicknamed "Mecklenburg Switzerland" due to its low moraine hills, the municipality of Hohen Demzin is known for its palaces, the grandest of which is the Neo-Classical Burg Schlitz. Built in the 1820s for Count Schlitz, it is now a luxury hotel that stands within beautifully landscaped parkland. Near its

chapel is the Secessionist nymph fountain, cast in 1903 for a Berlin department store. A copy of the fountain stands in New York's Central Park.
🚗 *Continue south on the B108 to Waren; drive into Zentrum for car parks around the harbour.*

⑥ Müritz-Nationalpark
Mecklenburg-Lower Pomerania; 17192
Covering an area of 322 sq km (124 sq miles), the Müritz-Nationalpark is famous for its birdlife and boating facilities. Foreign visitors, however, have not yet discovered the tiny glacial lakes, forests and abundant birdlife of this sparsely populated and quiet backwater destination.
A half-timbered town on the north shore of the Müritzsee (Lake Müritz), **Waren** is an ideal base for tourists with its beaches, hiking and boating options *(03991 153 40; www.mueritzfischer.de)*. At 115 sq km (44 sq miles), Müritzsee is Germany's largest lake after Constance. Visitors can find a bench at the harbour and enjoy the bustle as motorboats and small yachts tie up at the wharf or embark on a cruise on the lake *(Weisse Flotte Müritz, Kietzstrasse 17; 03991 12 26 68;*

Winged Wonders
Renowned for its birdlife, the Müritz-Nationalpark is a popular destination for those who want to spot the ospreys and sea eagles that breed here. Visitors can get information about sightings from the park centre at Federow, where there is an observation station. The spectacular avian show in the second half of October should not be missed. Thousands of cranes can be seen migrating south. The marshland around the Rederangsee, south of Federow, is a favourite roosting area.

www.weisse-flotte-mueritz.de) aboard a vintage steamer. The **Müritzeum** (03991 63 36 80; www.mueritzeum.de), at the eastern edge of the old town, houses the nation's largest freshwater aquarium and has displays on ecology.

Return from the centre to locate brown signs for the Müritz-Nationalpark on the B192. After 1 km (half a mile), turn right, following parking signs on Mecklenburger Strasse and head to **Federow**. Visitors can pick up maps from the park centre in Federow (May–Oct: open daily) and then continue to the hamlet of **Speck** on the banks of the Specker See (Lake Speck); it is possible to spot ospreys on a 2.5-km (1.5-mile) circuit of the lake. Another walk ascends to a viewing platform on the Käflingsberg Hill; the trail head is just over 1 km (half a mile) from the end of the paved road.

For a long walk, continue walking on the track beyond Speck, then turn left at the crossroads to the farming villages of **Granzin** and **Dalmsdorf**, where residents sell smoked fish by the roadside. Canoes can be hired (Kormoran Kanutouring, Granzin 28a, 17237 Kratzeburg-Granzin; 03982 22 98 88; www.kormoran-kanutouring.de), between April and early October to view the scenery around the lake.

🚍 *Return to Waren and turn right on to the B192. At Möllenhagen, turn right again following signs to Ankershagen, Peckatel and then turn left on B193 for Blumenholz. Turn right on to the B96 and take the Neustrelitz/Kiefernheide exit to Neustrelitz.*

⑦ Neustrelitz
Mecklenburg-Lower Pomerania; 17235
Designed in the 1730s as the Residenzstadt, or residence town, of a minor Mecklenburg duchy, the origins of Neustrelitz as a custom-built capital are evident in its unique and symmetrically designed Markt or marketplace, with streets that radiate like spokes from the corners. Visitors can better appreciate the square's perfect geometry from a viewing platform in the Baroque town church and then take the Schlosstrasse to the **Schloss**. This ducal palace was destroyed in World War II, but its gardens retain their naturalistic English style as designed by Peter Josef Lenné, the great Prussian garden designer of the 19th century. The orangery also remains intact and is now a restaurant. Its interiors were designed by the 19th-century master architect Karl Schinkel and Prussian court sculptor Christian Daniel Rauch.

Above Reed beds in the Muritzsee, renowned for its birdlife **Below** Nymph fountain, Burg Schlitz

EAT AND DRINK

GÜSTROW
Café Küpper *inexpensive*
Close to the Schloss, the small Café Küpper offers soups, snacks and gateau.
Domstrasse 15, 18273; 03843 68 24 85

BURG SCHLITZ
Wappen-Saal *expensive*
Housed in the spectacular Neo-Classical hall in Burg Schlitz , this restaurant serves French and Italian cuisine with an Asian touch. Book in advance.
Schlosshotel Burg Schlitz, 17166; 03966 127 00; closed Sun, Mon & Feb

AROUND MÜRITZ-NATIONALPARK
Fischerhof *moderate*
Located behind the high street off the main square, this small courtyard restaurant specializes in fresh Müritzsee fish.
Neuer Markt 19, 17192 Waren (3 km/ 2 miles north of Müritz-Nationalpark); 03991 66 98 15; closed Sun & Mon

NEUSTRELITZ
Luisenstube *moderate*
Situated just off the Markt, this cosy restaurant serves freshwater fish.
Seestrasse 8, 17235; 01764 157 79 20; www.luisenstube.de

DAY TRIP OPTIONS
Start from Schwerin or Waren.

Historical romance
In Schwerin ②, visit Staatliches Museum, then drive to Güstrow ④ for lunch. Explore the Dom and Schloss and head to Wismar ①. End the day on Zippendorf's ③ beach.

Take the B104 northwards from the Schloss in Schwerin to Güstrow. Return on the B104 to Prüzen, turn right to Bützow and head to Steinhagen, Neukloster. Then turn right on to the B192. Go left at Zurow to the B105 to reach Wismar. Follow the driving instructions to reach Zippendorf.

Outdoor escapes
Spend a day in Waren and explore the Müritz-Nationalpark ⑥. Visit the park centre in Federow or go on a hike up the Käflingsberg. Drive to Granzin to go canoeing before strolling around the Schloss gardens of Neustrelitz ⑦.

Follow instructions to Neustrelitz. Retrace the route to Waren.

Bremen •   • Hamburg

Hannover •   • Berlin

Dortmund •
Köln •   GERMANY   • Leipzig

• Frankfurt

Saarbrücken •
            • Nürnberg
Stuttgart •

• München

TRIP 5

HISTORY AND REVOLUTIONS ALONG THE ELBE

Havelberg to Lutherstadt Wittenberg

HIGHLIGHTS

Magnificent churches
Tour the impressive churches that
dot the banks of the Elbe river

School of modern design
Visit the Bauhaus design school, the inspiration
behind modern art and architecture

Charming country gardens
Wander around the landscaped gardens of Wörlitz
in the heart of eastern Germany

Historic town
Delve into history at Lutherstadt Wittenberg, a lovely
getaway with relics of the Protestant Reformation

Majestic interior of the Gothic Schlosskirche, Lutherstadt Wittenberg

HISTORY AND REVOLUTIONS ALONG THE ELBE

This tour loosely follows the Elbe, a major river that runs through Saxony-Anhalt (Sachsen-Anhalt), a state dotted with historic sights. In the 7th century, the river formed a natural frontier between Germans in the west and Slavic tribes in the east. In the 10th century, however, the German Saxons made a concerted effort to colonize and Christianize the east, to which end they built a series of great churches and abbeys in Magdeburg, Havelberg and Jerichow. With a new border secured, river trade helped settlements flourish – in particular the town of Tangermünde, whose half-timbered core has been wonderfully preserved. Further south along the Elbe, the small town of Lutherstadt Wittenberg is renowned as the birthplace of Protestantism. History is not the only attraction on this route: large portions of the Elbe are part of a UNESCO-designated biosphere reserve that offers good hiking, as do the wonderful country gardens of Wörlitz.

Above Scenic road to Havelberg, *see p70*

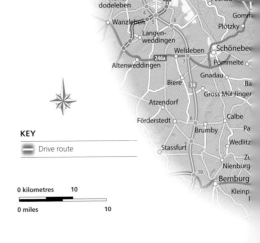

ACTIVITIES

Enter the zany world of architect Friedensreich Hundertwasser at the Grüne Zitadelle building in Magdeburg

Take a boat trip on the Elbe river

Explore the palatial Wörlitz gardens on foot or by gondola

Climb the stairs of Lutherstadt Wittenberg's castle tower for glorious views of the town

KEY

🌊 Drive route

0 kilometres   10

0 miles   10

Above Central lake, Wörlitz gardens, *see p72*
Below Magnificent late-Gothic gate, Neustädter Tor, Tangermünde, *see p70*

PLAN YOUR DRIVE

Start/finish: Havelberg to Lutherstadt Wittenberg.

Number of days: 3 days, allowing half a day to explore Lutherstadt Wittenberg.

Distance: 222 km (138 miles).

Road conditions: All major and minor roads are well paved and well signposted.

When to go: The month of June is the best time to visit.

Opening times: Most attractions open daily. Shops are open from 9am to 5pm, Monday to Friday, but close early on Saturdays. Shops and services are closed on Sundays. Restaurants generally close around 10pm.

Main market days: Magdeburg: Tue–Sat; **Lutherstadt Wittenberg:** Wed.

Shopping: In Lutherstadt Wittenberg, look out for *Lutherbrot*, a tasty gingerbread with chocolate and sugar icing.

Major festivals: Havelberg: Pferdemarkt (horse market and funfair), early Sep; **Lutherstadt Wittenberg:** Luther's Hochzeit (Luther's wedding festival), late Jun; Reformationstag (Reformation day), 31 Oct.

DAY TRIP OPTIONS

The northern part of this tour along the Elbe will appeal to **history buffs** who wish to see the great Saxon churches built as missionary outposts. The southern part of the Elbe, which takes in the Bauhaus School and the landscaped gardens of Wörlitz, will engage those interested in **design and architecture**. Exploring Lutherstadt Wittenberg, associated with the **Protestant Reformation**, can take a whole day. For full details, *see p73*.

Above Scenic view of the old town from Dom St Marien, Havelberg **Above right** Half-timbered houses lining the streets of Tangermünde **Below** Gothic Dom St Mauritius und St Katharina, Magdeburg

WHERE TO STAY

TANGERMÜNDE

Schloss Tangermünde *moderate*
Located in the castle, this is the town's most prestigious lodging. Facilities include a sauna and steam room. The restaurant here is also the best in town.
Auf der Burg, Amt 1, 39590; 03932 273 74 51; www.schloss-tangermuende.de

MAGDEBURG

Herrenkrug Parkhotel *moderate*
Lovely four-star hotel offering spacious and modern rooms. There is also a fine spa and a reputed restaurant.
Herrenkrug 3, 39114; 03918 50 80; www.herrenkrug.de

Hotel Ratswaage Magdeburg *moderate*
Situated in the city centre, this large hotel has 174 rooms, several bars, a restaurant, an indoor pool and a sauna.
Ratswaageplatz 1–4, 39104; 03915 92 60; www.ratswaage.de

Hotel Stadtfeld *moderate*
This three-star hotel near the city centre has simple rooms and a bar.
Maxim-Gorki-Strasse 31–37, 39108; 03915 066 60; www.hotelstadtfeld.de

Residenz Joop *moderate*
This bed-and-breakfast is an easy walk from the town centre.
Jean-Burger-Strasse 16, 39112; 03916 26 20; www.residenzjoop.de

DESSAU

Bauhaus Studio Building *inexpensive*
The design school has turned its former student dormitories into guest rooms, some equipped with kitchens.
Gropiusallee 38, Dessau, 06846; 03406 50 80; www.bauhaus-dessau.de

① Havelberg
Saxony-Anhalt; 39532

Havelberg's old town occupies a small island in the Havel river close to its confluence with the Elbe. This town was founded as a Christian missionary outpost in 948 by Emperor Otto I, who sensed a perfect defensive position in heathen Slav territory. Medieval houses still cluster in the old town, and above them looms the sombre **Dom St Marien** *(closed Mon)*, built between 1150 and 1170. The cathedral was destroyed in a huge fire in the 13th century, and its present appearance is the result of Gothic additions to its Romanesque core, with impressive results. Its most remarkable feature is a 14th-century stone choir screen carved with scenes from the New Testament.

🚗 *Turn right in the direction of Genthiner Strasse and stay on the B107 to Jerichow. Turn right at the town entrance to the Abbey car park.*

② Jerichow Abbey
Saxony-Anhalt; 39319

Like the Dom at Havelberg, Jerichow Abbey *(closed Mon)* was built during a spate of mid-12th-century ecclesiastical expansion. This Premonstratensian convent was founded in 1144, making it one of northern Germany's oldest brick buildings. The **abbey museum** displays the brick building methods that became typical of the region as it was settled in by the Germans.

🚗 *Retrace back along the B107, turn left on the B188 westwards to Tangermünde. Leave the B188, going south on Arneburger Strasse. Bear right on Lindenstrasse, left on Grete-Minde, to park on Lange Strasse.*

③ Tangermünde
Saxony-Anhalt; 39585

Central Tangermünde is a snapshot of the early 17th century – almost all the half-timbered houses along its central cobblestoned Lange Strasse replaced those lost in a fire in 1617. The fire was blamed on an innocent Grete Minde, who was thought to want revenge after the town's court refused her inheritance. She was soon after burned as a witch, but is now celebrated by a bronze statue that stands to the left of the **Rathaus**, one of the few buildings to escape the blaze. Built in the 1430s, it bristles with gables and ornamentation. A stroll down Kirchstrasse reveals a series of timber-framed houses en route

Statue of Grete Minde, Tangermünde

to the late-Gothic **St Stephanskirche**, completed at the end of the 15th century. The church was built by Charles IV, King of Bohemia, who used the town as his second royal residence after Prague. Behind the church are the remains of his castle, which was destroyed in 1640 by a Swedish campaign in the Thirty Years'War.

🚗 *Turn left to Lüderitz on to the B189, which becomes the B71 in Magdeburg. Follow signs to Zentrum, then the Dom to reach the Domplatz for on-street parking.*

Friedensreich Hundertwasser

The Grüne Zitadelle in Magdeburg was the last work of Austrian architect and designer Friedensreich Hundertwasser (1928–2000). Inspired by Antonio Gaudí and Gustav Klimt, Hundertwasser is famed for his rejection of straight lines in favour of unruly shapes, bright colours and chaotic designs. Fascinated by spirals, he called straight lines "the devil's tools".

④ Magdeburg

Saxony-Anhalt; 39104

Established as a trading post by Charlemagne in the 9th century, Magdeburg became the main residence of Emperor Otto I in the 10th century. The town was brutally sacked in 1631 by Catholic imperial forces, while World War II levelled most of it. However, Magdeburg is not without reminders of its glorious past. The Gothic **Dom St Mauritius und St Katharina** *(open daily)* has distinctive octagonal turrets and spires. Its construction began in 1209, vastly

enlarging an earlier monastery church founded by Otto I in 926. Look out for the emperor's tomb, sculptor Ernst Barlach's 1929 memorial to the dead of World War I and the sculpture of the *Magdeburger Virgins* (1240), illustrating the Parable of the Ten Virgins. In contrast, the most celebrated building is the **Grüne Zitadelle** *(tours: daily)*. With its playful curves and colours, this apartment complex, designed by Austrian architect Friedensreich Hundertwasser, is a key landmark.

🚗 *Turn right along Ernst-Reuter-Allee and continue on the Brückstrasse, which becomes the B1, continue further at Heyrothsberge, and turn right on to the B184. In Dessau, turn right on Rosslauer Allee, then right on to Antoinettenstrasse, which becomes Puschkinallee, then left on Gropiusallee to the car park.*

⑤ Dessau

Saxony-Anhalt; 06846

Built in 1925, The **Bauhaus School** in Dessau continues to be a design school. The work of architect Walter Gropius, this white concrete building is famed for the Bauhaus logo and the innovative balconies at the back of the building. The building also offers tours to the other Bauhaus attractions: the **Meisterhäuser** (masters' houses) and the **Siedlung Dessau-Törten**, a 1920s prototype housing estate, 7 km (4 miles) southeast of central Dessau. In the town centre, the **Bauhaus Museum** *(closed Mon)* has displays showcasing the application of Bauhaus theory to many areas of art and design.

🚗 *Go back to Puschkinallee, turn right and follow the street to the T-junction with Friedrichstrasse. Turn left then right on to Kavalierstrasse. Turn left to Vockerode, and at the T-junction turn left to Wörlitz. Turn left on Seespitze and follow signs to the car park.*

Bauhaus

The Bauhaus movement was begun in 1918 by painter Max Pechstein to utilize art for revolutionary purposes. One of its members, architect Walter Gropius, founded the design school at Weimar, though it later moved to Dessau. At odds with the Nazis during World War II, many members went into exile in the US.

Above Striking Grüne Zitadelle complex, Magdeburg **Below** Elegant Meisterhäuser, the masters' houses, Dessau

EAT AND DRINK

HAVELBERG

La Dolce Vita *moderate*
This restaurant offers superb town views from its terrace and serves Italian dishes and delicious ice cream.
Domplatz 2, 39539; 03938 720 83 40; www.cucina-italia.de

TANGERMÜNDE

Schulzens Brauerei *moderate*
A lively brewery restaurant serving goulash, roast beef and seasonal dishes.
Lange Strasse 34, 39590; 03932 24 41 45; www.schulzens.info; closed Mon & Tue

MAGDEBURG

Le Frog *moderate*
Set in Stadtpark, the town's main park, Le Frog's offers schnitzel, suckling pig in aspic and good salads.
Heinrich-Heine-Platz 1, 39104; 03915 31 35 56; www.lefrog-md.de

Petriförder *moderate*
A large, riverside restaurant with an extensive international menu that includes standard Italian options.
Petriförder 1, 39104; 03915 97 96 00; www.petrifoerder.de

Die Saison *expensive*
The restaurant of the Herrenkrug Parkhotel serves gourmet treats such as red mullet fillet and prawns on mussel risotto and broccoli rabe, along with a variety of delicious desserts.
Herrenkrug 3, 39114; 03918 50 80; www.herrenkrug.de

DESSAU

Kornhaus *moderate*
Housed in an elegant Bauhaus building overlooking the Elbe, this restaurant serves German and Mediterranean cuisine.
Kornhausstrasse 146, Dessau, 39104; 03406 501 99 63; www.kornhaus-dessau.de; closed Mon & Tue

Above Serene lake and 18th-century country gardens of Wörlitz

WALKING AROUND WÖRLITZ

The 56-km (35-mile) Gartenreichtour Fürst Franz hiking and biking trail travels through the nearby UNESCO biosphere reserve. Signposted from Wörlitz car park, the closest point of interest along the route is the fishing village of Vockerode and the adjacent royal woodland, Sieglitzer Park, both around 6 km (4 miles) to the west of Wörlitz. *www.gartenreich.de; www.dessau-tourismus.de*

WHERE TO STAY

WÖRLITZ
Pension Zum Hauenden Schwein *inexpensive*
This traditional place has clean and bright rooms and a good wine bar. *Erdmannsdorffstrasse 69, 06786; 03490 53 01 90; www.zumhauendenschwein.de*

LUTHERSTADT WITTENBERG
Alte Canzley *moderate*
The former chancellery building has been revamped to create a spotless, upmarket hotel. Facilities include a sauna. *Schlossplatz 3-5, 06886; 03491 42 91 90; www.alte-canzley.de*

Best Western Soibelmanns *moderate*
The most exclusive hotel in town has modern luxuries, including a sauna. *Collegienstrasse 56/57, 06886; 03491 42 50; www.stadtpalais. bestwestern.de*

Ringhotel Schwarzer Baer *moderate*
A central hotel in a 500-year-old building with free parking. *Schlossstrasse 2, 06886; 03491 420 43 44; www.stadthotel-wittenberg.de*

⑥ Wörlitz
Saxony-Anhalt; 06786
Many splendid residences set in landscaped gardens were built around Dessau in the 18th and 19th centuries. Of these, the most impressive is Wörlitz, where Gothic follies and mock-Classical statues dot manicured lawns, while swans and rowing boats bob on a tranquil lake. Prince Leopold III of Anhalt, along with his court architect Friedrich Wilhelm von Erdman, built the gardens in the second half of the 18th century. At the centre stands the Neo-Classical **Schloss Wörlitz** (*open Mar–Oct; closed Mon*) with its muted Baroque decor. Behind the palace, the central lake spreads out and gondola tours pass beneath an array of bridges around the lake. Other park attractions include the **Gotisches Haus**, the prince's Neo-Gothic residence, the mock Italian landscape **Insel Stein** and a **synagogue** (*all open Mar–Oct; closed Mon*) modelled on the Temple of Vesta in Rome.

🚗 *Turn left on Erdmannsdorff Strasse, then right on Dorfstrasse on to Wittenberger Strasse to join the B2. Turn right at the B187, then left at Elsterstrasse and right on Am Hauptbahnhof to exit on Lutherstrasse. Turn left at Neustrasse for the car park.*

⑦ LUTHERSTADT WITTENBERG
Saxony-Anhalt; 06886
Clinging to a scenic stretch of the Elbe, the tidy little town of Lutherstadt Wittenberg is named after its most famous resident, Martin Luther, who came here in 1508 and sparked the Protestant Reformation. It now basks in this golden era, celebrating the homes and graves of those who together created the "Protestant Rome".

A two-hour walking tour
From the Neustrasse car park turn left on to Mittelstrasse and follow it to Collegienstrasse, where, beside a small park, lies the **Lutherhaus** ① (*Apr–Oct: open daily; Nov–Mar: closed Mon*), formerly the Augustinian monastery into which Luther entered on arriving in the town. Dissolved during the Reformation, one of the monastery's wings served as the Luther family residence. Today it contains a collection of Reformation relics: Luther's desk, pulpit and first editions of many of his books. Outside the Lutherhaus, and on the corner of Lutherstrasse and Am Hauptbahnhof, grows an old oak, the **Luthereiche** ②, which was planted in 1830 on the spot where Luther displayed his

Exterior detail, Lutherhaus

Left Impressive interior of the Gothic Schlosskirche, Lutherstadt Wittenberg
Below Luthereiche outside the Lutherhaus, Lutherstadt Wittenberg

conviction in 1520 by publicly burning the papal bull threatening his excommunication. Further along Collegienstrasse from the Lutherhaus is the Renaissance **Melanchthonhaus** ③ *(open Apr–Oct; Nov–Mar: closed Mon)*, the former house of Humanist Philipp Melanchthon, Luther's closest associate and the author of *Augsburg Confession*, a statement of belief that became the Protestant constitution. Further on, Collegienstrasse ends at the **Marktplatz** ④, where 19th-century statues of Luther and Melanchthon stand. To their right, an alley cuts through a row of town houses to the **Stadtkirche St Marien** ⑤ *(closed Mon)*, where Luther married Katharina von Bora and their six children were

Luther's Living Room
Look out for Luther's living room in the Lutherhaus. Left as bare as it was in 1535, it is easy to imagine his students gathered here for the religious conversations that were later compiled in the book *Table Talk*. Luther's views on many religious and social matters are candidly outlined in the book.

baptized. This church dates from 1300 and contains an altar (1547) painted by the artist Lucas Cranach the Elder and his son. On the southern side of the Marktplatz is the **Cranach-Haus** ⑥, once the residence of the artist, now housing a historical print shop and the Cranach's World exhibition *(open Apr–Oct; Nov–Mar: closed Mon)*. Further left, Schlossstrasse leads to the old palace and the Gothic **Schlosskirche** ⑦ *(open daily)*. On 31 October 1517, Luther is said to have pinned his 95 theses on its door, which has since been replaced with a bronze door with the theses inscribed in Latin. His tombstone lies below the pulpit, opposite that of Melanchthon. The stairs up Schlossturm (castle tower) next door offers views over the town. Take the Schlossstrasse to Collegienstrasse and turn left into Mittelstrasse to the car park.

VISITING LUTHERSTADT WITTENBERG

Parking
The most convenient place to park is the outdoor car park on Neustrasse at the corner of Mittelstrasse, though there is plenty of on-street parking in the vicinity, if this is full.

Tourist Information
Schlossplatz 2, 06886; 03491 49 86 10; www.lutherstadt-wittenberg.de

EAT AND DRINK

WÖRLITZ
Gastwirtschaft im Küchengebäude *moderate*
This restaurant is the only real option inside the park grounds.
Schloss Wörlitz, 06786; 03495 02 23 38; www.gastwirtschaft-woerlitz.de

Pension Zum Hauenden Schwein *moderate*
A traditional wine bar and restaurant.
Erdmannsdorffstrasse 69, 06786; 03490 53 01 90; www.zumhauendenschwein.de

LUTHERSTADT WITTENBERG
Alte Canzley *moderate*
An excellent organic restaurant, with a menu featuring deer ragout with potato noodles, and salad bowls.
Schlossplatz 3-5, 06886; 03491 42 91 90; www.alte-canzley.de

Cafe Klatschmohn *moderate*
Enjoy the fabulous organic cakes, coffee and relaxed atmosphere here.
Kirchplatz 9, 06886; 03491 50 66 50; closed Mon & Tue

Kartoffelhaus Wittenberg *moderate*
An old-fashioned dark-wood pub specializing in potato preparations.
Schlossstrasse 2, 06886; 03491 41 12 00; www.wittenberg-kartoffelhaus.de

DAY TRIP OPTIONS
A variety of day trips are possible along this route, taking in ecclesiastical outposts, trading towns and landscaped gardens. Also discover Lutherstadt Wittenberg's many links with the Protestant Reformation.

The ecclesiastical frontier
Visit the red-brick abbeys and churches at Jerichow ❷ and Havelberg ❶ and then wander around the half-timbered houses of

Tangermünde ❸. The last two can also be reached by sailing up the Elbe on a day trip from Magdeburg ❹.

Take the B1 and turn left on to the B107 to Jerichow and then Havelberg.

Landscape and architecture
Follow the tour from Magdeburg ❹ to the Bauhaus design school ❺. Next, head for the charming, English-style gardens of Wörlitz ❻. If the weather is bad, visit the other

Bauhaus buildings in Dessau; if it is fine, enjoy a picnic in Wörlitz.

Follow the driving instructions from Magdeburg.

In the footsteps of Reformation
Children will love the Lutherhaus, as it offers plenty of engaging audio-visual games. Be sure to climb the stairs of the Schlossturm and then relax with coffee and cake at Cafe Klatschmohn.

Take the B184 and then the B187.

TRIP 6

PRUSSIAN SPLENDOUR
Schloss Charlottenburg to Filmpark Babelsberg

HIGHLIGHTS

Lakeside palaces
Discover the palaces and gardens around the scenic
lakes and forests to the southwest of Berlin

Royal retreat
Explore Park Sanssouci – Frederick the Great's retreat
and one of Europe's most beautiful royal complexes

Cultural haven
Visit the characterful Dutch and Russian quarters
in Potsdam, the historic lakeside state capital

Regional cuisine
Enjoy typical, hearty Berlin and Huguenot cuisine
with a beer in one of Potsdam's many
traditional restaurants

Sculptures in the palace gardens of Park Sanssouci

PRUSSIAN SPLENDOUR

Potsdam, the historical residence of the Prussian royals, is one of Germany's most attractive cities. Visitors from all over the world come to see its pretty royal summer castle, Schloss Sanssouci, built for the Prussian king, Frederick the Great. This is a tour through the countryside between Berlin and Potsdam, with beautiful landscapes, inviting lakes and extravagant Prussian residences. Its highlights are the Schloss Charlottenburg, Schloss Glienicke and its surrounding lakes, and the breathtaking Potsdam palaces and the churches in the historic city.

KEY

Drive route

PLAN YOUR DRIVE

Start/finish: Schloss Charlottenburg to Filmpark Babelsberg.

Number of days: 1–2 days, allowing half a day to explore Park Sanssouci.

Distance: 36 km (23 miles).

Road conditions: The roads along this trip are in very good condition.

When to go: The best time to visit the region is between late spring and early autumn.

Opening times: Most attractions open daily, while shops are open from 9am to 5pm, Monday to Saturday.

Major festivals: Park Sanssouci: Potsdamer Schlössernacht (night of Potsdam's palaces), Aug; Hollandisches Viertel: Potsdamer Tulpenfest (tulip festival), Apr.

Below Avenue leading to the Neues Palais, Park Sanssouci, see pp78–9

① Schloss Charlottenburg
Berlin; 14059

The Charlottenburg castle *(closed Mon)* was designed as a summer home for Sophie Charlotte, Elector Friedrich III's wife. Construction of the **Altes Schloss**, the old castle, designed by the German architect Johann Arnold Nering (1659–95), began in 1695 and the **Neuer Flügel** *(closed Mon)*, or new wing, was added in the 18th century. The interior of the building was fully restored after World War II.

The **Nering-Eosander-Bau** *(closed Mon)*, the palace in the Altes Schloss, contains the suites of Friedrich III and his wife. Its highlights include the Oak Gallery and the early 18th-century palace chapel. The Neuer Flügel is famous for its **Goldene Galerie**, a huge golden ballroom, and for its paintings by Watteau, Chardin and Pense.

The park behind the castle was originally French Baroque, but was reconstructed after World War II. Full of interesting buildings, it is open to visitors all year round and offers a scenic refuge for city dwellers, joggers and families.

Golden griffin sculpture, Klein Glienicke

🚗 *Leave the car park and turn right on Spandauer Damm to take the A115 towards Potsdam and turn on to Spanische Allee, which becomes Wannseebadweg, following signs to Strandbad Wannsee.*

② Strandbad Wannsee
Berlin; 14129

The public lido Strandbad Wannsee *(mid-Apr–late Sep: open daily)*, was constructed at the beginning of the 20th century and is big enough to accommodate 40,000 people on its artificial sandy beach. Its buildings, including the changing rooms, eateries and bathrooms, were built in the straightfoward, functional *Neue Sachlichkeit*, or New Objectivity style, spearheaded by the architect Martin Wagner. Alternatively, stroll down Wannseebadweg to explore the nearby **Schwanenwerder Island**, which is home to some stunning villas.

🚗 *Return to the A115 towards Potsdam and take the exit to Wannsee. Follow the B1 and continue westwards to reach Klein Glienicke.*

③ Klein Glienicke
Berlin; 14129

For centuries, the Hohenzollern Dynasty, who first ruled as Prussian electors and kings and later as emperors, transformed the sandy glades, pine forests and lakes south-west of Berlin into picture-perfect *Kulturlandschaft* – man-made landscapes of parks and palaces. Among the most brilliant of these is Klein Glienicke, built for Prince Karl of Prussia in the early 19th century. The vast park comprises the **Schloss Glienicke** *(Apr–Oct: closed Mon; Nov–Mar: open Sat & Sun, guided tours only)*, the **Jagdschloss Glienicke**, or Glienicke Hunting Lodge, and a number of smaller buildings. The palace and park were declared a UNESCO World Heritage Site in 1990.

The simple Neo-Classical façade of the charming **Schloss Glienicke** has a solemn dignity about it that was once admired by Goethe *(see p108)*. Inside, the atmosphere is rich, with many lovely paintings, colourful walls and rooms that are elegantly appointed with the architect Schinkel's furnishings and lit by bright, golden chandeliers. The proportions are perfect, giving the entire ensemble a particularly harmonious look.

The adjoining park has a mock monastery, or Klosterhof, a coach house, and the **Grosse Neugierde**, a Neo-Classical pavilion that offers splendid views of the Havel river.

🚗 *Return to the B1 and then continue on it towards Potsdam. Once in the city, follow the signs and take B273 towards Park Sanssouci.*

Above Impressive entrance to the Schloss Charlottenburg, Berlin

WHERE TO STAY

AROUND SCHLOSS CHARLOTTENBURG
Schlosspark Hotel *moderate*
A good business-style hotel with balconies that overlook the palace grounds. Amenities include a pool and discounted parking.
Heubnerweg 2a, 14059 Berlin (2 km/1 mile northwest of the palace); 030326 90 30; www.schlossparkhotel.de

Patrick Hellmann Schlosshotel *expensive*
This luxury hotel has a gourmet restaurant, bar and spa.
Brahmsstrasse 10, 14193 Berlin (6 km/4 miles southwest of the palace); 03089 58 40; www.schlosshotelberlin.com

EAT AND DRINK

AROUND SCHLOSS CHARLOTTENBURG
Kleine Orangerie *moderate*
This inviting café, set right next to the Schloss, offers tea, coffee and cake, but is most popular for its beer garden and tempting Sunday breakfast buffet.
Spandauer Damm 20, 14059 Berlin (west of the castle); 03032 220 21; www.kleineorangerie.de; closed Mon & Tue

KLEIN GLIENICKE
Blockhaus Nikolskoe *moderate*
Commissioned by Friedrich Wilhelm III according to a Russian design, this historic restaurant has a changing menu of traditional regional cuisine.
Nikolskoer Weg 15, 14109 Berlin; 03080 529 14; www.blockhaus-nikolskoe.de

Lutter & Wegner Schloss Glienicke *expensive*
The restaurant in the former castle stables serves modern versions of traditional German dishes. .
Königstrasse 36, 14109 Berlin; 030805 40 00; www.schloss-glienicke-berlin.de; closed Mon–Thu

VISITING PARK SANSSOUCI

Parking
Ample parking space is available at Neues Palais outside the entrance to the park.

Tourist Information
Am Neuen Palais 3, closed Tue;
An der Orangerie 1, closed Mon

WHERE TO STAY

AROUND PARK SANSSOUCI

Hotel am Luisenplatz *moderate*
A harmonious and unique ambience awaits guests at this very stylish hotel located in the historic centre of Potsdam. The rooms and suites of this four-star hotel are elegantly appointed.
Luisenplatz 5, 14471 Potsdam (2 km/ 1 mile south of the park); 0331 9 719 00; www.hotel-luisenplatz.de

Maxx by Steigenberger Sanssouci *moderate*
Right next to Park Sanssouci's eastern entrance, this hotel has bright, modern rooms. Guests get a free Potsdam travel card.
Allee nach Sanssouci 1, 14471 Potsdam (adjacent to the park); 0331 9 09 10; www.maxxhotel.com

Below Outdoor exhibits in Filmpark Babelsberg **Bottom** Schloss Cecilienhof in the Neuer Garten, Park Sanssouci

④ PARK SANSSOUCI

Brandenburg; 14469

A vast collection of ornate gardens, water features and follies, Park Sanssouci is also home to fantastic Neo-Classical, Baroque and Rococo palaces and pavilions. The first building on the site was the enchanting Schloss Sanssouci, built for the Prussian King Frederick the Great in 1745. Over the next 150 years, the park was transformed into one of the finest royal complexes in Europe.

A two-hour walking tour

Fountain head at the Neues Palais

Arrive early at Park Sanssouci in order to avoid the crowds. Georg Wenzeslaus von Knobelsdorff (1699–1753) built this complex between 1745 and 1747. From the car park, walk to the small **Schloss Sanssouci** ① *(closed Mon)*, which served the art-loving Frederick the Great as a retreat from wars and daily politics. Start the tour through the park at this Rococo palace, set atop terraced lands with grapevines. To the east of the palace stands the **Bildergalerie** ②, home to the king's collection of 17th-century Italian and Dutch paintings, including works by Caravaggio, Rubens and Van Dyck. To the west of the palace is the **Neue Kammern** ③ *(Apr–Oct: open Tue–Sun; closed Nov–Mar)*, the new chambers, formerly used as a guesthouse by the royal family.

Cross the Maulbeerallee and follow signs to **Orangerieschloss** ④ *(Apr: open Sat & Sun; May–Oct: closed Mon)*, which dates back to 1860 and now houses the tourist information centre for the park. The **Neues Palais** ⑤ *(closed Tue)*, or New Palace, is much larger and grander than Schloss Sanssouci. It is

accessed by following Hauptallee, the straight avenue that runs through Park Sanssouci. This palace was built after the Seven Years' War (1756–63) as a symbol of the strength and stability of Frederick's reign in the wake of the conflict. Highlights of this palace include the Grotto Hall where marble walls and columns are decorated with marine motifs. The upper gallery has paintings by 17th-century masters and the theatre is still used to host performances of classical music.

Take the path to the south of the Neues Palais to Schloss Charlottenhof, *(May–Oct: open Tue–Sun, guided tours only)*, a palace built in 1826 during the reign of Friedrich Wilhelm IV by architect Karl Friedrich Schinkel in Neo-Classical style. From here, walk to the Römische Bäder *(May–Oct: closed Mon)*, or Roman Baths, and the **Chinesisches Haus** ⑥ *(May–Oct: closed Mon)*. Designed in an imitation Chinese style that was fashionable in 1757, this Rococo teahouse used to host royal tea parties. An exhibition of porcelain is now housed here. Walk eastward from here and across the canal to the **Italienische Friedenskirche** ⑦, home to a

12th-century Byzantine mosaic. This Neo-Romanesque church is modelled on the Basilica of San Clemente in Rome. Walk back to the main avenue and follow signs back to the car park.

Visitors can also opt for a detour to Schloss Cecilienhof *(closed Mon)*, built for Crown Prince Wilhelm in 1913. It is located in the Neuer Garten, or New Garden, a section of the park that borders on Heiliger See. The palace is famous for having hosted the Potsdam Conference in 1945, when the heads of the Allied nations discussed the fate of post-war Germany. Cecilienhof is near the Russische Kolonie, a 15-minute drive east of the Neues Palais car park, or walk east on Voltaireweg and Alleestrasse.

🚗 *From Schloss Sanssouci, follow signs towards Babelsberg on B2 and then on Reiterweg to Alexandrowka to reach the Russische Kolonie.*

5 Russische Kolonie and Holländisches Viertel
Brandenburg; 14467

A short drive from the Neuer Garten, Russische Kolonie, the Russian colony, is a charming residential area known for its wooden log cabins, each with an enchanting little garden. It was built in 1826 for the singers of a Russian choir – a present from Tsar Alexander I of Russia to Prussia. In turn, the Prussian king built the Russian-style houses so that the choir would feel more at home in Potsdam. Follow Jägerallee to the **Holländisches Viertel**, or Dutch Quarter. It has 134 red-brick gabled houses along cobblestoned alleys that were built

by Dutch craftsmen in the first half of the 18th century, during the reign of Friedrich Wilhelm I.

🚗 *Follow signs on Gutenbergstrasse towards Nuthestrasse crossing Humboldtbrücke to take the exit toward Babelsberg. Turn right onto Daimlerstrasse to follow signs to the Filmpark Babelsberg.*

6 Filmpark Babelsberg
Brandenburg; 14482

This film park *(closed Mon & Tue)* was laid out on the site where Germany's first films were produced in 1912. The major films created in these studios were *Metropolis*, by the Austrian-American film-maker Fritz Lang, and *Blue Angel*, which turned the actress Marlene Dietrich into a star. The film park was also used for the production of Nazi propaganda films during Hitler's rule. Today, it is one of Europe's largest studio complexes and the source of blockbusters such as Quentin Tarantino's *Inglourious Basterds*. Visitors can admire some of the sets as well as stuntmen in action.

Above left Picturesque path flanked by trees leading to Neues Palais, Park Sanssouci **Above** Red-brick gabled house in Holländisches Viertel **Below** Neo-Classical Schloss Charlottenhof, Park Sanssouci

EAT AND DRINK

AROUND PARK SANSSOUCI

Assaggi *moderate*
Near the eastern end of Park Sanssouci this refined Italian restaurant has excellent meat, pasta and dessert options.
Luisenplatz 3, 14471; 03312 879 54 52; www.assaggi-potsdam.de

RUSSISCHE KOLONIE AND HOLLÄNDISCHES VIERTEL

Poffertjes en Pannekoeken *inexpensive*
Housed in a historical building in the Dutch Quarter, this café serves traditional Dutch pancakes with sweet or savoury toppings.
Mittelstrasse 32, 14467; 03316 008 03 86; www.poffertjes-en-pannekoeken.de

Maison Charlotte *expensive*
Tucked away in an old building in the Dutch Quarter, Maison Charlotte is an old wine bar with an excellent wine list and robust French cuisine. The traditional country-style cooking uses seasonal produce from France.
Mittelstrasse 20, 14467 Potsdam (1 km/0.6 mile east of the park); 03312 80 54 50; www.maison-charlotte.de

TRIP 7

GRAND OLD PRUSSIAN AVENUES
Schloss Rheinsberg to Freilandmuseum Lehde

HIGHLIGHTS

Sleepy rural haven
Explore the picturesque Schloss Rheinsberg, once
the retreat of kings, writers and poets

Sobering memorial
Take a sombre tour of the former concentration
camp of Sachsenhausen

Tropical paradise
Enjoy an unlikely getaway provided by a
Zeppelin hangar at Tropical Islands

Punts and Sorbs
Go punting on the mellow waterways of the Spreewald
and discover the culture of the Sorbs, Germany's
only Indigenous ethnic minority

GRAND OLD PRUSSIAN AVENUES

Around Berlin, scores of venerable, tree-lined Prussian avenues slice through the flat countryside to connect a series of varied attractions. Amid the forested rolling hills between Brandenburg and Mecklenburg-Western Pomerania in the north is Rheinsberg, a pretty town with a modest palace that was once a favourite of Frederick the Great. A short drive south is the former concentration camp of Sachsenhausen. More pleasant reminders of the past lie to the east, including the 13th-century monastery at Chorin and a remarkable Prussian ship hoist at Niederfinow. To the south, the leafy hills around Buckow are perfect for hiking, while the myriad waterways that crisscross the UNESCO-designated biosphere reserve of Spreewald can be explored in a punt. The Spreewald region also bears remnants of the Sorbian culture that prevailed before the 10th-century German conquest.

ACTIVITIES

Cruise the lakes around Rheinsberg in a rowing boat or kayak

Experience being lowered in a boat by an old Prussian ship hoist at Niederfinow

Explore the scenic woodlands around Buckow

Luxuriate, swim, slide and play in the warm temperature inside an old Zeppelin hangar in Tropical Islands

Go punting or paddling on the Spreewald waterways

Savour the famous Spreewald gherkin in the region that produces 40,000 tonnes (44,092 tons) of the pickled cucumbers per year

0 kilometres 10

0 miles 10

KEY

Drive route

Below Beautiful scenery en route to the Tropical Islands, *see p87* **Below right** Colourful boats and canoes, perfect for exploring Lübben, *see p87*

Above Broad avenue to Chorin, *see p85*

PLAN YOUR DRIVE

Start/finish: Schloss Rheinsberg to Freilandmuseum Lehde.

Number of days: 3 days, allowing half a day to explore Buckow.

Distance: 300 km (186 miles).

Road conditions: Generally well paved and straight minor roads.

When to go: Summer is best for attending music festivals and visiting Buckow and the Spreewald region. In winter, allow plenty of time in the warmth of Tropical Islands.

Opening times: Most attractions open daily, while shops usually open from 9am to 5pm, Monday to Friday but close early on Saturdays. Shops and services are closed on Sundays. Restaurants generally close around 10pm.

Main market days: Schloss Rheinsberg: Wed & Sat; Lübben: Wed & Fri.

Shopping: In Rheinsberg, look out for traditional pottery with its trademark dark blue and cream glazes.

Major festivals: Schloss Rheinsberg: Rheinsberger Musiktage (music days), May/Jun; Kammeroper Schloss Rheinsberg (opera festival), late Jun/mid-Aug; Kloster Chorin: Choriner Musiksommer (classical music festival), Jun; Buckow: Literatursommer (literary summer festival), May–Aug.

DAY TRIP OPTIONS

Families will enjoy **boating** in Spreewald before taking a splash in Tropical Islands. **History enthusiasts** can head to the **monastery** in Chorin, followed by a visit to the **ship hoist** at Niederfinow and, later, take a **walk** around Buckow. Visitors could also begin with an exploration of the Sachsenhausen before unwinding in Rheinsberg. For full details, *see p87*.

Right Schloss Rheinsberg, one of the town's main attractions **Below** Grim exterior of the former concentration camp at Sachsenhausen

BOATING AROUND RHEINSBERG

Much of Rheinsberg's charm lies in its adjacent tranquil wooded lakes. These can be explored with **Reederei Halbeck** *(033931 386 19; www. schiffahrt-rheinsberg.de)*, who operate half-day cruises of local lakes from the quay behind the palace. They also rent out rowing boats and kayaks.

WHERE TO STAY

AROUND SCHLOSS RHEINSBERG
Der Seehof *moderate*
A mid-18th-century former farmhouse just north of Schloss Rheinsberg, offering bright rooms with lake views.
Seestrasse 18, 16831 Rheinsberg; 03393 140 30; www.seehof-rheinsberg.de

Pension Holländermühle *moderate*
This comfortable B&B has a novel location in a 125-year-old windmill, just a couple of minutes' drive south of Schloss Rheinsberg.
Holländer Mühle 1, 16831 Rheinsberg (1 km/0.6 miles south of Rheinsberg); 03393 123 32; www.hollaender-muehle.de

Zum Jungen Fritz *moderate*
This centrally located inn has cheerful hosts and tidy rooms. Free passes to the local gym are also provided.
Schlossstrasse 8, 16831 Rheinsberg; 03393 121 68; www.junger-fritz.de

AROUND KLOSTER CHORIN
Haus am See *inexpensive*
Beautifully situated in the woods north of the monastery grounds, this family-run hotel has simple, floral rooms.
Neue Klosterallee 12, 16230 Chorin; 03336 65 31 11; www.haus-am-see-chorin.de

AROUND THE SCHIFFSHEBEWERK
Am Schiffshebewerk *inexpensive*
A guesthouse with clean and spacious en-suite rooms located in quiet, rural surroundings. Famous for traditional meals and homemade cakes.
Hebewerkstrasse 43, 16248 Niederfinow; 03336 27 00 99; www.hotel-schiffshebewerk.de

① Schloss Rheinsberg
Brandenburg; 16831

According to Frederick the Great, king of Prussia, his happiest days were spent in the Schloss Rheinsberg *(closed Mon)*, located in a sedate little town of the same name. Here, in the early 18th century, he studied for the throne, wrote flute sonatas and gave occasional concerts. Later, the palace served as a sanatorium. It has since been renovated and has become a popular attraction with lovely gardens; some of the elegant palace rooms can be visited. Highlights include the Spiegelsaal (mirror hall), with its dizzying ceiling fresco by court painter Antoine Pesne, and the Baroque Muschelsaal (shell hall) with its maritime theme. The north wing of the palace houses the **Tucholsky Literaturmuseum** *(closed Mon)*, which examines the life of pacifist and left-wing journalist Kurt Tucholsky (1890–1935).
🚗 *From Schlossstrasse, drive toward Herzberg to reach Köpernitz.*

Rheinsberg and Kurt Tucholsky
The picturesque setting of Rheinsberg provided Kurt Tucholsky with inspiration for his novel *Rheinsberg: Ein Bilderbuch für Verliebte* (Rheinsberg: A Picture Book for Lovers), a cheerful love story laced with criticism of bourgeois thought and nationalism. This made it one of the books burned by the Nazis once they came to power, though by then Tucholsky had already left Germany. He died in exile, in Sweden, before the World War II he had predicted broke out.

At Köpernitz, turn left in the direction of Gransee. From here, turn right and get onto the B96 to Nassenheide. Take the exit towards Oranienburg-Nord, then turn left on Granseer Strasse toward Sachsenhausen. Turn left on to the Friedrichsthaler Strasse, and almost at the roundabout, exit on to Sophie-Scholl-Strasse, which becomes Aderluch. Turn left on Schäferweg to reach the car park at the former camp gates.

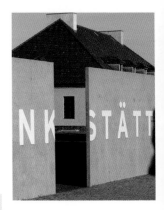

② Gedenkstätte Sachsenhausen
Brandenburg; 16515

A poignant reminder of one of the most oppressive regimes of the 20th century, the Gedenkstätte Sachsenhausen, or memorial *(open daily; museums: closed Mon)*, portrays the atrocities that occurred here when it was converted into a concentration camp during World War II. The Sachsenhausen became a model for most other Nazi camps. Though it was never designated a full-blown "death camp", around half of its 220,000 prisoners were killed. Inside, several museums detail the lives and fates of the prisoners and document the horrors of systematic executions. Take a tour of the hall that examines the Soviet Special Camp (1945–50) which existed here after World War II, when the Russians imprisoned 60,000 suspected Nazis and killed at least 12,000 of them, although most of them were probably innocent.

🚌 *Turn left from the car park on Strasse der Nationen and then right on to Strasse der Einheit. Take the B273 to Wandlitz, then turn left in the direction of Bisenthal and continue toward Eberswalde. In Ebers**walde**, turn right on to the B167, then left over the canal towards Angermünde. Finally, turn left into the signed cloister car park.*

③ Kloster Chorin
Brandenburg; 17279
Founded in 1258 by Cistercian monks, Chorin cloister *(open daily)* is studded with decorative brickwork. One of the grandest red-brick structures in Germany, its scale is impressive even today; it is hard to imagine what its impact would have been in the 12th century. Dissolved in 1542, the monastery slowly crumbled until the 19th century, when its slender arches, graceful windows and step gables were renovated during the Romantic movement. The surrounding parkland beside a pretty lake offers an idyllic walk.

🚌 *Return via Angermünder Strasse and, just before Eberswalde, turn left on Oderberger Strasse, which becomes Macherslust, then turn right on to Hebewerk Strasse. Park at car park beside the ship hoist.*

④ The Schiffshebewerk
Brandenburg; 16248
A huge iron sentinel perched amid rolling green hills, the Schiffshebewerk Niederfinow (ship hoist) has a framework of gigantic girders designed for lifting boats 36 m (118 ft) between the Oder river and the Oder-Havel canal, two vital regional waterways. The ship hoist cuts the process of transferring giant barges from several tedious hours to just 20 minutes. On its completion in 1934, it was the largest of its kind and remains impressive, particularly when viewed from the upper platform *(open daily)*, a vantage point which provides good views. It is also possible to be a part of the experience by being lifted or lowered in a boat, such as those belonging to Fahrgastschiffahrt Neumann *(03334 244 05; www.finow kanalschiffahrt.de)*, whose ticket booth is in the Schiffshebewerk car park information kiosk. An adjacent visitors' centre *(open daily)* details the €500 million new boat lift that opens in 2022.

🚌 *Turn left out of the car park, then at the T-junction turn left briefly on to the B167, then right following signs to Prötzel. In Prötzel, turn left on to the B168, then right at a roundabout to Bollersdorf. Shortly after Bollersdorf turn right to Buckow and then left on Schulstrasse to reach the public car park.*

Above Sculptures adorning the garden, Schloss Rheinsberg **Below** Pretty red-brick Kloster Chorin

EAT AND DRINK

AROUND SCHLOSS RHEINSBERG
Zum Alten Fritz *moderate*
Bustling wood-clad restaurant in an old inn specializing in traditional German food, including wild boar, venison, duck and salmon dishes. The wine selection is great too, and the restaurant is always busy, so booking is advisable at the weekend. *Schlossstrasse 11, 16831 Rheinsberg; 03393 120 86; www.alterfritz-rheinsberg.de*

Other options
For a unique local gastronomic experience, pay a visit to **Eis-Zauberei** *(Kurt-Tucholsky-Strasse 36, 16831; www.eiszauberei.de)*, an ice-cream maker with a wide range of highly unusual yet refreshing flavours, which include onion-honey, garlic-pickles-dill and macha-mango.

AROUND KLOSTER CHORIN
Alte Klosterschänke *moderate*
This traditional restaurant, a short walk from the monastery, uses fresh, seasonal and local organic produce. It also offers a good selection of German wines. *Amt Chorin 9, 16230 Chorin; 03336 653 01 00; www.alteklosterschaenke.de; closed Mon–Thu*

Above The charming Brecht-Weigel-Haus

VISITING BUCKOW

Parking
The P1 car park lies just off Schulstrasse.

Tourist Information
Sebastian-Kneipp-Weg 1, 15377; 03343 15 00 31; www.maerkischeschweiz.eu; closed Mon

WALKING AROUND BUCKOW

For a long walk around Buckow, take the 7.5-km (5-mile) path bordering the Schermützelsee. It is well marked and takes about two hours to complete.

WHERE TO STAY

BUCKOW

Bergschlösschen *moderate*
This late 19th-century villa offers comfortable rooms with valley views.
Königstrasse 38, 15377; 03343 35 73 12; www.bergschloesschen.com

Zur Märkischen Schweiz *moderate*
A reasonably priced traditional inn.
Hauptstrasse 73, 15377; 03343 34 64; www.hotel-maerkische-schweiz.de

TROPICAL ISLANDS

Tropical Islands *moderate*
Rent a tent, stay in a lodge inside the heated hall, or sleep on the beach.
Tropical-Islands-Allee 1, 15910 Krausnick, 15910; 03547 760 50 50; www.tropical-islands.de

AROUND LÜBBEN

Hotel Schloss Lübbenau *moderate*
Lübbenau's palace has elegant *fin-de-siècle* rooms and a relaxing spa.
Schlossbezirk 6, 03222 Lübbenau (14 km/ 8 miles south of Lübben); 03542 87 30; www.schloss-luebbenau.de

Zur Bleiche *expensive*
A boutique hotel with luxurious suites.
Bleichstrasse 16, 03096 Burg im Spreewald (30 km/19 miles southeast of Lübben); 03560 36 20; www.hotel-zur-bleiche.com

⑤ BUCKOW

Brandenburg; 15377
With its rolling hills, trickling streams and languid lakes, the sleepy little spa town of Buckow has long been a popular getaway from Berlin. Poet and playwright Bertolt Brecht was among those drawn here, spending several summers in an idyllic lakeside cottage. The house now makes an interesting stop on a walk around the three lakes between which Buckow nestles.

A 90-minute walking tour

From the car park turn left down to Schulstrasse, left again along Hauptstrasse and then look for a right turn down Erlenweg to the lovely lakeside promenade. Follow this around the Buckowsee lake, turn right at a junction in the path to arrive at the **Brecht-Weigel-Haus** ① *(open Wed–Sun)*, where the artist couple Brecht and his wife, Helene Weigel, spent many summers in the mid-1950s. It is now a memorial to their time spent here. The interior of the house displays rustic furnishings alongside photo exhibits and the famous covered wagon used in Brecht's play *Mother Courage and Her Children*. From the house, follow Werderstrasse uphill, then turn left up Bertolt-Brecht-Strasse, which climbs steeply to offer superb lake views. Buckow's ritziest homes are found

here. Most are attractive **pre-World War II villas** ② built with Art Nouveau touches. Turn left down Ringstrasse and left again on to the shores of the Schermützelsee, Buckow's largest lake. Here, **Strandbad Buckow** ③, a popular swimming beach, provides facilities as well as opportunities for renting rowing boats *(open May–Sep; 01723 21 58 60)*. The hour-long lake tours by Seetours *(Apr–Oct: open daily; 03343 32 32; www.seetoursms.de)* also begin from here.

A signposted path behind and uphill from the beach leads up the side of **Schlossberg** ④, a small hill that provides pretty views of the town. This leads back down to follow the banks of Griepensee to a small bridge beside the **Schweizer Haus** ⑤, a visitors' centre that has a series of information boards and interactive displays about the local ecology and hiking routes. It faces Lindenstrasse, which leads to Königstrasse and into **Buckow's centre** ⑥, with its smattering of shops. Return to the car park by walking left along Hauptstrasse and turning left again into Schulstrasse.

🚗 *Return to the B168 and continue to Müncheberg, then to Beerfelde. Follow the B168, bypassing Fürstenwalde, then turn right on to Hauptstrasse, following signs to Alt Schadow. Take Lubbener Strasse, which becomes Dorfstrasse to Schlepzig. Turn left, go past Krausnick, then turn right to the car park at the Tropical Islands.*

❻ Tropical Islands
Brandenburg; 15910

Occupying a former Zeppelin hangar, Tropical Islands *(open daily)* is a landscaped indoor park complex which contains water-based attractions, such as pools, lagoons, whirlpools, waterfalls and saunas as well as restaurants. Enjoy the lush landscape and look out for the tropical birds that thrive in the constant 27° C (81° F) temperature of the complex.
🚗 *Return to Krausnick and head to Schlepzig. From here turn right, then right again to get on to the B87 to park at the harbourside car park in Lübben.*

❼ Lübben
Brandenburg; 15907

The second largest Spreewald town, Lübben bustles with hotels and restaurants. Its most popular attraction is the Schloss *(Apr–Oct: closed Mon; Nov–Mar: open Wed–Fri & Sun)*, which houses a regional history museum. Behind the palace is the Schlossinsel, an artificial

archipelago with gardens and a leafy maze. Nearby, the harbour area buzzes with punts, or *Kahn*, which cruise the surrounding waterways. A number of operators *(www.bootsverleihpetrick.de)* offer tours and canoe or kayak rentals.
🚗 *From the car park turn left on to the B87, then left again, following signs to Lübbenau. From Lübbenau turn left at Dammstrasse and park in central Lübbenau for a 4-km (2-mile) walk to the Freilandmuseum.*

❽ Freilandmuseum Lehde
Brandenburg; 03222

Popular for punting and canoeing trips, the village of Lehde is dominated by the Freilandmuseum Lehde *(Apr–Oct: open daily)*. This museum re-creates a traditional Sorbian village, using original houses and farmhouses. Inside there are simple, rustic furnishings, including some beds designed to sleep a whole family.

The Sorbs
Germany's only Indigenous ethnic minority, the Sorbs, now just 60,000 in number, can trace their ancestry back to the Slavic Wends, who, in the 5th century, settled in the Lusatia swamps between the Oder and Elbe rivers. In the 10th century, this region was conquered and forcibly Germanized. Yet Sorbian is still spoken in the region, most street signs are bilingual and popular Sorbian festivals are still observed.

Above Canoes in the Spreewald town of Lübben **Centre left** Open-air Freilandmuseum, set in Lehde

EAT AND DRINK

BUCKOW

Fischerkehle *moderate*
An elegant choice, famous for simple local dishes featuring fish and game. *Fischerberg 7, 15377; 03343 33 74*

Stobbermühle *moderate*
A former watermill, this charming restaurant serves regional and national dishes. It is a favourite with locals, especially for its terrace in summer. *Wriezener Strasse 2, 15377; 03343 668 33; www.stobbermuehle.de*

LÜBBEN

Strubel's *inexpensive*
Enjoy traditional cuisine here. Try the local fish and the perch, eel and pike platter. *Dammstrasse 3, 15907; 03542 27 98; www.ferienwohnung-strubel.de*

Im Alten Gärtnerhaus *moderate*
Mediterranean and local Spreewald dishes served in a cosy small restaurant with a beer garden. *Ernst-von-Houwald-Damm 6, 15907; 03546 18 69 56; www.altesgärtnerhaus-lübben.de; closed Mon*

DAY TRIP OPTIONS
This route offers a wide range of day trips.

Spreewald delights
Begin the day by punting or canoeing in the canals of Lübben ❼, then indulge in watersports at the relaxing Tropical Islands ❻.

From Lübben, take the Frankfurter Strasse and then the Dorfstrasse to the Tropical Islands.

A monastery and a ship hoist
Tour the monastery at Chorin ❸ and explore the remarkable Schiffshebewerk ❹ at Niederfinow before visiting the peaceful woods and lakes at Buckow ❺.

From Chorin take the Angermünder Strasse to Britz, then turn on to Oderberger Strasse and further on to Coderberger Strasse, then An der Schleusentreppe and Hebewerk Strasse to Niederfinow. Take the B167 to Sternebech, which joins the B35.

Then take the Hauptstrasse following signs to Buckow.

History and architecture
Visit the memorial at Sachsenhausen ❷ before heading to the delightful Schloss Rheinsberg ❶.

Take the B96 to Gransee. Take the Sonnenberger Strasse and then the Rheinsberger Strasse to Koppernitz, following signs to Rheinsberg.

TRIP 8

PALACES AND CASTLES OF MÜNSTERLAND

Kalkar to Münster

HIGHLIGHTS

Historical romance

Tour the grand moated castles of Münsterland, from
swaggering Baroque palaces surrounded by trim
gardens to grizzled stone castles whose painted
halls hint at Renaissance courtly life

Cultural capital

Wander around Münster, a bustling, prosperous
university town whose lanes abound with
historic architecture

Country cooking

Sample hearty Westphalian fare, including smoked
hams, strongly flavoured sausages and heavy
stews, in rustic beamed inns

PALACES AND CASTLES OF MÜNSTERLAND

The plains on the German-Dutch border see few visitors except those who stop by Westphalia's (Nordrhein-Westfalen) capital, the lively university city of Münster. Yet, with its short distances and straight roads, Münsterland provides perfect back roads touring. It is a sparsely populated landscape of half-timbered farmsteads, windmills and woods as well as of spires that soar above neat market squares. The countryside is dotted with numerous moated castles and manor houses on artificial islets -- the hundred or so *Wasserschlösschen* (water castles) from a feudal past still largely privately owned by noble families. Starting at the historic town of Kalkar, this tour takes drivers to the architecturally rich city of Münster.

PLAN YOUR DRIVE

Start/finish: Kalkar to Münster.

Number of days: 2 days, allowing half a day to explore Münster.

Distance: 156 km (97 miles).

Road conditions: The region has well-signposted roads. There is some congestion during rush hour in the short section of the road into Münster.

When to go: It is best to visit this region in late spring or summer, when palace gardens are in full bloom.

Opening times: Most restaurants are closed either on Mondays or Tuesdays.

Main market days: Kalkar: Thu; Xanten: Mon, Thu & Sat; Münster: Wed & Sat (produce and crafts market).

Major festivals: Münster: Send (funfair and crafts market) early Mar, mid-Jun & late Oct.

Above Rapeseed flowers on the road to Schloss Lembeck, *see p91*

① Kalkar
North Rhine-Westphalia; 47546
Cafés and shops occupy the patricians' houses on Kalkar's cobbled Marktplatz, dominated by the 15th-century **Rathaus**. The square is a fine place to sit and soak up the atmosphere of this historic town. Highlights include **St Nikolaikirche** *(open daily)*, whose stunningly intricate altars date from Kalkar's golden age in the 15th and 16th centuries; the high altar was created by three craftsmen over 12 years.

🚗 *Leave the town on Altkalkarer Strasse to the left of the church. Turn left at the roundabout on to the B57 towards Xanten. Parking is available in the Archäologischer Park and in Xanten's Ostwall and Markt.*

② Xanten
North Rhine-Westphalia; 46509
Located by the mighty Rhine river, Xanten was once a Roman metropolis known as Colonia Ulpia Traiana. Today's walled town was established around a memorial church, **Dom St Victor**. Built on top of the grave of the martyr St Victor, the church was first named *Ad Sanctos* (by the saints), which was soon shortened to Xanten.

On the outskirts of the town is the **Archäologischer Park** *(open daily)*, which, with its reconstructed Roman public buildings, hints at the scale of this 1st-century port, which housed 10,000 people. A museum by the baths has displays on the town's Roman past.

🚗 *Continue on the B57 and turn left on Weseler Strasse towards Wesel. Follow the B58 through Wesel to turn left on to the B70 crossing Brünen to Raesfeld. Park at the Schloss.*

③ Schloss Raesfeld
North Rhine-Westphalia; 46348
The 17th-century moated palace of Count Alexander II von Velen, Schloss Raesfeld, was described as a "trumpet blast in stone". It has a Baroque altar in its chapel. A riverside walk through the garden leads to a ruined watermill.

🚗 *Drive through Raesfeld and take the B224 at the roundabout on the outskirts of the town. Turn left at Erle on Rhader Strasse to reach Lembeck. Follow signs to the Schloss.*

Chateaux of Münsterland
Without a defensive hill anywhere on the plains of Münsterland, feudal rulers in the Middle Ages turned to water for protection. Broad moats were dug to encircle their *Wasserschlösschen*. More powerful cannons and peace rendered such defences obsolete in the 17th century, so aristocrats re-created their strongholds as chateaux-style status symbols. Around 100 of these remain within a 100-km (50-mile) radius of Münster, of which 40 are still owned by the original noble families.

④ Schloss Lembeck
North Rhine-Westphalia; 46286
The formidable gatehouse of Schloss Lembeck *(Mar–Nov: open daily)* belies the Baroque elegance inside. The architect Johann Conrad Schlaun introduced Italianate style to the castle in the 17th century, when he redesigned the **Festsaal** (Celebration Hall). Do visit the rhododendron park.

🚗 *Turn right from the entrance of the castle and on Wulfener Strasse turn left at T-junction on to the B58. Drive through Haltern, turn left in Lüdinghausen at the white signpost for "Burgen" and park at the castle.*

Above left Reconstructed Roman ruin in the Archäologischer Park, Xanten **Above** Moated entrance to Schloss Raesfeld

VISITING XANTEN

Parking
Parkplatz Nordwall off Rheinstrasse is placed between the town centre and the Archäologischer Park.

Tourist Information
Kurfürstenstrasse 9, 46509; 02801 77 22 00; www.xanten.de; open daily

WHERE TO STAY

XANTEN

Van Bebber *moderate*
Housed in a Baroque town house, this friendly family hotel has spacious rooms with antique-style furnishings, as well as an excellent restaurant that specializes in game.
Klever Strasse 12, 46509; 02801 66 23; www.hotelvanbebber.com

AROUND SCHLOSS RAESFELD

Hotel am Schlos *moderate*
Small, cosy rooms, some with views of the Schloss directly across the moat.
Freiheit 21, 46348, Raesfeld; 02865 959 50; www.hotel-am-schloss-raesfeld.de

EAT AND DRINK IN XANTEN

Café de Fries *inexpensive*
Sweet and savoury pancakes, waffles, salads and light meals are served in this café.
Kurfürstenstrasse 8, 46509; 02801 20 68; www.cafe-defries.de

Gotisches Haus *moderate*
One of Xanten's oldest inns, this atmospheric place is spread over four floors. In summer, the beer garden in its courtyard is open.
Markt 6, 46509; 02801 70 64 00; closed Mon

Above Burg Vischering, a magnificent moated castle **Above right** Wooden doors of the Überwasserkirche, Münster **Below** Quiet road leading to Münster

WHERE TO STAY IN MÜNSTER

Hof zur Linde *moderate*
Located on the riverside in the Handorf suburb, the Hof zur Linde is a traditional hotel with modern furnishings and fittings.
Handorfer Werseufer 1, 48157; 0251 327 50; www.hof-zur-linde.de

Martinihof *moderate*
A simple but good-value modern hotel above a pub, the Martinihof is situated close to Prinzipalmarkt.
Hörsterstrasse 25, 48143; 0251 418620; www.hotel-martinihof.de

Mauritzhof *moderate*
A boutique hotel on the ring road around the city centre, the Mauritzhof has a designer look that compensates for its compact standard rooms.
Eisenbahnstrasse 17, 48143; 0251 417 20; www.mauritzhof.de

Schloss Wilkinghege *expensive*
Historic style meets modern comfort in the individually decorated rooms of this 18th-century *Wasserschloss*.
Steinfurter Strasse 374, 48159; 0251 14 42 70; www.schloss-wilkinghege.de

⑤ Burg Vischering
North Rhine-Westphalia; 59348
Burg Vischering *(closed Mon)* is one of the oldest and best-preserved castles in Münsterland. Founded in 1271, it was extended in the 16th and 17th centuries. Across a drawbridge from agricultural outbuildings, the palace retains its loopholes (arrow slits in the walls) and battlements. The castle also has Oriel windows, gables and sandstone fireplaces inside its painted halls. Walk through the surrounding woodland for views of the castle reflected in the moat.

🚗 *Return to the B58 and follow signs to Nordkirchen. Follow signs from the town centre to "Wasserschloss". Parking is available at the castle.*

⑥ Schloss Nordkirchen
North Rhine-Westphalia; 59394
The vast, moated Schloss Nordkirchen *(open Sun for guided tours only)*, nicknamed the "Westphalian Versailles", is a perfectly symmetrical French Baroque castle. It was designed by the German architect Johann Conrad Schlaun (1695–1773) as an aristocratic status symbol. Now a school of finance, it has Baroque gardens *(open daily)* sprinkled with white statuary.

🚗 *Return to Lüdinghausen to reach the B235. Continue further on B235 past Senden, turn right on Osthofstrasse towards Albachten. Continue further once past Roxel, turn left to park at Burg Hülshoff.*

⑦ Burg Hülshoff
North Rhine-Westphalia; 48329
The writer and poet Annette von Droste-Hülshoff, the most celebrated member of the aristocratic Hülshoff Dynasty, was born at Burg Hülshoff in 1797. The castle's ground floor *(open Wed–Sun)* is a shrine to the writer, who is viewed as Germany's very own Emily Brontë – both writers died unmarried and penned sombre tales steeped in their personal tragedies. There are splendid views of this Renaissance manor rising from its moat from the adjoining park, restored to re-create the gardens in which Hülshoff found inspiration.

🚗 *Return to Roxel, turn left on to Roxeler Strasse to Münster. Continue on Einsteinstrasse and Wilhelmstrasse, turn right at the B219 junction. Park in front of Schloss Münster.*

Revolution in Münster
Religious disaffection during the Reformation led to one of the most colourful episodes in Münster's history. A fundamentalist Anabaptist regime seized control of the city in 1534, with a Dutchman named Jan van Leiden at its head – money was made obsolete, property communal and polygamy a duty. However, the city was recaptured in 1535 and van Leiden and his lieutenants were executed and their bodies hung in cages from the Lambertikirche spire as a warning to others.

⑧ MÜNSTER

North Rhine-Westphalia; 48143

Steeped in centuries of learning, the capital of Westphalia is the university city par excellence. World War II saw 90 per cent of the old town laid to ruins, but most of it has now been rebuilt. In 2004, the UN Environmental Programme hailed Münster as the world's most livable city. For visitors, its shops and fine cuisine add to its appeal and complement the impressive monuments and museums.

A 90-minute walking tour

The car park is located in the forecourt of **Schloss Münster** ①, the palace of Münster's Prince-Bishop rulers. Designed by the court's master-architect Johann Conrad Schlaun, the Baroque residence is now the main university building. From the car park, cross the road into Frauenstrasse. Turn left into Jüdefelderstrasse to the **Kuhviertel** ②, a cosy nest of lanes full of student drinking dens. Walk back to Frauenstrasse and turn left to the Gothic Liebfrauenkirche, the Church of Our Lady, popularly called **Überwasserkirche** ③, or church over water, after the Aa river behind it.

Continue down the road and cross the Aa to reach a cobbled lane framed by the twin spires of the **Dom St Paul** ④, built in the 13th century to replace the monastery that gave Münster its name. Inside is a painted 16th-century astronomical clock by painter Ludger Tom Ring and a frieze in the Romanesque vestibule

Detail on the door of the Schloss Münster

illustrating the labours of the months. Opposite the cathedral, the **LWL-Museum für Kunst und Kultur** ⑤ *(closed Mon)* displays art and sculpture from the medieval to the modern ages. It includes religious sculptures by Münster's Heinrich Brabender that survived the Anabaptist purges. Walk across Domplatz to Prinzipalmarkt, a former merchants' street that now has some of the finest shops. Ahead is the gabled Gothic **Rathaus** ⑥ *(closed Mon)* where the Catholic faction brokered a peace deal to end the Thirty Years' War. Walk down the main street to the 15th-century **Lambertikirche** ⑦. The three iron cages attached to its spire were used to display the executed Anabaptist revolutionaries. Turn right in front of the church to stroll down Salzstrasse. Go past the **Stadtmuseum** ⑧ *(closed Mon)* at No. 28, which has Anabaptist exhibits, to the Promenadenring parkland that circles the city. A stroll along the promenade leads back to the car park.

Above Thirteenth-century twin-spired Dom St Paul, Münster

VISITING MÜNSTER

Parking
The city's largest parking areas are at the Schloss on Schlossplatz. Central car parks on Königstrasse and Heinrich-Brüning-Strasse are busy at weekends.

Tourist Information
Heinrich-Brüning-Strasse 7, 48143; 0251 492 27 10; www.tourismus.muenster.de; closed Sun

EAT AND DRINK IN MÜNSTER

Kleiner Kiepenkerl *moderate*
This upmarket family-run inn offers regional fare such as sausage platters. Tables are set on a terrace in summer. *Spiekerhof 47, 48143; 0251 434 16; www.kleiner-kiepenkerl.de; closed Mon*

Pinkus Müller *moderate*
In the Kuhviertel is Münster's last surviving and oldest microbrewery specializing in draught beers and regional cuisine such as veal ragout Töttchen. *Kreuzstrasse 4–10, 48143; 0251 451 51; www.pinkus-mueller.de; closed Sun*

Gabriel's im Kaiserhof *expensive*
Münster's leading gourmet restaurant serves first-class dinners in the Kaiserhof hotel just outside the centre. *Bahnhofstrasse 14, 48143; 02514 17 86 00; www.kaiserhof-muenster.de; closed Sun–Tue*

TRIP 9

MYSTICAL MOUNTAINS

Burg Falkenstein to Rammelsberger Bergbaumuseum

HIGHLIGHTS

Medieval towns
Wander around the lovely half-timbered towns
of Quedlinburg and Goslar

Witches and folklore
Spark the imagination with tales
of witches at the Hexentanzplatz
and the Brocken

Delightful steam trains
Chug up the Harz mountain range to reach the
Brocken on Europe's largest narrow-gauge network

Mining heritage
Explore the old mines that were for centuries a way of
life in the Harz at the Rammelsberger Bergbaumuseum

A steam train on the Brockenbahn railway in the Harz

MYSTICAL MOUNTAINS

A popular outdoor retreat for northern Germans, the scenic Harz mountain range lies where Saxony-Anhalt (Sachsen-Anhalt), Thuringia (Thüringen) and Lower Saxony (Niedersachsen) meet. Soaring peaks are absent here, but thickly wooded mountains abound, with pretty villages and modest resort towns tucked between them. The Harz's highest peak, the Brocken, is also its centrepiece, not least for its long-standing mystical associations with witchcraft. Mining too has been an integral part of life here, and old mines have now been made into attractions, but the Harz is famous mostly for hiking and cycling opportunities in summer and tobogganing and skiing in winter. The old narrow-gauge railway network, complete with steam trains, is ideal for exploring the gateway towns of Quedlinburg and Goslar, both UNESCO World Heritage Sites.

ACTIVITIES

Watch cuckoo clocks being made at the Harzer Uhrenfabrik in Gernrode

Hike in the deep and verdant Bode Valley for a picturesque view of the Harz Mountains

Explore the atmospheric limestone caverns at the Rübeland Caves

Take a steam train to the top of the Harz Mountains on the Brockenbahn railway

Enjoy skiing, tobogganing, hiking and mountain biking on the Wurmberg

Journey into the dark depths of the Rammelsberger silver mine near Goslar

Above Hillside surrounding the Hexentanzplatz, *see p99* **Below left** Pastel-coloured half-timbered houses in the town of Quedlinburg, *see pp98–9* **Below right** Steam train to the Brocken peak, *see p99*

PLAN YOUR DRIVE

Start/finish: Burg Falkenstein to Rammelsberger Bergbaumuseum.

Number of days: 2–3 days, allowing half a day to explore Goslar.

Distance: 139 km (86 miles).

Road conditions: Well paved, though many roads through the mountains tend to be steep and winding.

When to go: It is possible to visit year-round, but minor roads are occasionally snowbound from December to March. Winter is best for skiing and sledging.

Opening times: Most attractions open daily, while shops open from 9am to 5pm, Monday to Friday, but close earlier on Saturday. Most shops and services are closed on Sunday. Restaurants generally close around 10pm.

Main market days: Quedlinburg: Wed & Sat; **Goslar:** Tue & Fri.

Shopping: Look out for wood carvings such as marionettes of witches or cuckoo clocks at Harzer Uhrenfabrik. Local crafts are available at Goslar's Kunsthandwerkermarkt (early Aug).

Major festivals: Quedlinburg: Musiksommer (classical music festival), Jun–Sep; **Mount Brocken:** Walpurgisnacht (witches' night), 30 Apr.

DAY TRIP OPTIONS

Using Quedlinburg as a base, **nature enthusiasts** can spend a day **hiking** in the southern Harz, then ride on the **steam train** up the Brocken. Those interested in **history** can explore Goslar's half-timbered old town before returning on a scenic route via the Rübeland Höhlen. For full details, *see p101.*

Halberstadt

Langenstein

81

79

Ditfurt

Münchenhof

23

24

25

Westerhausen

36

Hoym

Blankenburg

QUEDLINBURG ❸

11

Gersdorfer Burg

Badeborn

26

Wedersleben

81

Wienrode

Bode

Thale

Neinstedt

Rieder

Asmusstedt

Ermsleben

185

THE HEXENTANZPLATZ ❹

Bad Suderode

Gernrode ❷

Ballenstedt

HARZER UHRENFABRIK

185

Meisdorf

BURG FALKENSTEIN

❶

Wieserode

Mägdesprung

Selke

Pansfelde

Stangerode

Bodetal

0 kilometres 5

0 miles 5

Above Aerial view of Burg Falkenstein and the surrounding forest **Below** Entrance to the Rübeland Höhlen

WHERE TO STAY

AROUND BURG FALKENSTEIN

Hotel Nordmann *moderate*
A lovely country hotel whose facilities include a spa with pool and sauna, and a wildlife park with deer, camels and bison..
Deistrasse 23, 06543 Stangerode (19 km/ 12 miles southeast of Burg Falkenstein); 03474 295 30; www. nordmannharz.de

QUEDLINBURG

Am Brühl *moderate*
This country-house-style hotel in a half-timbered building on the edge of the old town serves regionally inspired food.
Billungstrasse 11, 06484; 03943 961 80; www.hotelambruehl.de

Schlossmühle *moderate*
A smart hotel with fine castle views from its snug, spotless modern rooms.
Kaiser-Otto-Strasse 28, 06484; 03943 78 70; www.schlossmuehle.de

AROUND THE HEXENTANZPLATZ

Hotelpark Bodetal *moderate*
Neat little holiday apartments with a pool and spa.
Hubertusstrasse 9–11, 06502 Thale (7 km/4 miles north of the Hexentanzplatz); 03947 776 60; www.ferienpark-bodetal.de

AROUND THE BROCKEN

Regiohotel Am Brocken *moderate*
A family-run hotel with modern rooms and impressive views over Braunlage. Its restaurant serves local cuisine.
Hermann-Löns-Weg 1, 38879 Schierke (10 km/6 miles south of the Brocken); 05322 95 01 90

① Burg Falkenstein
Saxony-Anhalt; 06543
Sitting on a rocky outcrop, the stocky Burg Falkenstein *(open Thu–Sun)* provides views over wooded hills and the eastern plains of Saxony-Anhalt, making it the most attractive castle in the Harz. Built between 1120 and 1180, it has since been expanded. Inside, the chapel is a highlight, as is the walk around its interiors, which include a museum. Falconry displays *(Apr–Sep)* are an added attraction.

🚗 *Follow signs to Ballenstedt and turn left on to the B185. At the T-junction, turn right to Rieder. In Gernrode, turn right on Bergstrasse to Lindenstrasse. Park at Harzer Uhrenfabrik.*

② Harzer Uhrenfabrik
Saxony-Anhalt; 06507
Woodcarving has long been a traditional craft in the Harz, which is known for its cuckoo clocks. The Harzer Uhrenfabrik factory *(open daily)* is one of the few places in Germany where visitors can watch clocks being made. A few paces down Lindenstrasse lead to the **Stiftskirche St Cyriakus**. An early pioneer of the Romanesque style, it is one of the country's best-preserved churches.

🚗 *Head back towards Rieder, but turn left on to Quedlinburger Strasse before the town of Quedlinburg. In Quedlinburg's town centre, turn left on to Steinbrücke, then left again on to Carl-Ritter-Strasse car park.*

③ Quedlinburg
Saxony-Anhalt; 06484
Set in the rolling foothills of the Harz, the town of Quedlinburg dates back to its foundation as a fortress in 922, after which it became the favourite residence of Saxon emperors. The town flourished as a centre for dyes, paper production and engineering in the Middle Ages, when most of its half-timbered houses were built. Reached by continuing along Carl-Ritter-Strasse from the car park, then turning left up Finkenherd, the **Schlossberg** *(closed Mon)* is a knuckle of rock that served as the foundation for a 16th-century Renaissance castle constructed around the **Stiftskirche St Servatius** *(closed for renovation)*, built between 1070 and 1129. The adjacent **Schlossmuseum** *(closed Mon)* has local treasures dating back to the Stone Age. To the right of the castle gates is a row of half-timbered houses with a courtyard that hosts the **Lyonel-Feininger-Galerie** *(closed Tue)*, where the 1920s works of this Bauhaus artist are displayed. To the left of

Carl-Ritter-Strasse, on Wordgasse, lies the **Fachwerkmuseum** *(open Apr–Oct; closed Thu)*, Germany's oldest half-timbered house, built in 1310, now a construction museum. Turn left for a short walk to the Markt. One of its many attractive buildings is the Rathaus, parts of which date back to 1320.

 Leave Quedlinburg on Gernröder Weg, which becomes Suderöder Chaussee, then turn right on Suderöder Strasse for Thale. In Thale, turn left, then right to Hexentanzplatz car park.

Left Scenic train ride to the Brocken
Below Sixteenth-century Renaissance castle atop the Schlossberg, Quedlinburg

HIKING IN THE BODE VALLEY

The Hexenstieg, or Witches'Trail, along the Bode Valley offers great views, passing gnarled trees that are centuries old. This path is best explored by first taking a bus No. 18 from Thale's train station to the village of Treseburg, then walking the 10 km (6 miles) back downstream, which takes 2–3 hours. For a longer walk, take the chairlift to Hexentanzplatz, then walk the 10-km (6-mile) trail to Treseburg, stop for lunch, then return to Thale via the Hexenstieg – a walk of 4–5 hours. Maps are available at the tourist information office *(Bahnhofstrasse 1, 06502 Thale; 03947 776 800; www.bodetal.de)*.

EAT AND DRINK

QUEDLINBURG

Himmel und Hölle *inexpensive*
A cosy restaurant in a small hotel, Himmel und Hölle is known for its *Flammkuchen*, a pizza-like dish topped with crème fraiche, onion and bacon. *Hölle 5, 06484; 03946 52 86 55; www.himmelundhoelle-qlb.de*

Theophano *expensive*
Tucked beneath the cellar arches of a 360-year-old half-timbered house, this restaurant serves modern regional cuisine with an international touch, as chef Sebastian Vogel and his team experiment with various cooking styles. *Kornmarkt 6, 06484; 03946 81 00 50; www.restaurant-theophano.de*

AROUND THE BROCKEN

Bahnhofsbaude Schierke *inexpensive*
Dishes and hearty snacks from the Harz region are served here. *Am Bahnhof, 38879 Schierke; 03945 55 83 45; www.schierke-am-brocken.de*

Walpurgisnacht
Walpurgisnacht (30 April) probably began as a Celtic festival celebrating spring, but developed a reputation for black magic. Legends grew of witches and warlocks flying up to the Brocken to recount the past year's evil deeds before holding an orgy that included the devil himself. So powerful were these legends that for centuries church bells would toll on Walpurgisnacht to deter evil forces.

---

④ The Hexentanzplatz
Saxony-Anhalt; 06502
The Hexentanzplatz, or "witches' dance place", probably began life as a spiritual place used for Celtic rituals and sacrifices. Later, it became known as an occult centre, where witches were said to gather before flying to the Brocken on Walpurgisnacht. Today, revellers arrive on the same night to enjoy the celebrations. A modest museum, the

Sculpture of a goblin, the Hexentanzplatz

Walpurgishalle *(May–Oct: open daily)*, explains pagan worship in German with vivid drawings and a ghoulish Germanic sacrificial stone.

 From Thale return to the T-junction and turn left. Continue on the same road and turn right on to the B81. In Blankenburg, turn left on to the B27 to the car park left beyond the caves.

⑤ Rübeland Höhlen
Saxony-Anhalt; 38889
Since its chance discovery by a 15th-century miner, the 600,000-year-old **Baumannshöhle** *(Nov–Mar: closed Mon)* has attracted visitors keen

to tread in the footsteps of Stone Age inhabitants and Ice Age bears, some of whose skeletons remain here. The adjacent **Hermannshöhle** *(closed Nov–Apr)* has stalagmites and stalactites.

 Continue on the B27, turn right at Elend and continue to Schierke; park at the railway station.

⑥ The Brocken
Saxony-Anhalt; 38879
The ascent of the Brocken (1,141 m/ 3,747 ft), the highest peak in the Harz, is a vital part of any Harz itinerary. The easiest way to reach the top is by the narrow-gauge Brockenbahn railway, which climbs steeply to a height of 1,125 m (3,691 ft). Trains depart from Schierke for the short journey. Here, the **Brockenhaus** *(open daily)* displays exhibits on the mountain's geology and mythology. An easy 2.5-km (1.5-mile) path loops the summit, offering superb views.

 Return to the B27 and turn right. In Braunlage, turn right down Pfaffenstieg and right again on to the Wurmberg chairlift car park.

Steam Trains in the Harz
Steaming through 140 km (87 miles) of track through the mountains, the **Harzer Schmalspurbahn** *(www.hsb-wr.de)* is the largest narrow-gauge network in Europe. Many of the steam trains are from the 1950s, but one has been in service since 1887. The railway lines link Quedlinburg, Nordhausen and Wernigerode with the Brocken. Round trips depart daily.

---

7 The Wurmberg
Lower Saxony; 38700

The Harz's second-highest peak, the Wurmberg (971 m/3,186 ft) is a venue for many outdoor sports (open daily). In winter, the ski lift (www.wurmberg-seilbahn.de) of the resort town of Braunlage is used by snowboarders. In summer, the Wurmberg's chairlift carries hikers to a good selection of trails. Hiking from the summit to the base takes around 1.5 hours.

🚗 *Turn right on to Pfaffenstieg, left on to Am Amtsweg, then right on Harzburger Strasse. Turn right on the B4, and in Bad Harzburg turn left on to Harzburger Strasse. Take the B498 and get on to the B241 to Goslar. In Goslar, turn right and then left to the car park.*

Above Charming town of Goslar on the northwestern slopes of Harz Mountains

VISITING GOSLAR

Parking
The multi-storey car park at Bäckerstrasse 100 on the eastern side of Goslar and the parking space near Kaiserpfalz are among the most convenient of several car parks.

Tourist Information
Markt 7, 38640; 05321 780 60; www.goslar.de; open daily

WHERE TO STAY

AROUND THE WURMBERG

Echtzeit *moderate*
Set on Wurmberg, this comfortable designer hotel offers a variety of outdoor activities. It features a restaurant that serves simple, regional fare, alongside ready-to-eat snacks throughout the day.
Elbingeröder Str. 4, 38700 Braunlage; 05520 776 44 34; www.echtzeit-hotel.de

GOSLAR

Altstadt-Hotel Gosequell *moderate*
This family-run hotel in the town's historic centre is housed in a restored heritage building. The restaurant serves local specialities.
An der Gose 23, 38640; 05321 340 50; www.hotel-gosequell.de

Kaiserworth *moderate*
A historic hotel in a former 15th-century guildhall near Goslar's marketplace, the Kaiserworth has rooms decorated in a range of styles. The restaurant has a seasonal regional menu.
Markt 3, 38640; 05321 70 90; www.kaiserworth.de

8 GOSLAR
Lower Saxony; 38640

One of Germany's most attractive towns, Goslar is famous for its half-timbered houses. The discovery of silver in the 10th century made it one of Europe's leading towns but it fell into decline after the Duke of Braunschweig-Wolfenbüttel claimed the mine in 1532. Much of the town has been preserved, along with its Romanesque palace.

A two-hour walking tour

Exit the car park on Bäckerstrasse, turn right then left on to Fischemäkerstrasse and follow it to Goslar's **Markt** ①, where a group of half-timbered buildings surround a 13th-century fountain on which Goslar's imperial eagle puffs out his chest. The old treasury building to the left is famed for its 18th-century carillon (open daily) in which parading figures tell the story of mining history. Opposite, the 15th-century Rathaus with its Gothic gables looks most impressive at night. Behind it is the Romanesque market church or Marktkirche. The 16th-century half-timbered **Brusttuch Haus** ②, with its excellent woodwork, lies behind the church. From the left of the house, Hoher Weg leads to the **Historisches Zinnfigurenmuseum** ③ *(closed Mon; www.zinnfigurenmuseum-goslar.de)*, one of the best miniature tin figure museums in Germany. Just off Hoher Weg, a path to the left follows the Abzucht stream, which leads to the **Goslarer Museum** ④ *(closed Mon)*. Inside, the Goslarer Evangeliar, a jewel-encrusted book of gospels, and the Bergkanne, a stein with figures of miners, are displayed. Back to Hoher Weg, the **Grosses-Heiliges-Kreuz** ⑤ *(closed Mon & Tue)*, a former hospice, is now a crafts centre. At the end of Hoher Weg is the Domhalle, the vestibule of a church that once housed the Kaiserstuhl, the imperial throne. Down the street to the right is the **Kaiserpfalz** ⑥ *(open daily)*, the 11th-century imperial palace of Heinrich III. Later, it was used as a granary, until it was rescued by Kaiser Wilhelm I in 1868 for the Second Reich. Inside, the Ulrichskapelle is the resting place of Heinrich III's heart in a gilt box. From

Kaiserpfalz go left to Bergstrasse. On the opposite corner is the Baroque **Siemenshaus** ⑦ *(guided tours only)*, the family home of the Siemens industrialist family. A short walk from here to Jakobistrasse leads to **Mönchehaus Museum** ⑧ *(closed Mon)*, which displays the work of artists including Willem de Kooning. Continue down Jakobistrasse to the car park.

🚗 **Turn right on to Vogelsang, left on to Bäckerstrasse, then right on to Mauerstrasse and left on to Okerstrasse. Turn right on to the B241 and left on to Rammelsberger Strasse to the museum.**

⑨ Rammelsberger Bergbaumuseum
Lower Saxony; 38640
For a millennium the Rammelsberger silver mine formed Goslar's economic backbone. Closed down in 1998, it has since become the **Bergbaumuseum** *(open daily)*, which chronicles the mine's history. Visitors can don overalls and tour the 18th- and 19th-century shafts.

Above left Fountain in the Markt, Goslar **Above** Outdoor cafés in Goslar with the Marktkirche looming behind **Below** Old mine at the Rammelsberger Bergbaumuseum

EAT AND DRINK IN GOSLAR

Aubergine *moderate*
A luxury restaurant serving French and Italian cusine. Good for fresh fish and lamb. The mocha mousse dessert is a house speciality. *Marktstrasse 4, 38640; 05321 421 36; www.aubergine-goslar.de*

Die Worthmühle *moderate*
Harz's speciality restaurant offers rustic nooks and dishes such as iberico pork schnitzel and duck breast, alongside *Goslarer Gosebier*, a fruity local beer. *Worthstrasse 4, 38640; 05321 434 02; www.worthmuehle.de; closed Sun*

Other options
Goslar is filled with atmospheric cafés, but look out for the Baroque-style **Café Anders** *(Hohe Weg 4, 38640; 05321 238 14; www.barockcafe-anders.de)*, which offers homemade truffles and great Harz views.

DAY TRIP OPTIONS
The Harz is compact and within range of day trips. Quedlinburg is a good base and is well served by the narrow-gauge railway.

Castles and caves
From Quedlinburg ③, head to Thale and walk along the Bode Valley. If there is time to spare, the Harzer Uhrenfabrik ② at Gernrode is a good wet-weather option, along with the Burg Falkenstein ① or the Rübeland Höhlen ⑤.

Follow the route to Thale and continue to the T-junction after Neinstedt. Turn right and head to Gernrode, then take the road to Ballenstedt and continue to Burg Falkenstein. For the caves, head from Thale to Blankenburg and on to the B27.

Magical Brocken
Enjoy a ride on the narrow-gauge trains from Quedlinburg ③ to the summit of the Brocken ⑥.

Quedlinburg's railway station is at the end of Bahnhofstrasse; from the

market walk along Steinbrücke and then turn right down Bahnhofstrasse.

Picturesque Harz
Explore Goslar ⑧, a pretty town with 1,800 half-timbered houses, and then head to the interesting Rammelsberger Bergbaumuseum ⑨ to visit the old silver mine and learn about the history of mining in this region.

Follow the route to Goslar, then the B241 to Rammelsberger Bergbaumuseum.

TRIP 10

HILLTOP CASTLES AND LUSH LANDSCAPES
The Wartburg to Schloss Belvedere

HIGHLIGHTS

Iconic castle
Tour the Wartburg, whose fairy-tale looks
match its romantic past

Sleepy towns
Walk around the half-timbered old towns
of Schmalkalden and Arnstadt, nestled
in wooded hills

Highland hiking
Escape to the hills in the Thuringian Forest to hike
the trails, or to follow in Goethe's footsteps in
a day-long expedition

Cultural jewel
Explore the museums and palaces of the
UNESCO-listed town of Weimar

Mighty gates of the medieval castle Wartburg, Eisenach

HILLTOP CASTLES AND LUSH LANDSCAPES

Hilltop ski resorts, spa towns and the network of hiking trails through the Thuringian Forest (Thüringer Wald) have transformed the "green heart" of Germany into a holiday playground. Yet, thanks to its fragmentation into a patchwork of small duchies in the 16th and 17th centuries, Thuringia (Thüringen) is just as rich in history and art. References to luminaries such as composer Johann Sebastian Bach, reformer Martin Luther and writer and polymath Johann Wolfgang von Goethe appear regularly on a route that begins at a fairy-tale castle in Eisenach and winds deep into the Thuringian Forest, a wooded upland where cosy timber-framed towns and ducal palaces nestle beneath pine-clad hills. The route emerges from this timeless landscape to veer east toward its final stop, Weimar, a cradle of culture that appeals to head and heart alike.

ACTIVITIES

Hike into the high country on the 20-km (13-mile) stretch from Ilmenau or just take a walk around Grosser Inselsberg

Go skiing in winter and summer at Oberhof

Try Thuringian bratwurst, grilled over hot charcoal, available throughout the region

Explore Goethe's house in Weimar

KEY

〰️ Drive route

PLAN YOUR DRIVE

Start/finish: The Wartburg to Schloss Belvedere.

Number of days: 3–4 days, allowing half a day to explore Weimar.

Distance: 250 km (155 miles).

Road conditions: Roads are generally good in the Thuringian Forest. In winter, snow can be a problem.

When to go: The best time to visit is summer (June to August), when flowers carpet the meadows, festivals are in full swing and hiking is idyllic. The ski season is from mid-December to February.

Opening times: Most shops are open from 9am to 5pm Monday to Friday. Many museums in Weimar are closed on Mondays.

Main market days: Eisenach: Wed & Thu; Ilmenau: Fri; Arnstadt: Tue, Fri & Sat; Erfurt: Mon–Sat; Weimar: Mon–Sat.

Major festivals: Erfurt: Krämerbrückenfest (merchant's bridge medieval festival), Jun; DomStufen-Festspiele (music/theatre festival), Jul–Aug; Weimar: Wine Festival, Aug; Weimarer Zwiebelmarkt (onion festival), Oct.

DAY TRIP OPTIONS

Meiningen is an ideal base for **outdoor activities** in the Thuringian Forest, with **skiing** in Oberhof and **walks** around Ilmenau. Visit Weimar to see **splendid art galleries**, and **aristocratic palaces**, then stop by Erfurt's **Gothic cathedral** and take a side-trip to Arnstadt. For full details, *see p111*.

Above left Straw bales on a meadow, Drei Gleichen, *see p108* **Above right** Shops and cafés on Krämerbrücke, Erfurt, *see p109* **Below** Sculpture at Dom St Marien, Erfurt, *see p109*

Above Bachhaus with its lovely garden, Eisenach **Below** The Wartburg, perched on top of a hill, Eisenach

VISITING THE WARTBURG

Parking
Park in the castle's car park. Alternatively, visitors can park in Eisenach's old town and take mini-trains or bus No. 10 from the main square.

Tourist Information (Eisenach)
Markt 24, 99817; 03691 792 30; www.eisenach.info; closed Sat & Sun

VISITING GROSSER INSELSBERG

Tourist Information
Tabarz, Theodor-Neubauer-Park 3, 99891; 03625 96 10 87; www.bad-tabarz.de

Hiking
03613 74 20; www.thueringen-tourismus.de

WHERE TO STAY

THE WARTBURG
Hotel auf der Wartburg *expensive*
This luxurious small hotel has individually styled rooms.
Auf der Wartburg 2, 62298; 03691 79 70; www.wartburghotel.de

SCHMALKALDEN
Patrizier *moderate*
The rooms here are decorated with floral wallpaper and antique-style furnishings.
Weidebrunner Gasse 9, 98574; 03683 60 45 14; www.stadthotel-patrizier.de

MEININGEN
Gästehaus Schlundhaus *moderate*
Just off the Marktplatz, this guesthouse offers cosy rooms.
Schlundgasse 4, 98617; 01765 592 41 99; www.uwe-klein-hotels.de

① The Wartburg
Thuringia; 99817
Clasped to a ridge south of Eisenach, the Wartburg *(open daily)* is a well-spring of German identity. The castle's Romanesque Palas, or Great Hall, is rich with 19th-century murals and mosaics. According to legend, medieval bards once battled for their lives in singing contests romanticized in Wagner's opera, *Tannhäuser*. The exiled Martin Luther hid here while translating the New Testament into German in 1521. In 1817, student fraternities from across the country gathered here to demonstrate for a united Germany. Drive to the old town of Eisenach on the B19 to pay tribute to Johann Sebastian Bach, by visiting the **Bachhaus** *(open daily)*, the museum built on what was thought to be the site of his birth.

🚗 *Follow signs for Naturpark-Route Thüringer Wald on the B7 then the B88. At Thal, take the B88 to Seebach, Tabarz and then Friedrichroda. Turn right at the T-junction and park on the main square.*

② Friedrichroda
Thuringia; 99894
Spa waters have attracted visitors to Friedrichroda for the past two centuries. In 1835, Britain's Princess Victoria came here to take a cure and fell in love with Duke Albert of Saxe-Coburg-Gotha, her future husband. Tour the gardens of the Neo-Gothic **Schloss Reinhardsbrunn** *(guided tours; www.erlebniswelt-reinhardsbrunn.de)*, where the two royals met. Return to Tabarz to visit the **Marienglashöhle** *(open daily)* grotto. It literally means "Mary's Glass Cave", which alludes to the gypsum crystals found here that were mined for altar decoration.

🚗 *Return to Tabarz, then turn left at the brown panorama symbol and drive through the town centre. Drive uphill, following signs to turn right towards Grosser Inselsberg.*

③ Grosser Inselsberg
Thuringia; 98599
A patchwork of woodland and meadow spreads out beneath one of the highest mountains in the Thuringian Forest. At 918 m (3,012 ft), it has forested hills to the south and foothills rolling north to Eisenach. Well-known as a winter ski resort, Grosser Inselsberg is also a popular destination in summer. Adventure enthusiasts can try walking a section of the Rennsteig, Germany's most popular long-distance footpath, to climb to the summit or whizz downhill through the pine trees on a summer toboggan run *(Mar–Oct: open daily)*.

🚗 *Return to the main road and head to Brotterode. Turn left in the town centre, following signs to Schmalkalden. Parking is available in the Pfaffenwiese car park, past the roundabout.*

Forest Train to Gotha

A novel way to visit Gotha and Schloss Friedenstein (see p109) and do some sightseeing is on the Thüringerwaldbahn from Friedrichroda. The Thuringian Forest Train (tram No. 4) takes 50 minutes to cover the 20-km (12-mile) journey northward to Gotha. Trams depart twice an hour in summer and once an hour in winter from Friedrichroda.

❹ Schmalkalden

Thuringia; 98574

So quaint are its timber-framed buildings that it is hard to believe that Schmalkalden was briefly the epicentre of European politics. An imperial meeting was convened here in 1537 to reconcile the continent's Catholic rulers with Protestant princes and Martin Luther. Up the high street from the Altmarkt town square – which is a mosaic of historic buildings – is the Lutherhaus. This was Martin Luther's residence during the Imperial Diet. The Reformation also changed **Schloss Wilhelmsburg** (Nov–Mar: closed Mon). This castle's chapel was one of the first to represent Luther's elevation of the spoken word over decoration.

🚗 *Continue along Recklinghäuser Strasse then the Hauptstrasse, turn right at the T-junction to take the B19 to Meiningen. Drive into the centre, and at Sächsischer Hof hotel, turn right to park on Klostergasse or park past the Schloss in the Zentrum West car park.*

❺ Meiningen

Thuringia; 98617

A past life as the Residenzstadt or royal seat of the Saxe-Meiningen dukes lends Meiningen an aristocratic air. Romantic composers such as Franz

Liszt and Johannes Brahms conducted the town's orchestra, and its court theatre was acclaimed across Europe. Today, the town retains a reputation for ballet, theatre and classical music (www.das-meininger-theater.de). The Ducal Riding Hall (closed Mon), which stands next to Schloss Elisabethenburg (closed Mon), displays backdrops from 19th-century theatre productions. Do not miss the castle's stuccoed café.

🚗 *Follow the one-way system to Neu-Ulmer-Strasse and turn right towards Rohrer Strasse to Suhl. In Rohr, follow signs to Benshausen, then to Zella-Mehlis on the B62. Take the Bahnhofstrasse then the Oberhofer Strasse, which becomes the Heinrich-Ehrhardt-Strasse, to Oberhof and turn toward Oberhof-Sud to park beside the Haus des Gastes.*

❻ Oberhof

Thuringia; 98559

Spread over a ridge at an elevation of 860 m (2,822 ft), Oberhof is the main winter playground of the Thuringian Forest. Skiers and snowboarders have a choice of slopes, and non-skiers can swish downhill in rubber rings or on a toboggan. Cross-country skiing is possible even in summer, on a 2-km (1-mile) long circuit in the DKB-Skisport-Halle (open daily; www.oberhof-skisporthalle.de). Visitors can also hike through the surrounding high meadows on circular trails; maps are available in the Haus des Gastes.

🚗 *Leave Oberhof via Crawinkler Strasse and follow signs to Ohrdruf. Turn right towards Crawinkel, then take the B88 to Ilmenau, via a short section of the A71. Leave the A71 at Ilmenau West to park beside Erfurter Strasse, just before the sign to the Rathaus.*

Above Scenic road to Oberhof, through the Thuringian Forest **Below left** Half-timbered building, Eisenach **Below right** Statue of Bach at Bachhaus, Eisenach

EAT AND DRINK

FRIEDRICHRODA

Brauhaus *moderate*
A 19th-century inn, Brauhaus offers country cooking, such as game roulade, and beers brewed in-house. It also has five rooms and a beer garden.
Bachstrasse 14, 99894; 03623 30 42 59; www.brauhaus-friedrichroda.de

SCHMALKALDEN

Ratskeller *moderate*
Traditional dishes such as *Eisbeinsülze* (salted pork knuckle) and fresh trout are served here, inside the town hall.
Altmarkt 2, 98574; 03683 27 42

MEININGEN

Schloss-Stuben *moderate*
Housed inside Schloss Elisabethenburg, this restaurant serves hearty German dishes such as venison goulash with Thuringian dumplings or pike-perch fillet.
Schlossplatz 1, 98617; 03693 50 23 44; www.schloss-stuben-mgn.de; closed Mon

Above Houses and shops around Krämerbrücke, Erfurt **Below** Schloss Wachsenburg above Holzhausen

WHERE TO STAY

ILMENAU

Berg & Spa Hotel Gabelbach *moderate*
Located midway along the Goethewanderweg path, this comfortable spa hotel in the woodland south of Ilmenau is well placed for walkers.
Am Gabelbach 1, 98693; 03677 86 00; www.gabelbach.com

ARNSTADT

Hotelpark Stadtbrauerei *moderate*
This understated design hotel was renovated from a brick brewery and has an attached microbrewery/restaurant. Located south of the old town, it provides free bikes for guests to explore the region.
Brauhausstrasse 1–3, 99310; 03628 60 74 00; www.hotelpark-arnstadt.de

ERFURT

Hotel Zumnorde *moderate*
Extra-large beds come as standard in the classic, modern rooms of this smart and efficient hotel in the city centre.
Anger 50–51, 99084; 0361 568 00; www.hotel-zumnorde.de

7 Ilmenau
Thuringia; 98693

"I was always happy to spend time here," wrote JW Goethe, 18th-century playwright and philosopher, about this university town. Ilmenau returned the compliment by dedicating the **Goethe Stadtmuseum** *(closed Mon)* to the father of the German Enlightenment. The museum is located in the Baroque Amtshaus on the Markt, where a bronze of Goethe rests on a bench.

🚗 *Take the Erfurter Strasse, following signs to Martinroda, Neusiss and Dosdorf to Arnstadt. Go straight over the roundabout into Plauesche Strasse towards the tower and park on Ried.*

8 Arnstadt
Thuringia; 99310

A medieval watchtower at Arnstadt's entrance hints at the charm of this old town at the forest's edge. Full of half-timbered houses and tangled lanes, it is a great place to explore. The **Markt** has a Renaissance town hall and the Bachkirche. Arnstadt was the home of the composer Johann Sebastian Bach, who, at the age of 18, scandalized the congregation of the Bachkirche with his contrapuntal style on the organ. In the **Schlossmuseum** *(closed Mon)* on Erfurter Strasse are 18th-century doll tableau and porcelain displays.

🚗 *Return to the roundabout and turn left on to Lindenallee, following signs to Zentrum. Turn left at the roundabout on to Wachsenburgallee, then right and then left on to Ohrdrufer Strasse towards Gotha to reach Holzhausen.*

Johann Wolfgang von Goethe

The Frankfurt-born son of a wealthy family, Goethe (1748–1832) found fame at the age of 26 as the author of *The Sorrows of Young Werther*. This tale of obsessive love not only became the bestseller of the early Romantic movement, but also led to Goethe's appointment as ducal adviser in Weimar in 1775. Yet, to label Goethe as just a writer is inadequate. Between court duties, he conducted scientific experiments, studied geology, designed palaces and gardens, collected antiquities and penned his masterpiece, *Faust*. Author Thomas Mann dubbed him "the greatest German of all".

9 Drei Gleichen
Thuringia; 99869

Three castles, collectively known as Drei Gleichen, crown the hills en route to Gotha. The 17th-century **Wachsenburg** is the best preserved after its restoration as a hotel and restaurant; it is worth a visit for the view from its perch above Holzhausen village. Continue for 5 km (3 miles) on the road to reach Thuringia's oldest castle, the **Mühlberg** *(Mar–Oct: open daily, Nov–Feb: castle grounds open daily)*, a ruin located above its sleepy village. A further 2 km (1 mile) drive northward toward Wandersleben leads to the ruined **Burg Gleichen** *(Apr–Oct: open daily)*, which still retains its impressive defensive walls.

🚗 *From Mühlberg, continue to Gotha via Wechmar and Günthersleben. Turn right on to the B247 and follow signs to Gotha and brown signs to Schloss Friedenstein.*

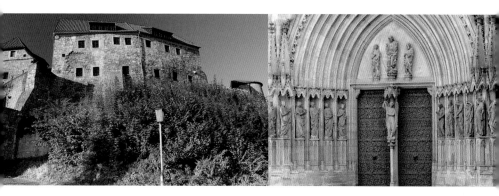

In Goethe's Footsteps

While JW Goethe admired Ilmenau town, it was the local countryside that inspired his artistic and scientific work. Many visitors come solely to walk "auf Goethes Spuren" (in Goethe's footsteps) on the Goethewanderweg. The appeal of this 20-km (13-mile) hike to Stützerbach is its scenic variety. Marked by Goethe's "g" monogram, the trail begins in Ilmenau's Markt and passes cliffs and caves before it ascends into high country. Goethe museums lie en route – the cabin in which he wrote *Wanderers Nachtlied* on Kickelhahn Hill and the ducal hunting lodge Jagdhaus Gabelbach *(closed Mon)*, which has exhibits on his science studies. The Ilmenau tourist office *(www.ilmenau.de)*, in the Amtshaus, stocks maps of the walk.

⑩ Schloss Friedenstein

Thuringia; 99867

The dynastic residence of the House of Saxe-Coburg *(closed Mon; www.stiftungfriedenstein.de)* – better known in Britain as the House of Windsor – holds interest for everyone. Works by Cranach the Elder and a sumptuous oil painting of 15th-century suitors, *Gotha Lovers*, star in an art gallery. The floors above have fabulously stuccoed period rooms, museums of antiquities and regional culture, and the perfectly preserved court theatre, Eckhof-Theater. One of the oldest stages in Europe, it hosts a drama festival in July and August.

🚗 *Continue on Stieler Strasse, across the B247, to take the B7 to Erfurt. At the B7/B4 junction, turn left on to Heinrichstrasse towards the Dom. Park in Domplatz's underground car park.*

⑪ Erfurt

Thuringia; 99084

Bursting with history and university life, Erfurt is a splendid little city and the capital of the Thuringian state. It is also the oldest settlement in the region, with its earliest historical records dating from AD 729. Ascend the sweeping steps from Domplatz to the **Dom St Marien**. This cathedral has a low-lit High Gothic choir, with original choir stalls, 14th- and 15th-century stained-glass windows and Wolfram, a Romanesque bronze candelabrum (c. 1160) shaped like a man. The adjacent five-nave **Severikirche** has more Gothic furnishings and the sarcophagus of St Severus. The high street off Domplatz, Marktstrasse, leads to Fischmarkt, surrounded by Renaissance patricians' houses. The picture-perfect "merchant's bridge", **Krämerbrücke**, spans the Gera river and has dozens of inhabited buildings.

🚗 *Return to the B4/B7 junction to take the B7 to Weimar. Follow signs to Zentrum and park at the Goethehaus car park on Ackerwand.*

Above left Well-restored Wachsenburg, Drei Gleichen **Above** Sculptures around the ornate entrance to the Dom in Erfurt **Below** Pretty buildings lining Fischmarkt, Erfurt

VISITING ERFURT

Parking
Parking is available in the underground car park in Domplatz and in a car park beside the cathedral on Domstrasse.

Tourist Information
Benediktsplatz 1, 99084; 03616 64 00; www.erfurt-tourist-info.de

EAT AND DRINK IN ERFURT

Zum Goldenen Schwan *moderate*
Hearty fare such as *Rostbrätel* (roast pork with onions) and home-brewed beers are served in this traditional inn. *Michaelisstrasse 9, 99084; 03612 62 37 42; www.zum-goldenen-schwan.de; Jan–Feb: closed Sat & Sun*

Zum Wenigemarkt 13 *moderate*
This restaurant features traditional Thuringian cooking along with some modern dishes; try the beef roulade with dumplings. *Wenigemarkt 13, 99084; 03616 42 23 79; www.wenigemarkt-13.de; closed Mon*

Top Modest façade of the Schillerhaus in Weimar **Above** Town hall and cafés on the Markt in Weimar

VISITING WEIMAR

Parking
Parking is available at the Goethehaus car park on Ackerwand.

Tourist Information
*Markt 10, 99423; 03643 74 50;
www.weimar.de*

WHERE TO STAY IN WEIMAR

Amalienhof *moderate*
A good-value hotel near Goethe's house, which offers spacious rooms and breakfast. It also has a rooftop terrace.
*Amalienstrasse 2, 99423; 03643 54 90;
www.amalienhof-weimar.de*

Grand Hotel Russischer Hof *moderate*
Sumptuously decorated, Russischer Hof was once the haunt of the composers Franz Liszt and Robert Schumann. The hotel's suites are similarly grand and its standard accommodation is very comfortable.
*Goetheplatz 2, 99423; 03643 77 40;
www.russischerhof-weimar.de*

Elephant *expensive*
A rendezvous for artists, poets, intellectuals and statesmen since the 16th century, Elephant is a superbly sited and elegant Art Deco hotel.
*Markt 19, 99423; 03643 80 20;
www.hotelelephantweimar.de*

⑫ WEIMAR

Thuringia; 99423

For outsiders, Weimar is synonymous with the Weimar Republic government of Germany in the 1920s. At home, however, the erstwhile court-town is lauded as a cradle of German culture, a former home to poets, artists, composers and philosophers, a wellspring of the German Enlightenment and the birthplace of Bauhaus design.

A 90-minute walking tour

Walk to Ackerwand from the car park and turn right into the pedestrianized Frauenplan to reach **Goethes Wohnhaus** ① *(closed Mon)* on the corner of Seifengasse. Goethe occupied this Baroque house for 50 years as an adviser to the Saxe-Weimar court. Displays in its rooms include sculpture and art acquired during his Italian travels and a piano on which composer Felix Mendelssohn showcased work-in-progress after dinner. An adjacent museum *(closed Mon)* details court life in contemporary Weimar. Walk down to the end of Seifengasse to see the **Platz der Demokratie** ②. Surrounded by ducal Baroque palaces, this square helps visitors gauge the former glory of Weimar. The centrepiece of the square is an equestrian statue of Goethe's aesthete employer, Duke Carl August. To the right of the square is the **Grünes Schloss** ③ *(closed Mon; limited number of tickets)*, home to one of Europe's finest Rococo libraries,

established by the duke's wife, Duchess Anna Amalia. Walk west across the square to reach the **Markt** ④, which has a Renaissance fountain; houses, including that of the great German painter Lucas Cranach the Elder; and the Neo-Gothic town hall. Walk across the Markt and turn left into Frauentorstrasse and then right into Schillerstrasse, named after the dramatist Friedrich von Schiller. At No. 12 is **Schillerhaus** ⑤ *(closed Mon)*, a relatively modest residence compared to that of Schiller's friend, Goethe. Schillerstrasse arcs into **Theaterplatz** ⑥, which has a famous statue of Goethe and Schiller by sculptor Ernst Rietschel and the theatre in which the German National Assembly ratified the liberal Weimar Republic in 1919. Opposite is the **Wittumspalais** ⑦ *(closed Tue)*, where at a round table, the duchess hosted soirées attended by Weimar's intellectual luminaries. Its Neo-Classical interiors are the town's finest. Walk for ten minutes along Goetheplatz to the new

Left Approach to the Baroque Schloss Belvedere near Weimar **Below** Goethes Gartenhaus, the summerhouse given as a gift to Goethe, Weimar

EAT AND DRINK IN WEIMAR

Crêperie du Palais *moderate*
Galettes (savoury crêpes), crêpes and Breton cider are served in this cosy side street French café near Herderplatz.
Am Palais 1, 99423; 03643 40 15 81; www.creperie-weimar.de; closed Mon–Wed

Zum Weissen Schwan *moderate*
Regional fare such as *Sauerbraten* (marinated beef) with *Klösse* (dumplings) plus Goethe's favourite dish, boiled beef in green herb sauce, is served in the writer's local inn.
Frauentorstrasse 23, 99423; 03643 90 87 51; www.weisserschwan.de; closed Sun & Mon

Weinbar Weimar *expensive*
Try masterchef Marcello Fabbri's five-course tasting menu, or choose from a selection of small dishes to share at this convivial wine bar. It also offers excellent wines.
Humboldtstrasse 2, 99423; 03643 469 95 33; www.weinbar-weimar.de; closed Sun & Mon

Bauhaus-Museum. Zeughof threads between the two and joins Rittergasse to emerge at Herderplatz, on which is the **Kirche St Peter und Paul** ⑧. The church's sumptuous triptych was painted by Cranach. This painting serves as an introduction to the art in the **Stadtschloss** ⑨ *(closed Mon)* at the end of Vorwerksgasse, which runs behind the church. Rebuilt in Neo-Classical style on Goethe's advice, this palace houses the Saxe-Weimar dynasty's gallery, including Cranach's wedding portraits of Johann Friedrich and his bride. On leaving the palace from the southern side, emerge at its original Renaissance gateway and tower. Walk behind the palace and cross the Ilm to reach a broad park. Follow signs to the **Goethes Gartenhaus** ⑩ *(closed Tue)* beside the Ilm. This summerhouse was given to Goethe for drawing up the plans for Weimar. Cross the river on a footbridge to the left of the house, and turn right. Beyond a folly, on Marienstrasse, lies Liszthaus *(closed Tue)*, home of the Romantic composer Franz Liszt. Turn right into Ackerwand to return to the car park.
🚗 *Turn left on to Marienstrasse and continue on it to reach the Schloss Belvedere.*

⑬ Schloss Belvedere
Thuringia; 99425
The summer palace of Duke Carl August, the Baroque Schloss Belvedere has a cheery canary-yellow colour scheme. Some of its outbuildings have been modernized as a music school, but the rooms in the main residence *(Apr–Oct: closed Mon)* have been restored as a historical backdrop for displays of porcelain, glass and furniture. Learn about the lovely gardens in the west pavilion before exploring the 43 ha (106 acres) of greenery, landscaped into the naturalistic English style of the late 1700s.

DAY TRIP OPTIONS
Meiningen is an ideal base for exploring the Thuringian Forest, while Weimar makes an excellent base for most sights along this drive.

Outdoor pursuits
Explore Meiningen ⑤ before driving to the half-timbered houses in Schmalkalden ④, leaving time for the palace chapel before setting off to ski or hike in Oberhof ⑥, and to work up an appetite for lunch in Arnstadt ⑧. Stroll its streets or drive

to Ilmenau ⑦ for a walk on the Goethewanderweg.

Follow the B19 to Schmalkalden, then retrace the route to Meiningen and take the B62 and Heinrich-Ehrhardt-Strasse to Oberhof. Follow the route to Arnstadt, and then retrace the route to Ilmenau.

Classics and culture
In Weimar ⑫, tour Goethe's house before travelling back in time with Erfurt's ⑪ Krämerbrücke and cathedral, both medieval showpieces of the state's capital

city. Next, browse the art in Schloss Friedenstein ⑩, then return east past Drei Gleichen ⑨ to Arnstadt ⑧. Drivers can then travel back to Weimar to spend time in Schloss Belvedere's ⑬ gardens.

Follow the B7 to Erfurt, then continue on it to Schloss Friedenstein. Follow the tour in reverse order to Arnstadt and then retrace the entire route back to Weimar to reach Schloss Belvedere.

TRIP 11

ON THE TRAIL OF THE SUN KING
Zwickau to Bautzen

HIGHLIGHTS

Local folk crafts

Explore the historic mining towns in the Erzgebirge
and buy beautiful wooden toys and traditional
Christmas decorations

Baroque Dresden

Tour the rebuilt grand palaces and impressive churches
that spread the fame of the "Florence of the Elbe"

Riverside beauty

Cruise down the Elbe on a vintage paddlesteamer,
stopping off along the way at pretty spa villages

Magical scenery

Visit the Bastei to see the fantastical gorges
and plateaus of Saxon Switzerland

ON THE TRAIL OF THE SUN KING

Saxony (Sachsen) promotes itself as the "state of the arts" and its brooding castles, Gothic hall churches and opulent palaces are fine representatives of centuries of artistic brilliance. This is a state as rich in landscapes as it is in culture. There is a real sense of transition on this route, as it emerges from the Erzgebirge, an upland whose old towns are full of mining history, folk crafts and charm, to follow the trail of Augustus the Strong, an 18th-century Saxon Sun King who erected some of the most sensational Baroque architecture around his capital, Dresden. The mood changes again as the route travels east along the Elbe into Saxon Switzerland, a realm full of fantastical rock plateaus and mystery.

ACTIVITIES

Shop for traditional wooden toys in the towns of the Erzgebirge

Sample Saxon wines in an old town *Weinstube* in Meissen

Stroll through elegant Baroque gardens at Schloss Moritzburg and Gross Sedlitz

Hike in the beautiful forests from Festung Königstein

Take a historic paddlesteamer from Dresden, then walk through the Bastei

Go ghost-hunting in the cellars of Burg Stolpen

KEY

Drive route

PLAN YOUR DRIVE

Start/finish: Zwickau to Bautzen.

Number of days: 5–6 days, with at least a day each in Dresden and around Saxon Switzerland.

Distance: 284 km (177 miles).

Road conditions: There are good, well-signposted roads throughout the region.

When to go: The best time to visit the region is between late June and September, when small town festivals are in full swing, gardens are in bloom, steamboats ply the Elbe and the hiking season is on. However, Dresden is busy at this time. Christmas markets are charming in December.

Opening times: Shops open from 9am to 6pm Monday to Friday. Most museums and monuments are closed on Mondays.

Main market days: Zwickau: Thu & Fri; Erzgebirge: Wed & Fri (Schneeberg); Tue & Fri, (Annaberg-Buchholz); Freiburg: Thu; Meissen: Wed & Sat; Dresden: Thu-Sat; Pirna: Wed & Sat; Bautzen: Tue, Thu & Sat.

Shopping: Wooden toys and traditional Christmas decorations are available in stores throughout the Erzgebirge, while wines and porcelain can be purchased around Meissen.

Major festivals: Erzgebirge: Bergstadtfest (mining festival), last Sat & Sun in Jun; Schneeberg (Bergstreittag Miners' Parade), 22 Jul; Weihnachtsmarkt (Christmas markets), first three weeks of Advent; Dresden: Dixieland Festival, early May; Musikfestspiele (classical music festival) mid-May–early Jun; Bautzen: Sorbischer Ostereiermarkt (Easter egg market), five weeks before Easter; Osterreiten (Sorb Easter Sunday parade), Easter Sun.

DAY TRIP OPTIONS

With Dresden as a base, day trips can be made to the **Baroque palaces** and **beautiful gardens** in Schloss Pillnitz, while Bad Schandau provides access to the brooding **castles** and the **small village-resorts** on the Elbe. For full details, *see p123*.

Above Meadows on the way to Bad Schandau, *see p122* **Below** Cobbled street in the old town, Meissen, *see p118*

Right Rock formations along the Sächsische Silberstrasse

① Zwickau
Saxony; 08056

Music and motor cars have made Zwickau famous. In 1810, Romantic composer Robert Schumann was born in what is now the Robert-Schumann-Haus on **Hauptmarkt** *(closed Mon)*, a block across from the **Dom St Marien**. This church's richly decorated Gothic altar was made by the tutor of the Renaissance master-artist Albrecht Dürer. In more recent history, Zwickau was renowned for the cars produced by the Horch factory – Audis, Daimlers and Trabants, the 500 cc steel and plastic workhorses of Eastern Bloc transport. Some of these models are displayed in the **August Horch Museum** *(closed Mon)*.

🚗 *From the Zentrum car park, turn right on to the B173/Dr-Friedrichs-Ring, a one-way system. At the T-junction, turn left towards Schneeberg on the B93. Park on the Markt.*

② Erzgebirge
Saxony; 08289, 09456, 09427, 09573 & 09599

Rich deposits of silver, tin, copper and cobalt earned the uplands along the Czech border the name "Ore Mountains". When these reserves waned, the miners turned to folk crafts, so this route along the Sächsische Silberstrasse (Saxon Silver Route) offers both historical romance and an opportunity to buy beautiful handicrafts such as wooden toys and lace.

① **Schneeberg**
An enormous Markt boxed in by Baroque town houses and signs declaring *Glück auf* – the traditional "good luck" salutation of miners – are reminders of the wealthy past of this silver-mining town. Another testament to Schneeberg's former status is **St Wolfgangkirche** at the top of the Markt, a late-Gothic hall church whose altarpiece is by the Renaissance artist Lucas Cranach the Elder (1472–1553). The **Museum für bergmännische Volkskunst** *(closed Mon)* beneath the church contains examples of the miners' folk crafts.

🚗 *Retrace the route to B93, then take the B169 to Aue. Take the B101 past Schwarzenberg and Raschau to Annaberg-Buchholz. Turn left on to the Sehmatalstrasse at the sharp right bend before the viaduct and park at Frohnauer Hammer car park.*

② **Annaberg-Buchholz**
One of the major attractions in this hilltop town is the **Frohnauer Hammer** *(tours daily)*. Visitors will probably hear this mechanical marvel before seeing it. Inside a shingle-roofed building, a 17th-century contraption harnesses energy from a stream to power three hammers that weigh up to 250 kg (551 lb) each. It is the last forge of its kind in Europe and until 1904 it produced iron and copper products,

samples of which are on display in an exhibition room above. Drive back to the B101, go beneath the viaduct and then turn left at the roundabout. Around a tight bend, turn right into the Altstadt and park at the Markt. In Annaberg-Buchholz's old town, grand town houses suggest a place of some importance. The richest silver seams in the area funded both its main square and **St Annenkirche**, whose rough exterior belies a beautiful interior. Notoriously superstitious, miners hoped their lavish outlay would find favour with St Anne, the profession's patron saint. Prayers were said just before a shift in a contemporary shaft, now accessed via a mining museum *(open daily)* opposite the church door.

🚗 *Continue north on the B101 and turn left on to the B95 towards Chemnitz. Turn left in central Ehrenfriedersdorf towards Greifensteine for the entrance.*

③ Greifensteine
Around 300 million years ago, magma bubbling up through fissures in the Earth's crust wore away the surrounding sandstone to leave these strange granite outcrops, which appear unexpectedly in a pine forest like fortifications of a fantastic castle. Walk around their bases before ascending a walkway for a panoramic view. Long mined as a quarry by locals, the rocks are put to better use today as a natural amphitheatre for musicals and opera in summer *(www.greifensteine.com)*.

🚗 *Back in Ehrenfriedersdorf, turn left at the T-junction and then right towards Dreibach and Scharfenstein to Zschopau. Drive through the town centre to Waldkirchen and turn left to Augustusburg; park below the Schloss.*

④ Schloss Augustusburg
Several sights in one courtyard castle make this 16th-century royal hunting lodge *(open daily)* a family favourite. Visitors can buy a combination ticket to access a trio of museums: former banqueting chambers whose displays on hunting are upstaged by murals of gambolling hares; displays of vintage motorbikes; and the fairy-tale carriages of Saxony's rulers in the old stables. Also of interest are the historic rooms of the **Lindenhaus** *(tours daily)* and a dungeon full of grisly torture instruments. Displays of falconry staged by the drawbridge offer a glimpse of the castle's past *(open daily)*.

🚗 *Continue north, following signs to Flöha and join the B180 then the B173 to Freiberg. Follow signs to Zentrum and park on Schlossplatz.*

⑤ Freiberg
Historic and postcard-pretty, old Freiberg is a delight. Having emerged from World War II unscathed, the main square, **Obermarkt**, crowded by narrow 17th-century merchants' houses, is a slice of bygone Germany. The town's name literally means "Free Mountain", as the wealth from silver mining was all tax-free. Silver also funded Freiberg's architectural treasure, the late-Gothic **Dom St Marien** *(open daily)*, which has a sculpture of a miner gesturing up to its Tulip Pulpit (1505). A town and mining museum, **Stadt-und Bergbaumuseum** *(closed Mon)*, stands opposite the cathedral.

🚗 *Turn right from Schlossplatz and then right again on to Leipziger Strasse to find the B101 to Nossen, then Meissen. Park beside the river on Hochuferstrasse.*

Above Pretty pastel-hued houses, Augustusburg village **Centre left** Sculptures on the walls of Dom St Marien, Zwickau **Below** Schloss Augustusburg, on its wooded perch above the town

EAT AND DRINK IN ERZGEBIRGE

Ratskeller *moderate*
With its panelled dining room and dishes such as Erzgebirge trout pan-fried in butter, this local institution is a bastion of traditional dining.
Obermarkt 16, 09599 Freiberg; 03731 221 51; www.ratskeller-freiberg.de

Ratskeller Schneeberg *moderate*
As the name suggests, this restaurant is situated beneath the old town hall. It is good for both formal dining and casual outdoor eating. The menu offers several deer dishes as well as a variety of pork options.
Markt 1, 08289 Schneeberg; 03772 224 84; www.ratskeller-schneeberg.de

Right Panoramic view of the charming town of Meissen **Below** Frauenkirche's ornate cupola, Dresden

VISITING DRESDEN

Parking
Ample parking is available on Schiessgasse and in Neumarkt.

Tourist Information
Neumarkt 2 (QF Passage), 01067; 03515 016 01 60; www.dresden.de

WHERE TO STAY

MEISSEN
Fuchshöhl *inexpensive*
Personality abounds in this homely pension in a half-timbered house, whose artist owner cherishes a relaxed atmosphere and charmingly mismatched furnishings.
Hohlweg 7 (top of Burgstrasse), 01662; 03521 833 99 77; www.fuchshoehl.de

Goldener Löwe *moderate*
The decor in this small, pleasant hotel just off the Markt is reminiscent of Baroque grandeur.
Heinrichsplatz 6, 01662; 03521 411 10; www.goldener-loewe-meissen.com

DRESDEN
Bülow Palais *moderate*
Formerly the Baroque palace of Augustus the Strong's master-architect, this Relais & Chateaux hotel is all old-world opulence and faultless service.
Königstrasse 14, 01097; 03518 00 30; www.buelow-palais.de

Taschenbergpalais Kempinski *expensive*
Housed in the palace where Augustus the Strong installed his mistress, this hotel affords five-star luxury. "Kurfürsten" deluxe rooms offer the best views of the Residenzschloss or Zwinger.
Taschenberg 3, 01067; 03514 91 20; www.kempinski-dresden.de

③ Meissen
Saxony; 01662
Known for porcelain, Meissen is also worth visiting for its cobbled lanes. In the town's Domplatz, a High Gothic cathedral with a ducal chapel and an altarpiece by Lucas Cranach the Elder adjoins the 16th-century **Albrechtsburg**. In 1710, Augustus the Strong converted the palace into the first porcelain factory outside East Asia. Meissen china is now manufactured at a factory *(tours daily)* 1.5 km (1 mile) south of the centre, where there is an exhibition centre and a shop.

🚗 *Turn right beneath Albrechtsburg to cross the river on the B101.*
Follow signs to Moritzburg crossing Weinböhla; park at the palace.

④ Schloss Moritzburg
Saxony; 01468
Unimpressed by a small hunting lodge he had inherited, Augustus the Strong ordered his court architect Matthäus Daniel Pöppelmann to build him a Baroque pleasure palace. The finest craftsmen in Saxony were hired to create the decadent interiors *(Apr–Oct: tours daily; Nov–Mar: tours Tue–Sun)*. Highlights include a banqueting hall with hunting trophies and the royal four-poster bed with iridescent feather tapestries.

🚗 *Follow signs to Dresden and to Innere Altstadt, crossing the Elbe on Carolabrücke. Go over Rathenauplatz on to St Petersburger Strasse and turn right for the car park.*

⑤ Dresden
Saxony; 01067
So devastating was an Allied air raid in February 1945 that, for most, the name of Saxony's capital is synonymous with destruction. In fact, Dresden is better understood in terms of its resurrection. After decades of Communist neglect, the old town's Baroque monuments are being rebuilt and the "Florence of the Elbe" is regaining its former glory.

A one-hour walking tour
From the car park on Schiessgasse, walk up Landhausstrasse to reach the epicentre of Dresden's rejuvenation, the Neumarkt, and the symbol of its revival, the **Frauenkirche** ①. After it was rebuilt, thousands gathered to celebrate the reconsecration of this Baroque church in October 2005. Original fire-blackened blocks stand out in its new sandstone. The crucifix in its interior was forged by a Coventry silversmith whose father flew in the Allied raid – a poignant symbol of reconciliation. A rear entrance provides access up the bell-like cupola *(open daily)* for views over the cafés of the Neumarkt. Turn right on to Salzgasse to admire sculpture and art from the 19th century in the Albertinum *(closed Mon)*, or simply stroll on the **Brühlscher Terrasse** ②, the handsome riverfront belvedere that was revered as the "balcony of Europe" in Dresden's heyday. Ascend a staircase, to the left, to access the Brühlscher Terrasse atop the town's fortifications where visitors can explore casements and cannon rooms at the Festung Xperience.

Above Baroque Zwinger, the showpiece of Dresden **Below** Field of flowering crops along the road to Dresden

EAT AND DRINK

MEISSEN

Zum Löwen *moderate*
Try the pasta, meat, fish and vegetarian dishes at this hotel restaurant. For a large appetite, try the Argentinian steak.
Heinrichsplatz 6, 01662; 03521 411 10; www.goldener-loewe-meissen.com

Vincenz Richter *moderate*
This restaurant, housed in a snug 16th-century tavern, has been run by over four generations of the Richter family, who also sell their own wines.
An der Frauenkirche 12, 01662; 03521 45 32 85; closed Sun & Mon

DRESDEN

Sophienkeller *moderate*
Enjoy hearty fare such as roast suckling pig in this restaurant in the stone cellars opposite the Zwinger.
Taschenburg 3, 01067; 0351 49 72 60; www.sophienkeller-dresden.de

Alte Meister *expensive*
Modern international dishes such as grilled fish with saffron risotto are served in this stylish café-restaurant at the back of the Zwinger.
Theaterplatz 1a, 01067; 03514 81 04 26; www.altemeister.net

Villandry *expensive*
A relaxed locals' restaurant and bar specializing in Mediterranean cuisine.
Jordanstrasse 8, 01099; 03513 097 28 77; www.villandry-dresden.de; closed Sun & Mon

---

Continue down the terrace, towards the tiered spire of the Hofkirche and the Schlossplatz, beside the State Parliament. First, though, turn left on to Augustusstrasse for the **Fürstenzug** ③, a 102-m (335-ft) long frieze, made of 24,000 Meissen china tiles, which depicts eight centuries of Saxon rulers in a medieval pageant. Behind this is the Renaissance courtyard of the royal stables, the **Johanneum** ④, which houses a transport museum *(closed Mon)*. Return to the Schlossplatz. The Italian-designed Catholic **Hofkirche** ⑤ was Augustus's bid to appease the Pope, who had begun to suspect that the elector's conversion to Catholicism was just a ruse to claim the Polish crown. Take a look at its all-German interior, furnished with a Rococo pulpit by court sculptor Balthasar Permoser. Then walk round to Theaterplatz and the prestigious **Semperoper** ⑥, which replicates the opera house where composer Richard Wagner premiered works such as *Tannhäuser*. The showpiece of Dresden is the Baroque palace, **Zwinger** ⑦, next door. Ascend via its outstanding Wallpavillon gateway to walk the balustrade. It has three museums *(closed Mon)*: the Gemäldegalerie Alte Meister, Rüstkammer and Porzellansammlung. Exit via the Glockenspielpavillon, named

Sculpture on a dome in Dresden

for its carillon of porcelain bells, and pass the former palace guardhouse, now a ticket booking centre, to reach the **Residenzschloss** ⑧ *(closed Tue)*, the colossal electors' palace. Augustus's treasury (Grünes Gewölbe) within has many bejewelled gold and porcelain trinkets. Ascend the tower *(late Mar–Oct: closed Tue)* for a view over the skyline. Exit left from the palace to see the antithesis of such decadence, the renovated Kulturpalast, an example of stark 1960s Modernism with a striking mural. Walk alongside it to return to Neumarkt to relax in its cafés, and then take Landhausstrasse back to the car park.

🚗 *Follow signs for Pillnitz on Käthe-Kollwitz-Ufer along the south bank of the river, across a bridge and then along the north bank for about 6 km (4 miles). Parking is available at the Schloss on the left.*

Above Wall and tower of the Festung Königstein **Above right** Spire of the Stadtkirche St Marien towering over rooftops, Pirna **Below** Gross Sedlitz, on the outskirts of Pirna

CRUISING THE ELBE

River cruisers ply the Elbe three times a day, stopping at various destinations along the river. At Königstein, **Kanu Aktiv Tours** *(03502 159 99 60; www. kanu-aktiv-tours.de)* rents canoes and kayaks. The modern cruisers of **Sachsische Dampfschiffahrt** *(www. saechsische-dampfschiffahrt.de)* depart regularly on stately cruises up the Elbe to Bad Schandau via all the destinations included in this tour.

WHERE TO STAY IN PIRNA

Deutsches Haus *moderate*
Old-fashioned furnishings meet modern, friendly service in this small hotel installed in a Renaissance courtyard residence. It makes a fine base for visiting Dresden and Saxon Switzerland and has a good restaurant. *Niedere Burgstrasse 1, 01796; 03501 468 80; www.romantikhotel-pirna.de*

⑥ Schloss Pillnitz
Saxony; 01326

A drive along the Elbe offers views of the 19th-century villas and palaces on the river's northern bank. The inspiration for these buildings was Schloss Pillnitz, an extraordinary ensemble begun in 1720 to host the summertime revels of Augustus the Strong. Architect Pöppelmann reflected the ruler's admiration for autocratic Oriental emperors in the chinoiserie of the facing wings, one of which contains a crafts museum *(May–Oct: open Tue–Sun; closed Nov–Apr)*. Learn about the complex's creation in the **Neues Palace** *(Apr–Oct: closed Mon; closed Nov–Mar)*, then explore the gardens *(open daily)* to find a large palm house and the Triton Gondola in which Augustus' son cruised the Elbe.

🚗 *Continue on north bank road to reach the main road and the B172 to Pirna-Zentrum. In the town centre, turn right following signs to Gross Sedlitz, and park at Barockgarten.*

⑦ Gross Sedlitz
Saxony; 01809

Fountains and flowerbeds, parterre patterns and statues of antique deities make this the most grandiose of Augustus's pleasure gardens *(closed Nov–Mar)*. A synthesis of late-Baroque Italian and French styles, its symmetry reflects the Age of Reason (the 17th century flourishing of philosophical thought). It opens on to an immaculate green where Augustus the Strong played bowls, then sweeps down to a lower terrace, a radiant green divided by channels and backed by the rhythmic arches of an orangery full of fragrant Tuscan orange trees.

🚗 *Return to Pirna and drive over the B172 into the Zentrum. Park beside the river in the car park P6, or on Markt beyond the viaduct.*

Wines of Saxony

The northern slopes of the Elbe are sufficiently sun-drenched to allow viticulture. Müller-Thurgau (also called Rivaner), fresh and characterful, is the most popular variety of grape cultivated here, followed by Riesling and Weissburgunder (Pinot Blanc). This region's white wines are generally medium-dry and sprightly, while reds such as Traminer and Blau Spätburgunder tend to be aromatic. Although locally produced wines can be tasted in a *Weinstube* in Meissen, aficionados should visit the acclaimed Schloss Wackerbarth estate *(open daily; www.schloss-wackerbarth.de)* in Radebeul, near Dresden.

Left Breathtaking view from Festung Königstein Below Cannon on the fortified walls of Festung Königstein

VISITING FESTUNG KÖNIGSTEIN

Tourist Information
Pirnaer Strasse 2, 01824; 03502 16 82 61; www.koenigstein-sachsen.de; May–Oct: open daily, Nov–Apr: open Mon–Sat

EAT AND DRINK IN PIRNA

Deutsches Haus *moderate*
Fine German cuisine is served in a charming country-styled dining room – old wood furniture and glass lamps – or in the beer garden. *Niedere Burgstrasse 1, 01796; 03501 468 80; www.romantikhotel-pirna.de*

Felsenbirne *moderate*
Traditional regional cuisine is cooked with a twist here, with vegan and vegetarian produce taking centre stage. Try the caramelized Altenburg goat cheese, or the roasted char fillet with spinach. *Lange Strasse 34, 01796; 03501 759 97 91; www.felsenbirne-restaurant.de; closed Tue & Sun*

❽ Pirna
Saxony; 01796
A chequerboard of Baroque streets shaded in dusty pastels, the town of Pirna is centred on the cobbled **Markt**, seemingly unchanged since it was painted by the Italian artist Canaletto in 1754; a copy of the painting is in the tourist office at No. 7. Carved portals still front handsome merchants' mansions; the town hall continues to be the town's centrepiece, even though its Renaissance looks suffered during 19th-century renovations; and **Schloss Sonnenstein** remains on a hill above. The town's church, **Stadtkirche St Marien** *(open daily)*, is worth visiting for its vaulted roof and a Renaissance pulpit adorned with coquettish cherubs.

🚗 *Return to the B172, going left towards Bad Schandau. After 12 km (8 miles) turn right to reach Festung Königstein; tourist trains ascend to the fortress from the car park.*

❾ Festung Königstein
Saxony; 01824
This mountain fortress *(open daily)* looks so impregnable that no attempt has been made to conquer it in over 600 years. The stronghold is 240 m (787 ft) above the Elbe, with unscalable 42-m (138-ft) tall walls. Visitors can peer down a 152-m (499-ft) deep well dug by Augustus the Strong and tour the prison where he imprisoned an alchemist to force him to create gold from base metals. These experiments resulted in the creation of his "white gold" – porcelain. If inspired by the views, visitors can drive 2 km (1 mile)

east to Königstein village for walks to the **Lillienstein** (435 m/1,427 ft) or **Pfaffenstein** (415 m/1,362 ft) plateaus; maps are available at the fortress's ticket office *(03502 16 46 07; www.festung-koenigstein.de)* and the village information centre.

🚗 *Take the B172 and cross the river to reach Bad Schandau. Park by the river.*

Augustus the Strong
Frederick Augustus (1670–1733) was nicknamed "Augustus the Strong" either because of his physical strength or his rumoured 370 illegitimate children. Impressed by France's Palace of Versailles, Augustus styled himself as a Saxon Sun King and began to transform his capital to mirror his own magnificence. His admiration for omnipotent Oriental rulers also made him covet Asian porcelain. His alchemist, Johann Friedrich Böttger, cracked the secret of "white gold" while incarcerated in Festung Königstein.

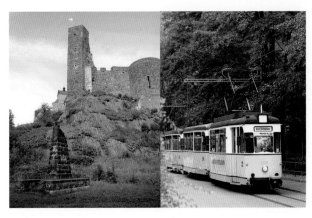

Above Ruins of Burg Stolpen on a basalt ridge **Above right** Kirnitzschtalbahn tram running through Bad Schandau **Below** Verdant scenery around the Bastei

HIKING AROUND BAD SCHANDAU

Tourist Information
Markt 12, 01814; 03502 29 00 30; www.bad-schandau.de

WHERE TO STAY

BAD SCHANDAU
Elbresidenz *expensive*
Five town houses have been conjoined to create a smart five-star retreat with tastefully and stylishly decorated rooms; the best have views of the Elbe. Guests can relax in the large spa and wellness centre.
Markt 1, 01814; 03502 291 90; www.elbresidenz-bad-schandau.de

AROUND BASTEI
Hotel Elbiente *moderate*
Set beside the ferry landing directly below the Bastei, this hotel offers modern rooms overlooking the river. It also has a restaurant and a small spa.
Wehlener Weg 1, 01824 Rathen; 03502 47 55 00; www.elbiente.de

BAUTZEN
Goldener Adler *moderate*
Rather dated furnishings do not detract from the appeal of the spacious rooms of this hotel, housed in a grand town house in a central location. Guests should visit the romantic wine cellar.
Hauptmarkt 4, 02625; 03591 486 60; www.goldeneradler.de

⑩ Bad Schandau
Saxony; 01814
Spa waters have attracted visitors to this gentle riverside resort for over a century. Take the **Personenaufzug** *(open daily)*, the 50-m (164-ft) iron lift built in 1904, to a spectacular viewing platform. It is advisable to carry walking boots – an hour's walk east leads to another viewpoint at **Schrammsteineaussicht**, which offers sweeping views of the area's most fissured plateau. For another walk, take the **Kirnitzschtalbahn** *(open daily)*, the historic tram from the Kurpark, for a rickety ride up a wooded valley. Alight at Lichtenhainer Wasserfall to walk to the waterfall and a rock arch called *Kuhstall*, or cowshed.
🚗 *Return toward the bridge, but turn right before it toward Bastei via Porschdorf, then a left turn at the main road towards*

Lohmen. If the inner car park is full, park by the turn off and use the shuttle bus.

⑪ Bastei
Saxony; 01847
The astonishing sandstone formations at Bastei were created millions of years ago by water erosion. Popular with 19th-century Romantics, the area was featured in the fantasy film *The Chronicles of Narnia: The Lion, the Witch and the Wardrobe*. A footbridge connects the pinnacles that jut high above pinewoods and leads to the remains of a 13th-century fortress, the Bastei *(open daily)*, from where there are panoramic views over the river to Festung Königstein. Arrive early before it gets crowded; there are postcard views from the path ascending to the left, before the bridge. Return to the main road to drive 3 km (1 mile) east to Hohnstein village, in an idyllic setting beneath a castle that is now a youth hostel.
🚗 *Retrace the route toward Lohmen, and then turn right to Stolpen (left after Rathewalde if driving from Bastei). Park on Marktplatz.*

⑫ Burg Stolpen
Saxony; 01833
A picture book-pretty Marktplatz offers no hint of Stolpen's sombre history. Countess von Cosel (1680–1765), once wooed passionately by Augustus the Strong as a mistress and mother to three of his children, was imprisoned in the lofty 17th-century stronghold of Burg Stolpen *(open daily)* for 49 years.

Left Fortified town of Bautzen **Below** Burg Stolpen, rising above the town of Stolpen

EAT AND DRINK

BAD SCHANDAU

Elbterrasse *moderate*
Housed in the Elbresidenz hotel, this restaurant offers the best summer terrace in the area, as well as classic Saxon cooking with dishes such as *Sauerbraten* (marinated pot roast).
Markt 1, 01814; 03502 291 90; closed Sun & Mon

AROUND BASTEI

Landgasthaus zum Schwarzbachtal *expensive*
The rustic ambience of this restaurant belies the quality of the food that chef Barbara Siebert prepares from the freshest ingredients. Expect handwritten menus of modern German and regional dishes.
Niederdorfstrasse 3, 01848 Lohsdorf-Hohnstein (10 km/6 miles east of Bastei); 03597 58 03 45; www.schwarz bachtal.de; closed Thu, Jan & Feb

BAUTZEN

Mönchshof *moderate*
Wine in earthenware jugs, waiters in sackcloth and meaty recipes from 1560 make this medieval-themed inn very popular.
Burglehn 1, 02625; 03591 49 01 41; www.moenchshof.de; closed Mon & Tue

Wjelbik *moderate*
Traditional specialities such as ox fillet with horseradish sauce are served in this Sorbian restaurant behind the Dom.
Kornstrasse 7, 02625; 03591 420 60; www.wjelbik.de; closed Mon

Courtiers, fearing her influence over the besotted ruler, had plotted to have the 36-year-old black-eyed beauty incarcerated in what was already a decaying castle. She died here at the age of 84. Indeed, some say that the countess still roams the castle – her ghost is said to haunt a dark cellar.
🚗 *Follow the one-way road from Marktplatz to the T-junction, turn left toward Dresden, then right after 4 km (2 miles) on to the B6 to Bautzen. Park in the Kornmarkt-Center car park on Lauengraben, 300 m (329 yards) across the river.*

⑬ Bautzen
Saxony; 02625
The view of tightly packed medieval defence towers and spires seen on the drive across the Spree river is the finest introduction possible to the cultural capital of the Slavic Sorbs, Germany's only Indigenous minority. Known mainly for its top-security jail for political prisoners during the German Democratic Republic era, today Bautzen enchants visitors with its beautifully reconstructed old town. The winding streets with their original houses, the city walls, the curiously crooked Reichenturm tower and the Baroque town hall in the town square, all form an attractive complex. Take a riverside path past fortifications to see Slavic folk crafts and costumes in the **Sorbisches Museum** *(closed Mon)*, located beside the late-Gothic Schloss Ortenburg. The **Dom St Petri's** interior is curious – its nave bends to gain extra space on the square, and is divided and used by both Catholics and Protestants. A cathedral treasury *(open Mon–Fri)* is located behind in the Baroque Bishopric.

DAY TRIP OPTIONS

Follow the cultural trail left by Augustus the Strong from Dresden, or choose Bad Schandau to explore the outdoors of Saxon Switzerland.

Grace and grandeur
In Dresden ⑤, visit the Zwinger and treasury, then drive to Schloss Pillnitz ⑥ and Augustus' garden, Gross Sedlitz ⑦, then head for lunch in Pirna ⑧. Walk it off with a tour of the monarch's hunting lodge, Schloss Moritzburg ④, then go west to Meissen ③ to end the day with a taste of local wines in a *Weinstube*.

Follow the driving instructions to Pirna. Return to the dual carriageway and continue north to Radeburg, across the A4 and then follow signs to Moritzburg. Follow instructions in reverse to Meissen.

Mountains and valleys
From Bad Schandau ⑩, drive to the Bastei ⑪ with a packed picnic to enjoy views. Drive to Burg Stolpen ⑫, then head south to Pirna ⑧ for lunch and window-shopping along the cobbled lanes of its Baroque grid.

Follow the driving instructions to Stolpen, return via the road to Lohmen, then continue to Pirna.

TRIP 12

IN THE LAND OF THE BROTHERS GRIMM

Wiesbaden to Steinau an der Strasse

HIGHLIGHTS

Nineteenth-century opulence

Explore Wiesbaden, with its grand opera house
and hotels that evoke the imperial swagger
of the Kaiser's day

Chocolate-box charm

Visit the pretty half-timbered towns in Hesse,
from ancient Limburg an der Lahn to
charming Steinau an der Strasse

Impressive palace and gardens

Admire Kassel's Wilhelmshöhe, a magnificent palace
with a landscaped 18th-century park

Cultural extravaganza

Marvel at Hesse's contribution to world culture, from
Goethe and Heidegger to the Brothers Grimm

IN THE LAND OF THE BROTHERS GRIMM

The hilly, wooded landscape of Hesse (Hessen) is dotted with perfectly preserved medieval towns and crowned with castles of fairy-tale charm. If at times this most quintessentially German of regions seems like a storybook brought to life, that is no surprise, since it nurtured the careers of the Brothers Grimm and of Germany's greatest writer, JW Goethe. These literary giants have left their mark on Hesse, but so have the landgraves and churchmen who held sway over it. Lovers of architecture will be enchanted by the area's many quaint small towns, those interested in art will take to the Baroque glories of Kassel or Fulda, and for those who wish to unwind, the region's lazy waterways and spa towns offer plenty of opportunities for relaxation.

Above Carolingian burial chapel of Michaelskirche, Fulda, *see p135*

ACTIVITIES

Pamper yourself with a day at one of Hesse's elegant spas

Take a walk on one of the long-distance footpaths that crisscross the region

Explore the Fulda and Lahn rivers by canoe

Cycle through the gentle valleys of the Fulda and Lahn rivers

Climb up the steep steps to the great cascade at the Schlosspark Wilhelmshöhe

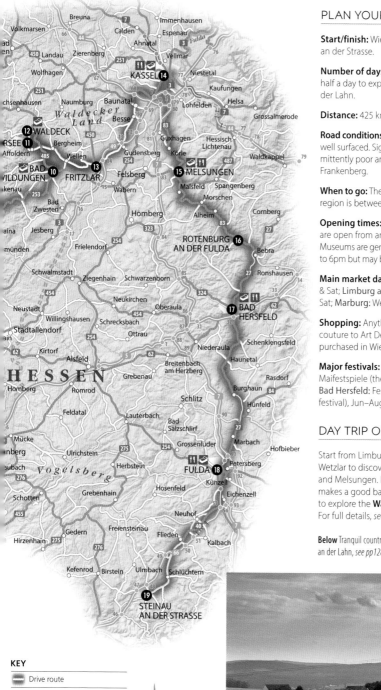

PLAN YOUR DRIVE

Start/finish: Wiesbaden to Steinau an der Strasse.

Number of days: 5–6 days, allowing half a day to explore Limburg an der Lahn.

Distance: 425 km (287 miles).

Road conditions: The roads are mostly well surfaced. Signposting is intermittently poor around Marburg and Frankenberg.

When to go: The best time to visit this region is between Easter and October.

Opening times: In larger cities, shops are open from around 9am to 6pm. Museums are generally open from 9am to 6pm but may be closed on Mondays.

Main market days: Wiesbaden: Wed & Sat; **Limburg an der Lahn:** Wed & Sat; **Marburg:** Wed & Sat.

Shopping: Anything from vintage couture to Art Deco glass can be purchased in Wiesbaden.

Major festivals: Wiesbaden: Maifestspiele (theatre festival), May; **Bad Hersfeld:** Festspiele (theatre festival), Jun–Aug.

DAY TRIP OPTIONS

Start from Limburg an der Lahn or Wetzlar to discover the **Lahn Valley** and Melsungen. Bad Wildungen makes a good base from which to explore the **Waldecker Land.** For full details, *see p135.*

Below Tranquil country landscape near Limburg an der Lahn, *see pp128–9*

KEY

🚗 Drive route

0 kilometres   10

0 miles   10

Above Country road leading to Limburg an der Lahn

VISITING LIMBURG AN DER LAHN

Parking
The Alstadtparkhaus is on the corner of Grabenstrasse and Sackgasse.

Tourist Information
Barfüsserstrasse 6, 65549; 06431 61 66; www.touristinfo-limburg.de; Apr–Oct: open daily; Nov–Mar: closed Sun

WHERE TO STAY

WIESBADEN

Nassauer Hof *expensive*
Kings, princes and the Russian novelist Fyodor Dostoevsky are among the illustrious past guests of Wiesbaden's grandest hotel. Rooms are furnished in a crisp but conservative style. The hotel also has a Michelin-starred fine dining restaurant called Ente.
Kaiser-Friedrich-Platz 3-4, 65183; 0611 13 30; www.nassauer-hof.de

LIMBURG AN DER LAHN

Dom Hotel *moderate*
This long-established hotel occupies a central site close to the Altstadt. Rooms are tastefully decorated in contemporary style with en-suite bath or shower, wireless Internet and TV.
Grabenstrasse 57, 65549; 06431 90 10; www.domhotellimburg.de

Nassauer Hof *moderate*
A comfortable three-star hotel right on Limburg's Alte Lahnbrücke, Nassauer Hof was destroyed during World War II but reconstructed in 1991. There is a good restaurant and a pretty terrace overlooking the Lahn river.
Brückengasse 1, 65549; 06431 99 60; www.nassauerhof-limburg.de

① Wiesbaden
Hesse; 65183
The 19th-century architecture of Hesse's leafy capital recalls its hey-day as Kaiser Wilhelm II's favourite watering hole. The focal point here is the colonnaded bowling green, fringed by the Neo-Classical **Kurhaus**, the **Casino** *(open daily)*, and the Neo-Baroque **Hessiches Staatstheater**, or Hessian State Theatre, which has a Neo-Rococo foyer. The best spa facility is the **Kaiser Friedrich Therme** *(open daily; Langgasse 38–40; 0611 31 70 60)*. Opened in 1913 on the site of a hot spring, it has retained its original Jugendstil (Art Nouveau) interior.

🚗 *Leave Wiesbaden along Taunusstrasse and Nerotal, following the road uphill to reach the B417 to Limburg an der Lahn.*

Shopping in Wiesbaden
Wiesbaden's elegance extends to its shops, from the designer bou-tiques along Wilhelmstrasse to the antique shops and fine-art galleries of Taunusstrasse, where visitors can buy anything from vintage couture or antiquarian books to Art Deco glass. In keeping with the city's refined, "old money" ambience, established and independent firms prevail.

② LIMBURG AN DER LAHN
Hesse; 65549
There is a powerful sense of antiquity to be discovered in the exceptionally well-preserved centre of Limburg an der Lahn. In this lovely city, tall half-timbered houses built between the 13th and 16th centuries lean across narrow, meandering lanes and are overshadowed in turn by the seven-towered St Georg's Dom. This cathedral was built in the 13th century on a dramatic site high above the Lahn river and is visible from miles around.

A two-hour walking tour
Exit the car park and walk up Grabenstrasse and right along Konrad-Kurzbold Strasse on to the **Alte Lahnbrücke** ①, a medieval stone bridge over the Lahn. It dates from 1315–54 and is crowned by an early 14th-century watch tower. The bridge, damaged towards the end of World War II, was restored and widened between 1946 and 1947.

There is a wonderful view of the Dom high above the river on a crag, with the ancient Altstadt huddled at its base. Return across the bridge, bear-ing slightly left up **Brückengasse** ② to reach the Altstadt. The 18th-century house at No. 2 was once an office belonging to the postal service of the aristocratic Thurn and Taxis Dynasty. Continue uphill into Rütsche, lined with tall, gabled half-timbered houses.

Left St Georg's Dom in its lovely setting above Lahn river, Limburg an der Lahn **Below** Detail in the main hall of the Kaiser Friedrich Therme, Wiesbaden

EAT AND DRINK

Benner's Bistronomie *expensive*
Set in the Kurhaus, this elegant bistro offers modern cuisine such as salmon tartare, wasabi tempura prawns and crêpe Suzette flambéed.
Kurhausplatz 1, 65189; 0611 53 62 00; www.benner-s.de

WIESBADEN

Ente *expensive*
The Nassauer Hof's gourmet restaurant oozes class, from the understated elegance of its ocean liner-like decor to the 600-bottle wine cellar and the creative menu, which offers the likes of Scottish scallops with corn crème brûlée, green asparagus and coconut jelly.
Kaiser-Friedrich-Platz 3-4, 65183; 0611 13 36 66; www.nassauer-hof.de; closed Sun–Tue

Other options
Wiesbaden's traditional high temple of cake and coffee is **Café Maldaner** (*Marktstrasse 34, 65183; 0611 30 52 14; www.maldaner1859.de*), founded in 1859. Head to **Fritz Kunder** (*Wilhelmstrasse 12, 65185; 0611 30 15 98; www.kunder-confiserie.de; closed Sun*) to sample *Wiesbadener Ananastörtchen* (refined bitter chocolate with a pineapple jelly filling).

LIMBURG AN DER LAHN

Twins *moderate*
A cosy restaurant in the Nassauer Hof hotel, Der kleine Prins serves a seasonal menu of creative German dishes and a selection of fine wines. Eat outside on the terrace in summer.
Brückengasse 1, 65549; 06431 99 60; www.nassauerhof-limburg.de; closed Mon–Wed

The **Werner Senger Haus** ③ at No. 5, built in the 13th century, is one of the oldest in Limburg. With a lofty, beamed hall on the ground floor, typical of the Altstadt's houses, it is now a hotel and restaurant. Turn left into **Römer** ④, dominated by a beautifully restored 13th-century Gothic Hallenhaus. Archaeological excavation at the site of this hall house has unearthed the remains of a Jewish ritual bath or mikvah. Turn right at the end of Römer and take the steps up to Domstrasse. Cross the road to reach **Diözesanmuseum** ⑤ (*Apr–Dec: closed Mon*). The museum's collection of ecclesiastical treasures includes the Staurothek, a 10th-century Byzantine cross reliquary. Leaving the museum, turn right up Domstrasse on to the Domplatz to visit the magnificent red-and-white bulk of **St Georg's Dom** ⑥. The cathedral was built in the early 13th century with the wealth accrued by Limburg's merchants in the Crusades. Its architecture is a blend of Rhenish Romanesque and early French Gothic. The interior has some early medieval frescoes.

Return to the Domplatz and walk along the southern walls of the cathedral to reach the **Schloss** ⑦. Though built on a superb defensive site high above the river, it is hard to imagine anything less forbidding than the castle's picturesque collection of stone and half-timbered buildings grouped around a central courtyard. Return to Domplatz, turning left down the atmospheric Grosse Domtreppe, the great cathedral steps, to reach **Bischofsplatz** ⑧. On the right, tall half-timbered houses lean at giddy

Sculpture in Limburg an der Lahn's old town

angles and on the left is the Stadtkirche or parish church, built around 1300. From Bischofsplatz follow Barfüssergasse and Salzgasse through the bustling heart of the Altstadt, stopping to admire the antiques and gift shops on the way to **Fischmarkt** ⑨. This contains the most impressive concentration of beautiful early-medieval houses in Limburg, including the Altes Rathaus, with its fine beamed hall and lovely spiral staircase. The old town hall now houses the municipal art collection *(open during exhibitions only)*. Turn into Sackgasse to reach the car park on the corner with Grabenstrasse.

🚗 **Leave the city on Eschhöfer Weg, following signs to Runkel.**

③ Runkel
Hesse; 65594
The Lahn Valley narrows and becomes steeper at Runkel, where the mighty **Burg** (*Apr–Oct: closed Mon*) overlooks a 15th-century stone bridge. The older, upper fortress was left a ruin by Austrian troops during the Thirty Years' War, while the 13th-century Unterburg, the lower castle, contains a museum and is the seat of the Wied family. On the opposite bank of the river stands another castle, **Burg Schadeck**. Known as the "swallows nest", it was built as a result of a dispute within Runkel's founding family.

🚗 **Leave Runkel on Borngasse following signs to Villmar and Aumenau. At Aumenau, turn right on to Elkerhäuser Strasse, then follow route to Weilburg. Use the Parkdeck Rathaus close to the tourist office to park.**

Above Garden, Schloss Weilburg **Above right**
Landgrafenschloss in the town of Marburg

VISITING WETZLAR

Parking
There is limited on-street parking on
the Domplatz. The entrance to the
Dom Garage car park is on the square.

Tourist Information
*Domplatz 8, 35578; 06441 99 77 55;
www.wetzlar.de; open daily*

Canoeing along the Lahn river
Canoes can be hired with **Kanu Lahn-
Dill** *(Dammstrasse 52, 35576 Wetzlar;
06445 601 99 70; www.kanulahn-dill.de)*

WHERE TO STAY

WEILBURG

Schlosshotel Weilburg *moderate*
The individually decorated rooms in this
four-star hotel feature en-suite bath or
shower, TV and minibar.
*Langgasse 25, 35781; 06471 509 00;
www.schlosshotel-weilburg.de*

WETZLAR

Bürgerhof *moderate*
This hotel occupies an 18th-century
house and has en-suite rooms with
cable TV and Wi-Fi.
*Konrad-Adenauer-Promenade 20,
35578; 06441 90 30; www.buergerhof-
wetzlar.com*

HERBORN

Hohe Schule *moderate*
Set in the 16th-century buildings of
Hohe Schule, this hotel has nine rooms.
*Schulhofstrasse 3–5, 35745; 02772 927
90; www.hohe-schule.de*

FRANKENBERG

Die Sonne *expensive*
Located in the former Stadtweinhaus,
Die Sonne has luxurious rooms, a spa
and a gourmet restaurant.
*Marktplatz 2-4, 35066; 06451 75 00;
www.sonne-frankenberg.de*

④ Weilburg
Hesse; 35781

Tucked into a loop of the Lahn
so tight that just one gate guards
the entrance to its compact
Altstadt, Weilburg is dominated
by its sprawling **Schloss** *(closed Mon)*.
The castle's surviving Renaissance
core was expanded in the 18th
century to create a suitably palatial
Residenz, or seat, for the counts of
Nassau-Weilburg. The lovely complex stretches 400 m (438 yards)
along the hillside above the river,
and there is a sunny Baroque garden *(open daily)* complete with
an orangery and a café.

🚗 *Cross the Steinerne Brücke below
Weilburg's old town, then turn left and
follow Bahnhofstrasse and Löhnberger
Weg to Löhnberg. At Löhnberg, follow
signs to Wetzlar, turning right on
the B49 to Lahnbahnhof. From
here, take Mühlengrund to the
town of Braunfels.*

⑤ Schloss Braunfels
Hesse; 35619

With its impressive forest of
towers rising high above the
half-timbered town of Braunfels
huddling at its gate, **Schloss
Braunfels** *(tours Apr–Oct: open daily;
Nov–Mar: open Sat, Sun)* looks every
inch the romantic medieval fortress,
though it owes its present fairy-tale
appearance to a 19th-century
Neo-Gothic rebuild. The seat of
the Counts of Solms since the 13th
century, it remains in the hands
of the Solms-Braunfels family.

🚗 *Leave Braunfels along Wetzlarer
Strasse. After crossing Oberndorf,
take Braunfelser Strasse to Wetzlar.*

Goethe in Wetzlar
Wetzlar was the seat of the highest
civil court of the Holy Roman Empire.
This was the reason the young law-
yer Goethe travelled here in the
summer of 1772. During his brief
stay, Goethe formed an unrequited
attachment to Charlotte Buff, who
was already engaged. This unhappy
romance formed the basis for *The
Sorrows of Young Werther*, the novel
that brought him international fame.
Charlotte's family home is now a
museum, the Lottehaus *(closed Mon)*.

⑥ Wetzlar
Hesse; 35573

Rising steeply from the banks of
the Lahn, Wetzlar's hilly **Altstadt**, or
old town, with its sloping squares
and lanes graced by attractive half-
timbered houses, requires leisured
exploration. The main focus here
is the peculiar-looking **Dom** *(open
daily)*, in which parts of the original
Romanesque Stiftskirche coexist
with incomplete sections of the
grander 13th-century Gothic hall
church intended to replace it.
Both Catholic and Protestant
congregations use the church.

🚗 *Leave Wetzlar along
Hermannsteiner Strasse. Follow signs
to Dillenburg/B277 until Herborn.*

⑦ Herborn
Hesse; 35745

Nestling beneath its 13th-century
castle, Herborn has a beautifully
preserved historic core. The stubby
16th-century **Rathaus** seems half
fortress, and there is an impressive
parade of five-storey houses along
Hauptstrasse, half-timbered or

shingle-hung, with gables facing the street. Also worth a visit is the 17th-century tannery and the neighbouring hangman's house in Schmaler Weg. Herborn's now defunct **Hohe Schule** was once an educational institution of international repute; the upper floors now house a museum *(closed Mon, Tue & Fri)* with displays relating to archaeology, war and weaponry in the region.

🚘 *Leave Herborn along Bahnhofstrasse, following signs for Marburg to reach the B277, then follow the B255 signposted to Marburg turning right at Gladenbach.*

Above Intricate Gothic entrance to the Elisabethkirche, Marburg

8 Marburg
Hesse; 35037

Marburg is home to the world's oldest Protestant university, Philipps Universität, and with its arty cinemas,

cheap cafés and student bars, the hilly, attractive **Oberstadt**, or upper town, has a classic university town atmosphere. Crowning the heights above it is the impressive **Landgrafenschloss**, former home of the Hessian Landgraves and now a museum *(closed Mon)*. In the Unterstadt, or lower town, the **Elisabethkirche** *(open daily)* is Germany's oldest purely Gothic hall church, dedicated to Elisabeth of Thuringia.

🚘 *Take the B3 as far as Cölbe, then take the B62 signposted Münchhausen/Bottendorf, then on to B252 via Münchhausen to reach the town of Frankenberg.*

9 Frankenberg
Hesse; 35066

An attractive base from which to discover the unspoiled wooded hills of the Waldecker Land *(www.waldecker-land.de)*, Frankenberg has a half-timbered old town, the **Altstadt**, tumbling downhill from its ten-towered early 16th-century **Rathaus**. The town hall's busy outline includes eight oriel windows and an eight-sided stair tower dating from 1535. Neustadt – the present-day town centre at the foot of the hill – was once a separate municipality with its own, much more modest Rathaus.

🚘 *Leave Frankenberg along Hainstrasse, then follow the B253 to Bad Wildungen. There is paid on-street parking in the Altstadt.*

Above Half-timbered houses in Wetzlar
Below Boats moored along Marburg canal

VISITING MARBURG

Parking
The Parkhaus Oberstadt at Pilgrimstein 17 is close to the tourist information office and convenient for the lift up to Oberstadt.

Tourist Information
Biegenstrasse 15, 35037; 06421 991 20; www.marburg-tourismus.de; closed Sun

EAT AND DRINK

WEILBURG

Alte Reitschule *expensive*
Fresh produce is used at the Schlosshotel's restaurant. Specialities include roast duck breast in port wine sauce and *Spätzle* (Swabian noodles).
Langgasse 25, 35781; 06471 509 00; www.schlosshotel-weilburg.de

WETZLAR

Zum Kesselchen *moderate*
Enjoy German specialities such as beef goulash from a kettle, Maultaschen dumplings and apple cake.
Silhöfer Str. 28, 35578; 06441 209 22 08; www.zum-kesselchen.de; closed Tue

MARBURG

Ratsschänke *moderate*
A fabulous traditional restaurant on the main square with pork *Schnitzel*, *Käsespätzle* (cheese noodles) and steak on the menu; booking advised.
Markt 3, 35037; 06421 138 34; www.ratsschaenke-marburg.de; closed Wed

FRANKENBERG

Restaurant Philipp Soldan *expensive*
This restaurant serves haute cuisine with French and Mediterranean touches based around regional ingredients.
Marktplatz 2–4, 35066; 06451 75 08 00; www.sonne-frankenberg.de; open Fri, Sat & Sun lunch

Above Striking view of Fritzlar from
St Petri Dom **Below** Stunning Edersee
Below right Old fortress of Schloss Waldeck

ACTIVITIES ON EDERSEE

Boat rental & Water-skiing
*Seestrasse/Bringhäuser Bucht, 34549
Edertal; 05623 25 82; www.wind
surfing-edersee.com*

Sailing
*Randstrasse 3, 34549 Edertal-Edersee;
05623 49 01; www.sun-fun.de*

WHERE TO STAY

WALDECK
Schlosshotel Waldeck *expensive*
Set inside the castle, this four-star
hotel features modern rooms.
*Schloss Waldeck 1, 34513; 05623 58 90;
www.schloss-hotel-waldeck.de*

KASSEL
Schlosshotel Bad Wilhelmshöhe
expensive
This four-star spa hotel is set in a park
that is a UNESCO Heritage Site.
*Schlosspark 8, 34131; 05613 08 80;
www.schlosshotel-kassel.de*

⑩ Bad Wildungen
Hesse; 34537
The town's half-timbered Altstadt
crowns a hilltop overlooking its spacious 19th-century spa quarter. The
14th-century Lutheran **Stadtkirche**
(open daily) blends Hessian and
Westphalian influences and contains
a beautiful winged altar by the medieval artist Conrad von Soest (1394–
1422). North of the old town is the
Baroque **Schloss Friedrichstein**, which
houses a museum *(tours only; Apr–Oct:
closed Mon; Nov–Mar: open Fri–Sun)* of
Hessian military history and hunting.
🚗 *Leave Bad Wildungen following
brown signs for Edertalsperre on
B485. Turn left for Affoldern then
follow Randstrasse to reach the
right bank of the Eder Dam.*

⑪ Edersee
Hesse; 34549
One of Germany's largest reservoirs,
the 27-km (17-mile) long Edersee
enjoys a scenic position amid the
wooded hills of the Naturpark

Kellerwald-Edersee. It is known for
outdoor activities such as angling,
sailing, water-skiing, hiking, mountain
biking and Nordic walking; other
pastimes include cruises on the lake
(www.personenschifffahrt-edersee.de).
The dam here is famed as one of
the targets of the 1943 Dambuster
raids, though it was swiftly repaired
and looks as solid today as when it
was completed in 1914.
🚗 *Continue beside the reservoir on
the Randstrasse, turning right on to
Abelauf/Seestrasse to reach Waldeck.*

Above Hochzeitshaus, the most impressive
half-timbered house in Fritzlar

⑫ Waldeck
Hesse; 34513
Although it is little more than a
couple of streets lined with half-
timbered houses, Waldeck attracts
many visitors thanks to the town's
scenic position high above the
Edersee. Its castle, **Schloss Waldeck**

Far left Grand façade of Schloss Wilhelmshöhe, Kassel **Left** Karlsaue garden and orangery, Kassel **Below left** Relief sculpture of St Martin on the walls of the medieval town hall, Fritzlar **Below** Majestic Herkules-Oktagon, Kassel

VISITING KASSEL

Parking
Street parking is available in front of the Hessisches Landesmuseum, a short walk from the tourist information office.

Tourist Information
Wilhelmsstrasse 23, 34117; 05617 077 07; www.kassel-marketing.de; open Mon–Sat

EAT AND DRINK IN KASSEL

Schlosshotel Bad Wilhelmshöhe
moderate
Wiener Schnitzel, grilled sea bass fillet and Kasnudeln (Austrian cheese noodles) are paired with refreshing wines at this hotel restaurant.
Schlosspark 8, 34131; 05613 08 84 12; www.schlosshotel-kassel.de; open daily

Kaskadenwirtschaft Grischäfer
expensive
A strategically located restaurant and café at the foot of the Wasserkünste, Kaskadenwirtschaft Grischäfer has a wide terrace and a prettily furnished, formal interior. It serves a broad menu, from coffee and cake to rustic regional fare and refined international cooking.
Schlosspark 22 am Kaskadenteich, 34131; 05612 88 77 44; www.kaskaden wirtschaft.de; Jan–Mar: open Sat & Sun; Apr–Dec: open Tue–Sun

---

(Apr–Oct: open daily, Nov–Mar: open Sun), was once the seat of the counts of Waldeck. The views over the lake from its battlements are breathtaking.

🚗 *Leave Waldeck via Bahnhofstrasse. Turn right on to the B485 towards Bad Wildungen, before turning left at the roundabout on to the Lieschensruh through Bergheim to Fritzlar. Parking is available outside the town walls.*

🔟 Fritzlar
Hesse; 34560
The beautiful town of Fritzlar has preserved its original, nearly complete ring of medieval walls with watchtowers and bastions. Snug behind these lofty walls, Fritzlar has over 450 half-timbered houses from various periods, the grandest of which is the Renaissance Hochzeitshaus or wedding house. Built between 1580 and 1590, it now houses the **Regionalmuseum** *(closed Mon)*. In the 8th century, the Anglo-Saxon apostle St Boniface had the holy oak of the Germanic god Donar cut down to build a chapel here. This was later replaced by the **St Petri Dom** *(open daily)*. The church's interior is rich in historic treasures. Adjacent to the church is a lovely 14th-century cloister and the **Domschatz** or cathedral treasury *(open daily)*; tickets for the Domschatz also allow a visit to the beautiful Romanesque crypt.

🚗 *Leave Fritzlar along Kasseler Strasse, following the yellow signs for Kassel and Gudensberg, avoiding the A49 Autobahn. At Gudensberg, take Besser Strasse past Besse, following signs to Kassel and Kassel-Wilhelmshöhe, then to Zentrum.*

🔢 Kassel
Hesse; 34117
Ravishing garden landscapes are the legacy of Kassel's 18th-century heyday. The most impressive is the Neo-Classical **Schlosspark Wilhelmshöhe** *(open daily)*, dominated by the **Herkules-Oktagon**, a hilltop folly from which 750,000 liters (198,129 gallons) of water is released down the **Wasserkünste** cascades to power a 52-m (170-ft) high fountain *(operates Wed & Sun)*. The castle houses the **Gemäldegalerie Alte Meister** *(closed Mon)*, a gallery whose collection of Old Masters is particularly strong on Flemish and Dutch artists. Kassel has the **Grimmwelt Museum** *(closed Mon)*, dedicated to the fairy tales, lives and times of the Grimm Brothers.

🚗 *Take the B3/ Frankfurter Strasse, briefly joining the A49 towards Frankfurt and Hannover before exiting for Kassel-Waldau signposted Melsungen. Then turn right on to the B83 for Melsungen.*

Right Quaint town of Steinau an der Strasse
Below The monastery ruins viewed from the
tower of the town church, Bad Hersfeld

VISITING FULDA

Parking
Paid on-street parking is available
close to the tourist information office.
Drivers can also use the underground
car park on Heertorplatz.

Tourist Information
*Bonifatiusplatz 1, 36037; 06611 02 18
14; www.tourismus-fulda.de; open daily*

Canoeing and biking along the
Lahn river
Canoes and bikes can be hired with
Rhön-Adventures *(Karlstrasse 33,
36037 Fulda; 06612 50 26 23: www.
rhoen-adventures.de).*

WHERE TO STAY

MELSUNGEN

Centrinum *moderate*
This smart hotel in Melsungen's Altstadt
offers a blend of historic half-timbered
architecture and glossy modernity.
There are just 12 tastefully decorated
rooms as well as an apartment.
*Rosenstrasse 1, 34212; 05661 92 60 60;
www.centrinum.de*

BAD HERSFELD

Zum Stern *moderate*
A traditional four-star hotel with original
beams, stripped stonework and warm
wood panelling as well as more contemporary touches. Each of the 45
en-suite rooms is unique; those in the
annexe are furnished in farmhouse style.
*Linggplatz 11, 36251; 06621 18 90;
www.zumsternhersfeld.de*

FULDA

Hotel Zum Ritter *moderate*
With a boutique hotel ambience,
the 130-year-old Zum Ritter is in
a quiet sidestreet a few minutes' walk
from Fulda's principal sights. The hotel
has just 33 rooms.
*Kanalstrasse 18–20, 36037; 06612
508 00; www.hotel-ritter.de*

Goldener Karpfen *expensive*
This long-established four-star hotel
in Fulda's attractive old town has an
excellent restaurant. The rooms vary
from slick minimalism to more traditional styles, complete with antiques.
All rooms have free wireless Internet.
*Simpliziusbrunnen 1, 36037; 06618 68
00; www.hotel-goldener-karpfen.de*

⑮ Melsungen
Hesse; 34212
A 16th-century stone bridge
crosses the Fulda at the little spa
town of Melsungen. The town has
a beautiful **Altstadt**, in which, with
the exceptions of the stone-built
Landgrafenschloss and late-Gothic
parish church, almost all buildings
are half-timbered. Pride of place on
the central market square goes to
the dignified 16th-century **Rathaus**.
🚗 *Continue along the B83 to reach
Rotenburg an der Fulda.*

⑯ Rotenburg an der Fulda
Hesse; 36199
Pretty, half-timbered Rotenburg
an der Fulda straddles the Fulda river
and is dominated by the Landgraves'
castle, the **Schloss Rotenburg**, which
is now a college of law and finance.
The town preserves poignant
reminders of small-town Jewish life
in Germany before the Holocaust,
including the former Jewish school

at No. 15 Brotgasse as well as
the half-timbered building on the
riverside that housed the **mikvah**,
or ritual bath, which is now a small
museum *(Brauhausstrasse 2; 06623
24 82; May–Oct: open on the first Sun
or by appointment).*
🚗 *Continue on the B83 to Bebra,
then take the B27 to Bad Hersfeld.*

⑰ Bad Hersfeld
Hesse; 36251
The austere ruins of Bad Hersfeld's
Benediktinerabtei *(closed Mon)*
provide a memorable setting for the
spa town's summer theatre festival,
the Festspiele. The museum *(closed
Mon)*, located next to the abbey, has
exhibits on the history of the town
and the region. Bad Hersfeld also has
a splendid twin-gabled **Rathaus** in
the Weser Renaissance style as well
as many fine half-timbered houses.
🚗 *Leave Bad Hersfeld along
the B27/Frankfurter Strasse and
follow this road to Fulda.*

18 Fulda

Hesse; 36037

Fulda was once an independent prince-bishopric, and its 18th-century **Barockviertel**, or Baroque Quarter, retains the air of a capital city. Its grand, twin-towered **Dom** was designed by Bavarian architect Johann Dientzenhofer. The cathedral holds the tomb of St Boniface, the Anglo-Saxon apostle of the Germans. The neighbouring **Dommuseum** (closed Mon) displays Boniface's ghoulish skull reliquary. The **Stadtschloss** (closed Mon, guided tours only), former residence of Fulda's bishops, has a cabinet of mirrors.

🚗 Leave Fulda's Aldstadt along the B254/Frankfurter Strasse, joining the B27 to the B40. This runs parallel to the Autobahn as far as Flieden; thereafter, the road has been declassified and is no longer signposted as a trunk road, but continues via Schlüchtern to Steinau an der Strasse.

19 Steinau an der Strasse

Hesse; 36396

The childhood home of the Brothers Grimm certainly looks the part, with a stern-looking castle presiding over a quaint, half-timbered **Altstadt**, untouched by time. The Renaissance **Amtshaus** in which the family lived is one of the most impressive houses in the town; it is now a museum, the **Brüder Grimm-Haus** (open daily). The Amtshaus's former barn now hosts the **Museum Steinau** (open daily), a well-laid-out local history museum.

The Brothers Grimm

Born in Hanau, near Frankfurt, in 1785 and 1786, Jacob and Wilhelm Grimm achieved fame thanks to their collection and popularization of traditional folk tales, nurturing the image of a make-believe Germany that has much in common with their Hessian homeland. They grew up in Steinau an der Strasse and studied law at Marburg University before working as librarians at the elector's court in Kassel. However, political disfavour forced them to move to Göttingen and they finally settled in Berlin. Though best known for stories such as *Hansel and Gretel*, *Rumpelstiltskin* and *Snow White*, the brothers were serious academics who also wrote a German dictionary together.

Above Stately façade of the Stadtschloss in Fulda

Left Baroque Dom housing the tomb of St Boniface, Fulda

EAT AND DRINK

MELSUNGEN

Rathaus Café *inexpensive*
The Rathaus Cafe is known for dishing up excellent German staples.
Am Markt 22, 34212; 05661 92 37 33

Ratskeller *moderate*
Located in Melsungen's marketplace, the Ratskeller serves wholesome, homemade fare.
Am Markt 1, 34212; 05661 908 89 30; www.ratskellermelsungen.de

BAD HERSFELD

L'étable *expensive*
Zum Stern's gourmet restaurant features creative modern European cooking. Try the Black Angus steak in Barolo vinegar gravy, or the fillet of sea bass in saffron and cockle broth.
Linggplatz 11, 36251; 06621 18 90; www.zumsternhersfeld.de; closed Mon & Tue

FULDA

Restaurant zum Ritter *moderate*
Seasonal produce sets the tone at Zum Ritter's traditional dining room, where there is a wide selection of *Schnitzel* (pork fillet) and steaks.
Kanalstrasse 18–20, 36037; 06612 508 01 13; www.restaurant-ritter.com; closed Sun

Goldener Karpfen *expensive*
This restaurant's menu changes seasonally, serving dishes such as crispy corn balls with red-wine onions and roasted sea bass fillet on kohlrabi and carrots.
Simpliziusbrunnen 1, 36037; 06618 68 00; www.hotel-goldener-karpfen.de

---

DAY TRIP OPTIONS

Enjoy a series of day trips with either Limburg an der Lahn or Bad Wildungen as a base.

Castles and historic towns
Explore Limburg an der Lahn ❷ before driving to the two castles near Runkel ❸. Stop by the castle in Weilburg ❹ and the medieval Schloss Braunfels ❺ before heading to see Wetzlar's ❻ hilly Altstadt.

Follow signs from Limburg an der Lahn to Runkel and then to Weilburg. Then follow the route through Schloss Braunfels to Wetzlar.

Unspoiled natural beauty
With Bad Wildungen ❿ as a base, drive to the Edersee ⓫ and take a boat cruise on one of Germany's largest reservoirs, then visit Schloss Waldeck ⓬, perched above the Edersee. Continue to Fritzlar ⓭ with its half-timbered houses.

Follow the route from Bad Wildungen to Edersee and then to Schloss Waldeck. Then take Bahnhofstrasse, turn right on to the B485 and follow signs to Fritzlar.

TRIP 13

ROMAN RUINS AND FINE WINES
Remagen to Trier

HIGHLIGHTS

Thrilling motorsport
Get an adrenaline rush at the Nürburgring, where rural
tranquillity and vehicles hurtling at breakneck speeds
combine to provide a unique experience

Fantasy castles
Explore the Mosel Valley's fairy-tale castles, which are
every bit as impressive as those on the Rhine

World-class wine
Sample some of Germany's best wines,
particularly the Mosel vintages

Historic ruins
Visit some of Europe's greatest Roman ruins – from an
isolated country house to Trier's magnificent sites

ROMAN RUINS AND FINE WINES

The Ahr and Mosel, tributaries of the Rhine, carve their way through the Eifel uplands, creating deep and twisted valleys. Despite being in the middle of Western Europe, these valleys remain among Germany's rural backwaters and the attractions along these major rivers offer a quieter version of those on the romantic Rhine. Although the Ahr valley is recovering from the devastating flood of 2021, both valleys still offer the classic German mix of atmospheric medieval castles, such as the magnificent Burg Eltz, and pretty half-timbered towns surrounded by steep vineyards that produce wonderful full-bodied wines. The tour visits the Nürburgring, the famous Formula One race car track, and finishes at the venerable city of Trier, the region's southern gateway, with its major collection of interesting Roman ruins.

Above Boats cruising along the Mosel at Bernkastel-Kues, see p142

KEY

 Drive route

ACTIVITIES

Enjoy the thrill of motor-racing on the hallowed asphalt of the Nürburgring

Explore Burg Eltz, tucked away in a quiet valley beside the Mosel

Sample some of Germany's finest wines in the quintessential wine town of Bernkastel-Kues

Tour Trier to get a glimpse of Roman culture among the most spectacular remains north of the Alps

Cruise the Mosel by boat or enjoy a hike on vineyard paths with views of the winding river

PLAN YOUR DRIVE

Start/finish: Remagen to Trier.

Number of days: 3–4 days, allowing half a day to explore Trier.

Distance: 261 km (162 miles).

Road conditions: Roads are paved and in good condition; most are relatively minor and twist along the Ahr Valley and over the Hunsrück Mountains.

When to go: It is possible to tour the area all year round, but the drive is particularly good during the wine festivals (late summer–early autumn).

Opening times: Most attractions open daily, while shops are open from 9am to 5pm, Monday to Friday, but close early on Saturdays. Most shops and services are closed on Sundays. Restaurants generally close around 10pm.

Main market days: Trier: Mon–Sat.

Shopping: Pick up local wines, particularly those of small vineyards that are not widely exported.

Major festivals: Bernkastel-Kues: Weinfest (wine festival), first weekend, Sep; Trier: Mosel Musikfestival (Moselle music festival), Jul–Oct; Weinfest (wine festival), late Aug; Trierer Weihnachtsmarkt (Christmas market), late Nov–late Dec.

DAY TRIP OPTIONS

Families should not miss a visit to the Nürburgring, where they can enjoy **motor-racing** before a relaxing stop at Burg Eltz. **Wine lovers** can explore one of Germany's best **wine-producing regions**, which can also be toured on **river cruises**. For full details, see p143.

Below Viewpoint near the attractive town of Cochem, *see p141*

0 kilometres 10

0 miles 10

Above Vineyards near Altenahr

WHERE TO STAY

AROUND RÖMERVILLA
Hohenzollern *moderate*
A short walk from the Römervilla
leads to this smart hotel with fine views.
*Am Silberberg 50, 53474 Ahrweiler
(west of Römervilla); 02641 97 30;
www.hotelhohenzollern.com*

ALTENAHR
Gasthaus Assenmacher *moderate*
This family-run hotel has simple
and bright rooms.
*Brückenstrasse 12, 53505; 02643 18 48;
www.gasthaus-assenmacher.de*

AROUND NÜRBURGRING
Motorsporthotel *moderate*
Located close to the main grandstand,
this hotel offers stylish rooms and is a
hub for motorsports enthusiasts.
*Hauptstrasse 34, 53520 Nürburg
(north of Nürburgring); 02691 920 00;
www.motorsporthotel.de*

COCHEM
Alte Thorschenke *moderate*
This central guesthouse dates back to
1332. Many of the rooms are in the
hotel's modern wing.
*Brückenstrasse 3, 56812; 02671 91 79
41; www.thorschenke.de*

Below The charming old town in Ahrweiler,
Ahr Valley **Below right** Ruins of Burg Are on
a craggy hill, Altenahr

① Remagen
Rhineland-Palatinate; 53424
The Ahr river flows into the Rhine
just south of Remagen, but the
town is better known for its pivotal
position in World War II. It was here
that American forces captured a
bridge across the Rhine, in an act
that was celebrated as a strategic
victory. Located in the former
bridgehead on the Rhine's left bank,
the **Friedensmuseum Brücke von
Remagen**, or bridge museum *(early
Mar–early Nov: open daily)*, details the
history of the bridge and its conquest.

🚗 *From the cul-de-sac road
beside the museum, turn left
down Goethestrasse, then right
down Südallee to take the B9 toward
Koblenz. Turn right on the B266 to
Ahrweiler. Get on to the B267, and
follow signs to the Römervilla car park.*

The Bridge at Remagen
The capture of the Ludendorff
Bridge at Remagen by American
forces in March 1945 has been seen
as a turning point in World War II,
since this was the last remaining
bridge over the Rhine. President
Eisenhower declared the bridge
"worth its weight in gold" and Hitler
had the officers in charge of the
bridge shot. Yet there were further
crossings over the Rhine, and 10
days later the bridge collapsed. Its
symbolic significance has grown
over time, partly due to the 1969
film *The Bridge at Remagen*.

---

② Römervilla
Rhineland-Palatinate; 53475
In 1980, road construction at the
base of vineyards just north of
Ahrweiler chanced upon the
foundations of an ancient building.
Closer examination revealed this
to be part of a 3rd-century Roman
country mansion, now protected
by the **Museum Römervilla** *(late
Mar–mid-Nov: closed Mon)*, where
the building's foundations can be
seen. Evidence suggests that the
place, preserved under a 5th-cen-
tury landslide, was inhabited from
at least as early as the middle of
the 1st century. After exploring the
museum, walk down Am Silberberg
and turn left along Walporzheimer
Strasse for a stroll into the charming
half-timbered centre of Ahrweiler.

🚗 *Turn left out of the car park,
then right on the B267. Pass through
a tunnel into Altenahr and park
by the river or up Rossberg street
below the castle.*

③ Altenahr
Rhineland-Palatinate; 53502
Surrounded by vineyards and wooded
crags, the town of Altenahr is wrapped
around a couple of bends of the Ahr
river. Take a ten-minute walk uphill via
Rossberg to the ruined 11th-century
Burg Are. Higher up the hillside, the
Rotweinwanderweg *(www.rotwein
wanderweg.de)* is a signposted red
wine walking trail that can be followed
for a pleasant hour or two of hiking
*(tourist office: Altenburger Strasse 1a; www.
altenahr-ahr.de, www.ahrtal.de; closed
Sat & Sun)* around Altenahr.

🚗 *Turn left on to the B257 and follow
it past Breidscheid to turn left in the
direction of Nürburgring. Turn right
on the B258 to the car parks beside
the Nürburgring grandstand.*

Left Impressive Burg Eltz perched on a hilltop **Below** Nürburgring, the famous Formula One race track

EAT AND DRINK

AROUND RÖMERVILLA

Eifelstube *moderate*
Quality traditional German food such as venison in elderberry sauce with *Spätzle* (Swabian noodles) is served here. *Ahrhutstrasse 26, 53474 Ahrweiler (east of Römervilla); 02641 348 50; www.eifelstube-ahrweiler.de; closed Mon & Tue*

Zur Alten Post *expensive*
Chef Hans Stefan Steinheuer and his family create sensational dishes at this fine-dining restaurant. Upstairs there are several stylish guest rooms too. *Landskroner Strasse 110, 53474 Bad Neuenahr-Ahrweiler (6 km/4 miles east of Römervilla); 02641 948 60; www.steinheuers.de; closed Tue & Wed*

ALTENAHR

Weingut Sermann *moderate*
This charming restaurant along the Ahr serves award-winning food and homemade Burgunder and Riesling wines. It has a few guest rooms as well. *Seilbahnstrasse 22, 53505; 02643 71 05; www.sermann.de; closed Wed*

AROUND BURG ELTZ

Schlossstube im Schlosshotel Petry *expensive*
Housed in a castle, this restaurant serves specialities such as ox medallions with *foie gras* on asparagus risotto. *St-Castor-Str 80, 56253 Treis-Karden (south of Burg Eltz); 02672 93 40; www.schloss-hotel-petry.de*

COCHEM

Alte Thorschenke *moderate*
Traditional German food is served in this atmospheric restaurant. *Brückenstrasse 3, 56812; 02671 91 79 41; www.thorschenke.de*

④ Nürburgring

Rhineland-Palatinate; 53520
Dubbed by British motor-racing driver Jackie Stewart as "Green Hell", the Nürburgring is revered as one of the world's most difficult and treacherous motor-racing circuits. Completed in 1927, its 73 curves have claimed dozens of lives. By the 1970s, the course was deemed too dangerous for top-class racing but in 1984 Formula One returned to a safer loop. The track is regularly used for motorsports and novelty events, such as old-timer races, but at other times it is possible to drive the course in one's own vehicle. There are no speed limits on some sections, though passing on the right is prohibited. To experience speeds of up to 320 kph (199 mph), book a seat in the **RingTaxi** *(book in advance: 02691 93 17 70; www.ringtaxi.com; children must be at least 12 years old and taller than 150 cm/5 ft)*. Otherwise, visit the visitor centre **Ring Werk** *(open daily; 02691 302 66 07; www.nuerburgring.de)*, with high-tech racing simulators, films and exhibits that will keep children busy.
🚗 *Return to the B258 and continue on it. Turn right on to the B262 to Naunheim. From here, turn right again on to a minor road signed "Burg Eltz" to reach the castle car park.*

⑤ Burg Eltz

Rhineland-Palatinate; 56294
Tucked in a hidden valley, Burg Eltz *(02672 95 05 00; Apr–Oct: open daily)* is one of Germany's most attractive castles. The construction of its cluster of archetypal turrets on a knuckle of rock began in the 12th century and,

Coat of Arms, Burg Eltz

though plenty of additions followed, it has never been destroyed or rebuilt. It survived a 2-year siege and was saved during the French campaigns of 1689 by having a member of the von Eltz family in the French Army. The interiors are preserved as they were in medieval times. The treasury displays valuables of gold and silver, while the armoury has many lethal-looking weapons.
🚗 *Return to Münstermaifeld and turn right to Hatzenport. Then turn right on to the B416 along the Mosel, which becomes the B49. In Cochem, use the car park beneath the Mosel bridge.*

⑥ Cochem

Rhineland-Palatinate; 56812
Half-timbered Cochem is striking, but can sometimes be overrun by visitors. From the town, a 15-minute signposted walk leads up to the town's main landmark, the **Reichsburg** *(mid-Feb–Nov: open daily)*. A turreted medieval-style castle built in 1877, albeit on 11th-century foundations, its antique-filled interior can be explored. Take the chairlift, **Cochemer Sesselbahn** *(Apr–mid-Nov: open daily)*, to the summit of Pinnerkreuz hill. Located along Endertstrasse, the main road through the town, the chairlift offers great valley views as well as a chance to walk downhill between vineyards back into town.
🚗 *Continue eastward on the B49, which becomes the B53, to follow the Mosel. At Traben-Trarbach follow signs to Bernkastel-Kues turning left on B50. Continue further on B50 and then to B53 to park beside the Mosel bridge.*

Right Steep vineyards near the twin town of Bernkastel-Kues

VISITING TRIER

Parking
The multi-storey car park is just off Simeonstiftsplatz, near the Porta Nigra.

Tourist Information
Simeonstrasse 55, 54290; 06519 780 80; www.trier-info.de; open daily

WHERE TO STAY

BERNKASTEL-KUES

Doctor Weinstube *moderate*
This half-timbered guesthouse with renovated rooms has a sauna and a restaurant with a Biergarten.
Hebegasse 5, 54470; 06531 966 50; www.doctor-weinstube-bernkastel.de

Gasthaus Burkhard *moderate*
A pleasant guesthouse with modern rooms as well as an excellent restaurant.
Burgstrasse 1, 54470; 06531 23 80; www.gasthaus-burkard.de

TRIER

Beckers *expensive*
Located in a wine-producing suburb, this is a stylish pension with sleek rooms.
Olewiger Strasse 206, 54295; 06519 380 80; www.beckers-trier.de

Villa Hügel *expensive*
This highly recommended Art Nouveau villa offers cheerful rooms.
Bernhardstrasse 14, 54295; 06519 371 00; www.hotel-villa-huegel.de

⑦ Bernkastel-Kues
Rhineland-Palatinate; 54470
On a serpentine bend in the river, among woods and vineyards, the twin-towns of Bernkastel-Kues have the perfect Mosel setting. They have many crooked houses, some of which house wine taverns, specializing in the local *Bernkasteler Doctor*. Bernkastel clusters behind the **Pfarrkirche St Michael**, once part of the town's defences. The **Marktplatz** is surrounded by half-timbered houses. Taste local wines and enjoy views at the Weinstube

in the **Burg Landshut** *(mid-Mar–Nov; closed Wed; www.burglandshut.de)*, a half-ruined, 13th-century castle. From the Marktplatz, follow Mandatstrasse to a 3-km (2-mile) hiking trail to the castle, or take the hourly shuttle bus *(Apr–Oct: open daily)* from the tourist office.

🚗 *Turn right out of the car park on to the B53 crossing Wintrich, then Mehring. In Trier, turn left on to Kaiser-Wilhelm-Brücke and then right on to Martinsufer to Friedrich-Ebert-Allee to Nordallee. Turn right at Simeonstiftsplatz to park on the left.*

⑧ Trier
Rhineland-Palatinate; 54290
Founded in 15 BC, Trier has northern Europe's greatest collection of Roman remains. It became the capital of the Western Roman Empire in the 3rd century. Today, the town's wine culture, combined with its proximity to Luxemburg, provides a cosmopolitan feel.

A two-hour walking tour
An alley from the Simeonstiftsplatz car park leads to the colossal 2nd-century **Porta Nigra** ① *(open daily)*, the last of Trier's four city gates. Named for its blackening, which had already occurred by the Middle Ages, it is remarkable for its ingenious design – the structure is supported by just a few iron rods. It was inhabited by a Greek hermit, Simeon, after 1028. Turned into a church after his death and sanctification, it was dissolved along with the adjoining monastery by Napoleon in 1802. South of the gate, Simeonstrasse leads to the **Hauptmarkt** ②, the hub of the old town where the sculpted fountain Petrusbrunnen lies encircled by grand houses including the vivid red Baroque Rotes Haus and the 15th-century Steipe, once a banqueting hall now housing Germany's oldest pharmacy, the Löwenapotheke.

A block east of the Hauptmarkt lies Trier's Romanesque **Dom St Peter** ③ *(open daily)*. Technically the oldest church in Germany, it was once a basilica, but since the late 3rd century it has been a bishops' seat. The current building originated in the 11th century and contains a robe believed to have been worn by Christ at his crucifixion, though this has not been scientifically authenticated. Housed in the extravagant Baroque Heiltumskammer, the robe has not been on display since 2012.

North of the church, the Bischöfliches Dom und Museum am Dom *(closed Mon)* is famed for an early 4th-century Roman fresco removed from the palace that once stood where the Dom does today. Turn left then right for a walk down Liebfrauenstrasse to the **Konstantinbasilika** ④ *(Nov–Mar: closed Mon, Apr–Oct: open daily)*. It originally provided a throne hall for Emperor Constantine in the 4th century but later became a Protestant church for the prince-electors who resided in the Baroque **Kurfürstliches Palais** ⑤, or Electoral Palace next door. The formal gardens beside the palace lead to the **Rheinisches**

Sculpture, Trier's Electoral Palace

Landesmuseum ⑥ *(closed Mon)*, a Roman archaeology museum with many treasures, including coins and mosaics. A walk south through the gardens leads to the **Kaiserthermen** ⑦ *(open daily)*, once the largest baths in the Roman world. Their foundations remain intact, making it easy to visualize the scale of this 4th-century complex. The scale also impresses at Trier's **Amphitheater** ⑧ *(open daily)*, a signposted ten-minute walk southeast along Olewiger Strasse from the underpass at the southeast corner of Kaiserthermen. This 20,000-capacity arena was built for gladiatorial and animal fights around AD 100, making it Trier's oldest Roman structure.

Return to the Kaiserthermen, turn right along Weberbach, left down Wechselstrasse, right again on Neustrasse, then left on Viehmarktstrasse to arrive at the Viehmarktplatz. The glassy cube in the centre protects the **Thermen am Viehmarkt** ⑨ *(closed Mon)*, the smallest and oldest of Trier's Roman baths. From the opposite side of Viehmarktplatz, turn right down Stresemannstrasse, then left down Brückenstrasse to **Karl-Marx-Haus** ⑩ *(open daily)* where Marx was born and grew up in the 19th century. Now a museum, it focuses on Marx's ideas. From here, turn left and walk along Fleischstrasse to the Hauptmarkt. Return via Simeonstrasse to Porta Nigra and turn left along the alley to the Simeonstiftsplatz car park.

Left Porta Nigra, Roman gateway into Trier
Below Entrance to Kaiserthermen, Trier

CRUISING THE MOSEL

Mosel cruise operators **Personenschifffahrt Gebrüder Kolb** *(06512 66 66; www.moselfahrplan.de)* operates excursions and roundtrips from Bernkastel-Kues, Trier and Cochem.

EAT AND DRINK IN TRIER

Weinstube Kesselstatt *moderate*
Enjoy regional dishes and wines in one of the prettiest settings in Trier.
Liebfrauenstrasse 10, 54290; 06514 11 78; www.weinstube-kesselstatt.de

Zum Domstein *moderate*
Dishes with a regional twist, as well as some inspired by old Roman recipes, are served here.
Hauptmarkt 5, 54290; 06517 44 90; www.domstein.de

Other options
Many restaurants in Trier have lively wine bars in the basement. One such is the **Ratskeller zur Steipe** *moderate (Hauptmarkt 14, 54290; 06517 50 52; www.ratskeller-trier.de)*, which serves local and Russian dishes.

DAY TRIP OPTIONS

Trier is a good base along this drive. Visitors can also consider staying in atmospheric Bernkastel-Kues. This tour can be covered along the A1 motorway on a two-day trip from both places.

Fantastic thrills
Unmissable for those travelling with children, the Nürburgring ❹ offers

plenty of motor-racing and has an excellent visitor centre. Then head to the fantasy castle, Burg Eltz ❺.

From Trier, follow signs to Koblenz and drive north to the end of the A1. Follow signs to Nürburgring.

Enchanting Mosel Valley
From Burg Eltz ❺, drive to Cochem ❻, then drive back along the Mosel

river to visit Bernkastel-Kues ❼. Wine lovers should consider heading straight to the twin-town via a cruise from Trier ❽ to sample the wines without having to drive later.

From Trier, follow signs to Koblenz, but leave the A1 at exit 123 to take the signed route to Bad Bertrich, then head to Cochem.

TRIP 14

THE ROMANTIC RHINE
Koblenz to Mainz

HIGHLIGHTS

Castle hopping
Explore the Rhine's many fairy-tale castles, such as
Rheinfels, Pfalzgrafenstein and Rheinstein

Rhine wine
Cosy up in a half-timbered inn at Bacharach and
sample the famous Rhineland wines

History in print
Admire some of the world's earliest printed books in the
town of Mainz, where Gutenberg invented the process

Craggy cliffs
Appreciate cascading vineyards and sweeping views of
the Rhine Gorge, a spectacular stretch of Germany's
most celebrated river

THE ROMANTIC RHINE

Slicing through the Taunus and Hunsrück hills, Germany's mighty Rhine river has sculpted a craggy and dramatic gorge classified by UNESCO as a World Heritage Site. Here, near-perfect wine-growing conditions and the lucrative tolls on passing river traffic gave rise to a multitude of wealthy castles during the Middle Ages. Many of these were destroyed in the 17th century and then rebuilt in the 18th and 19th centuries during the Romantic movement, which celebrated the valley as a source of Germanic identity. This tour visits many of these grand fortresses and explores the sleepy and traditional towns of Marksburg and Bacharach, where half-timbered houses have survived alongside Roman fortifications. Scores of local wines await discovery all along the way.

ACTIVITIES

Cruise the most scenic stretches of the Rhine at Koblenz aboard a pleasure boat

Taste flinty Rieslings, dry reds and sparkling wines on a wine-tasting tour at Boppard

Ascend the chairlift to the Vierseenblick at Boppard for extraordinary views of the Rhine

Explore the labyrinthine fortifications of the mighty Burg Rheinfels

Hike steep twisting paths to the Loreley Rock for views of the most treacherous part of the Rhine

Learn to print at the Druckladen workshop in Mainz, home of the printing press inventor Johannes Gutenberg

Below The Rhine flowing past lush green forested hills in the Rhineland-Palatinate

Above Pretty town centre of Bacharach, *see p152* **Above right** Pfalzgrafenstein, a toll castle built on an island in the Rhine, *see p152*

KEY

Drive route

PLAN YOUR DRIVE

Start/finish: Koblenz to Mainz.

Number of days: 3–4 days, allowing a day to explore Koblenz, Mainz and the major castles along the route.

Distance: 116 km (72 miles).

Road conditions: Well paved and signposted alongside the Rhine.

When to go: A good drive year-round, this route is particularly attractive in August and September, when wine festivals abound.

Opening times: Most attractions open daily; shops are open between 9am and 5pm, Monday to Friday, but close early on Saturdays. Shops and services are closed on Sundays. Most restaurants close their kitchens by 10pm.

Main market days: Boppard: Fri; Mainz: Tue, Fri & Sat.

Shopping: Pick up local wines, such as Rieslings, in Bacharach or Rüdesheim. In Mainz, browse the hand-printed posters, cards and flyers of the Druckladen for gifts or souvenirs.

Major festivals: Koblenz: Rhein in Flammen (Rhine in flames – a fire-works spectacular), Aug; Boppard: Weinfestwochenende Boppard (weekend wine festival), Sep/Oct; Loreley: Rhein in Flammen, late Sep; Oberwesel: Weinmarkt Oberwesel (wine market), mid-Sep; Rüdesheim: Rhein in Flammen, early Jul; Rüdesheimer Weinfest (wine festival), late Aug; Mainz: Mainzer Fastnacht (carnival), mid-Feb; Mainzer Johannisnacht (midsummer night), late Jun.

DAY TRIP OPTIONS

Wine lovers will appreciate not having to drive after a visit to Bacharach for **wine tasting**. Visitors can explore both banks of the Rhine separately, avoiding the use of car ferries. The high-lights on both banks are the chairlift-assisted **walks** and **castles**. On the **right bank**, the walk leads from Rüdesheim to Assmannshausen after a visit to the **Marksburg**. On the **left bank**, the chairlift climbs to **hikes** around Vierseenblick before a visit to **Burg Rheinstein**. For full details, *see p155*.

Above Restaurant terrace along the Rhine, Koblenz

BOATING ON THE RHINE

Several boats chug up and down the Rhine, allowing one to enjoy the scenery as well as sample wines. The largest company, **Köln-Düsseldorfer** *(0221 208 83 18; www.k-d.com)*, has five sailings daily from Koblenz.

VISITING KOBLENZ

Parking
The most convenient car park, the Schloss-Tiefgarage, is in the corner of Stresemannstrasse and Neustadt, just northeast of the Kurfürstliches Schloss.

Tourist Information
Forum Confluentes, Zentralplatz 1, 56068; 0261 1 29 16 10; www.koblenz-touristik.de

WHERE TO STAY

KOBLENZ
Diehl's Hotel *moderate*
This riverside hotel has pastel-coloured rooms, complete with claw foot bath-tubs. Facilities include a pool and sauna.
Rheinsteigufer 1, 56077; 0261 19 70 70; www.diehls-hotel.de

Kleiner Riesen *moderate*
Housed in a modern building, this guesthouse has elegant rooms. A continental breakfast buffet is served too.
Januarius-Zick-Strasse 11, 56068; 0261 30 34 60; www.hotel-kleinerriesen.de

AROUND MARKSBURG
Zum Weissen Schwanen *moderate*
This family-owned country hotel has interesting themed rooms. Two of them are inspired by the work of 19th-century Austrian artist Friedensreich Hundertwasser, who stayed here.
Brunnenstrasse 4, Braubach, 56338 (2 km/1 mile north of Marksburg); 02627 98 20; www.zum-weissen-schwanen.de

1 KOBLENZ
Rhineland-Palatinate; 56001
Located at the confluence of the Rhine and Mosel, Koblenz marks the northern end of the Rhine Gorge. Built in 9 BC as a Roman settlement, the city was repeatedly fought over for many centuries because of its strategic riverside location. Following its comprehensive destruction during World War II, it was rebuilt in a mix of old and new. Its pedestrianized centre has many pavement cafés and is surveyed from across the Rhine by the grandiose Ehrenbreitstein citadel.

A 90-minute walking tour

From the car park at the Kurfürstliches Schloss turn left down Stresemannstrasse to the Rhine, then left, following the river to its confluence with the Mosel. Known as the **Deutsches Eck** ①, or "German corner", the headland is presided over by a giant equestrian statue of Emperor Wilhelm I. Behind it, the Deutschherrenhaus was once the 13th-century head-quarters of the Teutonic Knights, but the building is now home to the Ludwig Museum *(closed Mon)*, displaying modern and contemporary art. Walking west along the thin strip of parkland from the Deutsches Eck, the picturesque old town, Altstadt, comes into view. To the right is the arresting castle **Alte Burg** ② on the banks of the Mosel. The first fortress here was built in the Middle Ages by the von

Madonna and Child, Liebfrauenkirche

Arken family, but in 1277, it was taken over by the archbishop of Koblenz, who sought to protect himself from the city's citizens, who were seeking independence. The fortress now houses the town archives. Walk through the archway just to the right, up a flight of stairs and left on Burgstrasse for the short walk o the **Florinsmarkt** ③. One f several focal points in the Altstadt, the Romanesque-Gothic church of Florinskirche *(mid-May–Oct: open daily)* is known, above all, for the Augenroller, a figure that rolls its eyes and sticks out its tongue every half-hour from its perch below the clock. From the Florinsmarkt, head south on Münzstrasse, which becomes Löhrstrasse before intersecting with **Am Plan** ④. Koblenz's most famous street corner. Here, the 17th-century buildings on each corner, Vier Türme, are celebrated for their ornate façades. Am Plan once

Left Medieval Marksburg, Braubach
Below Deutsches Eck, the spur between
the Mosel and the Rhine

EAT AND DRINK

KOBLENZ

Weindorf *inexpensive*
This "wine village", set around a mock
village square beside the Rhine promenade, is a fun place to sample local
wines and traditional German food.
*Julius-Wegeler-Strasse 2, 56068; 02611
33 71 90; www.weindorf-koblenz.de;
closed Mon & Tue*

Augusta *moderate*
Located on the Rhine, this restaurant
uses local produce and serves wines
from nearby vineyards. The lunch
specials include regional dishes.
*Rheinstrasse 2a, 56068; 0261 91 44
68 22; www.augusta-koblenz.de*

Weinhaus Hubertus *moderate*
This traditional wine tavern in the old
town offers an excellent range of local
wines. Sample the black pudding and
liver sausage with potatoes or the
Flammekuchen (Alsatian pizza topped
with créme fraîche, bacon and onions).
*Florinsmarkt 6, 56068; 0261 311 77;
www.weinhaus-hubertus.de; closed Tue*

Schiller's Restaurant *expensive*
Housed in Hotel Stein, this restaurant
offers three- to six-course menus of
seafood and world cuisines.
*Mayener Strasse 126, 56070;
0261 963 530; www.hotel-stein.de*

AROUND MARKSBURG

Zum Weissen Schwanen *moderate*
The hotel Zum Weissen Schwanen has
an excellent restaurant for local fish
and veal dishes in particular.
*Brunnenstrasse 4, Braubach, 56338
(2 km/1 mile north of Marksburg);
0262 798 20; closed Mon–Wed*

served as a butcher's market, the city's
main execution site and the venue for
medieval tournaments. An alley off its
left side leads to the **Liebfrauenkirche**
⑤, Koblenz's main church. Despite its
Baroque onion domes and Gothic
choir and chancel, the church is
Romanesque in origin. Just to the
south on Zentralplatz, the Mittelrhein-
Museum *(closed Mon)* is a regional
history museum with some 19th-
century paintings. Check out the
works of 18th-century Rococo painter
Januarius Zick, who lived in Koblenz.

With the Liebfrauenkirche to the
right, follow Braugasse east, turn
left onto Entenpfuhl and then right
along Firmungstrasse to head back
to the Rhine. Alongside the river,
the **Rheinpromenade** ⑥, a pleasant
promenade, stretches south and is
worth strolling down as far as the
quaint wine village **Weindorf** ⑦.
Back near the junction of Rheinstrasse,
a passenger ferry *(Easter–mid-Nov:
open daily)* crosses to the right bank
of the Rhine. From here, turn left then
right down the Charlottenstrasse
and Obertal to the funicular *(Easter–
Oct: open daily)* up to the **Festung
Ehrenbreitstein** ⑧ *(open daily)*, which
has a commanding position over the
city. First built in AD 1000, the fortress
was extended by the archbishop of
Trier, who lived here between 1648
and 1768 until its destruction by
Napoleonic troops in 1801. Today's
version, a Prussian rebuild from 1832,
houses the Landesmuseum *(open
daily)*. The state museum looks at
local trade, including car manufac-
ture in a tribute to Audi, which
was founded nearby. Return to the
Rheinpromenade using the cable car
(Apr–Oct & Dec: open daily) that takes

you across the river, and turn right on
to Stresemannstrasse to the car park.
🚗 *From the Kurfürstliches Schloss
turn left and get on to B49. Turn right
on to B42 in the direction of Lahnstein.
Follow signs to the Marksburg car park.*

② Marksburg
Rhineland-Palatinate; 56338
The huddle of towers and turrets
high above the delightful half-
timbered town of Braubach belongs
to the Marksburg *(open daily)*. Built
in 1117, it is one of the Rhine's most
impressive castles, and is particularly
remarkable for being the only
medieval castle in the region never
to have been destroyed. It is easy to
imagine lively banquets in its Gothic
grand hall, while its armoury and
array of torture instruments recall
a more gory past.
🚗 *Return to B42 and turn left. Take
the Kamp-Bornhofen-Boppard ferry
across the Rhine; then in Boppard,
turn left along Rheinallee for car park.*

season's first ripe grapes in a niche outside the church, beside the Traubenmadonna, or Grape Madonna, to gain her blessing. At the northern end of Boppard – a 20-minute walk along the promenade – a chairlift *(Apr–Oct: open daily)* ascends to a fine lookout known as the **Vierseenblick**, or Four Lakes View, because the four sections of the Rhine visible from here look unconnected. Several hiking trails fan out from here, and bus No. 34 takes an easy one-hour route back into Boppard.

🚗 *Turn right from the car park and right again to turn left on to Mainzer Strasse and on to B9 to Sankt Goar, then follow signs up Schlossberg to the Burg Rheinfels car park.*

Above The Rhine meandering between forested hillsides **Below** Sculpture of the mythical siren beside the Rhine, the Loreley

WHERE TO STAY

BOPPARD

Weinhaus Heilig Grab *moderate*
This 200-year-old historic wine tavern in the town centre has been converted into a hotel with a few basic rooms and a lovely garden.
Zelkesgasse 12, 56154; 06742 23 71; www.heiliggrab.de

AROUND BURG RHEINFELS

Loreley Weinstubchen *inexpensive*
Set close to the Loreley, this charming pension offers simple, cosy rooms and great hospitality.
Bahnhofstrasse 16, 56346 Sankt Goarhausen (2 km/1 mile east of Burg Rheinfels); 06771 70 68; www.loreley weinstuebchen.de

OBERWESEL

Burghotel Auf Schönburg *expensive*
An unusual opportunity to stay in a castle overlooking the Rhine. A castle has stood here since the 10th century, though this is a 1914 rebuild of the one burned down by French troops in 1689. Rooms have a glamorous, turn-of-the-20th-century feel.
Auf Schönburg, 55430; 06744 939 30; www.hotel-schoenburg.com; closed Jan–mid-Mar

❸ Boppard
Rhineland-Palatinate; 56154

Just two horseshoe bends upstream from Braubach and on the opposite bank of the Rhine, the atmospheric town of Boppard gathers around a riverfront promenade. Located beside the ferry terminal, the **Alte Burg** is the most impressive building on the waterfront. Built as a stronghold and tollhouse in 1340, it now houses the **Museum der Stadt Boppard** *(closed Mon)*, which celebrates local cabinet-maker Michael Thonet (1796–1871), who invented bentwood furniture. By soaking layered strips of wood veneer in hot glue and then bending them into shape in metal moulds, he created elegantly curved furniture that became hugely popular in the mid-19th century.

A block southeast lies Boppard's marketplace and the tourist office *(May–Sep: closed Sun; Oct–Apr: open Mon–Fri)*, which organizes wine tastings *(from Apr–Oct; www. boppard-tourismus.de)* at local vineyards. Just beyond, crossing Oberstrasse, the town's main shopping street, a short walk down Kirchgasse leads to the **Römer-Kastell**, where four of Boppard's 4th-century Roman watchtowers are preserved.

Back on Oberstrasse, a few minutes' walk west leads to the Karmeliterstrasse and its church, **Karmelitenkirche**. Local farmers place the

❹ Burg Rheinfels
Rhineland-Palatinate; 56329

The Rhine's largest castle, **Burg Rheinfels** *(closed mid-Nov–mid-Mar)* is a maze of sprawling passages, trenches and tunnels and ruined battlements (a torch is handy for exploration). Equally incredible is the fact that the castle was once five times its present size and mighty enough to survive a 14-month siege by 9,000 troops in 1255 and repel an army of 28,000 in 1692. It would never be taken by force, for in 1794 it was handed over without a shot to the French Revolutionary

Army who soon set about demolishing the citadel.

🚗 *Return to Sankt Goar, turn right down B9 and park at the Sankt Goar-Sankt Goarshausen ferry terminal. Leave the car here and board the ferry across the Rhine as a foot passenger if intending to walk or take the shuttle bus up the Loreley, since the tour returns this way.*

❺ Loreley

Rhineland-Palatinate; 56346
The giant rock outcrop on the opposite side of the Rhine from Sankt Goar, and above Sankt Goarshausen, is known as the Loreley. Visitors can either hike, drive or take a shuttle bus *(Apr–Oct: hourly)* from the ferry terminal to the summit for breath-taking views. The visitors centre *(Loreley Besucherzentrum; www.loreley-besucherzentrumtouristik.de)* has an English-language exhibition on the region's past and natural history.

The Legend of Loreley

The name Loreley is thought to originate from the old German and Celtic words for "lure" and "rock" and the legend of a lady who threw herself into the Rhine near St Goarshausen in despair over a faithless lover. On dying, she transformed herself into a bewitching siren and sat on the rock singing alluring songs. Distracted sailors would then fall foul of the undercurrents and rocky riverbed beneath the giant cliff that marks the narrowest point on the Rhine between Switzerland and the North Sea.

🚗 *Return to Sankt Goar on the ferry and turn left on to B9. In Oberwesel, park on riverfront.*

❻ Oberwesel

Rhineland-Palatinate; 55430
Located on the left bank of the Rhine, the charming wine town of Oberwesel has a well-preserved 3-km (2-mile) long medieval wall around the old town that makes for a good walk. The local history museum in the central **Kulturhaus** *(closed Mon)* has a good collection of 19th-century engravings of the sort that helped romanticize the Rhine and photographs of the local ladies who have been crowned *Weinhexe* – the good "wine witch" who protects the wine harvest – every April since the 1940s, following a local tradition.

🚗 *Continue on the B9 to the Kaub-Langscheid ferry. Leave the car and cross the Rhine on ferry as a foot passenger and take the passenger boat to Burg Pfalzgrafenstein.*

Above left Remains of a Roman military camp, Boppard **Above** Marktplatz and Romanesque Severuskirche, Boppard **Below** Outer walls of the formidable Burg Rheinfels

EAT AND DRINK

AROUND BURG RHEINFELS
Gasthaus Zur Krone *moderate*
Feast on traditional German dishes such as Rheinland pot roast and cheese noodles with roast onions.
Oberstrasse 38; 56329 St. Goar (south of Burg Rheinfels); 06741 15 15; www.kronegoar.de

Loreley Weinstubchen *moderate*
A snug place with fresh fish and an excellent *Rieslingschnitzel* (veal in wine).
Bahnhofstrasse 16, Sankt Goarhausen, 56346 (2 km/1 mile east of Burg Rheinfels); 06771 70 68; www.loreley weinstuebchen.de; Nov-Mar: closed Thu

Zum Goldenen Löwen *moderate*
The top-notch German cuisine here includes specialities such as *Braten vom Spanferkal* (roasted suckling pig).
Heerstrasse 3, Sankt Goar, 56329 (south of Burg Rheinfels); 06741 16 74; www.hotelzumgoldenenloewen.com

Schloss-Restaurant Auf Scharffeneck *expensive*
An elegant restaurant in Hotel Schloss Rheinfels offering game from the nearby Hünsrück highlands.
Schlossberg 47, Sankt Goar, 56329 (south of Burg Rheinfels); 06741 80 20; www.schloss-rheinfels.de

OBERWESEL
Hotel Weinhaus Weiler *moderate*
Enjoy modern Thai cuisine and local wines at this half-timbered restaurant.
Marktplatz 4, 55430; 06744 70 03; www.weinhaus-weiler.de

Burghotel Auf Schönburg *expensive*
This restaurant serves regional recipes made from fresh, seasonal ingredients.
Auf Schönburg, 55430; 06744 939 30; www.burghotel-schoenburg.de; closed Mon & Jan–mid-Mar

Right Burg Stahleck towering over the town of Bacharach **Below** Cannons facing the Rhine Valley, Burg Rheinstein

WHERE TO STAY

BACHARACH

Burg Stahleck/Jugendherberge Bacharach *inexpensive*
The budget alternative to Auf Schönburg in Oberwesel, Burg Stahleck is a 12th-century castle that once served as the seat of the Count-Palatinate of the Rhine and is now a stunning youth hostel. One does not need to be a member to stay, and most of the basic rooms are en suite and sleep between one and six people.
Bacharach, 55422; 06743 12 66; www.diejugendherbergen.de

Rhein Hotel *moderate*
This family-run half-timbered hotel beside the town walls has spotless, plain and compact rooms.
Langstrasse 50, 55422; 06743 12 43; www.rhein-hotel-bacharach.de; closed mid-Dec–Mar

RÜDESHEIM

Central Hotel *moderate*
A smart family-run place in the centre of Rüdesheim with bright, immaculate rooms and bathrooms and an excellent buffet breakfast.
Kirchstrasse 6, 65385; 06722 91 20; www.centralhotel.net; closed Dec–Mar

Hotel Felsenkeller *moderate*
A charming hotel in the town centre with a good restaurant; some of the rooms offer views of the Rhine.
Oberstrasse 39/41, 65385; 06722 942 50; www.felsenkeller-ruedesheim.de; closed Dec–Mar

🄻 Burg Pfalzgrafenstein
Rhineland-Palatinate; 56349
One of the most beautifully situated castles in Europe, the mighty fortress of Burg Pfalzgrafenstein *(mid-Mar–Oct: open Tue–Sun; closed Nov–mid-Mar)* stands in the middle of the Rhine river. With its unusual island perch, the castle was built to levy tolls on Rhine shipping. Constructed in 1325 by Ludwig the Bavarian, the castle's gun bastions and its present shape are the result of Baroque refurbishments in the 17th and 18th centuries.
🚗 **Exit the ferry terminal car park and turn left on to the B9. In Bacharach, park in the riverside car park.**

🄼 Bacharach
Rhineland-Palatinate; 55422
The pretty town of Bacharach has a unique complex of historic buildings, with fortified town walls, the church of St Peter, the ruins of the Gothic chapel of St Werner, and **Burg Stahleck** – the 12th-century castle towering over the town. Once the seat of the Count-Palatinate of the Rhine, today it is an impressive youth hostel.
A gate in the town wall, opposite Bacharach's main car park, provides access to its 14th-century fortifications, with views of the huddle of half-timbered buildings. Among these is the celebrated old house, **Altes Haus** on Oberstrasse 61, which is so wonky that it seems to lean in all directions at once. This building and many others house wine taverns, which serve up local wines such as Hahnenhof Riesling.

🚗 *Turn right out of the Bacharach car park on to the B9. Park at the signed car park beside the B9 in Trechtingshausen.*

🄽 Burg Rheinstein
Rhineland-Palatinate; 55413
The compact castle of **Burg Rheinstein** *(mid-Mar–mid-Nov: open daily; mid-Nov–mid-Dec: open Sat & Sun; mid-Dec–mid-Mar closed; www.burg-rheinstein.de)* sits in a spectacular location 82 m (270 ft) above the Rhine. After falling into ruin, the 13th-century castle was acquired by Prince Friedrich Ludwig of Prussia and given a complete makeover in 1820. This helped begin a Romantic architectural trend, which swept across Germany and saw many medieval ruins rebuilt as castles in an age in which fortifications no longer served a practical purpose. Here, the pastel-coloured interior rooms seem out of place in a castle, but convey a good sense of early 19th-century taste.
🚗 *Continue south on the B9, turn left over a bridge into Fruchtmarkt, then Vorstadt and Espenschiedstrasse/Mainzer Strasse. Follow ferry signs left down Hafenstrasse. Take the ferry across the Rhine. Turn right to Rüdesheim, then left down Burgstrasse to the roadside car park opposite the Rheingauer Weinmuseum.*

🄾 Rüdesheim
Hesse; 65385
Enjoying a picturesque location on the banks of the Rhine, Rüdesheim has a long history going back to Roman times. The town is famous for its main street, the Drosselgasse,

Left Panoramic view of the Rhine from Burg Rheinstein **Below left** Quirky Altes Haus, Bacharach **Below** Picturesque Burg Pfalzgrafenstein on its island in the Rhine

lined with wine bars and shops. There are also the remains of three castles: the Boosenburg, the Vorderburg and the 12th-century Brömserburg, which houses a wine museum. The **Rheingauer Weinmuseum Brömserburg** (closed for renovations until 2023; www.rheingauer-weinmuseum.de) has a wide array of wine-making items from Roman times, particularly aged wine presses, but also antique amphorae, wine coolers and goblets. Walking up Burgstrasse from the museum and turning right along Oberstrasse leads to the centre of Rüdesheim and Drosselgasse, the tourist hub where strings of souvenir shops peddle their wares. The top of the lane is close to the chairlift (Mar–Nov: open daily) to viewpoints above, while around its base are many lanes lined with wine taverns offering samples of the celebrated local Riesling.

Rüdesheim also has several historic mansions, including the half-timbered **Brömserhof** (1559), with a collection of musical instruments, and the early 16th-century Klunkhardshof.

Above the town towers the **Niederwalddenkmal**, a huge 38-m (125-ft) statue of Germania, built to commemorate German unity and the foundation of the German Reich in the wake of the country's victory in the Franco-Prussian War of 1870–71.

🚗 *Return to the B42 in the direction of Wiesbaden/Eltville to Hattenheim. Turn left at Schlossergasse, left on to Hauptstrasse, then right on to Eberbacher Strasse to signs for Kloster Eberbach car park.*

Walk to Assmannshausen

Taking the chairlift from the centre of Rüdesheim allows for an excellent two-hour hike to Assmannshausen, from where it is possible to get a boat or bus back to Rüdesheim; the boat is included in the price of a "Ringtour". The chairlift climbs to the impressive Niederwalddenkmal, after which the hiking trail passes through a series of fine Rhine viewpoints before descending past vineyards into Assmannshausen.

EAT AND DRINK

BACHARACH

Weingut Friedrich Bastian, Zum Grünen Baum *moderate*
For a good wine tavern experience, try Zum Grünen Baum, which offers a well-priced 15-wine sampler.
Oberstrasse 63, 55422; 06743 12 08; www.weingut-bastian-bacharach.de

Stueber's Restaurant *expensive*
This excellent restaurant in the Rhein Hotel is particularly good for its *Rieslingbraten* – a pot roast marinated for three days in Riesling and mustard – served with *Spätzle* (Swabian noodles).
Langstrasse 50, 55422; 06743 12 43; www.rhein-hotel-bacharach.de; closed mid-Dec–Mar

RÜDESHEIM

Breuer's *moderate*
Despite its location on the tourist strip, Breuer's is a stylish rustic restaurant specializing in classic regional cuisine such as venison *Schnitzel* (fillet) in mushroom sauce or fried trout in butter sauce.
Steingasse 10, 65385; 06722 905 00; www.ruedesheimer-schloss.com

Above Pretty rose garden in the town of Eltville **Below** Café in the grounds of Kloster Eberbach **Below right** Gutenberg-Museum, a tribute to Mainz's most famous resident, Johannes Gutenberg

WHERE TO STAY

KLOSTER EBERBACH

Gästehaus Kloster Eberbach
moderate
This hotel offers simple rooms in one of the outlying monastery buildings. It is set in peaceful wooded surroundings and serves a sumptuous buffet breakfast.
Eltville, 65346; 06723 917 82 90; www.kloster-eberbach.de

MAINZ

Hotel Schwan *moderate*
The elegant Hotel Schwan, housed in a 16th-century town building, has spacious rooms with Baroque touches.
Liebfrauenplatz 7, 55116; 06131 14 49 20; www.mainz-hotel-schwan.de

⑪ Kloster Eberbach
Hesse; 65346
The monastery of Kloster Eberbach *(open daily)* is best known as the Romanesque setting for the medieval murder mystery film *The Name of the Rose* (1986). Its most impressive feature is its austere basilica. Here, a steep staircase in the north transept climbs to the dormitory where monks slept on pallet-like beds. The walk around the cloisters to the lay refectory passes massive wine presses built of timbers sturdy enough for galleons; its shop has excellent wines.

🚗 *From the car park, head south to the T-junction, turn left towards Erbach and follow signs to Eltville. On arriving in the town, turn right and park at the Schwimmbad, then walk down to the riverfront and turn left toward the town centre.*

⑫ Eltville
Hesse; 65343
The oldest town in the region, Eltville is gathered around a cosy nest of lanes, but it is best known for its many rose beds, whose perfume thickens the summer air. Many rose bushes line the Rhine promenade and grow in the moat of the adjacent 14th-century castle, the **Burg** *(open daily)*, which was laid to waste by fierce Swedes during the Thirty Years' War (1618–48). Stirred up by the Counter-Reformation, this war between the Protestant Union and Catholic League raged across Europe. Only the four-storey residential tower of the Burg survived and climbing it provides a glimpse of a stained-glass window celebrating Johannes Gutenberg, as well as fine views of the town's waterfront.

🚗 *Turn right out of the car park, following Wallufer Strasse, turn right again at the next junction. Head south to Mainz-Amöneburg. Take the B40, then the Theodor-Heuss-Brücke bridge over the Rhine into Mainz, then take the first left to a handy riverside car park.*

⑬ Mainz
Rhineland-Palatinate; 55001
As capital of Rhineland-Palatinate, and with good transport links to Frankfurt, large and cosmopolitan Mainz *(see p165)* has none of the sleepy atmosphere of the rest of the Rhineland. Originally a strategic settlement at the confluence of the Main and Rhine, by the 8th century it was the main religious centre north of the Alps. Its importance was enhanced by Johannes Gutenberg (c. 1400–68), who invented the printing press here in the 15th century.

Like Koblenz, Mainz suffered massive bombardment during World War II, though a large section of its half-timbered old town including the cathedral survived or was rebuilt to create an attractive town with many tempting traditional wine bars.

Mainz's majestic six-towered late-Romanesque **Kaiserdom** *(open daily)* is of 12th-century origin and unusual for sharing its exterior walls with adjoining houses. Inside, the highlight of the spartan cathedral is the Dommuseum and the adjacent **Gewölbehallen** *(open daily)*, which

Left Lovely view of the domed Christuskirche, Mainz **Below** Wine cellars, Kloster Eberbach

EAT AND DRINK

KLOSTER EBERBACH

Klosterschänke *moderate*
This restaurant at Kloster Eberbach serves plenty of uncomplicated hearty dishes such as pork ragout with potato dumplings and some lovely wines from the estate to wash them down with.
Kloster Eberbach, Eltville, 65346; 06723 917 82 90; www.kloster-eberbach.de

MAINZ

Altdeutsche Weinstube *moderate*
Traditional wine bars or *Weinstuben* abound in Mainz, but this cosy place beside the Hotel Schwan is the oldest in the region and worth seeking out.
Liebfrauenplatz 7, 55116; 06131 14 49 20; www.mainz-hotel-schwan.de

Heiliggeist *moderate*
Germany's oldest civil hospital has served as a restaurant since 1863. Enjoy quality local and Mediterranean specialities beneath the beautiful vaults; try the *Spundekäse* (a dip made from cheese, onion and cream with crusty bread).
Rentengasse 2, 55116;06131 22 57 57; www.heiliggeist-mainz.de

Zum Grünen Kakadu *moderate*
The Staatstheater's restaurant is a cultural hotspot with a small stage for events. Try Mainzer classics such as the local *Fleischwurst* (sausage), wild boar ragout or salmon with gnocchi.
Gutenbergplatz 3–5, 55116; 06131 285 12 81; www.zumgruenenkakadu-mainz.d

stores its treasures. These include sparkling reliquaries, intricate 15th- and 16th-century tapestries, a 13th-century rood screen by the Master of Naumburg, which vividly depicts Sin and Salvation, and some Rococo choir stalls.

Celebrating Mainz's most famous son, Johannes Gutenberg, the **Gutenberg-Museum** *(closed Mon)* on Liebfrauenplatz shows a reconstruction of his workshop from 1450 and has a rare copy of his first major work: the 42-line Bible, from 1455, which was named after the number of lines on each page. The museum also puts Gutenberg's invention in context with a look at Asian printing techniques and the hand copying of manuscripts, which he effectively turned into a dying art. For a hands-on experience, visit the nearby printing shop **Druckladen** *(closed Sun)*, where visitors can hand-set type (aprons are provided) to produce posters, cards and flyers. Enthusiastic staff offer guidance to those trying their hand at printing.

Invention of the Printing Press
In the early 15th century, goldsmith Johannes Gutenberg experimented with several technologies that led to the invention of the printing press. These included the development of movable metal type and moulds, oil-based inks and the mechanical printing press, for which he initially adapted wine presses. The resu Its changed the world forever, as information could spread more quickly. This gave more power to the masses and helped to spread the Protestant Reformation.

DAY TRIP OPTIONS

All the stops on this route can be visited on day trips. Koblenz in particular is a good base for boat trips.

Medieval castles and monasteries
Drive along the banks of the Rhine, stopping at the Marksburg **2**, the Rhine's most attractive castle, and the unusual islet-based Burg Pfalzgrafenstein **7** before arriving at the bustling

town of Rüdesheim **10** on the banks of the Rhine. Take its chairlift over the pretty vineyards to the excellent and downhill two-hour walk to Assmannshausen, with sweeping Rhine Valley views along the way. End the day with a sumptuous meal at the peaceful and atmospheric Kloster Eberbach **11**.
Take the B42 along the right bank of the Rhine.

Mighty fortifications
Explore Boppard **3**, with its remaining Roman walls, then ride the chairlift up to the Vierseenblick. Next, wander around the splendid medieval town fortifications of Oberwesel **6** and those of the quaint wine town of Bacharach **8** before a visit to the Gothic fantasy castle of Burg Rheinstein **9**.
Take the B9 along the left bank of the Rhine.

TRIP 15

THE GERMAN WINE ROUTE
Deutsches Weintor to Speyer

HIGHLIGHTS

Vintage wines
Sample the wines of Pfalz and Rheinhessen, from crisp
Rieslings to Auslese and barrique-aged Pinot Noir

Gourmet delights
Enjoy the region's restaurants, where regional specialities
such as Saumagen meet European sophistication

Rural idyll
Admire Pfalz's rustic beauty, from castle-topped hills to
the half-timbered villages of Leinsweiler and St Martin

Religion and culture
Visit the ancient Jewish cemeteries and cathedrals
at Oppenheim, which bear witness to its cultural
and historical legacy

A vineyard near the Katharinenkirche, Oppenheim

THE GERMAN WINE ROUTE

Set in gently rolling countryside between Pfälzer Wald's wooded hills and the Rhine, with the French Alsace to the south, the wine-growing regions of Pfalz and Rheinhessen are Germany's largest. This area has much in common with its southern neighbour, Alsace – from its architecture to the dialects spoken. They also share a history of alternating periods of French and German control. The trip follows an established and well-signposted wine route past picturesque vineyards, beautiful villages, chic hotels and top-quality restaurants. A gourmet experience is guaranteed. Visitors can look forward to tasting the different types of wine made by the numerous small vineyards scattered throughout the region. Other highlights include the ancient and historic cathedral cities of Mainz, Worms and Speyer.

Above Vineyards along the way to Nierstein, *see p165*

ACTIVITIES

Sample the wines on an oenophile's tour of the region's superb wineries

Take a hike in the unspoiled Naturpark Pfälzer Wald in St Martin

Scare yourself in the ossuary at Oppenheim and then tour the underground passages

Hike to the impressive ruins of Wachtenburg for spectacular views over the Rhine Valley

Acquire a taste for *Saumagen*, Pfalz's most famous regional speciality

Above Busy street, Neustadt an der Weinstrasse, *see p163*

KEY

Drive route

0 kilometres   10

0 miles   10

PLAN YOUR DRIVE

Start/finish: Deutsches Weintor to Speyer.

Number of days: 5 days, allowing half a day to explore Oppenheim.

Distance: 260 km (162 miles).

Road conditions: The region has well-paved minor roads with gentle gradients. The Deutsche Weinstrasse is well signposted; look for the grape symbol.

When to go: The tourist season begins with the Mandelblütenfest in March and continues until the end of October. Some attractions close for winter.

Opening times: Most attractions open daily, while shops are open 9am to 5pm Monday to Friday, but close early on Saturdays. Shops and services are closed on Sundays. Most restaurants close their kitchens by 10pm.

Major festivals: Neustadt an der Weinstrasse: Deutsches Weinlesefest (wine festival), Oct; **Gimmeldingen:** Mandelblütenfest (almond blossom festival), Mar/Apr; **Bad Dürkheim:** Wurstmarkt (sausage festival), Sep; **Mainz:** Mainzer Fastnacht (pre-Lent carnival), Feb; **Worms:** Nibelungen Festspiele (theatre festival), Jul; Backfischfest (folk and wine festival), late Aug/early Sep.

DAY TRIP OPTIONS

Lovers of **fine food** and **wine** will find the Weinstrasse at its most chic between Edenkoben and Freinsheim and enjoy the drive from Mainz to Worms, which is famous for **wine-growing villages**. For the lost-in-time charm of **sleepy villages** and **hilltop castles**, a drive from Bad Bergzabern to Burg Trifels is particularly magical. For full details, *see p167*.

Below Breathtaking view of the rocky outcrop from Burg Trifels, Annweiler, *see p161*

Right Schloss of the Counts Palatine of Zweibrücken, Bad Bergzabern **Centre right** Imposing Burg Trifels, Annweiler **Below** Sweeping view of Annweiler from Burg Trifels

WHERE TO STAY

AROUND BAD BERGZABERN

Zum Lam *moderate*
Located just off the Deutsche Weinstrasse, between Bad Bergzabern and Klingenmünster, this hotel is housed in an 18th-century half-timbered inn. It offers rustic but comfortable en-suite rooms as well as a decent restaurant serving Pfalz specialities.
Winzergasse 37, 76889 Gleiszellen-Gleishorbach (5 km/3 miles from Bad Bergzabern); 06343 93 92 12; www.zum-lam.de

LEINSWEILER

Hotel Rebmann *moderate*
This three-star hotel-cum-restaurant, in the centre of Leinsweiler, has refurbished en-suite rooms with pale maple furnishings.
Weinstrasse 8, 76829; 06345 954 00; www.hotel-rebmann.de

Leinsweiler Hof *expensive*
A four-star hotel in the countryside near Leinsweiler offering sweeping views over the surrounding vineyards. The elegant decor features modern and rustic touches. Facilities include a spa and indoor and outdoor pools.
Weinstrasse, Leinsweiler Hof 1, 76829; 06345 40 90; www.leinsweilerhof.de

ANNWEILER

Landhotel Sonnenhof *moderate*
Comfortable rooms in a lovely house 7 km (4 miles) east of Annweiler, with excellent service and a good breakfast, served on the terrace in summer.
Muhlweg 2, 76833 Siebeldingen; 06345 33 11; www.sonnenhof-siebeldingen.de

① Deutsches Weintor
Rhineland-Palatinate; 76889
Marking the start of the 85-km (53-mile) Deutsche Weinstrasse (German Wine Route) since 1936, the Deutsches Weintor or German Wine Gate *(closed Mon–Wed)*, located in the town of Schweigen-Rechtenbach, is a monumental sandstone gatehouse on the French border just north of the Alsatian town of Wissembourg. Visitors can taste and buy Pfalz wines here and there is a restaurant serving regional fare.
🚗 *Leave Schweigen-Rechtenbach on the B38 north, then turn left at the Deutsche Weinstrasse symbol to Bad Bergzabern and left on to Kettengasse to park.*

② Bad Bergzabern
Rhineland-Palatinate; 76887
With its leafy spa quarter and a charming historic centre focused on the **Schloss** of the Counts Palatine of Zweibrücken, Bad Bergzabern is the capital of the southern Weinstrasse. The ornate Renaissance **Gasthaus Zum Engel** (Angel's Inn) near the Schloss houses a local history museum *(Apr–Dec: open Tue–Sun)*. In the late 1930s, Bad Bergzabern formed part of the fortifications known as the **Westwall**; a bunker on Kurfürstenstrasse *(Apr–Oct: open Sun)* now houses a museum.
🚗 *Leave Bad Bergzabern along the B48/Weinstrasse north to Burg Landeck. Park at the Burg.*

③ Burg Landeck
Rhineland-Palatinate; 76889
There is a fairy-tale quality to the village of **Klingenmünster**, nestling beneath forested hills and dominated by the ruined fortress of Burg Landeck *(open daily)*, which towers 300 m (984 ft) above it. Built in the 13th century to defend a Benedictine abbey, it was destroyed by French troops in 1680 during the War of the Palatine Succession. It now houses a small museum and provides superb views.
🚗 *Return to the B48 north, turn left and then right, following signs to Slevogthof, to reach Leinsweiler.*

④ Leinsweiler
Rhineland-Palatinate; 76829
The arcaded town hall, the **Rathaus** of 1619, is the focus of this pretty, half-timbered village. Leinsweiler was the summer home of the German Impressionist painter Max Slevogt,

who died in 1932 and is buried here. Länsweiler is also home to a corkscrew museum, **Korkenzieher Museum** (*Sonnenberg 7, 76829; 06345 85 18; open by appointment*), which features a variety of interesting corkscrews.

🚗 *Continue to Birkweiler, take the slip road up to the B10, turning left for Annweiler. Take care as this is a dangerous junction. Park near the town hall and tourist information office.*

Wine Country
Vineyards dominate the picture-perfect landscape of the Pfalz and Rheinhessen region. Many local wine growers have a room set aside to sample and buy wines from the vineyard itself. However, German wineries tend to be family-run affairs, so it is wise to call before visiting. Dry white wines predominate – Rieslings are often excellent. Red wines made with the Spätburgunder (Pinot Noir) grape are also gaining popularity. The region also produces Sekt (sparkling wines) and small quantities of *Tresterbrand*, the German equivalent of the spirit grappa.

5 Annweiler
Rhineland-Palatinate; 76855
A former Free City of the Holy Roman Empire, Annweiler lies on the Queich river, which was once harnessed to provide power for the town's tanneries. The **Gerberviertel** (tannery district) is particularly picturesque, with its watermill and half-timbered houses, three of which house the local history museum, the **Museum unterm Trifels** (*closed Mon & Tue*).

🚗 *Leave the town of Annweiler along Altenstrasse, turning left on to Trifelsstrasse and follow signs to Burg Trifels. Park below the Burg.*

6 Burg Trifels
Rhineland-Palatinate; 76855
Perched on a narrow crag 300 m (984 ft) above Annweiler, Burg Trifels (*Feb–May & Nov: open Sat & Sun; May–Oct: open daily; Dec & Jan: closed*) is reached after an ascent through the forest. First mentioned in the 11th century, the castle was where the Salian emperors kept the imperial regalia of the Holy Roman Empire; Richard the Lionheart was briefly a prisoner here in 1193. The ruined castle was extensively restored between 1938 and 1942. Visitors can also explore two more castle ruins – Scharfenberg and Anebos – which crown neighbouring crags.

🚗 *Return to Annweiler on Trifelsstrasse, leaving Annweiler on Landauerstrasse. Rejoin the B10 and then turn on to Weinstrasse to reach the village of Siebeldingen.*

Above Scenic view of the countryside from Burg Landeck, Klingenmünster **Below** Dense forest near Burg Trifels

EAT AND DRINK

DEUTSCHES WEINTOR
Deutsches Weintor Restaurant *moderate*
Elegantly modern, the restaurant at the Deutsches Weintor serves creative dishes based on regional and seasonal ingredients accompanied by red and white Pfalz wines.
Weinstrasse 4, 76889 Schweigen-Rechtenbach; 06342 922 78 88; www.weintor.de; closed Mon–Wed

AROUND BURG LANDECK
Freiraum *moderate*
Housed inside Klingenmünster's Stiftsgut Keysermühle hotel, this restaurant focuses on regionally sourced, sustainable "slow food". It offers vegetarian and vegan options too.
Bahnhofstrasse 1, 76889 Klingenmünster (1 km/0.5 mile from Burg Landeck); 06349 993 90; closed Sun–Tue

LEINSWEILER
Leinsweiler Hof *expensive*
This restaurant provides lovely views across the countryside of the southern Weinstrasse. The menu emphasises regional and seasonal produce and includes refined versions of local specialities such as *Saumagen*.
Weinstrasse, Leinsweiler Hof 1, 76829; 06345 40 90; www.leinsweilerhof.de

ANNWEILER
s'Reiwerle *inexpensive*
Housed in a lovely half-timbered house in the centre of Annweiler, this traditional *Weinstube* (wine bar) and restaurant serves dishes such as *Saumagen* or lamb sausages with savoy cabbage.
Flitschberg 7, 76855; 06346 92 93 62; www.reiwerle.de; closed Mon & Tue

Right Deidesheim town centre **Far right** Vineyards around Villa Ludwigshöhe, Edenkoben **Below** Ruins of Wachtenburg in the town of Wachenheim

VISITING NEUSTADT AN DER WEINSTRASSE

Parking
The car park in the Hetzelgalerie shopping centre is convenient for reaching the tourist information office.

Tourist Information
Hetzelplatz 1, 67433; 06321 92 68 92; www.neustadt.eu; Apr–Oct: open Mon–Sat; Nov–Mar: open Mon–Fri

WHERE TO STAY

EDENKOBEN

Pfälzer Hof *moderate*
This well-established hotel offers a cosy atmosphere and beautiful views of the surrounding landscape. It also has a fine restaurant.
Weinstrasse 85, 67480; 06323 93 89 10; www.pfaelzerhof-edenkoben.de

MAIKAMMER

Gasthaus zum Winzer *moderate*
This hotel, in a Baroque former *Weingut* (winery), has five non-smoking, Mediterranean-style double rooms with hypoallergenic furnishings. It also has an excellent restaurant and offers free wireless Internet access.
Weinstrasse Süd 8, 67487; 06321 54 10; www.gasthaus-zum-winzer.de

ST MARTIN

St Martiner Castell *moderate*
A hotel-cum-restaurant situated in the old part of St Martin offering single, double or three-bedded rooms, all with en-suite baths and some with balconies.
Maikammerer Strasse 2, 67487; 06323 95 10; www.hotelcastell.de

GIMMELDINGEN

Weingut Mugler *moderate*
The Weingut Mugler has eight stylish, modern guest rooms. Diners can sample Mugler's wines along with the regional fare at their Kutscherhaus restaurant across the street.
Peter-Koch-Strasse 50, 67435; 06321 660 62; www.weingut-mugler.de

DEIDESHEIM

Deidesheimer Hof *expensive*
Dating from the 18th century, this inn is set in one of the Weinstrasse's most chic villages. The rooms and spacious suites are comfortable and tastefully furnished.
Am Marktplatz 1, 67146; 06326 968 70; www.deidesheimerhof.de

7 Siebeldingen
Rhineland-Palatinate; 76833
The village of Siebeldingen lies on the Queich river, which once formed France's northeast military frontier. Among the village's wine growers, the **Ökonomierat Rebholz** *(open Mon–Sat; www.oekonomierat-rebholz.de)* is the most distinguished, producing *Grosses Gewächs* wines – the German equivalent of the French *premier cru*.

🚗 *Follow the Deutsche Weinstrasse beyond Frankweiler and continue via Burrweiler to Hainfeld. Watch out for the sharp left turn in Hainfeld. Villa Ludwigshöhe is west of Edenkoben along Villastrasse.*

8 Edenkoben
Rhineland-Palatinate; 67480
Edenkoben was Bavarian territory from 1816 until 1945. On the outskirts of the town, Bavarian King Ludwig I built his residence, **Villa Ludwigshöhe** *(closed for renovations until 2023; www.schloss-villa-ludwigshoehe.de)*, which was designed by Friedrich Wilhelm von Gärtner in the style of a Roman villa. It was built between 1846 and 1852 on an idyllic site between woods and vineyards and contains a gallery devoted to the German Impressionist painter Max Slevogt. It is also the venue for chamber music concerts *(www.villamusica.de)*.

🚗 *From the villa, return to Deutsche Weinstrasse, continuing north through Edenkoben to Maikammer.*

9 Maikammer
Rhineland-Palatinate; 67487
With seemingly every second building a *Weingut* (winery), Maikammer is a Weinstrasse village *par excellence*. Grandiose 19th-century premises line the route from the village to its railway station; one of the finest buildings is home to **Weingut August Ziegler** *(open Mon–Sat; www.august-ziegler.de)*, which has thrice been declared German Winemaker of the Year. Alongside Riesling and Pinot Noir, the estate also produces varieties of wine quite unusual for Germany, including Shiraz and Sauvignon Blanc.

🚗 *St Martin is signposted from Maikammer along the minor road.*

⑩ St Martin

Rhineland-Palatinate; 67487

With a beautiful setting on the fringes of the **Naturpark Pfälzer Wald** (www. pfaelzerwald.de), a biosphere reserve, St Martin is among the loveliest villages in the region. With plenty of surviving half-timbered cottages and noblemen's houses, it is also the starting point for a number of hiking trails into the Naturpark Pfälzer Wald; one popular route ascends to the summit of the 673-m (2,208-ft) **Kalmit**, the highest hill in the district.

🚗 *Return to Maikammer and turn north towards Hambach. At Hambach turn left up Schlossstrasse to the Hambacher Schloss; the route is one-way. Continue on it, following signs to Hauptbahnhof (station) to Neustadt.*

⑪ Neustadt an der Weinstrasse

Rhineland-Palatinate; 67433

Neustadt is the most important urban centre on the Deutsche Weinstrasse, with a traffic-free historic core centred on the **Marktplatz** and its Gothic **Stiftskirche** and Baroque town hall, the **Rathaus**. The town's most famous sight is the **Hambacher Schloss** (open daily), a hilltop castle to the south, famous for the Hambacher Fest of 1832, during which a patriotic crowd hoisted the black-red-gold colours of German unity in one of the founding acts of German democracy.

🚗 *Leave Neustadt an der Weinstrasse along Karl-Helffenrich-Strasse, turn right on to Maximilianstrasse, taking Gimmeldinger Strasse, the middle of three roads, to reach Gimmeldingen. The village centre is a one-way system.*

⑫ Gimmeldingen

Rhineland-Palatinate; 67435

The pretty wine-growing village of Gimmeldingen lies on the edge of the Naturpark Pfälzer Wald and is the starting point for several hiking trails. The village is famous for its almond blossom, celebrated with an annual spring festival, the Mandelblütenfest.

🚗 *Continue along Meerspinnstrasse to reach Deidesheim.*

⑬ Deidesheim

Rhineland-Palatinate; 67146

Designer jewellery jostles for attention next to a butcher selling the local delicacy, *Saumagen*, on Deidesheim's

Marktplatz. The juxtaposition of rustic authenticity and metropolitan chic makes this one of the most intriguing villages on the Weinstrasse. The Rathaus houses the **Museum für Weinkultur** (museum of viticulture) (open Wed, Fri & Sat). Local wine growers include **Reichsrat von Buhl** (open daily), a renowned producer of Sekt (sparkling wine).

🚗 *Continue on the minor road along the B271, signposted to Wachenheim.*

⑭ Wachenheim

Rhineland-Palatinate; 67157

The impressive ruins of the 12th-century castle of **Wachtenburg** dominate Wachenheim. Constructed under the authority of Konrad von Hohenstaufen, half-brother of Emperor Frederick Barbarossa (1122–90), it was besieged in the 15th century, damaged in the Peasants' War of 1524–5 and finally blown up by French troops in 1689. Known as the "Balcony of the Pfalz" for the superb views it offers over the Rhine Valley, the castle ruins are a popular destination for hikers and are floodlit to spectacular effect at night.

🚗 *Continue on the minor road to Bad Dürkheim. Follow signs to Kurpark.*

Above Café tables on the main square of Siebeldingen **Below** Decorative sign outside a winery, Maikammer

EAT AND DRINK

MAIKAMMER

Gasthaus zum Winzer *expensive*
This Baroque former winery enjoys an attractive courtyard. The menu features modern European dishes.
Weinstrasse Süd 8, 67487; 06321 54 10; www.gasthaus-zum-winzer.de; open Wed–Sun

ST MARTIN

St Martiner Castell *moderate*
A handsome old hotel and restaurant with a menu which blends local and international influences.
Maikammerer Strasse 2, 67487; 06323 95 10; www.hotelcastell.de; closed Mon & Tue

GIMMELDINGEN

Netts *expensive*
Housed in a restored late Baroque village house, this modern restaurant and wine bar offers creative fare with outstanding wines.
Meerspinstrasse 46, 67435; 06321 601 75; www.nettslandhaus.de; open Wed–Sun

DEIDESHEIM

Turm Stüb´l *moderate*
Regional specialities and French dishes are served at this wine bar.
Turmstrasse 3, 67146; 06326 98 10 81; www.turmstuebel.de; closed Mon

Schwarzer Hahn *expensive*
The Deidesheimer Hof's Michelin-starred restaurant blends French, German and Mediterranean influences to impressive effect. The hotel also has a more traditional restaurant.
Am Marktplatz 1, 67146; 06326 968 70; www.deidesheimerhof.de; closed Sun–Tue & Jan

Above Ruins of Kloster Limburg, Bad Dürkheim **Above right** Vineyards around Nierstein **Below left** Village centre, Nackenheim **Below right** Wine cellar in Bockenheim

WHERE TO STAY

BAD DÜRKHEIM

Hotel Annaberg *moderate*
Surrounded by vineyards, this four-star hotel enjoys an idyllic location and has a delightful restaurant.
Annabergstrasse 1, 67098; 06322 940 00; www.hotel-annaberg.com

FREINSHEIM

Amtshaus *moderate*
A lovely boutique hotel with well-furnished rooms and modern bathrooms. The restaurant in the vaulted cellars is well worth a visit.
Hauptstrasse 29, 67251; 06353 501 93 55; www.amtshaus-freinsheim.de

Freinsheimer Hof *moderate*
A beautifully restored winery in the old town, this hotel has just four pretty rooms off an open verandah overlooking the lovely central courtyard.
Breite Strasse 7, 67251; 06353 50 804 10; www.freinsheimerhof.com

AROUND NACKENHEIM

Landhotel Battenheimer Hof *moderate*
This former wine estate from 1852 offers cosy rooms and a sauna. Breakfast is served in the conservatory or on the terrace in summer.
Rheinstrasse 2, 55294 Bodenheim (3km/ 2 miles north of Nackenheim); 06135 70 90; www.battenheimerhof.com

AROUND NIERSTEIN

Jordan's Untermühle *moderate*
The rooms are simple but attractive at this rustic half-timbered wellness hotel on the edge of Köngernheim, between Westhofen and Mainz. It has an outstanding restaurant.
Ausserhalb 1, 55278 Köngernheim (west of Nierstein); 06737 710 00; www.jordans-untermuehle.de

15 Bad Dürkheim
Rhineland-Palatinate; 67098
The spa town of Bad Dürkheim has a neat, traffic-free core fringing the **Kurpark**, a grassy park where the 33-m (108-ft) long **Gradierwerk** – a giant outdoor saline air purifier – is one of the largest of its kind in Germany. Dating from 1847, it is the sole survivor of five similar structures in the town. To the west of the town centre, on Luitpoldweg, are the ruins of the Romanesque Benedictine abbey of **Kloster Limburg** *(open daily).*

🚗 *Leave Bad Dürkheim along the B271 to Ungstein, turn right and then take the minor road signposted to Freinsheim.*

16 Freinsheim
Rhineland-Palatinate; 67251
Snug behind its surviving medieval walls, Freinsheim is a historic gem with a perfectly preserved old town focused on the diminutive yet dignified 18th-century **Rathaus**. Visitors can enjoy a walk around the inner circuit of the town's walls and discover houses built into them in

a picturesque fashion. A gastronomic hot spot, Freinsheim also has a number of interesting restaurants.

🚗 *Return to Ungstein, then turn right along the B271 to Bockenheim.*

Saumagen
Saumagen – stuffed pig's stomach is the Pfalz's great regional speciality. Like the Scottish dish haggis, it delights some and intimidates others; as with haggis, the stuffing is consumed, not the stomach itself. In the case of *Saumagen*, the filling is prepared with a mixture of potatoes, carrots and pork, flavoured with marjoram and often served sliced and seared.

17 Bockenheim
Rhineland-Palatinate; 67278
Situated beside a lake, the village of Bockenheim is supposedly built in the style of a Roman fort. The Deutsche Weinstrasse ends at Bockenheim, where the **Haus der Deutschen Weinstrasse**, or House of the German Wine Route, acts as the northern counterpart to the **Deutsches Weintor**

at the southern end of the route. The building spans the road and has a restaurant and tourist information office.

🚗 *Continue along the B271 Weinstrasse to Flörsheim, turning right on Wilhelm-Ternis-Strasse then left toward Westhofen.*

⑱ Westhofen
Rhineland-Palatinate; 67593
Enjoying a pretty setting, the vineyards surrounding the village of Westhofen are dotted with stone huts. These are characteristic of Rheinhessen's wine-growing country, and were originally built by vineyard workers to provide shelter during bad weather. **Weingut Wittmann** *(Mainzer Strasse 19; 06244 90 50 36; www.weingutwittmann.de; open Mon–Sat, by appointment)* produces top-notch dry Rieslings using organic methods.

🚗 *Leave Westhofen along Mainzer Strasse, signposted to Mainz taking the roundabout at B420 towards Köngernheim.*

⑲ Mainz
Rhineland-Palatinate; 55116
The capital of Rheinland-Pfalz, Mainz *(see pp154–5)* is dominated by the late Romanesque **Kaiserdom** *(open daily).* The magnificence of this imperial cathedral reflects the importance of the Prince-Bishops of Mainz, who were Electors of the Holy Roman Empire. The cathedral was burned down the day before its consecration in 1009 and again in 1081. It was rebuilt in the first quarter of the 12th century. Mainz was also the birthplace of printing pioneer Johannes Gutenberg. Exhibits in the **Gutenberg-Museum** *(closed Mon)* include a priceless Gutenberg Bible printed in Mainz in 1455.

🚗 *Leave Mainz along Rheinstrasse, following signs to Laubenheim. At Laubenheim continue through Bodenheim to Nackenheim.*

⑳ Nackenheim
Rhineland-Palatinate; 55299
Nackenheim is closely associated with the German playwright Carl Zuckmayer, who was born here in 1896. Nestled between vine-covered slopes and the Rhine, the village has a long history of producing wine. The long-established **Weingut Gunderloch** *(Carl-Gunderloch-Platz 1,*

06135 23 41; www.gunderloch.de; open Mon–Sat) produces traditional sweet wines of exceptional quality and some fine dry Rieslings.

🚗 *Leave Nackenheim on the Wormser Strasse, which joins the B9. Continue on the B9 to Nierstein, then turn left on to Pestalozzistrasse to the car park.*

㉑ Nierstein
Rhineland-Palatinate; 55283
Shuttered, half-timbered houses and *Strausswirtschaften* – temporary wine taverns run by the wine growers – characterize Nierstein. The village is famed for its Riesling and is focused on its central Marktplatz. Visitors can go on a signposted 14-km (8-mile) walk, the **Drei Türme Wanderweg** or Three Towers Walk *(www.nierstein.de),* which heads up into the vineyards of the **Roter Hang** above the village for views over the Rhine and the surrounding countryside.

🚗 *Continue south on the B9 to Oppenheim, then turn right on to Mainzstrasse and follow signs to Zentral Park-Platz to park.*

Discovering German Wines
Wine labels reveal much about the style and quality of German wine. Dry wines are labelled *Trocken*, semi-dry or slightly sweet wines are *Halbtrocken* and sweet wines are *Lieblich. Kabinett* refers to a wine made with fully ripened grapes; *Spätlese* means wine made from late-picked grapes, while *Auslese, Beerenauslese, Eiswein* and *Trockenbeerenauslese* are made with grapes picked progressively later, producing intense flavour and longevity. Many, though not all, quality wines display the symbol of the VDP *(Verband Deutscher Prädikatswein),* whose members include many of the nation's top wine growers.

Above left Outdoor café, Nierstein
Above Village gate of Nackenheim

VISITING MAINZ

Parking
The multi-storey car park in Weisslliliengasse is convenient for visiting the Kaiserdom and Gutenberg-Museum.

Tourist Information
Markt 17, 55116 ; 06131 24 28 88; www.mainz-tourismus.com; closed Sun

EAT AND DRINK

FREINSHEIM
Atable *expensive*
This restaurant serves classic French-inspired cuisine, which is accompanied by excellent local and French wines curated by the award-winning hosts. *Hauptstrasse 29, 67251; 06353 501 93 55; www.amtshaus-freinsheim.de; closed Sun & Mon*

Freinsheimer Hof *expensive*
Terracotta tiles and a vaulted ceiling provide a Mediterranean setting for this restaurant's special tapas meals. Book in advance. *Breite Strasse 7, 67251; 06353 50 804 10; www.freinsheimerhof.com; closed Wed & Thu*

AROUND NACKENHEIM
Gutschänke Battenheimer Hof *moderate*
Try regional dishes such as *Bodenheimer* pork with walnut pesto or goat's cheese salad with mustard. *Rheinstrasse 2, 55294 Bodenheim (3km/2 miles north of Nackenheim); 06135 709 40; www.battenheimerhof.com; closed Sun & Mon*

AROUND NIERSTEIN
Brot & Bouquet *moderate*
An award-winning restaurant of the Jordan's Untermühle hotel offers a good selection of wines. *Ausserhalb 1, 55278 Köngernheim (west of Nierstein); 06737 710 00; www.jordans-untermuehle.de*

Right Red sandstone Katharinenkirche, Oppenheim **Far right** Old city walls in the town of Worms **Below** Outdoor cafés in front of the Kaiserdom, Speyer

WHERE TO STAY

OPPENHEIM

Altes Amtsgericht *moderate*
Housed in a former district court building from 1903, this hotel has 14 modern and stylish rooms, some of which offer lovely views.
Amtsgerichtsplatz 1, 55276; 06133 572 49 63; www.altesamtsgerichtoppen heim.de

Hotel Zwo *moderate*
The 13 modern, stylish rooms in this boutique hotel have well-equipped bathrooms and wireless Internet.
Friedrich-Ebert-Strasse 84, 55276; 06133 94 94 35; www.hotelzwo-oppenheim.de

SPEYER

Domhof *moderate*
This charming hotel is very close to Speyer's cathedral, with 49 single and double rooms furnished in conservative style. It also has its own microbrewery.
Bauhof 3, 67346; 06232 132 90; www.hoteldomhof.de

㉒ OPPENHEIM

Rhineland-Palatinate; 55276
A ruined castle and a magnificent Gothic church are powerful reminders of Oppenheim's medieval heyday. Raised to the status of a Free City of the Holy Roman Empire in 1225, it lost its independence in the following century and was levelled by French troops during the War of the Palatine Succession (1688–97). This wine-growing town, on a pretty, sunny site overlooking the Rhine, also has an intriguing underground labyrinth to explore.

A one-hour walking tour

Park at the Zentralparkplatz, on the western edge of the Altstadt, before heading uphill along Gaustrasse and Burgstrasse. At the top of Burgstrasse ascend the Schlangenweg path to reach **Landskron** ①, a ruined imperial castle. At the far end of the castle, metal steps lead into a vineyard. Take the path through it, beyond the gate in the town wall at the far end. Cross the road to the Landskronhalle. The Nero's Steak & Meeresfrüchte is a good place for a snack. Follow the road downhill to the **Ruprechtsturm** ②, a mock-medieval folly built in 1903 on the site of a medieval tower destroyed during the French occupation. Continue downhill to Geschlechterbrunnen, a Renaissance well dating from 1546, and the arched entrance to the churchyard beyond it. Go through this, turning right to reach the **Michaelskapelle** ③, a

Winery sign, Oppenheim

13th-century Gothic chapel. In the basement is the Beinhaus (ossuary), where the bones of 20,000 citizens of Oppenheim who died between 1400 and 1750 lie neatly stacked. Further along the north wall is the Lapidarium, with gargoyles and Gothic carvings. Continue around the outside of the **Katharinenkirche** ④ *(open daily)*, a Protestant parish church, to enter on the south side. Construction began in 1225 in the Romanesque style, but most of what exists today is Gothic, including the 14th-century Rose of Oppenheim window. From the south side of the churchyard, go down the steps to Merianstrasse to the **Oppenheimer Stadtmuseum** ⑤ *(open daily)*, with displays on local history, and the tourist information office *(www.stadt-oppenheim.de)*, which organizes tours of the Oppenheimer

0 metres 150
0 yards 150

Nero's Steak & Meeresfrüchte

② Ruprechtsturm

① Landskron

Geschlechter-brunnen

Michaelskapelle
③

④
Katharinenkirche

Oppenheimer ⑤
Stadtmuseum

⑥ Marktplatz

ZENTRALPARK-PLATZ

Rathofkapelle ⑧

⑦ Deutsches
Weinbaumuseum

Kellerlabyrinth *(tours Mar–Oct daily; Nov–Feb: closed Sun)*, a subterranean network of cellars and passageways. Merianstrasse leads to the **Marktplatz** ⑥, dominated by the 17th-century Rathaus. Cross the square to reach the Catholic church of St Bartholomäus, once part of a Franciscan monastery. Follow Kirchstrasse to Wormserstrasse to the **Deutsches Weinbaumuseum** ⑦ *(Apr–Oct: closed Mon; www.dwm-content. de)*, with exhibits on Germany's winemaking history. Walk back up Wormserstrasse and turn left into Rathofstrasse, following the street around to the **Rathofkapelle** ⑧, a chapel which is now a restaurant. Beyond it, a plaque commemorates Oppenheim's Jewish community on the site of a synagogue destroyed on "Kristallnacht" in an anti-Jew attack in 1938 in Nazi Germany. At the end of the Rathofstrasse, turn left into Krämerstrasse, which ends at the Gautor, a surviving gate of the town walls, built in 1566. Exit through the gate to return to the car park.
🚗 *Leave Oppenheim along the B9/ Rheinstrasse to Guntersblum, turn right and continue through Alsheim and Osthofen to Worms.*

㉓ Worms
Rhineland-Palatinate; 67547
One of Germany's oldest cities, Worms is closely associated with Protestant reformer Martin Luther and the Legend of the Nibelungen from Germanic mythology. It has a 12th-century cathedral, the **Dom St Peter** *(open daily)*, and a Jewish cemetery, **Heiliger Sand**, where the oldest gravestone dates from 1076.
🚗 *Follow Ludwigstrasse to the B9, then follow signs for Speyer turning right for Frankenthal, further again turn right at Rheingönheim. At Speyer follow signs for Zentrum along the B39.*

Above Oppenheim's Marktplatz, lined with tall buildings

㉔ Speyer
Rhineland-Palatinate; 67346
The smallest of Pfalz's three cathedral cities is the best-preserved, with a broad main street, Maximilianstrasse, which runs west from the **Kaiserdom**. One of the finest surviving examples of Romanesque architecture in Europe, the imperial cathedral is a UNESCO World Heritage Site.

Above Heiliger Sand, an ancient Jewish cemetery in Worms

Jews of the Rhineland
Jewish culture was established in the region in the 10th century with settlements in Speyer, Worms and Mainz. The cities had a major influence on the development of Ashkenazi Jewish culture, since it was here in the early Middle Ages that the Yiddish language emerged as an offshoot of the Middle High German.

VISITING WORMS

Parking
The Parkhaus Am Dom at Koehlstrasse 7 is a two-minute walk from the Dom, Rathaus and Marktplatz.

Tourist Information
Neumarkt 14, 67547; 06241 853 73 06; www.worms-erleben.de; Apr–Oct: open daily; Nov–Mar: open Mon–Fri

EAT AND DRINK

OPPENHEIM
La Piazza *moderate*
An Italian restaurant overlooking the main square serves fresh Mediterranean food with a local twist at good prices. *Merianstrasse 5, 55276; 06133 614 28 42; www.lapiazza-oppenheim.de; closed Tue*

Restaurant Völker *moderate*
Enjoy delicious Flammkuchen, schnitzel and pasta dishes. Booking advised. *Merianstrasse 7, 55276; 01719 53 01 43; closed Mon*

SPEYER
Ratskeller *moderate*
Brick-vaulted cellar-restaurant beneath Speyer's 18th-century town hall. *Maximilianstrasse 12, 67346; 06232 786 12; www.ratskeller-speyer.de; closed Sun dinner, Mon & Tue*

Zum Alten Engel *moderate*
Cosy cellar-restaurant that is an adherent of the Slow Food movement. *Mühlturmstrasse 7, 67346; 06232 709 14; www.alter-engel-speyer.de; closed Sun & Mon*

DAY TRIP OPTIONS
The route can be broken down into day trips for those with less time or a special interest to follow.

Wine country
Food and wine lovers should head to Edenkoben ⑧ and stop at the restaurants and wineries along the route to Freinsheim ⑯. Oenophiles can take the drive from Mainz ⑲ to Worms ㉓ through some of the most popular wine-growing villages.

Follow the driving instructions from Edenkoben to Freinsheim, then follow the route to Mainz. From Mainz follow instructions to Worms.

Castles and villages
Those interested in art and architecture can explore fairy-tale castles and charming half-timbered villages along the route from Bad Bergzabern ❷ to Burg Trifels ⑥.

Follow the driving instructions from Bad Bergzabern to Burg Trifels.

TRIP 16

FRANCONIA OF THE PRINCE-BISHOPS
Bayreuth to Aschaffenburg

HIGHLIGHTS

Spiritual Franconia
Visit Franconia's palaces and churches, where spiritual
and temporal power meet divine inspiration

Crags and caves
Experience the strange, intriguing geology
of the Fränkische Schweiz, both above
and below the ground

Riverside landscape
from castle-topped hillsides to the vineyards
of the Mainschleife

Delectable tipple
Sample the delicious, distinctive beers of Bavaria's
traditional independent brewers

FRANCONIA OF THE PRINCE-BISHOPS

For many centuries, Franconia's Prince-Bishops held both spiritual and political power in this region. Drawn from the ranks of the nobility, they left a lasting cultural legacy in this fascinating corner of northern Bavaria (Bayern), which ranges from Bamberg's well-preserved historic core to the splendid Baroque and Gothic masterpieces throughout the region. Amidst the palaces and churches are traditional *Weinstuben* and old pubs where one can enjoy Franconia's distinctive food, wine and beer. Away from the cities, the smaller towns and villages often have a rustic, lost-in-time charm. This trip takes visitors through lovely landscapes ranging from the valley of the meandering Main river to the startling geology of Fränkische Schweiz and the unspoiled rural idyll of Naturpark Steigerwald.

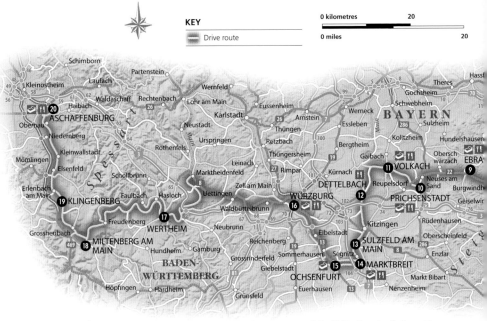

KEY

⸺ Drive route

0 kilometres 20

0 miles 20

Below Eighteenth-century Residenz, set in a magnificent park, Würzburg, *see p178*

ACTIVITIES

Test the waters with a relaxing day at Bayreuth's Lohengrin Therme spa

Raise your glass to Franconia's smoked beers and distinctive dry wines

Feel the rush on Pottenstein's snow-free summer toboggan run

Take a hike through Naturpark Steigerwald or among the Mainschleife's vineyards

Shop at the designer outlets in Wertheim village

Above Half-timbered houses and the Martinskirche on the Rathaus, Forchheim, *see p173*

PLAN YOUR DRIVE

Start/finish: Bayreuth to Aschaffenburg.

Number of days: 5 days, allowing a day to explore Bamberg.

Distance: 440 km (273 miles).

Road conditions: Roads are generally well paved and signposted and have gentle inclines. Snow and ice can be a problem in winter.

When to go: The region is at its best from May to October, when the weather is most agreeable. In some smaller villages, hotels and museums are closed in January or February.

Opening times: Shops are generally open from 9am to 8pm, while sights of interest are open from 9am to 6pm.

Main market days: Bamberg: Mon–Sat; Würzburg: Tue, Wed, Fri & Sat; Aschaffenburg: Wed & Sat (farmer's market).

Shopping: Souvenirs from the region include Rauchbier, the smoky local beer from Bamberg, and Franconian wines from Würzburg and Volkach.

Major festivals: Bayreuth: Bayreuther Festspiele (Wagner festival), Jul–Aug; Bamberg: Sandkerwa (folk festival), Aug; Dettelbach: Altstadt-Weinfest (wine festival), Jun; Würzburg: Kiliani Volksfest (procession in traditional costumes and funfair), Jul; Weinparade am Dom (wine festival), Aug/Sep; Clingenburg: Weinfest (wine festival), Apr/May; Aschaffenburg: Kulturtage (culture days), Jun–Aug.

DAY TRIP OPTIONS

The **castles**, **caves** and outdoor activities of Fränkische Schweiz will appeal to **families**, while **art** and **architecture buffs** will find much to admire between Vierzehnheiligen, Bamberg and Würzburg. **Epicureans** will relish the **wines** and the **food** in the villages of the Mainschleife. For full details, *see p179*.

Above Pompejanum villa, on the banks of the Main, Aschaffenburg, *see p179*

Right The countryside near Bayreuth
Below left Entrance to the Markgräfliches
Opernhaus, Bayreuth **Below right** Decorative
signpost in Tüchersfeld

VISITING BAYREUTH

Parking
There is a signposted public
underground car park (Tiefgarage
Rathaus) beneath the Rathaus
(town hall).

Tourist Information
Opernstrasse 22, 95444; 09218 85 88;
www.bayreuth-tourismus.de; Nov–Apr:
open Mon–Sat; May–Oct: open daily

WHERE TO STAY

BAYREUTH
Lohmühle *moderate*
Housed in two fine gabled houses on
the site of a former tannery, close to
the centre of Bayreuth, this hotel has
21 simple but comfortably furnished
en-suite rooms as well as a restaurant.
Badstrasse 37, 95444; 0921 530 60;
www.hotel-lohmuehle.de

Goldener Anker *expensive*
This old and rather grand family-run
hotel has 35 individually styled rooms
that are traditionally furnished. The
in-house restaurant has preserved
its original 1920s Art Deco interior.
Opernstrasse 6, 95444; 0921 787 77 40;
www.anker-bayreuth.de

BURG RABENSTEIN
Burg Rabenstein *expensive*
There are just 22 individually styled
rooms and suites in this historic castle,
varying in style from prettily rustic to
plush; some include beds with
tapestries and canopies.
Rabenstein 33, 95491; 0920 29 70 04
40; www.burg-rabenstein.de

FORCHHEIM
Hotel am Kronengarten *moderate*
A small and pleasant modern hotel on
the edge of Forchheim's historic old
town offering comfortable rooms,
some of which are singles and triples.
Bamberger Strasse 6a, 91301;
09191 725 00; www.hotel-am-
kronengarten.de

① Bayreuth
Bavaria; 95444
The city of Bayreuth came into its own
in the early 18th century, when it was
transformed into a fine stone-built
capital for Margravine Wilhelmine
(1709–58), sister of Frederick the Great
of Prussia. Her residence, the **Neues
Schloss** *(open daily; www.schloesser.
bayern.de)*, was built by Joseph Saint-
Pierre. The elongated three-storey
palace combines Classical lines
with a rustic ground floor.

Another highlight of the city is
the magnificent Baroque opera house,
the ornate **Markgräfliches Opernhaus**
(tours daily). Built in the 1740s, it has an
interior designed by Giuseppe Galli
Bibiena, who came from a famous
Bolognese family of theatre architects,
and his son Carlo. The city is associated
with composer Richard Wagner
(1813–83), who took up residence

here in 1872. His home, **Villa Wahnfried**
*(Jul & Aug: open daily; Sep–Jun: closed
Mon)*, is on the northeastern side of
Neues Schloss and is now a museum.
In the villa's garden are the tombs of
Wagner and his wife, Cosima, the
daughter of Franz Liszt. Each summer
Bayreuth hosts the Wagner festival,
the **Bayreuther Festspiele**, held in the
Festspielhaus, the imposing but
spartan theatre built in 1872–5 to
a design by Gottfried Semper.

Visitors to Bayreuth can also take a
cure at the **Lohengrin Therme** *(www.
lohengrin-therme.de)*, a thermal spa.

🚗 *Follow signs to Fränkische Schweiz/
Hollfeld, Erlanger Strasse, later signed
as B22, then turn left on to the road
signposted Pottenstein.*

② Pottenstein
Bavaria; 91278
Four valleys meet at Pottenstein,
yet the village feels almost walled
in by the high crags surrounding
it. One such rock is topped by the
region's oldest castle, **Burg Pottenstein**
*(Easter–Oct: open Wed–Sun; Jul & Aug;
also open Tue; www.burgpottenstein.de)*;
below ground are the **Teufelshöhle
Caves** *(Jun–Nov: open daily; Dec–May:
open Sun)*. Besides visiting these
sights, visitors can also enjoy the
snow-free summer toboggan
run *(www.sommerrodel bahnen-
pottenstein.de)* here.

🚗 *Head west from Pottenstein
along the B470/Forchheimer Strasse
to reach the village of Tüchersfeld.*

EAT AND DRINK

BAYREUTH

Lohmühle *moderate*
Regional produce forms the basis
for the award-winning Franconian
cooking in this rustic restaurant. The
trout, carp and catfish come from
its own ponds.
*Badstrasse 37, 95444; 0921 530 60;
www.hotel-lohmuehle.de*

Goldener Anker *expensive*
The Goldener Anker hotel's restaurant
offers refined Franconian cooking,
with a few Mediterranean influences,
matched with fine wines.
*Opernstrasse 6, 95444; 0921 787 77 40;
www.anker-bayreuth.de; open Wed–Sun
dinner only, daily during the Festspiele*

FORCHHEIM

Zollhaus *moderate*
Overlooking the Wiesent river, this
restaurant serves regional gourmet
dishes, such as braised ox shank.
*Hauptstrasse 4, 91301; 09191 97 09 90;
www.zollhaus-forchheim.de; closed
Mon & Tue*

Other options
Forchheim has a number of tiny
breweries, some of which operate traditional *Brauereigaststätten* – rustic old
pubs in which to sample the brew –
such as **Eichhorn** *(Bamberger Strasse 9;
09191 64 768; www.gasthaus-
eichhorn.de)* and **Hebendanz Keller**
*(Auf den Kellern 22, 0160 90251346;
www.hebendanz-keller.com)* with a
lovely Biergarten under the trees.

Above Canoeists on the banks of
the Püttlach river, near Tüchersfeld
Below Pottenstein's main street

③ Tüchersfeld
Bavaria; 91278
Looking as though its houses have
been dropped at random among
rocky pinnacles, tiny Tüchersfeld is
even more improbably scenic than
Pottenstein. The village is home to
the **Fränkische Schweiz Museum**
*(Apr–Oct: open daily; Nov–Mar: open Sun;
www.fraenkische-schweiz-museum.de)*,
which has peasant costumes, arts and
crafts, furniture, and an 18th-century
synagogue alongside displays on the
region's geology and archaeology.

🚗 *At the end of Tüchersfeld turn
left to Unterailsfeld. In Unterailsfeld,
turn right on to Oberailsfeld Strasse
to Oberailsfeld. Take Burgenstrasse
driving through the village of
Oberailsfeld; follow brown signs
signposted to Burg Rabenstein.*

④ Burg Rabenstein
Bavaria; 95491
Perched on a dramatic crag
overlooking the Ailsbach Valley
and with its oldest parts dating
from the 12th century, the
castle of Rabenstein *(guided tours:
Apr–Oct: Wed–Sun; Nov–Mar: Sat &
Sun; www.burgrabenstein.de)* looks
every inch the impregnable
medieval fortress, though much
of it was ruined during the Thirty
Years'War (1618–48). There are
regular interesting **falconry
displays** *(Apr–Oct: Tue–Sun)*
here. The **Sophienhöhle
Caves** *(guided tours: mid-
Mar–Oct: Tue–Sun & Nov–mid-
Mar: Sat & Sun)*, among the
most beautiful showcaves
in Germany, are just a ten-
minute walk away.

🚗 *Take the B470 and follow it
westwards to Forchheim. Parking is
available in the car park on Pradeplatz.*

Crags, Castles and Caves
The Franconian Switzerland
(Fränkische Schweiz) has long been
one of Germany's most popular
regions for its startling, craggy
natural beauty and dramatic castles
and pretty villages, as well as for the
opportunities it offers for outdoor
activities, from cycling and hiking
to rock climbing and canoeing.
The region's limestone geology
ensures the natural wonders continue underground in the form of
strikingly beautiful cave systems,
some of which can be visited.

⑤ Forchheim
Bavaria; 91301
With a historic core centred on
the tall, onion-domed tower of
Martinskirche and a 15th-century
half-timbered **Rathaus**, this lively
small town, with timber-framed
houses, is well worth exploring. It was the second seat
of the Bamberg Prince-Bishops
in the Middle Ages. Their palace,
the **Kaiserpfalz**, has precious
late-Gothic frescoes and is now
the **Pfalzmuseum** *(Dec: open daily;
closed Mon; www.kaiserpfalz.forchheim.
de)*, with sections devoted
to local history, archaeology
and folk costume.

🚗 *Leave Forchheim along
Bamberger Strasse, following
yellow signs for Bamberg.
This joins the B22. At Bamberg,
follow signs to Zentrum
to reach the car park.*

Pillar with sculptures
in Forchheim

Above Impressive façade of the Neue Residenz, Bamberg

⑥ BAMBERG

Bavaria; 96047

For centuries the seat of an independent Prince-Bishopric within the Holy Roman Empire, Bamberg has survived the turmoil of Germany's history relatively unscathed, with an exceptionally well-preserved historic core that was added to UNESCO's list of World Heritage Sites in 1993. The city centre is divided into three parts by the Main-Danube canal and the Regnitz river, but most of the major sights are in the hilly Bergstadt to the west of the river, dominated by a splendid four-spired cathedral. This walk explores the Bergstadt and the riverside areas of Bamberg.

VISITING BAMBERG

Parking
The City-Altstadt Tiefgarage, an underground car park, is located near the tourist office.

Tourist Information
Geyerswörthstrasse 5, 96047; 0951 297 62 00; www.bamberg.info; open daily

WHERE TO STAY IN BAMBERG

Messerschmitt *moderate*
Family owned since 1832, this beautiful hotel is a mix of traditional and modern, set in the house that belonged to the parents of the famous aviation pioneer, Willy Messerschmitt. The hotel also has a renowned restaurant.
Lange Strasse 41, 96047; 0951 29 78 00; www.hotel-messerschmitt.de

St Nepomuk *moderate*
This stylish hotel offers views of the Altes Rathaus. It has 23 rooms, a suite and two restaurants and a bar.
Obere Mühlbrücke 9, 96049; 0951 984 20; www.hotel-nepomuk.de

A two-hour walking tour

From the car park, walk to the tourist office, where visitors can pick up the key to the tower of **Schloss Geyerswörth** ① *(closed for renovations until 2023)*, which lies across the road from the office. There are fine views over Bamberg from the top of this 16th-century Prince-Bishop's residence.

Afterward, cross the river by the wooden footbridge. Then turn left into Schranne, right into Balthasargässchen, then left again to reach Judenstrasse, a street of historic town houses, including the **Böttingerhaus** ②, built for the privy councillor Ignaz Tobias Böttinger between 1707 and 1713. Take the left fork into Concordiastrasse to reach another of Böttinger's residences, Concordia, which dates from 1722.

Traditional biscuits, Bamberg

Return to Judenstrasse. Thirsty walkers can stop at Klosterbräu *(open daily)* on the right, which was once the Prince-Bishops' brewery.

At the end of Judenstrasse, turn left to head up Untere Kaulberg to reach the 14th-century **Pfarrkirche zu Unsere Lieben Frau** ③. The parish church of Our Dear Lady has a lovely tabernacle in the ambulatory and Tintoretto's *Assumption* just by the door. Cross the busy road in front of the church, descending the steps signposted Dom to reach Hinterer Bach. Follow this curving cobbled lane uphill, admiring the 17th-century Alter Ebracher Hof on the climb up. At the top is Domplatz, Bamberg's showpiece square. On the left is the 13th-century **Kaiserdom** ④ *(open daily)*, a cathedral filled with artistic treasures such as the Bamberger Reiter, an equestrian likeness of a medieval knight. The cathedral cloisters house the Diözesanmuseum *(closed Mon)*, with a remarkable collection of 11th-century clerical vestments. Beyond the Dom, on the left, is the elaborate Renaissance façade of the **Ratsstube** ⑤, a part of the Alte Hofhaltung, a rambling complex that once housed the Prince-Bishops' household. The Ratsstube houses the Historisches Museum *(Apr–Oct: closed Mon; Nov–Mar: temporary exhibitions only)*, with displays relating to Bamberg's history. Return to Domplatz and cross the road to reach the **Neue Residenz** ⑥ *(open daily)*, whose Baroque façade zigzags across the north side of the square. Work started on it in 1613, but the palace attained its current magnificence under Prince-Bishop Lothar von Schönborn between 1697 and 1703. The palace is the work of Leonhard

0 metres 200
0 yards 200

Dientzenhofer, from the Bavarian Dynasty, whose architectural influence reached as far as Prague. A guided tour goes through the richly decorated state rooms but visitors are free to admire the German medieval and Baroque paintings in the palace gallery at leisure. Don't miss the lovely rose garden behind the palace, with its pretty Baroque café *(open summer)* and excellent views over the old city.

Leave Domplatz along Obere Karolinenstrasse. On the corner of Domstrasse stands the **Missionshaus St Heinrich** ⑦, an elegant mansion that was once the Bamberg residence of Bayreuth's Margraves. Turn right down Michaelsberger Strasse, following the street uphill to the former Benedictine monastery of **Kloster St Michael** ⑧, whose church *(closed for renovations until 2029)* was rebuilt in the late-Gothic style after a fire in 1610. The Baroque monastery buildings contain a brewery museum, the Fränkisches Brauereimuseum *(open Wed–Sun)*. On leaving the museum, stop by the garden behind the monastery. Next, return to the Aufsess Strasse, which becomes Elisabethenstrasse, to reach the river. On the opposite bank is a picturesque huddle of fishermen's cottages known as **Klein Venedig** ⑨, or Little Venice. Turn back up Elisabethen Strasse and left into Obere Sandstrasse, which leads to Dominikanerstrasse. Bear right into Herrenstrasse, then left to the Obere Brücke, a bridge that passes through the **Altes Rathaus** ⑩, set on a mid-river island. The old town hall houses the Sammlung Ludwig *(closed Mon)* collection of Strasbourg and Meissen porcelain. Retrace the route, turn left on to Geyersworthplatz and then left again on to the wooden footbridge to the car park.

🚗 *Leave the town of Bamberg along the B4/Hallstädter Strasse. At Breitengüssbach, follow signs to Bad Staffelstein via Zapfendorf and Ebensfeld to Grundfeld. At Grundfeld, follow the road signposted to Vierzehnheiligen.*

Bishops and Empire

Formed from the eastern part of Charlemagne's empire in the 9th century and dissolved in 1806, the Holy Roman Empire was a loose alliance of states under the aegis of an emperor chosen by *Kurfürsten* (electors), though in practice the Habsburgs dominated. Bamberg and Würzburg were independent Prince-Bishoprics of the empire in which the bishops wielded temporal and spiritual power. Aschaffenburg was the second seat of the archbishops of Mainz, since the city dominated the largest of their territories.

⑦ Vierzehnheiligen
Bavaria; 96231
A worthwhile excursion from Bamberg, Vierzehnheiligen is best known for its splendid pilgrimage church, **Basilika Vierzehnheiligen** *(open daily)*, a masterpiece of southern German Baroque and Rococo styles. Designed by the Franconian architect Balthasar Neumann, it was built between 1743 and 1772 at the site where a shepherd had a vision of a crying child accompanied by the Holy Helpers – the Vierzehnheiligen – or 14 saints of intercession of the church's name.

🚗 *Return to Bamberg and take Unterer Kaulberg and Würzburger Strasse. Follow the yellow signs for Würzburg to reach the B22 and then signs to Pommersfelden and Schloss Weissenstein.*

Above left Riverside view of Bamberg and Kirche St Michael **Above** Visitors strolling along Obere Brücke, Bamberg **Below** Pretty Altes Rathaus, set on a mid-river island, Bamberg

EAT AND DRINK IN BAMBERG

Brudermühle *moderate*
Wild boar, venison, carp and trout are among the specialities on the menu of this atmospheric riverside restaurant. *Schranne 1, 96049; 0951 95 52 20; www.brudermuehle.de*

Messerschmitt *expensive*
Regional produce, including goose liver, duck and venison, features on the menu of the Messerschmitt's fine dining room. *Lange Strasse 41, 96047; 0951 29 78 00; www.hotel-messerschmitt.de; closed Sun & Mon*

Other options
Local *Brauereigaststätten* (brewery-owned restaurants) worth visiting include **Greifenklau** *(Laurenziplatz 20, 0951 532 19; www.greifenklau.de; closed Sun & Mon)*, **Spezial** *(Obere Königstrasse 10, 0951 243 04; www.brauerei-spezial.de)* and **Schlenkerla** *(Dominkanerstrasse 6; 09515 60 50; www.schlenkerla.de).*

CYCLING IN VOLKACH

Pick up maps of the Mainschleife for cycling routes from the tourist office in the town hall *(Rathaus, Marktplatz 1, 97332; 09381 401 12; www.volkach. de; May–Oct: open daily; Nov–Apr: closed Sun).*

WHERE TO STAY

AROUND SCHLOSS WEISSENSTEIN

Kellerhaus Pommersfelden *moderate*
A modern café-bistro just south of Schloss Weissenstein, with great views of it from the terrace. Try a *Flammkuchen* (Alsatian pizza) with local white wine.
Kellerberg 1, 96178 Pommersfelden; 09548 98 21 98; www.kellerhaus-pommersfelden.de; Apr–Sep: closed Mon, Oct–Mar: closed Mon & Tue

EBRACH

Klosterbräu Landidyll *moderate*
The 18th-century guesthouse of the former Cistercian abbey of Ebrach has simple but comfortable rooms.
Marktplatz 4, 96157; 09553 180; www. klosterbraeu.info; closed Mon–Wed, Jan & Feb

PRICHSENSTADT

Alte Post Neuses *inexpensive*
A traditional inn (Napoleon once stayed here) with 10 comfortable, classically furnished rooms. Frankonian dishes are served in the restaurant or in the Biergarten.
Neuses am Sand 19, 97357; 09383 71 55; www.alte-post-neuses.de

VOLKACH

Zur Schwane *moderate*
An old hotel and restaurant with wooden ceilings and cosy rooms furnished with antiques. It also has its own winery on the outskirts of Volkach.
Hauptstrasse 12, 97332; 09381 806 60; www.schwane.de

Above Main street of Prichsenstadt, lined with pretty houses **Below** Grand façade of Schloss Weissenstein

⑧ Schloss Weissenstein
Bavaria; 96178

The Prince-Bishops of both Bamberg and Würzburg were members of the Schönborn Dynasty, and the familiy's wealth and power are reflected in the splendour of their family seat, **Schloss Weissenstein** *(Apr–Oct: open daily)*. The design was a collaboration between the Bamberg court architect Johann Dientzenhofer and the celebrated Viennese Baroque master Johann Lukas von Hildebrandt. The palace was completed in 1718 and is notable for the ceremonial *Treppenhaus* (staircase) and its collection of Old Masters.

Sign for walking circuits, Prichsenstadt

🚗 **Return to the B22, following signs for Steppach and Burgebrach, turning left continue along it to Ebrach.**

⑨ Ebrach
Bavaria; 96157

Ebrach sits at the heart of the idyllic forested **Naturpark Steigerwald** *(www.steigerwald-info.de)*, offering scope for relaxing country walks. The village is dominated by the buildings of a former Cistercian abbey. The cathedral-like **Klosterkirche** *(Apr–Oct: open daily)* is an important work of the early Gothic period and has a beautiful rose window; the Baroque abbey buildings now house a prison, but the splendid *Treppenhaus* and **Kaisersaal** (imperial hall) can still be visited *(Apr–Oct: tour 1:45pm daily)*. Ebrach is an ideal base for exploring Naturpark Steigerwald, the

unspoiled upland landscape which is notable for its biodiversity.

🚗 **Continue west along the B22 to Neuses am Sand, where there is a signposted left turn that leads to Prichsenstadt.**

⑩ Prichsenstadt
Bavaria; 97357

With a well-preserved set of defensive walls and towers rising above vineyards to shelter its intact historic core, tiny Prichsenstadt is a gem, its appearance to this day reflecting the urban forms of the Middle Ages. The town has a nightwatchman who conducts guided tours *(Sat & Sun)* that can be booked from all hotels. Wine aside, Prichsenstadt is also known for its asparagus and strawberries.

🚗 **Leave Prichsenstadt on the road signposted to Volkach from the west gate of the old town.**

⑪ Volkach
Bavaria; 97332

With two lofty 13th-century town gates, a fine 16th-century Rathaus and numerous *Winzer* (wine growers), Volkach is the "capital" of the Mainschleife. Historic houses here include the splendid Baroque **Schelfenhaus** and Renaissance **Echterhof**. A short walk from the town is the late-Gothic pilgrimage church of **Maria im Weingarten** *(Apr–Oct: open daily; Mar & Nov: open Fri–Sun)*. Idyllically situated amid vineyards to the northwest of Volkach, this church has a *Madonna* by the Würzburg sculptor Tilman Riemenschneider.

🚗 *Follow Brückenstrasse to reach the bridge over the Main, then turn left after the bridge, on to Escherndorfer Strasse to reach the village of Dettelbach.*

⑫ Dettelbach

Bavaria; 97337

Dettelbach is another handsome village behind intact defensive walls. Tucked between the medieval **Rathaus** and the eccentric-looking parish church is **KuK** *(open daily)*, a modern cultural centre where visitors can sample local wines and learn about Dettelbach's religious tradition. The pilgrimage church of **Maria im Sand** lies east of the village centre. Visitors should not leave Dettelbach without sampling the delicious local *Muskazinen* – hard-baked biscuits similar to Italian *biscotti.*

🚗 *Follow the road leading southward along the Main to Kitzingen. In Kitzingen, follow signs for Ochsenfurt, then after the railway bridge for Sulzfeld and Marktbreit.*

⑬ Sulzfeld am Main

Bavaria; 97320

The picturesque wine-growing village of Sulzfeld has a remarkably complete medieval town wall dating from the 15th and 16th centuries. With 21 towers, it creates a convincing impression of a child's toy fort brought magically to life. The village's other main claim to fame is as the

birthplace of the *Meterbratwurst* – a giant sausage sold by length (half-metre or metre).

🚗 *Take the An der Staatsstrasse, which becomes Sulzfelder Strasse to Segnitz, where a signposted left turn brings drivers to the bridge to Marktbreit.*

The Mainschleife

The Mainschleife is a loop-like meander of the Main river east of Würzburg at a point where the landscape has a particularly gentle beauty, framed by low, vine-covered hillsides and dotted with attractive small villages. The local explanation for the Main river's eccentric course at this point is that it is here the river feels most at home. One excellent way to enjoy the area's beauty is by bicycle or e-bike (*Zweirad Weissensee, Im Seelein 14, Volkach; 09381 39 88; www.zweirad-weissensee.de*) on the annual car-free Sunday in mid-May.

Above Late-medieval Rathaus in Dettelbach
Below Meandering Mainschleife-Main river east of Würzburg

EAT AND DRINK

EBRACH

Klosterbräu *moderate*
Prize-winning interpretations of traditional Franconian cuisine are served in the abbey's 18th-century guesthouse. The large beer garden is a good place to try the home-brewed, dark Klosterbier, or the house wine.
Marktplatz 4, 96157; 09553 180; www.landidyll.com; closed Thu, Jan & Feb

PRICHSENSTADT

Zur Prichsenstadter Krone *moderate*
This modern family-run restaurant of the Weingut Wagner (winery) offers excellent Franconian dishes with Silvaner or Müller-Thurgau white wines and Regent and Acolon red wines.
Karlsplatz 11, 97357; 09383 6549; www.weingutwagner.de; closed Mon–Wed

VOLKACH

Weinstock *expensive*
Set in the Schwane Hotel, this classy gourmet restaurant features "aroma menus'" conjured by Michelin-starred chef Steffen Szabo. Enjoy delicious vegetarian dishes such as sweet potato, grapefruit and yogurt, or scallops with carrot and physalis.
Hauptstrasse 12, 97332; 09381 806 60; www.schwane.de; closed Mon–Wed & Aug

DETTELBACH

Café Kehl *inexpensive*
One of the nicest places to try Dettelbach's famous fat-free biscuits and the *Muskazinen*, the Café Kehl is a snug and rustic café that serves good coffee and cakes.
Eichgasse 5, 97337; 09324 973 00; www.cafe-kehl.de

Right Outdoor café outside tall, half-timbered houses, Ochsenfurt **Below** Vineyards near the small town of Marktbreit

VISITING WÜRZBURG

Parking
The 600-space Marktgarage underground car park, beneath the Marktplatz, is near the tourist information office.

Tourist Information
Falkenhaus, Marktplatz 9, 97070; 09313 723 98; www.wuerzburg.de; May–Oct: open daily; Nov–Apr: closed Sun & Mon

WHERE TO STAY

MARKTBREIT

Hotel Löwen *moderate*
Located close to the Rathaus, the rooms at this splendid half-timbered inn vary in style from rustic to elegant.
Marktstrasse 8, 97340; 09332 505 40; www.loewen-marktbreit.de

OCHSENFURT

Gasthof Bären *moderate*
This traditional hotel and restaurant at the entrance to Ochsenfurt's old town has 24 refurbished rooms, each with an en-suite bathroom and TV.
Hauptstrasse 74, 97199; 09331 86 60; www.gasthof-baeren-ochsenfurt.de

WÜRZBURG

Zur Stadt Mainz *moderate*
Established in 1403, this is the oldest hotel in town. It has comfortable rooms and a traditional restaurant.
Semmelstrasse 39, 97070; 09312 06 77 70; www.hotel-stadtmainz.de; closed Wed

Hotel Rebstock *expensive*
With a magnificent Rococo façade and a history that goes back to 1408, this hotel has individually designed rooms in a tasteful, contemporary style. The restaurant is one of Würzburg's best.
Neubaustrasse 7, 97070; 09313 09 30; www.rebstock.com

ASCHAFFENBURG

Wilder Mann *moderate*
On the edge of the old town, this is a historic four-star hotel that has 68 en-suite rooms. The 600-year-old, half-timbered Goldener Karpfen opposite is run by the same group.
Löherstrasse 51, 63739; 06021 30 20; www.hotel-wilder-mann.de

⑭ Marktbreit
Bavaria; 97340

Marktbreit was once a significant centre for trade between the Main and the Danube. With a splendid gabled Renaissance **Rathaus** of chateau-like proportions and a number of imposing merchants' houses, this town has an architectural heritage that outshines its relatively modest present-day importance. It was the birthplace of the psychiatrist and neuropathologist Alois Alzheimer (1864–1915), after whom the degenerative brain disease is named.

🚗 *Take Ochsenfurter Strasse, following signs for Stadtmitte (city centre) to Ochsenfurt's old town.*

⑮ Ochsenfurt
Bavaria; 97199

Though its outskirts are somewhat disfigured by the sugar works for which it is known, Ochsenfurt preserves a historic **Altstadt** (old town) behind high medieval walls. The focal point is the 16th-century **Rathaus**, with a clock upon which miniature figures perform each hour. The

14th–15th-century **Stadtpfarrkirche St Andreas,** St Andreas's church, contains a statue of St Nicholas by sculptor Tilman Riemenschneider (1460–1531), while alongside the wall is the **Palatium**, the seat of the Würzburg cathedral chapter between 1334 and 1810.

🚗 *Cross the Main on the B13 and continue to Würzburg.*

⑯ Würzburg
Bavaria; 97070

One of Franconia's finest historic cities, Würzburg rose from the ashes after being destroyed in World War II. It was the home of sculptor Tilman Riemenschneider and his woodcarvings can be seen at the **Museum für Franken** *(closed Mon)* in the **Marienberg** fortress above the city. The 18th-century **Residenz** *(open daily)* is Bavaria's enchanting Baroque palace, designed by the German architect Balthasar Neumann and the Viennese architect Johann Lukas von Hildebrandt for Prince-Bishop Johann Philipp Franz von Schönborn.

Sculpture in Würzburg's magnificent Residenz

🚗 *Take the B8, following signs to Marktheidenfeld. At Marktheidenfeld, take the signposted left turn to*

Franconian Wine
Würzburg's traditional *Weinstuben* (wine bars) are excellent places to try Franconia's dry white wines, which are as distinctive as the stubby *Bocksbeutel* in which they are bottled. The climate encourages the use of earlier-ripening grape varieties, with Silvaner being the best known; Müller-Thurgau, also known as Rivaner, and Bacchus are also popular as well. Red wines are grown in the western part of the region, close to Aschaffenburg.

Wertheim. Turn right on the road signposted to Wertheim. Parking is available along the riverside.

⑰ Wertheim
Baden-Württemberg; 97877
Wertheim has a pretty **Altstadt** on a wedge of land at the confluence of the Tauber and Main rivers. The town is overlooked by **Burg Wertheim** *(open daily)*, a castle that has been a ruin since the Thirty Years' War. Today, Wertheim is known above all for its shops, in particular at Wertheim Village *(open Mon–Sat)*, a shopping centre just east of town.
🚗 *Continue along the south bank of the Main to reach Miltenberg.*

⑱ Miltenberg am Main
Bavaria; 63897
Miltenberg am Main stands on a tight bend in the Main river and, until 1803, was part of the territories of the Mainz Prince-Bishops. The focal point of the Altstadt here is the **Marktplatz** (marketplace), fringed by half-timbered houses and with a Renaissance fountain, the **Marktbrunnen**, which dates from 1583. The statue in the centre depicts Justice.

🚗 *Cross the Main and then follow Brückenstrasse to reach Klingenberg.*

⑲ Klingenberg
Bavaria; 63911
Klingenberg lies at the foot of steep slopes on the **Fränkische Rotwein Wanderweg**, a footpath through the red wine country of Lower Franconia (Unterfranken). The ruins of the medieval Clingenburg castle host the annual wine festival. There's an observation tower *(open Sat & Sun)* for admiring the views across the valley.
🚗 *Follow the road along the river to Aschaffenburg.*

⑳ Aschaffenburg
Bavaria; 63739
Aschaffenburg is dominated by the Renaissance **Schloss Johannisburg** *(closed Mon)*, built for the Mainz Prince-Bishops between 1605 and 1614. Inside, visitors can see the princely apartments and admire a selection of Old Masters as well as the world's largest collection of cork architectural models. Overlooking the Main nearby is the **Pompejanum** *(Apr–Oct: closed Mon)*, a re-creation of a Roman villa built for the Bavarian King Ludwig I between 1840 and 1848.

Above left Spectacular fresco in the Residenz, Würzburg **Above** Imposing fortress of Marienberg, Würzburg

VISITING ASCHAFFENBURG

Parking
The underground car park at Stadthalle is near the tourist information office.

Tourist Information
Schlossplatz 2, 63739; 06021 39 58 00; www.info-aschaffenburg.de

EAT AND DRINK

MARKTBREIT
Löwen *moderate*
Seasonal produce from the region is the mainstay of this traditional dining room.
Marktstrasse 8, 97340; 09332 505 40; www.loewen-marktbreit.de; closed Mon

WÜRZBURG
Weinhaus Stachel *expensive*
Regional and organic produce are on the menu in this historic *Weinstube*.
Gressengasse 1, 97070; 09315 27 70; www.weinhaus-stachel.de; closed Sun & Mon

ASCHAFFENBURG
Theater Klause *moderate*
This place serves regional dishes with local beers and wine.
Metzgergasse 7, 63739; 06021 220 74; www.theaterklause-ab.de; closed Tue

---

DAY TRIP OPTIONS
Bayreuth and Bamberg make great bases for day trips around the region.

Architectural wonders
In Bamberg ❻, admire the frescoes on the old town hall and the Baroque architecture on a visit to Vierzehnheiligen ❼, and its pilgrimage church designed by Balthasar Neumann. Then head for Schloss Weissenstein ❽, the

ancestral home of the Schönborn family, who provided the region with many of its Prince-Bishops.
Head north to Vierzehnheiligen on the B4, returning to Bamberg to take the B22 towards Pommersfelden.

Wine and dine
Discover the scenic wine-growing country around Würzburg ⓰ with a day trip to the Mainschleife. Start at Prichsenstadt ❿ before lunch and

a winery visit at Volkach ⓫, then continue south to Dettelbach ⓬ to sample the delicious *Muskazinen* biscuits. Return to Würzburg for a leisurely dinner in one of the city's old traditional restaurants.

Head east to Prichsenstadt along the A3, continuing to Volkach, then south along the Main to Dettelbach. Return to Würzburg on the B22 and B8.

TRIP 17

JURASSIC CRAGS AND FEUDAL FIEFDOMS
Ingolstadt to Landshut

HIGHLIGHTS

Jurassic park
Discover Naturpark Altmühltal's dramatic
limestone crags and Jurassic fossils

Divine inspiration
Enjoy the rich artistic legacy of the region's
complex religious history

The Donaudurchbruch
Visit the lovely wooded stretch of the Danube,
where the pretty landscape is punctuated
with architectural delights

Beer culture
Look out for the region's distinctive hop-growing
frames before sampling the excellent local beers

JURASSIC CRAGS AND FEUDAL FIEFDOMS

Jurassic geology adds drama to the gentle landscapes of Bavaria's Naturpark Altmühltal, one of Germany's largest nature reserves. Castle-topped crags stand sentinel over the valley of the placid Altmühl river that flows east to join the Main-Donau canal and the Danube. Along the way, there are small towns of great historic and architectural interest, while the Danube has produced a landscape of extraordinary loveliness in the narrow gorge known as the Donaudurchbruch. Gourmets will enjoy the hearty regional fare served in rustic surroundings, while the Hallertau district to the south of Ingolstadt and Kelheim is the world's largest hop-growing region, supplying not only Munich's internationally renowned brands but also local brewers, whose beers are worth sampling.

ACTIVITIES

Admire Eichstätt's varied handicrafts, from ceramics and soap to jewellery

Take a hike on the Altmühltal Panoramaweg path at Solnhofen

Hire a canoe and paddle down the slow-flowing Altmühl river

Cruise the Danube on a boat trip through the Donaudurchbruch gorge near the Befreiungshalle

Take a tour of the breweries at Kelheim or Weltenburg to soak up the local culture

Above Panoramic view of the Willibaldsburg in Eichstätt, *see p186* **Below left** Cafés outside the old town hall, Ingolstadt, *see p184*

PLAN YOUR DRIVE

Start/finish: Ingolstadt to Landshut.

Number of days: 3 days, allowing half a day to explore Neuburg an der Donau.

Distance: 292 km (181 miles).

Road conditions: Roads have gentle inclines and are well signposted; snow and ice can be a problem in winter.

When to go: May to October is the best time to enjoy the scenery, while Christmas markets and snow ensure a magical atmosphere in December.

Opening times: Most attractions are open daily. Shops are open from 9am to 6pm, Monday to Friday, and close early on Saturdays.

Main market days: Ingolstadt, Neuburg an der Donau, Eichstätt: Wed, Sat; Landshut: Fri.

Major festivals: Beilngries: Bayerische Zwiebelmarkt (Bavarian onion market), biennial, Oct; Neuburg an der Donau: Schlossfest (castle festival), biennial, Jun–Jul, next in 2023; Landshut: Landshuter Hochzeit (Landshut wedding), every four years in Jun & Jul, next in 2023.

DAY TRIP OPTIONS

Art and architecture buffs will enjoy the historic **cathedrals**, **castles** and **museums** of Neuburg an der Donau and Eichstätt, while **families** can hunt for **fossils** in Eichstätt and Solnhofen. **Lovers of scenic grandeur** will appreciate the remarkable landscape of Eichstätt. For full details, *see p189*.

Below Brewer's dray, Kelheim, *see p188*

Above Imposing Neues Schloss in Ingolstadt **Above right** Baroque interior of St.-Maria-de-Victoria-Kirche, Ingolstadt

VISITING INGOLSTADT

Parking
Ample parking is available beneath the Stadttheater, along the northern Danube embankment.

Tourist Information
Moritzstrasse 19, 85049; 08413 05 30 30; www.ingolstadt–tourismus.de; Apr–Oct: open daily; Nov–Mar: closed Sat & Sun

VISITING NEUBURG AN DER DONAU

Parking
There is parking along Luitpoldstrasse, as well as in the underground Tiefgarage Schrannenplatz along Weinstrasse.

Tourist Information
Ottheinrichplatz A118, 86633; 08431 552 40; www.neuburg-donau.de; Good Friday–Oct: open daily; Nov–Good Friday: open Mon–Fri

WHERE TO STAY

INGOLSTADT

Altstadthotel moderate
Comfortable rooms, a sauna and a hot tub feature at this hotel. Of the 41 rooms, the larger ones facing the courtyard are recommended.
Gymnasiumstrasse 9, 85049; 08418 86 90; www.altstadthotel-ingolstadt.de

NEUBURG AN DER DONAU

Gasthaus Zur Blauen Traube inexpensive
This historic inn dates from 1701 and has a restaurant that serves traditional Bavarian fare.
Amalienstrasse 49, 86633; 08431 83 92; www.zur-blauen-traube.de

Hotel-Gasthof Bergbauer moderate
A few minutes' walk from the Obere Altstadt district, this hotel has modern decor as well as a restaurant.
Fünfzehnerstrasse 11, 86633; 08431 61 68 90; www.hotel-gasthof-bergbauer.de

❶ Ingolstadt
Bavaria; 85049
Located on the Danube, bustling Ingolstadt was once a formidable fortress and, in the Middle Ages, capital of the Duchy of Bayern-Ingolstadt. The town houses many important historic buildings, including the whitewashed Gothic **Neues Schloss** (closed Mon), home to Germany's oldest military museum; the brick-built Liebfrauenmünster (open daily), the largest late-Gothic hall church in Bavaria, with seven storeys of attics in its roof; and the Baroque church, **St.-Maria-de-Victoria-Kirche**, a masterpiece by the renowned Asam brothers of Munich.

🚗 *Leaving Ingolstadt, follow the B13/Neuburgerstrasse west, bearing left 8 km (5 miles) west of the town to Neuburg an der Donau.*

❷ NEUBURG AN DER DONAU
Bavaria; 86633
With a splendid Renaissance Schloss overlooking the Danube and a compact old town, this historic Residenzstadt, or feudal seat, has architectural glories that outstrip its modest present-day status. From 1505, it was the capital of the independent principality of Pfalz-Neuburg for 300 years. Be sure to sample the Schrobenhausen asparagus, harvested from mid-April to mid-June in the countryside to the south.

A two-hour walking tour
Park the car on Luitpoldstrasse at the foot of the Obere Altstadt (upper town), and ascend the broad stone steps to pick up a free map from the tourist office on Ottheinrichplatz. Turn right at the **Stadttheater** ①, a former ducal grain warehouse, following Residenzstrasse to reach the main portal of **Schloss Neuburg** ②. This magnificent Renaissance palace was built between 1530 and 1545 for Ottheinrich, the first Count Palatinate of Neuburg. Following a makeover, it became one of the earliest Baroque palaces in Germany.

Visit the **Schlosskapelle** ③ *(open daily)*, a little further to the right, before entering the palace. The first purpose-built Protestant church in Bavaria, it is decorated with frescoes. The arcaded inner courtyard, or *Schlosshof*, has faded murals depicting scenes from the Old Testament. Created by Hans Schroer some time after 1555, the murals remained long buried beneath a coat of paint and were only rediscovered in the 1960s. The palace houses the Schlossmuseum *(closed Mon)*, whose varied exhibits include the Bavarian state collection of Flemish Baroque painting, with works by Rubens and Jacob Jordaens. Inside the Schloss, the grandest room is the Renaissance Rittersaal, or Knights' Hall, in the north wing, with a heavy wooden ceiling and stout stone columns. Return to the palace entrance and stop for refreshments at the **Vivat** ④, a wine bar opposite, then ascend the gentle slope of Amalienstrasse, which is lined with town houses from the 16th–18th centuries. Halfway along Amalienstrasse is Karlsplatz, around which Neuburg's principal civic buildings are ranged. These include the late-Renaissance Hofkirche Unsere Liebe Frau (Court Church of Our Dear Lady), the **Rathaus** ⑤ or town hall – a Renaissance palazzo built by Josef Heintz and Alexander Pasqualini between 1603 and 1609 – and the Rococo **Provinzialbibliothek** ⑥ or provincial library *(May–Oct: guided tours Wed & Sun; 08431 552 40)*. Dating from 1731, it has a Baroque hall on its upper floor. The neighbouring **Weveldhaus** ⑦ is a fine example of a nobleman's town house. Built in 1517 and raised by one storey in 1713, it has graceful stucco ceilings and houses the Stadtmuseum *(closed Mon & Dec– mid-Mar)* with well-presented displays on the town's history. Continue along Amalienstrasse to reach the **Obere Tor** ⑧, a Renaissance gateway whose terracotta-coloured gable marks the western exit from the Obere Altstadt. Decorated with Neuburg's heraldic crest, it depicts Ottheinrich and his brother, Philipp. Pass through the gate

Column in Karlsplatz, Neuburg an der Donau

to Wolfgang-Wilhelm-Platz and the Hützeldörr, the southern portion of the garden. Return to the Obere Tor, pass through the gate and turn right into **Herrenstrasse** ⑨, which has some historic houses. It leads to the Luitpoldstrasse car park via Landschaftsstrasse.

🚗 *From Luitpoldstrasse, head north over Elisenbrucke, following signs for Eichstätt. After a few kilometres, turn left at the signpost for Bergen.*

Reformation and Counter-Reformation

Neuburg's pragmatic rulers straddled the religious divisions of 16th- and 17th-century Germany. Ottheinrich condemned Lutheranism in 1522 but converted in 1542; a later Count Palatinate, Wolfgang Wilhelm (1578–1653), converted back to Catholicism to inherit his mother's estate.

③ Bergen
Bavaria; 86633

Nestled in the rolling countryside between the Danube and Altmühl, this village has the **Heilig-Kreuz-Kirche** pilgrimage church, whose white-and-gold Baroque interior by the Eichstätt court architect Giovanni Domenico Barbieri dates from 1756. Visit the Romanesque crypt; water from the well in the north aisle was once believed to have healing properties.

🚗 *Return to the T-junction, then turn left and head to Nassenfels. Take Eichstätter Strasse, pass Adelschlag to get on to the B13, following signs to Eichstätt.*

Above Schloss overlooking the Danube, Neuburg an der Donau **Below** Arcaded courtyard of Schloss Neuburg, Neuburg an der Donau

EAT AND DRINK

INGOLSTADT
Gaststätte Daniel *inexpensive*
Ingolstadt's oldest restaurant, dating back to 1471, provides an atmospheric setting for traditional Bavarian cooking and Herrnbräu beers.
Roseneckstrasse 1, 85049; 08413 52 72; closed Mon

Zum Kuchlbauer *inexpensive*
Rustic beams and masses of brewing paraphernalia ensure that this "beer museum" lives up to its name. Try the roast pork marinated in strong beer with a mug of the delicious, dark Kuchlbauer Vollbier Dunkel.
Schäffbräustrasse 11a, 85049; 08413 55 12; www.zum-kuchlbauer-ingolstadt.de

NEUBURG AN DER DONAU
Neuwirt *moderate*
Seasonal produce, including Schrobenhausen asparagus, potatoes and game, feature on the menu of this restaurant, which serves local beers.
Färberstrasse 88, 86633; 08431 20 78; www.neuwirt-neuburg.de; closed Tue

Right The Altmühl Valley from Willibaldsburg, Eichstätt **Centre right** Bishop's palace in the Residenzplatz, Eichstätt **Below** Limestone crags, Altmühl Valley

VISITING EICHSTÄTT

Parking
On quiet days, it is relatively easy to find on-street parking in the town centre. Drivers can also use the Altstadt car park on Ostenstrasse.

Tourist Information
Domplatz 8, 85072; 08421 600 14 00; www.eichstaett.info; Apr–Oct: open daily; Nov–Mar: open Mon–Fri

WHERE TO STAY

EICHSTÄTT
Waldgasthof zum Geländer moderate
Situated in a tranquil forest clearing just north of Eichstätt, this three-star hotel offers comfortable modern rooms and excellent regional cuisine in its award-winning restaurant.
B13, Geländer 1, Eichstätt-Weissenburg 85132; 08421 93 77 70; www.waldgasthof-gelaender.de

PAPPENHEIM
Zum Goldenen Hirschen inexpensive
Tucked behind the gabled Renaissance façade of this 16th-century former brewery, in the heart of Pappenheim, are 14 atmospheric and tastefully renovated rooms and suites.
Marktplatz 4, 91788; 09143 434; www.gasthof-zum-goldenen-hirschen.de

BEILNGRIES
Der Millipp moderate
This stylish, half-timbered, 16th-century hotel in the historic town of Beilngries has 34 charming rooms.
Hauptstrasse 9, 92339; 08461 12 03; www.der.millipp.de

④ Eichstätt
Bavaria; 85072
The university town of Eichstätt, an independent Catholic bishopric for centuries, retains the feel of a miniature capital city. The **Dom** is remarkable for its Gothic Pappenheim altar, but Baroque architecture transformed the town after the Thirty Years' War. This is most apparent in the **Residenzplatz**, which is dominated by the bishops' palace. High above the town, the castle of **Willibaldsburg** houses the **Jura Museum** (closed Mon), with Jurassic-era fossils from the surrounding district.

Explore Eichstätt's dinosaur trails by picking up a map from the tourist office to follow the Fossilienpfad or fossil path, which leads to the fossil quarry at Blumenberg. Afterwards, ask at the tourist office for information about visiting the town's artist's studios and crafts workshops.

 Take the B13/ Weissenburger Strasse, turn left on to Rebdorfer Strasse after the bridge at the signpost for Solnhofen. Follow the road along the Altmühl Valley to the Zwölf Apostel. Continue past it to the car park just before Solnhofen village.

⑤ The Zwölf Apostel
Bavaria; 91807
The dolomite outcrops known as the Zwölf Apostel (Twelve Apostles) at Solnhofen are among the most impressive of the Altmühl Valley's Jurassic landforms. Easily reached along the Panoramaweg footpath from the car park west of the cliffs, this site is a nature reserve. The 200-km (124-mile) Altmühltal Panoramaweg hiking trail (www.naturpark-altmuehltal.de) is a relaxing way of discovering the valley. The area southwest of Solnhofen has yielded many of the region's fossils, while to the east, at **Dollnstein**, canoes can be hired on the Altmühl river (www.kanuvermietung-altmuehltal.de).

 Continue north to Pappenheim.

Fascinating Geology
Solnhofen's fossils were formed in a salty lagoon on the edge of the sea. The animals that died in the lagoon were well preserved due to the lack of oxygen in the water. Among the specimens found are those of the earliest known bird, archaeopteryx.

⑥ Pappenheim
Bavaria; 91788

With its picturesque setting and historic architecture, Pappenheim is one of the most attractive small towns in the region. Impressive 18th- and 19th-century houses line the main street, Deisingerstrasse, where the merchant's house at No. 16 has an inscription giving the date of its construction as the year 5608, according to the Jewish calendar. In the Middle Ages, Pappenheim was the seat of the Holy Roman Empire's field marshal, but today there is nothing warlike about this sleepy, ruritanian town. It is dominated by a romantic ruined **castle** (*closed Mon*) that hosts one of the region's most atmospheric Christmas markets. Pappenheim also has two stately palaces – the festive-looking Renaissance **Altes Schloss**, or old palace, and the Neo-Classical new palace, or **Neues Schloss**, built between 1819 and 1820 by Bavarian court architect, Leo von Klenze.

🚗 *Return to Eichstätt via Solnhofen, and enter the town on the B13. Turn left at the roundabout following signs for Kinding and Beilngries.*

Romans and Bavarians
The Limes – the frontier between the Roman Empire and the Germanic tribes – passed through the Altmühl region. A museum (*Apr–Dec: open daily; Jan–Mar: open Sun*) at Kipfenberg Castle, between Eichstätt and Beilngries, tells both sides of the story.

⑦ Beilngries
Bavaria; 92339

Children and adults alike will be charmed by the magical old toys and dolls at Beilngries's **Spielzeugmuseum** (*Apr–Oct: open daily; Nov–Mar: open Wed, Sat & Sun pm; www.museen-anno-dazumal.de*). Take a stroll around the picturesque **Innerer Graben** street in the old town, which reveals the toy-town dimensions of the medieval fortifications, complete with nine of the original twelve 15th-century towers. With its characterful old inns, the town is a good base for exploring this part of the Altmühl Valley.

🚗 *Take the Kelheimer Strasse/B299, then turn left following signs for Dietfurt/Kelheim. Continue beyond Dietfurt along the the the north bank of the Main-Donau canal to Prunn. At Prunn, turn left to get on to a minor road, which ascends to the castle car park.*

Left Tall Romanesque tower, a remnant of Beilngries's medieval fortifications **Below left** Willibaldsburg, perched on a hill above Eichstätt **Below right** Tomb of St Willibald at the Willibaldsburg in Eichstätt

SHOPPING IN EICHSTÄTT

Eichstätt has plenty of shops with fine handicrafts. At **Goldschmiede Berger** (*Marktplatz 9, 85072; 08421 84 38*), visitors can shop for exquisite gold jewellery. **Seifenmanufaktur Lau** (*Bahnhofplatz 11, 85072; 01511 740 33 40*) is a famous soap shop here. **Wölfl Huthaus** (*Marktplatz 12, 85072; 08421 16 20*) sells a wide range of hats.

EAT AND DRINK

EICHSTÄTT

Gasthof Krone *inexpensive*
Altmühl Valley lamb is the speciality of this snug, welcoming *Gasthof* (inn) opposite Eichstätt's cathedral. The emphasis here is on local and seasonal produce and there's a pleasant beer garden in summer. *Domplatz 3, 85072; 08421 44 06; www.krone-eichstaett.de*

BEILNGRIES

Der Millipp *moderate*
Regional produce dominates the menu of this historic old guesthouse and butcher's shop in the old town of Beilngries. The setting is simple but elegant, with pretty, rustic furniture, wood and pale colours. In summer, there is also a beer garden. *Hauptstrasse 9, 92339; 08461 12 03; www.der.millipp.de*

Right Gabled burghers' houses in the centre of Landshut **Below left** Paintings on a shop's façade in Landshut **Below right** Scenic view of the Danube and the Befreiungshalle

DANUBE BOAT CRUISES

Several boat cruises through the Donaudurchburch between Kelheim and Kloster Weltenburg are available daily from late March to the end of October. During the peak season, from late April to mid-October, there is at least one boat every 45 minutes in both directions, with greater frequency on weekends. *www.schiffahrt-kelheim.de*

WHERE TO STAY

AROUND THE BEFREIUNGSHALLE
Weisses Lamm *moderate*
A traditional small-town inn next to one of Kelheim's town gates, the Weisses Lamm has comfortable rooms. Its welcoming restaurant serves good regional dishes and Weltenburg beer.
Ludwigstrasse 12, 93309 Kelheim (east of the Befreiungshalle); 09441 200 90; www.weisses-lamm-kelheim.de

LANDSHUT
Goldene Sonne *moderate*
This smart and comfortable family-run hotel, housed in a gabled house with beams and attics, has views over the old town and Burg Trausnitz. The hotel's restaurant serves Bavarian and Italian cuisine.
Neustadt 520, 84028; 0871 925 30; www.goldenesonne.de

⑧ Burg Prunn
Bavaria; 93339

Its gravity-defying site atop a crag makes the medieval castle of Prunn *(Apr–Oct: open daily, Nov–mid-Mar: closed Mon; guided tours only)* perhaps the most photogenic of the Altmühltal's fortresses. In the Middle Ages, under the Frauenberg knights of Haag, it was an important cultural centre; fragments of frescoes survive from this period. Later, the castle passed to the Jesuits, who crafted the rich stuccowork in its chapel. The views from the castle, up the Altmühl Valley along the Main-Donau canal, are spectacular. Opposite the castle gates is a restaurant and café, the Burgschenke Schloss Prunn, serving snacks and cakes as well as full meals.
🚗 *From the car park, return to Prunn village, turn left and then continue to Kelheim. At Kelheim turn right over the bridge along Alleestrasse toward the town centre. Turn right again up Hienheimer Strasse to reach Befreiungshalle, which is signposted.*

⑨ The Befreiungshalle
Bavaria; 93309

High above the modest town of Kelheim lies the vast Neo-Classical Befreiungshalle, or Liberation Hall *(open daily)*, which guards the entrance to the Donaudurchbruch gorge. It was commissioned by the Bavarian King Ludwig I to commemorate victory over Napoleon's armies in the wars of 1813–15. The circular, domed interior has 34 winged angels of victory. Stairs lead to a viewing platform that has superb views over Kelheim and the gorge. Next, take a boat cruise *(late Mar–Oct: daily; www.schiffahrt-kelheim.de)* up the Danube, passing through the lovely **Donaudurchbruch gorge**. End the day exploring **Kloster Weltenburg** followed by a traditional meal paired with its monastery-brewed dark beer.
🚗 *Return to Kelheim, turn right along Alleestrasse and right again at the fork to reach the bridge across the Danube; on the south side, take the road to Weltenburg. Park in the riverside car park or in Kelheim and take the boat.*

Left Picturesque Kloster Weltenburg on the Danube near Kelheim

VISITING LANDSHUT

Parking
The well-signposted car park beneath the City Center mall is convenient for the old town's main sights.

Tourist Information
Altes Rathaus, Altstadt 315, 84028; 08719 220 50; www.landshut-tourismus.bayern; closed Sun

BREWERIES

Sample the local brew at the Schneider-Weisse brewery's **Weisses Bräuhaus** *(Emil-Ott-Strasse 3; 09441 34 80; www.weisses-brauhaus-kelheim.de)* in Kelheim or at Kloster Weltenburg's **Klosterschenke** *(Asamstrasse 32, Kelheim; 09441 675 70; www.klosterschenke-weltenburg.de; closed mid-Dec–mid-Mar)*, where the malty Barock Dunkel is a speciality.

EAT AND DRINK

AROUND THE BEFREIUNGSHALLE

Gasthof Berzl *inexpensive*
A traditional, family-run inn next to the Altmühl gate, this place offers excellent meat and homemade sausages.
Hafnergasse 2, 93309 Kelheim (east of the Befreiungshalle); 09441 14 25; www.gasthof-berzl-kelheim.de; closed Wed

LANDSHUT

Restaurant Stegfellner *moderate*
Tucked above a Gothic vaulted shop, this restaurant serves Bavarian cuisine.
Altstadt 71, 84028; 0871 280 15; www.stegfellner-landshut.de; closed Sun

Other options
Coffee with cake is a German ritual and can be enjoyed at **Café-Conditorei Belstner** *(Altstadt 295, 84028; 0871 221 90; www.cafe-belstner.de).*

Hop-growing
The Hallertau district between Kelheim and Landshut is the world's largest hop-growing region. Hops are climbing plants and the distinctive posts and wires of hop fields enable the plant to grow high. Flowers from the female plant are used in the brewing process.

⑩ Kloster Weltenburg
Bavaria; 93309
The Benedictine Abbey of Weltenburg has a Baroque chapel designed by the Asam brothers and the world's oldest abbey brewery *(tours Apr–Oct: open Sat & Sun)*. Its beautiful setting by the Danube is the highlight here. The most popular way to arrive is on a boat trip *(late Mar–Oct)* through the wooded gorge from Kelheim.

🚗 *Return to Kelheim, following Regensburger Strasse on the south bank of the Danube to the B16, before taking the road via Rohr in Niederbayern to Alzhausen. Here, the road continues via Rottenburg an der Laaber to Landshut and then on Altdorfer Strasse.*

⑪ Landshut
Bavaria; 84028
The broad main streets of Landshut's handsome old town are lined with fine gabled houses overlooked by the slender 130-m (427-ft) high brick tower of the Gothic **St Martinskirche**. The **Stadtresidenz** *(closed for renovations until spring 2023)*, or town palace, has a lovely inner courtyard in Italian Renaissance style. Looming over the town is **Burg Trausnitz** *(tours daily)*, the ancestral castle of Bavaria's royal family, the Wittelsbachs.

Above Pretty staircase in Burg Trausnitz, Landshut

DAY TRIP OPTIONS
Ingolstadt and Eichstätt are good bases for day trips.

Art and architecture
Explore Ingolstadt's ❶ historic old town, then head to Neuburg an der Donau ❷ to admire the impressive castles of the Counts Palatinate before continuing via the pilgrimage church at Bergen ❸ to the delightful cathedral city of Eichstätt ❹.

Head west from Ingolstadt on the B13. From Neuburg an der Donau, follow signs for Eichstätt and Bergen. From Bergen, follow signs to Eichstätt on the B13. Return to Ingolstadt on the B13.

Photographer's treat
Follow the fascinating dinosaur trail in and around Eichstätt ❹ before heading to inspect the spectacular Jurassic fossils at Eichstätt's Jura Museum in the attractive castle of Willibaldsburg. Next, head to Solnhofen to admire the impressive limestone crags, the Zwölf Apostel ❺.

Head west towards Solnhofen along the Altmühl Valley to reach Solnhofen, returning by the same route.

TRIP 18

THE NORTHERN ROMANTIC ROAD
Würzburg to Donauwörth

HIGHLIGHTS

Old-world charm
Experience the world of knights and princes, from
Würzburg's Residenz to Burg Harburg

Local wines
Taste the local Taubertal and Franconian wines in
one of Würzburg's traditional Weinstuben

Medieval time travel
Be enchanted by the medieval towns of Rothenburg
ob der Tauber, Dinkelsbühl and Nördlingen

Exquisite scenery
Enjoy the magnificent countryside, from vine-clad
slopes to wooded hills and the extraordinary
landscape of the Ries Crater

THE NORTHERN ROMANTIC ROAD

The northern section of Germany's most celebrated travel route is characterized by its breathtaking landscape. Rolling countryside provides a picturesque setting for small historic towns strung out along the rivers Tauber and Wörnitz. This tour passes through the medieval townscapes of Rothenburg ob der Tauber and Dinkelsbühl. Further south, Nördlingen combines spectacular beauty with its curious setting in the Ries Crater. This is by no means an unknown corner of Germany, but its popularity has not dimmed its charm: hotels are characterful, regional cooking is hearty, and there are crisp Baden or Franken wines from vineyards to enjoy along the way.

Above Cycle path beside the main road to Nördlingen, *see pp198–9*

ACTIVITIES

Take a hike past vineyards, castles and churches on the long-distance footpath that follows the "Romantic Road"

Sample the wines of the Tauber Valley, where a cycle route runs along the vineyard trail on the boundary between Bavaria and Baden Württemberg

Encounter wildlife at Bad Mergentheim's Wildpark, where the attractions include deer, lynx, brown bears and a pack of wolves

Discover Rothenburg ob der Tauber on an English-language evening walk with the town's night-watchman

Take a walk along the signposted footpaths of the Geopark Ries for a close view of the meteorite crater

Below Courtyard and well, Burg Harburg, *see p199*

Above Resplendent Schlossgarten, Weikersheim, *see p195*

PLAN YOUR DRIVE

Start/finish: Würzburg to Donauwörth.

Number of days: 3–4 days, allowing half a day to explore Rothenburg ob der Tauber.

Distance: 215 km (134 miles).

Road conditions: The route is marked with brown "Romantische Strasse" signposts. Roads are generally well paved, with gentle inclines. However, some stretches in the Tauber Valley are narrow.

When to go: May to October is a good time to drive along this scenic route. Lively Christmas markets are an added attraction in December.

Opening times: Most attractions are open daily, while shops are open from 9am to 6pm, Monday to Friday, and close early on Saturdays.

Major festivals: Rothenburg ob der Tauber: Meistertrunk (historical re-enactment), May; Feuchtwangen: Kreuzgangspiele (theatre festival), end May–Aug; Dinkelsbühl: Kinderzeche (children's and folklore festival), Jul; Nördlingen: Historisches Stadtmauerfest (town walls festival), every three years in Sep, next in 2022; Donauwörth: Schwäbischwerder Kindertag (children's historical procession), Jul.

DAY TRIP OPTIONS

The northern section of this wine-producing country will be of special interest to **wine lovers**, while history-lovers will enjoy a visit to the **historic towns** of Rothenburg ob der Tauber and Nördlingen. For **family fun**, the valley of the Wörnitz river offers plenty of opportunities for **angling**, **kayaking** and **boat trips**. For full details, *see p199*.

Above Bird's-eye view from the Türmersturm, Tauberbischofsheim **Above right** Rose garden in bloom, Schloss Weikersheim **Below right** Festung Marienberg, overlooking the Main river, Würzburg **Below far right** Façade of Deutschordensschloss, Bad Mergentheim

VISITING WÜRZBURG

Parking
The 500-space Marktgarage underground car park is located beneath the Marktplatz and is a convenient spot for visiting the tourist information office.

Tourist Information
Falkenhaus, Marktplatz 9, 97070; 09313 723 98; www.wuerzburg.de; May–Oct: open daily; Nov–Apr: closed Sun

WHERE TO STAY

WÜRZBURG

Steinburg *expensive*
This four-star country house hotel has 69 individually styled rooms. Facilities include an indoor pool and a sauna.
Mittlerer Steinbergweg 100, 97080; 09319 70 20; www.steinburg.com

TAUBERBISCHOFSHEIM

Badischer Hof *moderate*
Located in the town centre, this three-star hotel has well-equipped en-suite rooms, complete with wireless Internet, TV and, in some cases, a balcony.
Sonnenplatz, 97941; 09341 98 80; www.hotelbadischerhof.de

BAD MERGENTHEIM

Hotel Alte Münze *moderate*
The three-star Alte Münze offers 29 simple, modern rooms, including singles and doubles and three suites.
Münzgasse 12, 97980; 07931 56 60; www.hotelaltemuenze.de

WEIKERSHEIM

Laurentius *moderate*
This small hotel, with varying views over vineyards and the Schloss, has just 13 wine-themed rooms. All have a shower, flat-screen TV and Internet.
Marktplatz 5, 97990; 07934 910 80; www.hotel-laurentius.de

① Würzburg
Bavaria; 97070
The capital of Franconia's wine country, Würzburg became an independent prince-bishopric between 1168 and 1803. Occupying a picturesque position on the banks of the Main river, the town features many impressive churches. Of these, the most notable is the Romanesque **Dom St Kilian** *(open daily)*, which was built between 1040 and 1188. Towering above the town, the mighty castle, **Festung Marienberg**, is also worth a visit. One of the later Baroque additions to the fortress, the former arsenal now houses the **Mainfränkisches Museum** with a valuable collection of medieval art treasures *(closed Mon)*. However, Würzburg's greatest attraction is the Baroque **Residenz** *(open daily)*, a palace of the prince-bishops, now a UNESCO World Heritage Site. Built between 1720 and 1744, the centre-piece of the palace is the sumptuous emperor's chamber, the **Kaisersaal**.

🚗 *Take the Röntgenring, cross the Main river then bear left on the B27 as far as the A3, beyond which the Romantische Strasse continues to the* town of Tauberbischofsheim. Park at the back of the Rathaus on Ringstrasse.

② Tauberbischofsheim
Baden-Württemberg; 97941
Formerly part of the territories of the Mainz archbishops, Tauberbischofsheim has an Altstadt, or old town, focused on its **Marktplatz**. The market square is fringed by half-timbered houses and dominated by the Neo-Gothic town hall, or **Rathaus**. On the square is the Baroque house, the Rehhof (1702) and the old **Sternapotheke** (1670), or Star Pharmacy, in a house once occupied by Georg Michael Franck, grandfather of the Romantic poets Clemens and Bettina Brentano. The town's main symbol is the Türmersturm or Türmer's Tower, part of the **Kurmainzisches Schloss**. Dating from 1250, the castle now houses the **Tauberfränkisches Landschaftsmuseum** *(Easter–Oct: open Tue–Sun)*, whose collections include local *Tracht* (peasant costumes) and handicrafts.

🚗 *Take Würzburger Strasse, before turning right on to Mergentheimer Strasse. This becomes the B27 and then, after the A81, the B290.*

③ Bad Mergentheim

Baden-Württemberg; 97980
Set by the Tauber river, Bad
Mergentheim was home to the
Teutonic Knights from 1527 to 1809.
First built in the 12th–13th centuries,
the **Deutschordensschloss** dominates
this leafy little spa town. The castle
houses a **museum** *(closed Mon & Tue)*
with staterooms and displays relating
to the Knights' history. Just south of the
town, **Pfarrkirche** *(closed Mon & Tue)*, the
parish church at Stuppach, contains a
masterpiece, the *Stuppacher Madonna*
(1519), by German Renaissance painter Matthias Grünewald. Around 2 km
(1 mile) from the town is the **Wildpark
Bad Mergentheim** *(Mar–Oct: open
daily; Nov–Feb: open Sat & Sun; 07931
56 30 50; www.wildtierpark.de)*, which
is spread over 35 ha (86 acres), and
features more than 70 species in
a natural setting.

🚗 *Head east along the B19/
Igersheimer Strasse. From Igersheim,
turn right. Follow signs to Weikersheim.*

④ Weikersheim

Baden-Württemberg; 97990
Weikersheim's neat central square
acts as a picturesque frame for
Schloss Weikersheim *(closed Mon)*,
transformed in the 16th century,
on the orders of Count Wolfgang II
of Hohenlohe, into one of Germany's
most beautiful Renaissance palaces.
The highlight of the interior is the
Rittersaal, or knight's hall, a vast
banqueting hall with a magnificent fireplace and painted ceiling.
The Baroque palace garden,
Schlossgarten, is graced by many
fountains and more than 50 statues.

🚗 *Continue along the Tauber Valley.*

---

*Follow signs to Röttingen, taking the
same road to Bieberehren, then drive
south to Creglingen. Herrgottskirche
church is south of the junction with
Rothenburger Strasse; there is parking
on the side of the road.*

The Teutonic Knights

Formed at the end of the 12th
century to protect pilgrims in the
Holy Land, the Order of the Teutonic
Knights of St Mary's Hospital in
Jerusalem turned its attention to
Europe after the Crusades. In the
13th century, it took Christianity and
the German language to the Baltic,
creating the German colony of East
Prussia. After the Order's Grand
Master, Albert of Brandenburg, converted to Lutheranism in 1525, its
seat moved from Königsberg to Bad
Mergentheim. The Order's distinctive
black cross has become famous
as the model for the Iron Cross,
Germany's decoration for gallantry.

---

⑤ Creglingen

Baden-Württemberg; 97993
Upstream from Weikersheim, on
the Bavarian border, is the small
town of Creglingen. Just south
of its half-timbered centre is the
Herrgottskirche *(closed Mon & Jan)*.
This pilgrimage church shelters a
masterpiece by sculptor Tilman
Riemenschneider. Carved between
1493 and 1510, the **Marienaltar** was
so aligned that the central figure
of Mary is lit up through the chapel's
rose window on the Feast of the
Assumption on 15 August.

🚗 *Return to Creglingen, turning
right on to the Romantische Strasse
towards Rothenburg ob der Tauber.*

Centre left Stunning Marienaltar with
Mary as the central figure, Creglingen
Below Pretty rural landscape, Creglingen

HIKING NEAR THE
ROMANTISCHE STRASSE

A long-distance hiking trail runs parallel
to the Romantic Road, threading
through meadows and forests. Visitors
can contact the nearest local tourist
office *(www.romantischestrasse.de)*
for more information.

EAT AND DRINK

WÜRZBURG

Ratskeller *moderate*
The menu at this lovely, atmospheric
restaurant is a mix of steaks, salads
and hearty regional fare, such as
liver dumpling soup or Franconian
bratwurst, all accompanied by
delicious local wines.
*Langgasse 1, 97070; 09311 30 21;
www.wuerzburger-ratskeller.de*

TAUBERBISCHOFSHEIM

Badischer Hof *moderate*
Regional cooking using seasonal
ingredients typifies the menu at
the Badischer Hof, where dishes
such as roast stuffed pork with bread
dumplings or trout with potatoes are
accompanied by wines from the
surrounding district.
*Sonnenplatz, 97941; 09341 98 80;
www.hotelbadischerhof.de; closed Fri*

WEIKERSHEIM

Restaurant im Gewölbe *expensive*
A stone-vaulted cellar is the setting
for Sabine and Jürgen Koch's
gourmet cooking, which fuses
international sophistication with
regional ingredients in dishes such as
sweetbread and veal cheek ragout.
*Marktplatz 5, 97990; 07934 910 80;
www.hotel-laurentius.de;
closed Mon, Tue & Sun dinner*

Above Galgentor, an old execution place, Rothenburg ob der Tauber

VISITING ROTHENBURG OB DER TAUBER

Parking
There are paid car parks at the northern and southern ends of the old town, outside the town walls.

Tourist Information
Marktplatz 2, 91541; 09861 40 48 00; www.rothenburg.de; May–Oct & Dec: open daily; Nov & Jan–Apr: closed Sun

WHERE TO STAY

ROTHENBURG OB DER TAUBER

Eisenhut moderate
Located in the heart of the Altstadt, this old hotel occupies four 16th-century patrician houses. Some of its 78 individually styled rooms have four-poster beds. All have satellite TV, wireless Internet and en-suite bath or shower.
Herrngasse 3–7, 91541; 09861 70 50; www.eisenhut.com

Gasthof Goldener Greifen moderate
This family-run inn offers simple but charming accommodation. Rooms are well equipped.
Obere Schmiedgasse 5, 91541; 09861 22 81; www.gasthof-greifen-rothenburg.de

Burg Hotel expensive
A delightful hotel with lovely views over the Tauber Valley. There are 15 individually decorated rooms and suites, with en-suite bathrooms.
Klostergasse 1–3, 91541; 09861 948 90; www.burghotel.eu

SCHILLINGSFÜRST

Die Post moderate
This hotel offers views over the valley. The in-house distillery produces Obstwasser, the fruity schnapps of the region.
Rothenburger Strasse 1, 91583; 09868 95 00; www.hotel-diepost.de

⑥ ROTHENBURG OB DER TAUBER

Bavaria; 91541

Without the catastrophe of the Thirty Years' War (1618–48), Rothenburg ob der Tauber might have been very different, for the loss of population and vitality that followed the conflict helped preserve its medieval and Renaissance townscape. Once a Free City of the Holy Roman Empire, Rothenburg is now no more than a minor country town, but its exceptional architectural heritage and scenic position above the lovely Tauber Valley ensure that this perfect little time capsule is one of Germany's most beloved attractions.

A two-hour walking tour

Park outside the old town, Altstadt, on Bezoldweg and head to the **Klingentor** ①, one of several lofty gates that punctuate Rothenburg's well-preserved medieval defences. Built around 1400, the Klingentor also served as a water tower. Within the bastion is the late 15th-century fortified church of St Wolfgang, built into the town walls. Continue into the Altstadt, heading south along Klingengasse, with the Gothic bulk of the Lutheran parish church of **St Jakob** ② (open daily) ahead. The interior is worth visiting for the Heilig Blut Altar, or holy blood altar, by the Würzburg-based master-sculptor Tilman Riemenschneider. The altar's detailed portrayal of the Last Supper ranks as one of Riemenschneider's finest woodcarvings. Leave the church and turn left along Kirchplatz, to carry on

Eagle crest from the Rathaus

to the 12th-century **Weisser Turm** ③. Part of the original inner town wall, the "White Tower" is the highest point in the Altstadt. Next to it, the half-timbered Judentanzhaus, or Jewish dance hall, is a reminder of the town's importance as a centre of Jewish culture in the Middle Ages. The street leading east from Weisser Turm is known as Galgengasse, or Gallows' Lane, as it once led to the Galgentor, the town's gallows. Turn right down Pfarrgasse, then left into Rödergasse, looking right to admire the picturesque buildings around the Markusturm and Röder-bogen, a town gate and former prison built around 1200. Walk to the end of Rödergasse to the **Röderturm** ④ (Mar–Nov & Christmas Market: open daily), the only one of the town gates that can be climbed for views over the town. It contains an exhibition on the bombing of Rothenburg during World War II, of which barely a trace now remains. Head back to Markusturm, through the Markt, to see the splendid **Rathaus** ⑤ rising above. The town hall consists of two structures: the Renaissance building in front of the Markt dates from the late 16th century, while the Gothic structure behind it is much older. To the right, the gabled Ratstrinkstube, or City Councillors'Tavern, is graced by a 17th-century clock. Mechanical figures emerge on the hour *(10am–10pm)* to depict the story of the Meistertrunk, the drinking bet that spared the city during the Thirty Years' War. Return to the Markt, heading downhill along Obere Schmiedgasse.

to **Plönlein** ⑥, a charming little fork in the road, one of the most photogenic spots in Rothenburg. Return to the Markt, turning left into Herrngasse, which has the town's grandest patrician houses. A vaulted passageway leads through the Rathaus to the historic vaults, or **Historiengewölbe** ⑦ *(closed Jan; Feb: open Sat & Sun; Mar–Dec: open daily)*, where Rothenburg's travails during the Thirty Years'War are brought to life. Continue down Herrngasse to **Franziskanerkirche** ⑧ *(Jan–Mar: closed; Apr–Dec: open daily)*, which contains another Riemenschneider altar. Turn right into Trompetergässchen, and then left into Klosterhof to reach the **Reichsstadtmuseum** ⑨ *(open daily)*. Housed in a former convent, the imperial city museum's collections include the *Rothenburg Passion* paintings from the Franziskanerkirche and a section on the town's Jewish history.
🚗 **Head south on Nördlinger Strasse on to Rothenburger Strasse to Insingen. Turn left to Diebach for Schillingsfürst.**

⑦ Schillingsfürst
Bavaria; 91583
Lording over the countryside from the highest outcrop of the Frankenhöhe hills, the Baroque palace of **Schloss Schillingsfürst** *(Apr–Oct: open Tue–Sun)* is still the seat of the princes of Hohenlohe-Schillingsfürst. While its history dates back to the 11th century, the present building was built in the 18th century to designs by Darmstadt court architect Louis Rémy de la Fosse. Highlights include the Empfangssalon, or reception room, hung with Gobelin tapestries.
🚗 **Take the Frankenheimerstrasse. From Feuchtwanger Strasse turn right on to a minor road. Turn left to Wörnitz. Follow signs to B25/Feuchtwangen.**

Above left The lush medieval town of Rothenburg ob der Tauber **Above** Stately Rathaus, Rothenburg ob der Tauber **Below** Retable depicting *The Stigmatization of St Francis*, Franziskanerkirche

GUIDED TOURS

Wine Tours
Wine has been grown in the Tauber Valley since the 11th century, with Silvaner and Müller-Thurgau as the main grape varieties. Local tourist offices have a list of wineries that can be visited by making an appointment.

Night Walk
Listen to the story of this medieval town on a guided walk with the nightwatchman of Rothenburg ob der Tauber. *www.nightwatchman.de*

EAT AND DRINK

ROTHENBURG OB DER TAUBER
Eisenhut *expensive*
The Eisenhut hotel's dining room serves Franconian and international fare in comfortable surroundings. It uses regional and seasonal produce to create dishes such as roast wild boar in juniper cream with pickled cranberries or homemade gnocchi.
Herrngasse 3–7, 91541; 09861 70 50; www.eisenhut.com

Reichsküchenmeister *expensive*
This snug, traditional restaurant serves refined German cooking such as carp fillet in white wine sauce or *Schnitzel* (venison fillet in breadcrumbs).
Kirchplatz 8, 91541; 09861 97 00; www.reichskuechenmeister.com

SCHILLINGSFÜRST
Schlosscafe Schillingsfurst *moderate*
A stone-walled restaurant that serves Franconian specialities, notably desserts like *Schneeballen* ("snowballs" – balls of fried sugared pastry).
Am Wall 10, 91583; 09868 74 06; www.schlosscafe-schillingsfuerst.de; closed Mon & Tue

---

The Meistertrunk Legend
Protestant Rothenburg sided with the Swedes during the Thirty Years'War, but was occupied by Catholic troops under General Tilly in 1631. According to a legend, Tilly agreed to spare the town from destruction if a councillor could down a 3.25-litre (5-pint) tankard of wine in one draught; former mayor Georg Nusch did so and Rothenburg was saved. This tale forms the basis for the Meistertrunk Festival, a re-enactment of the mythical story, which takes place at Whitsun.

Right Patchwork of fields and forested hills near Harburg **Below** Burg Harburg, on a rocky hill overlooking the Wörnitz Valley, Harburg

WHERE TO STAY

FEUCHTWANGEN

Greifen-Post *moderate*
This lovely hotel occupies a pair of 14th- and 15th-century buildings on Feuchtwangen's marketplace. Facilities include a library, indoor pool, sauna and steam bath.
Marktplatz 8, 91555; 09852 68 00; www.hotel-greifen.de

DINKELSBÜHL

Deutsches Haus *moderate*
This 15th-century inn exudes character, from its lively, decorated wooden ceilings to the individually styled rooms with modern comforts, including Wi-Fi.
Weinmarkt 3, 91550; 09851 60 58; www.deutsches-haus-dkb.de

NÖRDLINGEN

Kaiserhof Hotel Sonne *moderate*
With a central location, this traditional hotel has peasant-style furniture in some rooms, all of which have bath or shower, TV and Internet. Past guests include four Holy Roman Emperors and the writer JW von Goethe.
Marktplatz 3, 86720; 09081 50 67; www.kaiserhof-hotel-sonne.de

HARBURG

Schlosshotel Harburg *moderate*
A hotel-restaurant with a rustic feel, located within the precincts of Harburg's castle, this has seven simple but pretty double rooms with en-suite shower.
Burgstrasse 1, 86655; 09080 15 04; www.burgschenke-harburg.de

DONAUWÖRTH

Goldener Hirsch *moderate*
The Goldener Hirsch offers comfortable en-suite rooms. Its restaurant serves Swabian specialities.
Reichsstrasse 44, 86609; 09063 124; www.goldener-hirsch-donauwoerth.de

8 Feuchtwangen
Bavaria; 91555
This city originated in the 9th century as a Benedictine abbey, which was dissolved during the Reformation. Feuchtwangen's attractive Altstadt (old town) is dominated by two churches; the larger of the two, **Stiftskirche**, is the former abbey church. Nestling alongside is a 12th-century **cloister**, the setting for the annual summer Kreuzgangspiele Theatre Festival. Feuchtwangen's **Fränkisches Museum** *(Jan & Feb: closed; Mar–Dec: open Tue–Sun)* is one of southern Germany's best folk art museums.

🚗 *Leave Feuchtwangen on the B25/ Dinkelsbühler Strasse to Dinkelsbühl.*

9 Dinkelsbühl
Bavaria; 91550
Though its peaceful setting on the Wörnitz river lacks the scenic splendour of Rothenburg ob der Tauber, Dinkelsbühl is one of the best-preserved medieval urban complexes in Germany, with lofty walls and towers encircling the Altstadt. At its heart is the soaring **Münster St Georg**, the town's 15th-century Gothic parish church. Its tower offers a fine view of the town. Opposite, on **Weinmarkt**, is a parade of tall, gabled houses as grand as any in Germany.

🚗 *Continue south along the B25. Pass Wallerstein and continue on the B25, which becomes the B29 to Nördlingen. Obtain a Parkscheibe (parking disc) from the tourist office car park for one hour for free. Park for free (no time restrictions) in car parks outside Altstadt near the gates.*

Above Colourful houses and tower gate in the old town centre in Dinkelsbühl

10 Nördlingen
Bavaria; 86720
This town stands at the centre of the Geopark Ries *(www.geopark-ries.de)*, in the Ries Basin, a huge crater over 100 m (110 yards) deep, formed millions of years ago by a meteor strike. With medieval walls encircling a well-preserved Altstadt, Nördlingen has its share of grandiose architecture. The late-Gothic **St Georgskirche** is a triple-nave hall church with round pillars and network vaults. It is possible to climb the 90-m (295-ft) high church tower, known as the **Daniel** *(open daily)*, for a bird's-eye view of the distant rim of the Ries Crater. Visit the **Rieskrater Museum** *(closed Mon)* to learn more

Far left Portcullis over the gateway, Burg Harburg **Left** Row of traditional buildings along Reichsstrasse, Donauwörth **Below** Pretty houses in the town of Nördlingen

about the meteorite strike that created the Ries.

🚗 *Continue along the B25 to Harburg.*

⑪ Harburg

Bavaria; 86655

Harburg nestles on the banks of the Wörnitz river, which can be crossed on a restored 18th-century stone bridge that offers views of the **Burg Harburg** *(mid-Mar–Oct: open daily)* that was owned by the princes of Oettingen-Wallerstein. One of the best-preserved medieval castles in Germany, it sprawls along the hilltop. The former 18th-century **synagogue** at Egelseestrasse 8 is a reminder that a quarter of Harburg's population was once Jewish.

🚗 *Continue south along the B25. Turn right on Nurnberger Strasse to Donauwörth. The Am Münster underground car park is well signposted.*

⑫ Donauwörth

Bavaria; 86609

Donauwörth was restored after its destruction in 1945. Its main street, Reichsstrasse, is lined with patrician houses that hint at the town's former importance as a Free City of the Holy Roman Empire. The abbey church of **Heilig Kreuz** is an example of southern German Baroque, while the wooden-galleried **Invalidenkaserne**

was originally built as barracks. From Reichsstrasse, a bridge leads through the **Rieder Tor** across a branch of the Wörnitz river onto the island of Ried. From here, visitors can get views of the town's medieval fortifications.

The Ries Crater

Around 15 million years ago, a meteorite 1 km (0.6 miles) in diameter slammed into what is now northern Bavaria at a speed of about 70,000 kph (44,000 mph). The impact had the force of 250 Hiroshima atomic bombs and left behind a crater 25 km (16 miles) in diameter, known as the Ries. When viewed from a suitable vantage point – such as the top of the Daniel in Nördlingen – the rim of the crater is still clearly visible.

EAT AND DRINK

FEUCHTWANGEN

Greifenstube *expensive*
This restaurant offers regional cooking with creative touches such as duck liver parfait in a *Baumkuchen* (layered cake) crust or fillet of young pork wrapped in savoy cabbage. There is a limited choice of vegetarian dishes.
Marktplatz 8, 91555; 09852 68 00; www.hotel-greifen.de; closed Sun dinner & Mon

DINKELSBÜHL

Deutsches Haus *moderate*
Local produce is to the fore at the 15th-century Deutsches Haus, where the rustic dining room offers an atmospheric setting for typical regional and Mediterranean dishes.
Weinmarkt 3, 91550; 09851 60 58; www.deutsches-haus-dkb.de

Luis Restaurant *moderate*
Set in the 16th-century, half-timbered Hezelhof hotel, this quirky restaurant features modern interiors. Meat-lovers can try regional sausages from the wood-fired grill, smoky South Tyrol bacon, steaks and burgers. There's ample choice for vegetarians too.
Segringer Strasse 4, 91550; 09851 589 68 60; www.luis-hezelhof.com

NÖRDLINGEN

Wirtshaus Meyers Keller *expensive*
Located on the southern outskirts of Nördlingen, Jockl Kaiser's Michelin-starred restaurant offers a choice of menus: a cosmopolitan degustation menu or a regional menu, which emphasises the culinary tradition of the Ries region.
Marienhöhe 8, 86720; 09081 44 93; www.meyerskeller.de; closed Mon & Tue

---

DAY TRIP OPTIONS

This beautiful region can be explored in a series of day trips.

Medieval Würzburg

In Würzburg ①, tour the Residenz before visiting Tauberbischofsheim ② and Bad Mergentheim ③ to see the local wineries.

Take the B27 as far as the A3, beyond which the Romantische Strasse continues to Tauberbischofsheim. Take the B27, then the A81 and the B290 to Bad Mergentheim.

Charming towns

Explore the charming town of Rothenburg ob der Tauber ⑥ before stopping to tour the

Schloss at Schillingsfürst ⑦. Head to Dinkelsbühl ⑨ and stroll around its medieval fortifications. Stop at Nördlingen ⑩ to see the Ries Crater.

Take Rothenburger Strasse to Schillingsfürst, take the B25 and continue on it to Dinkelsbühl. Continue on the same road, which becomes the B29 to Nördlingen.

TRIP 19

THE SOUTHERN ROMANTIC ROAD
Augsburg to Füssen

HIGHLIGHTS

Wealthy Augsburg
Admire the art and architecture paid for by Augsburg's
bankers, from exquisite gold- and silver-work to
the world's first social housing complex

Baroque and Rococo grandeur
Wonder at the architectural opulence, from Landsberg
am Lech to Wieskirche, a UNESCO World Heritage Site

Hiking landscape
Enjoy a wealth of activities, from walking in Pfaffenwinkel
to mountain hikes around Hohenschwangau

Romantic fantasy
Explore "Mad" King Ludwig's medieval
castle of Neuschwanstein

THE SOUTHERN ROMANTIC ROAD

The southern section of Germany's most famous tourist route begins at splendid Augsburg. The city's creative and architectural splendour was funded by its bankers, making it one of Europe's richest and most important cities at the height of the German Renaissance. Further south, a dream-like artistic vision prevails in the heavenly creations of Baroque and Rococo church builders and in the Wagnerian fantasies of "Mad" King Ludwig at Schloss Neuschwanstein, Germany's best-loved castle. Overshadowing everything is the majestic grandeur of the Alps, visible on a clear day even from Augsburg. Swabian cuisine hints at Italy's proximity, with ravioli-like *Maultaschen* and gnocchi-like *Spätzle* or *Kasspätzen* featuring on menus, although beer remains the drink of choice.

Above Lush, grassy slopes beside the road between Wildsteig and Rottenbuch, *see p206*

ACTIVITIES

Go on a mountain hike or opt for a ramble in the lovely walking country of Pfaffenwinkel in Schongau

Climb to the top of the town in Landsberg am Lech to see the imposing 15th-century Gothic Bayertor, or Bavarian Gate

Slide downhill on the popular 760-m (2,500-ft) summer toboggan run at Schwangau

Take off on a hang-gliding or paragliding course on the Tegelberg at Schwangau

Experience high-altitude scenic thrills on the Tegelberg cable cars

Above Schloss Neuschwanstein on a forested crag, Hohenschwangau, *see p207*

PLAN YOUR DRIVE

Start/finish: Augsburg to Füssen.

Number of days: 3 days, allowing a day to explore Augsburg.

Distance: 140 km (87 miles).

Road conditions: Roads are well surfaced and signposted with brown "Romantische Strasse" signs. Traffic can be heavy in the urban sections in and around Augsburg, where drivers should also watch out for trams.

When to go: This trip is best from May to October. There are a limited number of winter sports available in the Alpine south during winter.

Opening times: Museums often close on Mondays, while the royal castles at Hohenschwangau are open daily. Shops are closed on Sundays.

Major festivals: Augsburg: Plärrer (folk festival and funfair), Easter and late summer; Landsberg am Lech: Ruethenfest (children's folk festival), every four years, next in summer 2023.

DAY TRIP OPTIONS

Lovers of historic towns will enjoy Augsburg and Landsberg am Lech in the north, while for an unrivalled combination of **scenic grandeur** and **architectural fantasy**, the Romantic Road is at its **prettiest** in the south, between Schongau and the **royal castles** at Hohenschwangau. For full details, *see p207*.

KEY

🛤 Drive route

0 kilometres   10

0 miles   10

Above Shopping street in the town of Füssen, *see p207*

VISITING AUGSBURG

Parking
The Annahof underground car park is signposted off Fuggerstrasse and is close to the tourist information office.

Tourist Information
Rathausplatz 1, 86150; 08215 020 70; www.augsburg-tourismus.de; open Apr–Oct: daily; Nov–Mar: closed Sun

WHERE TO STAY IN AUGSBURG

Hotel am Rathaus *moderate*
Tucked in a discreet lane near Augsburg's Rathaus, this hotel has 31 rooms, each equipped with cable TV.
Am Hinteren Perlachberg 1, 86150; 08213 464 90; www.hotel-am-rathaus-augsburg.de

Hotel Maximilian's *expensive*
Augsburg's top address since the 17th century, this hotel with views along the main street has contemporary and stylish rooms and suites.
Maximilianstrasse 40, 86150; 08215 03 60; www.hotelmaximilians.com

Above right Fuggerei, the world's oldest social housing complex, Augsburg

❶ AUGSBURG
Bavaria; 86150
Founded by the Romans, Augsburg reached its zenith during the Renaissance. An important banking centre during this period, the city attained renown all across Europe for its artists and craftsmen, above all in England, where the Augsburg painter Hans Holbein the Younger (1498–1543) became King Henry VIII's court painter. The city also played a key role in the Reformation and its past glories are reflected in the architecture of its city centre.

A two-hour walking tour
Park in the Annahof underground car park and walk through the courtyard to the church of **St Anna** ① *(open daily)*, which contains the Renaissance burial chapel of the wealthy Fugger family. There is also an exhibition on Martin Luther, who stayed here in 1518 during his meetings with papal legate Cardinal Cajetan following the publication of his famous 95 Theses. Exit the church and head down Martin-Luther-Platz, then bear left to **Maximilianmuseum** ② *(closed Mon)*. Housed in a 16th-century merchant's house, the museum contains works by Augsburg's famed gold- and silversmiths and by the Dutch sculptor Adriaen de Vries (1556–1626), who was responsible for several of the city's fountains. From the museum, Phillippine-Welser-Strasse leads into **Rathausplatz** ③, or Town Hall Square. It is dominated by the façade of the Rathaus, one of Germany's finest town halls and one of the most important

secular Renaissance buildings north of the Alps. Built from 1615–20, it was designed by Elias Holl. Badly burned during World War II, it has since been restored. Inside, Goldener Saal, or Golden Hall *(open daily)*, is a masterpiece complete with a gilded walnut ceiling. Head north up Karolinenstrasse, cross Leonhardsberg to the northern Altstadt, or old town, and Augsburg's **Dom** ④, a blend of the Romanesque and Gothic styles with 12th-century stained-glass windows and altar panels by Hans Holbein the Elder, father of the celebrated portraitist. On the northern side of the cathedral is the Diözesanmuseum *(closed Mon)*, whose treasures include the cathedral's 11th-century bronze doors, illustrated with scenes from the Old Testament. North along Frauentorstrasse is the **Leopold-Mozart-Haus** ⑤ at No. 30 *(closed Mon)*, where Mozart's father Leopold was born in 1719, and which now houses an exhibition. Return to Rathausplatz and turn left down Perlachberg, past Elias Holl's gabled butcher's guild house, the Stadtmetzg, and left again into Auf dem Rain, where the **Brechthaus** ⑥ *(closed Mon)*, birthplace of the playwright Bertolt Brecht, is now a museum. Head back to the main road, and turn left along Jakoberstrasse to the **Fuggerei** ⑦. Founded by Jakob Fugger the Rich in 1521, this group of almshouses is thought to be the

The Fuggers

In three generations, the Fugger family went from being weavers to bankers to the mighty Habsburgs. The greatest of the dynasty was Jakob Fugger the Rich, the wealthiest businessman of his day, who funded Charles V's ascent to the throne of the Holy Roman Empire. His town palace in Augsburg hosted the meeting between Martin Luther and Cardinal Cajetan and is to this day home to the Fugger Privatbank. However, his most famous memorial is the Fuggerei, the world's first social housing complex.

world's oldest social housing complex. One of the apartments is preserved in its original condition as a museum *(closed Mon)*.

Head back to the city centre along Jakoberstrasse and turn left into Oberer Graben, on the far side of which is the artisans' quarter, or **Handwerkerviertel** ⑧, a district of winding lanes. It was in one of the houses in this district, at Vorderer Lech, that Hans Holbein the Younger was born; the house was destroyed in World War II. In its place stands the Kunstverein Augsburg *(closed Mon)*, which hosts temporary exhibitions of modern art. Continue along Vorderer Lech into Bäckergasse; at the end, turn right up Milchberg to **St Ulrich und Afra** ⑨, a late-Gothic church which dominates the southern part of the Altstadt. Begun in 1474, it was not completed until 1603 and contains the tombs of St Ulrich, St Afra and St Simpert. North from here stretches Maximilianstrasse, lined with mansions and cafés. Among the grandest mansions is the

Detail on the balustrade, Fugger Chapel

Schaezlerpalais ⑩, built in 1765 as the town palace of the banker Liebert von Liebenhofen and now a museum of German Baroque art *(closed Mon)*. The former palace's Rococo ballroom is the venue for concerts in summer. In front of the Schaezlerpalais stands the Herkulesbrunnen, or Hercules Fountain, one of three Renaissance fountains by Adriaen de Vries, completed around 1600. Go north along Maximilianstrasse, past the Fugger City Palace, or **Fugger-Stadtpalast** ⑪, to see the other fountains: Merkurbrunnen stands on Moritzplatz, a small square near the Rathausplatz, and Augustusbrunnen is in front of the Rathaus. Continue on the same road to the car park.

🚗 *Take the B2/Friedberger Strasse to Friedberg. Paid parking is next to the Rathaus.*

② Friedberg
Bavaria; 86316

Founded by King Ludwig II in 1264, Friedberg is set behind well-preserved town walls. The town's hilltop Altstadt has a 17th-century **Rathaus**. Beyond the fortifications is the **Wittelsbacher Schloss**. At the eastern end of Herrgottsruhstrasse stands **Herrgottsruh** *(open daily)*. Built between 1731 and 1753, this church is one of the finest examples of Bavarian Rococo. It contains murals by Cosmas Damian Asam, the most prolific painter in Bavaria of his time.

🚗 *Return along Augsburger Strasse and take the B300/ Haunstetter Strasse south from the city. Join the B17 and continue further along to Hurlach, then take left crossing Kaufering to reach Landsberg am Lech, where there is limited parking on the main square.*

Above Magnificent coffered ceiling of the Goldener Saal, Rathaus, Augsburg **Below left** Baroque Rathaus, Friedberg **Below right** Gardens at the rear of the Fuggerei, Augsburg

EAT AND DRINK IN AUGSBURG

Die Ecke *expensive*
Close to the Rathaus, this gourmet restaurant serves refined German cuisine. Enjoy French, Italian and German wines. *Elias-Holl-Platz 2, 86152; 08215 106 00; www.restaurant-die-ecke.de; closed Mon & Tue*

Maximilian's *expensive*
Changing seasonal and regional dishes are prepared in an open kitchen. Try tapas-sized culinary delights as well. *Maximilianstrasse 40, 86150; 08215 03 60; www.maximilians-augsburg.de; closed Sun*

Other options
König von Flandern *(Karolinenstrasse 12, 86152; 08211 580 50; www.koenig vonflandern.de)*, a microbrewery, serves beers and regional food. Try the **Ratskeller** in the vaulted cellar of the Rathaus *(Rathausplatz 2, 86150; 08213 198 82 38; www.ratskeller-augsburg.de)*. The cheapest meals are at the stand-up stalls in the **Stadtmarkt** *(closed Sun)* off Annastrasse – a lunchtime favourite with locals.

Above Old town walls, Schongau **Below** Breathtaking view of the green countryside along the road to Rottenbuch **Below right** Cafés lining a cobbled street in Füssen

WHERE TO STAY

LANDSBERG AM LECH

Arthotel Ana Goggl *moderate*
Dating back to 1667, this hotel close to the main square offers cosy rooms.
Hubert-von-Herkomer-Strasse 19–20, 86899; 08191 32 40; www.ana-hotels.com

SCHONGAU

Gasthof Blaue Traube *moderate*
This inn on Schongau's main street offers simple but attractive rooms.
Münzstrasse 10, 86956; 08861 30 60; www.blaue-traube-schongau.de

HOHENSCHWANGAU

Hotel Garni Schlossblick *moderate*
This hotel consists of a main building and an annexe, the Villa Jägerhaus. Rooms in both are comfortable.
Schwangauer Strasse 7, 87645; 08362 816 49; www.schlossblick-neuschwanstein.de

FÜSSEN

Hotel Schlosskrone *moderate*
A long-established hotel with well-equipped doubles and deluxe rooms.
Prinzregentenplatz 2, 87629; 08362 93 01 80; www.schlosskrone.de

Hotel Sonne *expensive*
The four-star Hotel Sonne has 50 rooms decorated in different styles.
Prinzregentenplatz 1, 87629; 08362 90 80; www.hotel-fuessen.de

➌ Landsberg am Lech
Bavaria; 86899

With a main square dominated by the town hall, the **Historisches Rathaus**, Landsberg am Lech has a well-preserved historic core. The façade of the town hall features stuccowork from 1719 to 1721 by Dominikus Zimmermann, who, with his brother Johann Baptist, was also responsible for the Wieskirche. The town also has many gate towers, most notably the Gothic 15th-century 36-m (118-ft) high **Bayertor**, located at the top of the steep, pretty Alte Bergstrasse.

🚗 *Take the Katharinenstrasse, turn left on to the B17 and continue to Schongau, where there is on-street parking in the Altstadt.*

Hitler in Landsberg am Lech
For all its timeless beauty, Landsberg am Lech's chief historical claim to fame is as the place where Hitler wrote *Mein Kampf*. At his trial, following the disastrous coup attempt in Munich in 1923, the future dictator was given a lenient sentence despite charges of high treason. The case, far from being a humiliation, proved to be something of a propaganda platform and Hitler used the months of confinement to complete his notorious political manifesto.

➍ Schongau
Bavaria; 86956

Perched above the Lech river in the district known as the **Pfaffenwinkel** (priests' corner), this former minor seat of the Wittelsbach Dynasty has an almost complete set of medieval town walls, which look particularly impressive when floodlit at night. The **Ballenhaus** in the centre of the old town is a former warehouse with a stepped gable, dating from 1420.

🚗 *Cross the Lech river to Peiting on the Peitinger Strasse and head south along the B23 to Rottenbuch. Parking is available in front of the church; follow signs to Ortsmitte.*

➎ Rottenbuch
Bavaria; 82401

Rottenbuch's former Augustinian monastery complex was secularized in 1803, although its appearance remains unaffected. The village's focus is the convent church of **Mariä Geburt**, which has an opulent interior in the Rococo style, with stuccowork dating from the mid-18th century.

🚗 *Continue south on the B23. Beyond Achen, turn right on to Steingadener Strasse to Wildsteig. After Wildsteig, take the signposted turning to Wies/Wieskirche. There is paid parking at the side of the road, close to the church.*

➏ Wieskirche
Bavaria; 86989

Located 5 km (3 miles) from Steingaden is the meadow church of **Wieskirche** *(open daily)*. Completed in 1754 at the spot where a farmer's wife had seen tears flow from the eyes of an abandoned statue of Christ, the church was the work of Dominikus Zimmermann. The building is a masterpiece of 18th-century southern German architecture.

🚗 *Return to the signposted turning. Continue to Steingaden, bearing left on to the B17. Follow brown signs, "Königsschlösser", to the castles at Hohenschwangau. There are paid car parks at the base of the village. Ascend to Schloss Neuschwanstein by shuttle bus, horse and cart or on foot.*

"Mad" King Ludwig II

Bavaria's famous monarch Ludwig II has become a revered figure since his drowning in the Starnberger See in 1886. Coming to the throne as a youth on the eve of Bavaria's defeat and incorporation into the Prussian-led German Empire, he was denied real power; instead, he lived out his absolutist fantasies in extravagant building projects that threatened to bankrupt the public purse. As a result he was forced to step down shortly before his untimely – and some still say suspicious – death, a few weeks before his 41st birthday.

❼ Hohenschwangau
Bavaria; 87645

Germany's most famous castle sits on a forested crag above Hohenschwangau. **Schloss Neuschwanstein** *(open daily)* was built for Ludwig II between 1869 and 1884. Guided tours take visitors through the richly adorned Singer's and Throne Hall as well as the king's royal lodgings. The Neo-Gothic **Schloss Hohenschwangau** *(open daily)* in the valley below is where Ludwig spent much of his childhood. Enjoy a summer toboggan run *(www.tegelberg bahn.de)* or a cable car ride to the top of the the Tegelberg summit *(www. tegelbergbahn.de)* for spectacular views.

🚗 *Exit Hohenschwangau and take Parkstrasse, turning left on to the B17 for Füssen. Park in one of the underground car parks close to the tourist office and the Altstadt.*

❽ Füssen
Bavaria; 87629

The Romantic Road ends at Füssen. The Altstadt is dominated by the late-Gothic **Hohes Schloss**, former summer palace of Augsburg's bishops, which houses two art galleries *(Apr–Oct: closed Mon; Nov–Mar: open Fri–Sun pm)*. The former Benedictine monastery of **Kloster St Mang** *(Apr–Oct: closed Mon; Nov–Mar: open Fri–Sun pm)* has Baroque staterooms, while the **Heilig Geist Spitalkirche**, or Church of the Holy Ghost, has a pretty painted façade.

An Operatic Fantasy

Conceived by theatre designer Christian Jank, Neuschwanstein is the ultimate fantasy castle, inspired by the castles of the Age of Chivalry, notably the Wartburg in Thuringia. Ludwig II was the patron of the composer Richard Wagner, whose operas provided inspiration for the decor. The Sängersaal, or Singers' Hall, is modelled on the hall at Wartburg – the scene of the singers' contest in Wagner's opera *Tannhäuser*.

Above left Scenic Schloss Hohenschwangau, Hohenschwangau **Above** Landsberg am Lech from across the Lech river

HIKING IN THE PFAFFENWINKEL

The Pfaffenwinkel has three major hiking trails – the Konig-Ludwig-Weg, Lech-Hohenweg and the Pralatenweg – crisscrossing the district. There are also 28 self-guided hikes that range from easy strolls to mountain hikes. *www.pfaffen-winkel.de*

EAT AND DRINK

SCHONGAU

Schlossgasthof Zum Hechten
moderate
Dark wooden tables and historic paintings provide an appropriate setting for hearty, traditional local fare such as *Schweinshaxn* (knuckle of ham). *Ritterstrasse 6, 87629; 08362 916 00; www.hotel-hechten.com*

FÜSSEN

Gasthaus zum Schwanen
moderate
Set in a beautiful old gabled house, this restaurant serves regional specialities from Swabia and the Allgäu, including *Maultaschen* (Swabian ravioli) and *Kasspätzen* (cheese-topped noodles) with roast onion and salad. *Brotmarkt 4, 87629; 08362 61 74; www. schwanen-fuessen.de; closed Tue*

DAY TRIP OPTIONS

Augsburg is a good base for exploring the northern section of the route, while Schongau and Füssen are excellent for discovering the southern part.

Historic towns

Explore historic Augsburg ❶ before heading to Friedberg ❷ to admire

the beautiful Herrgottsruh church. Stop at Landsberg am Lech ❸ to visit its Baroque town hall.

Head east to Friedberg along the B2, then south along the B300/B17 to Landsberg am Lech.

Scenic and architectural paradise

Stroll through Schongau's ❹ old town,

then head to Hohenschwangau ❼ to explore its royal castles, which stand amid superb Alpine scenery.

Head south to Rottenbuch on the B23. At Achen, the Steingadner Strasse branches off to Wildsteig. Look out for brown signs to the Wieskirche. Bear left at Steingaden on to the B17 and follow signs to the castles.

TRIP 20

MOUNTAIN ROADS AND VINEYARDS
Baden-Baden to Durbach

HIGHLIGHTS

Rejuvenating spas
Escape to the thermal baths in Baden-Baden,
celebrated for their healing qualities

Fine wines
Taste and buy the wines produced in the region
immediately south of Baden-Baden

Spectacular valley
Cruise through the Kinzig Valley on the
Schwarzwaldhochstrasse, which is dotted
with attractive villages and large
traditional farmhouses

Amusement park
Delight the kids at Europa-Park, Germany's
biggest theme park

MOUNTAIN ROADS AND VINEYARDS

The town of Baden-Baden, with its classy spas and air of 19th-century grandeur, defines the northern Black Forest, which is less wild and more accessible than the south. This tour follows the Schwarzwaldhochstrasse (Black Forest High Road), which rolls along the western edge of the mountain range, revealing fine views over the Rhine Valley. The road then leads to the eastern end of the Kinzig Valley, at the heart of the Black Forest, where pockets of traditional life have survived in small logging and farming villages. Of particular interest here are the brewery town of Alpirsbach and the half-timbered village of Schiltach. The tour finally takes drivers to the Badische Weinstrasse, a scenic road that meanders through an area known for its vineyards and wineries.

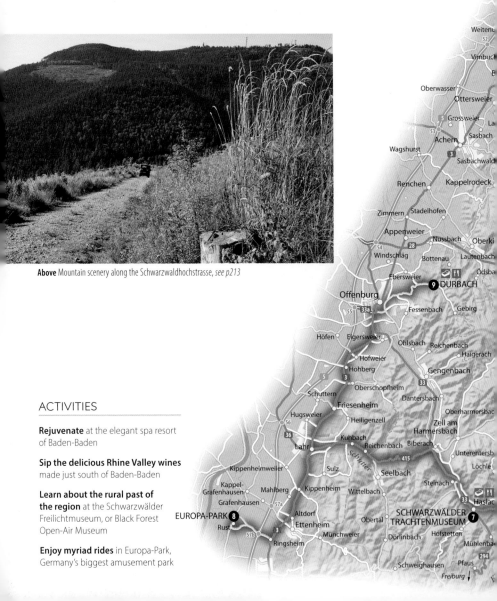

Above Mountain scenery along the Schwarzwaldhochstrasse, *see p213*

ACTIVITIES

Rejuvenate at the elegant spa resort of Baden-Baden

Sip the delicious Rhine Valley wines made just south of Baden-Baden

Learn about the rural past of the region at the Schwarzwälder Freilichtmuseum, or Black Forest Open-Air Museum

Enjoy myriad rides in Europa-Park, Germany's biggest amusement park

Above Logging on the banks of the Kinzig river, Schiltach, *see p214* Below Mural of the historic blaze on the Rathaus, Schiltach, *see p214*

KEY

Drive route

0 kilometres 5

0 miles 5

PLAN YOUR DRIVE

Start/finish: Baden-Baden to Durbach.

Number of days: 3 days, allowing half a day in Baden-Baden.

Distance: 220 km (137 miles).

Road conditions: Roads are well paved but often steep and twisting, though driving is not difficult. In winter, snow can cover higher portions of the drive.

When to go: This trip is possible throughout the year, although the higher points may be blocked by snow between December and March.

Opening times: Most attractions open daily. Shops open from 9am to 5pm on weekdays, and close early on Saturdays and remain closed on Sundays. Restaurants generally close at 10pm.

Main market days: Freudenstadt: Fri & Sat (Apr–Oct: also Tue).

Shopping: The boutiques of Baden-Baden sport an array of luxury goods, while the vineyards and wine sellers along the Badische Weinstrasse offer an excellent selection of local vintages.

Major festivals: Baden-Baden: Osterfestspiele (classical music), Apr; New Pop Festival, Sep.

DAY TRIP OPTIONS

Visitors interested in traditional rural life can follow the tour through the Gutach Valley where the **open-air museum** is a highlight, while **families** can head to Europa-Park, where there are many attractions to fill the day. **Wine lovers** can take a relaxed tour of the Badische Weinstrasse and Durbach, where lovely walks pass through **vineyards**. For full details, *see p215*.

Above Interior of the grand Trinkhalle, Baden-Baden

VISITING BADEN-BADEN

Parking
Baden-Baden has a dozen central car parks, of which several are underground. One such is the Kongresshausgarage on Augustaplatz.

Tourist Information
Kaiserallee 1, 76530; 07221 27 52 00; www.baden-baden.de; open daily

WHERE TO STAY

BADEN-BADEN
Heliopark Bad Hotel Zum Hirsch *moderate*
This historic old town hotel's fine public rooms include a splendid ballroom. Thermal spring water flows from the taps of its antique-furnished rooms. *Hirschstrasse 1, 76530; 07221 93 90; www.heliopark-hirsch.de*

Brenners Park-Hotel & Spa *expensive*
The best address in Baden-Baden, this hotel exudes 19th-century elegance. Its own park and an excellent modern spa and gym complex make it one of the finest hotels in the world. *Schillerstrasse 4-6, 76530; 07221 90 00; www.brenners.com*

FREUDENSTADT
Bären *moderate*
A friendly and traditional three-star choice a block east of the Marktplatz, this hotel has rooms that have a comfortably dated, vaguely 1950s feel. Some rooms have balconies and the hotel provides Internet access. *Lange Strasse 33, 72250; 07441 27 29; www.hotel-baeren-freudenstadt.de*

❶ BADEN-BADEN
Baden-Württemberg; 76530

Founded as a Roman bathing spot, and a particular favourite of the Roman Emperor Caracalla (188–217 BC), Baden-Baden has an idyllic location in the midst of gentle wooded hills. In 1810, the Baden Margraves built Neo-Classical thermal baths around the springs here, to serve an early 19th-century fashion for bathing. Its importance has faded since, yet something of these halcyon days continues to live on in the elegant villas, grand hotels, spas and manicured gardens.

A 90-minute walking tour

From the car park entrance turn left to cross the park and the Oos river on a small footbridge. Then turn right along Lichtentaler Allee, which becomes Kaiserallee. This leads to a large building in the greenery on the left known as the **Trinkhalle** ① *(open daily)*, the grandest of a series of 19th-century buildings and follies built alongside the Oos as social centres. Turning right out of the Trinkhalle, a path leads through parkland to the Neo-Classical **Kurhaus** ② *(open daily)*, the main venue for cultural and social events in Baden-Baden, which

Façade of the Neo-Renaissance Trinkhalle

includes a famous casino. Visits to the interior are possible on 20- minute tours held every 30 minutes. Outside the Kurhaus a bandstand marks the start of Kurgarten, an avenue of chestnut trees lined with expensive boutiques and the tourist information office. A right turn at the bottom of this leads back to **Lichtentaler Allee** ③, a 3-km (2-mile) long promenade. Down this avenue is the Kunsthalle *(closed Mon)*, home to international contemporary art. Walk along the promenade to Bertholdstrasse, which is on the left behind the Stadtmuseum, and turn right on to the footpath on the near side of the river. Over the next footbridge lie the thick beech hedges of the **Gönneranlage** ④. These are ornamental gardens where over 400 varieties of rose thrive. Exiting the gardens from the opposite side, take the left turn that leads down Ludwig-Wilhelm-Strasse to the car park at Augustaplatz. From here, turn left then right down Lichtentaler Strasse to the square on Sophienstrasse. Gernsbacher Strasse, which is across the square, leads into the old town, the **Altstadt** ⑤. This was reduced to ashes in 1689 during the Palatinate War of Succession; rebuilding it took a century. Follow Gernsbacher Strasse and turn left into an alley at Sonnenplatz. This leads to the marketplace, where villas surround the **Stiftskirche Liebfrauen** ⑥. This church's land-mark spire summarizes its architec-tural history, with a Romanesque square tower forming the base for an octagonal Gothic cap that carries Baroque cupolas. Behind the church, occasional wisps of steam drifting over the cobbled street announce the presence of the **Bäderviertel** ⑦ at the base of some stone steps. The baths quarter was established by the Romans and its ruins can still be seen at the Römische Badruinen *(open daily)*. The ruins lie in the basement of the spa Friedrichsbad *(open daily)*, which looks like a minor palace with its green copper cupolas and colonna-des. Return to Lichtentaler Strasse and Augustaplatz to reach the car park.

🚗 *Turn left out of the car park, right on to Lichentaler Strasse, which becomes Hauptstrasse. Turn right when this road meets the B500, which becomes the Schwarzwaldhochstrasse. Park at the roadside car park at Mummelsee.*

② Schwarzwaldhochstrasse

Baden-Württemberg; 77889
The Schwarzwaldhochstrasse, or Black Forest High Road (B500), climbs from Baden-Baden through meadows and valleys to the pine-covered hills that pave the way to Freudenstadt. Various viewpoints and belvederes along the route provide views to the rolling hills and vineyards of the upper Rhine Valley and beyond to the French Vosges Mountains. Visitors should allow time for several short hikes *(www.schwarzwaldhochstrasse.de)* includ-ing the 2-km (1-mile) loop around the Mummelsee. Continue down the B500 and then turn right into the road signposted to Allerheiligen. A 20-minute hike starts at the Gothic

ruin of the Allerheiligen monastery and leads to an attractive waterfall.

🚗 *From Allerheiligen return to the B500 and continue south, then left on to the B28. In Freudenstadt, turn left on to the B462 to reach the car park.*

③ Freudenstadt

Baden-Württemberg; 72250
Built on a high plateau, Freudenstadt was commissioned by Duke Friedrich I in 1599. The town's giant marketplace is the biggest square in Germany. The most imposing buildings here are the town hall and **Stadtkirche**, an oddly L-shaped church designed to segregate men and women.

🚗 *Return to the B28, turn left down Lauterbadstrasse and then take the B294 towards Freiburg. In Alpirsbach, turn right into Alleenstrasse to park on the Krähenbadstrasse.*

The Who's Who of Baden-Baden
Though still a playground for the extremely rich, Baden-Baden had its heyday in the late 19th century, when the international elite flocked here to promenade and recuperate. Visiting luminaries included statesmen and monarchs such as Queen Victoria, Kaiser Wilhelm I and Otto von Bismarck, composers such as Pyotr Ilyich Tchaikovsky and Johannes Brahms and novelists such as Leo Tolstoy and Fyodor Dostoevsky.

Above Fountains in Freudenstadt's town centre **Below left** Wooded hills surrounding the town of Baden-Baden **Below** Typical landscape, Schwarzwaldhochstrasse

EAT AND DRINK

BADEN-BADEN

Café König *moderate*
This is the place to enjoy afternoon coffee and cake, in particular the exquisite *Schwarzwalder Kirschtorte* (black forest cherry gâteau).
Lichtentaler Strasse 12, 76530; 07221 235 73; www.chocolatier.de; closed dinner

KurhausRestaurant *expensive*
The Kurhaus serves dishes such as roast duck breast marinated with blackberry paste, fried green asparagus and wild rice risotto.
Kaiserallee 1, 76530; 07221 90 70; www.kurhaus-badenbaden.de

Le Jardin de France *expensive*
An elegant restaurant in a courtyard off Lichtentaler Strasse, this serves creative, modern French cuisine using ingredients such as pak choi and northern Iberian sausage.
Lichtentaler Strasse 13, 76530; 07221 300 78 60; www.lejardindefrance.de; closed Mon

AROUND FREUDENSTADT

Schwarzwaldstube *expensive*
With lovely views and countless international awards to its name, this restaurant is full of gourmet surprises.
Tonbachstrasse 237, 72270 Baiersbronn (11 km/7 miles north of Freudenstadt); 07442 49 20; www.traube-tonbach.de; closed Mon–Tue

Above Farm mill in Vogtsbauernhof, Schwarzwälder Freilichtmuseum **Above right** Fountain outside a brewery, Alpirsbach **Below** The Marktplatz captured from the 16th-century Rathaus, Schiltach

WHERE TO STAY

SCHILTACH

Zum Weyssen Rössle *moderate*
A short walk from the marketplace, this traditional guesthouse features cheerful floral and modern rooms. It offers free Wi-Fi, as well as a good continental breakfast buffet.
Schenkenzeller Strasse 42, 77761; 07836 387; www.weysses-roessle.de

AROUND SCHWARZWÄLDER TRACHTENMUSEUM

Hotel Storchen *moderate*
The traditional half-timbered exterior of this guesthouse in Haslach suggests nothing of the eccentricities within. All its rooms are themed with concepts such as Oriental, aquatic, desert island and even a hot-air balloon.
Hauptstrasse 35, 77716 Haslach (east of Schwarzwälder Trachtenmuseum); 07832 97 97 97; www.hotel-storchen.de

DURBACH

Rebstock *moderate*
With lovely, individually decorated country-style or boutique rooms and suites, this family-run hotel has exquisite landscaped gardens that serve as a backdrop for its spa, which includes a sauna and steam room.
Halbgütle 30, 77770; 07814 820; www.rebstock-durbach.de

Hotel Ritter *expensive*
An upmarket, family-run boutique hotel, Ritter has tasteful decor and offers superb fitness and spa facilities.
Tal 1, 77770; 07819 32 30; www.ritter-durbach.de

④ Alpirsbach

Baden-Württemberg; 72275
Strung out along a tight valley, the town of Alpirsbach once basked in a medieval golden age that gave it the Romanesque Benedictine monastery **Kloster Alpirsbach** *(mid-Mar–May: open Tue–Sun; Jun–Oct: open daily; Nov–mid-Mar: open Thu–Sun)*, whose church was built of regional red sandstone in the 11th century. The interior has powerful nave capitals, which illustrate the forces of good and evil. The cold Dormitorium and calefactory of the monks are visited by hour-long tours that give a background about life in the monastery. Other tours visit the adjacent brewery, the **Alpirsbacher Klosterbräu** *(tours daily)*, which brews the fruity local beers.

🚗 *Return to the B294 from Krähenbadstrasse, turn right, following signs to Schiltach. Take the Schiltach-Ost entrance to the town, turn right at Hauptstrasse, then left on to Schramberger Strasse for*

on-street parking. Walk back to Hauptstrasse, turn left and take the alley on the right to the museum.

⑤ Schiltach

Baden-Württemberg; 77761
The picture-postcard town of Schiltach was built on the banks of the Kinzig river, where a reconstructed lumber mill houses the **Schüttesäge-Museum** *(Apr–Oct: open daily; closed Nov–Dec)*. The black-and-white photographs at this sawmill museum illustrate a bygone era when the town was the hub of the logging industry. A short walk along the river toward Hauptstrasse leads to a marketplace surrounded by half-timbered buildings, none of which date from before 1533, when a fire reduced the town to ashes. The **Rathaus** or town hall has murals of the blaze, including a depiction of the innocent girl blamed for the fire, who was mistaken as a witch and burnt at the stake.

🚗 *Continue on Schramberger Strasse and turn right on to the B294. Then turn right on to the B33 towards Villingen-Schwenningen. Park at the signed roadside parking beside the museum.*

⑥ Schwarzwälder Freilichtmuseum

Baden-Württemberg; 77793
Close to the Gutach's confluence with the Kinzig is the Schwarzwälder Freilichtmuseum *(end Mar–Nov: open daily)*, an open-air museum. The focus here is the **Vogtsbauernhof**, a 1612 farmhouse. Its roof is typical of the local building style. Arranged around the farm are 26 other traditional buildings, brought here from around the region to create a little village. Costumed guides and craft demonstrations bring the place to life. Visitors can follow signs on the B33 from the museum to the **Sommerrodelbahn** *(Mar–Oct: open daily)*, a summer toboggan run.

🚗 *Return to the B33, turning left to Hofstetten. Turn right at Ringstrasse in Haslach. Follow signs to the museum and park in the car park beside it.*

⑦ Schwarzwälder Trachtenmuseum
Baden-Württemberg; 77716
Packed with a comprehensive collection of local costumes, this folk museum *(Apr–mid-Oct: open Tue–Sun; mid-Oct–Dec & Feb–mid-Mar: open Tue– Fri; closed Jan)* in the town of **Haslach** includes items such as the *Bollenhut*, a straw bonnet clustered with pompoms once worn by the unmarried women of the Gutach Valley. Look out for some of the costumes worn at carnival. Behind the museum, the old town of **Haslach** is worth exploring for the cluster of half-timbered houses funded by a silver-mining boom.

🚗 *Return to the B33. At Biberach get on to the B415 towards Lahr. Drive through Lahr, turning left on to the B3 and then right on to the road signposted to the Europa-Park.*

⑧ Europa-Park
Baden-Württemberg; 77977
The largest amusement park in Germany, Europa-Park *(late Mar–Dec: open daily)* offers 50 rides, making it very popular with children. Its huge landscaped grounds are of interest

Ed Euromaus at the Europa-Park

too; the size of 80 football fields, they contain several fun villages themed by European countries.

🚗 *Return along the B3 and head north through Lahr. In Offenburg take the Hauptstrasse and follow signs to Durbach. There are many places to park along the road through Durbach.*

⑨ Durbach
Baden-Württemberg; 77770
An important stop on the Badische Weinstrasse, Durbach is of particular interest to wine lovers for its shop, the **Durbacher Winzergenossenschaft** *(open daily)*. This wine cooperative offers a great selection of distinguished and well-priced local wines and is liberal with its samples. The shop is signposted and lies to the right of the main road at Durbach's centre. It faces the **Schloss Staufenberg**, which looms over the town from a vineyard-draped hill. The occupants of this 11th-century castle have been documented as producing wine since 1391. Visitors are not allowed inside the castle but can sample its wines in its earthy wine bar or outdoors on a terrace with spectacular views.

Above left Sign for a restaurant serving wines from Baden-Baden **Above** Aerial view of the vineyards in Durbach

EAT AND DRINK

ALPIRSBACH
Zur Löwen-Post *moderate*
A traditional restaurant, Zur Löwen-Post also serves local innovations such as a salad garnished with roasted brewers malt and roast pork in black beer sauce. A full selection of the local Alpirsbacher beers is available.
Marktplatz 12, 72275; 07444 955 95; www.loewen-post.de; closed Tue

AROUND SCHWARZWÄLDER TRACHTENMUSEUM
Hellas *moderate*
Enjoy Greek specialities and traditional local dishes, ranging from schnitzel to gyros and calamari, at this hotel-restaurant.
Hauptstrasse 35, 77716 Haslach (east of Schwarzwälder Trachtenmuseum); 07832 97 97 97; www.hotel-storchen. de; closed Wed

DURBACH
[maki:'dan] im Ritter *expensive*
Housed in Hotel Ritter, this gourmet restaurant serves tapas-sized dishes. Try the redfish with cabbage and cardamom, or the oat root with trumpet mushroom and orange, paired with excellent wines.
Tal 1, 77770; 07819 32 30; www.ritter-durbach.de

DAY TRIP OPTIONS
Baden-Baden (just off the A5 motorway) is a great base for day trips.

Past in the present
Spend the day at the Schwarzwälder Freilichtmuseum ⑥ to learn about life on a farm in the 16th century.

From Baden-Baden follow the tour to the museum.

Themes and thrills
With attractions to fill a day, Europa-Park ⑧ near Rust is ideal for families.

Take the tour to the Schiltach and then to Rust. Follow signs to the park.

Wines and vineyards
Try a relaxed tour of the Badische Weinstrasse, following it from the spa town of Baden-Baden ① to Durbach

⑨, where lovely walks through vineyards will enable visitors to appreciate the region. Take a break and taste the local wines at Durbacher Winzergenossenschaft, the wine cooperative shop in Durbach.

Take the route to the B500, then turn in the direction of Karlsruhe, then turn left on to the B3 following signs to Durbach.

TRIP 21

CUCKOO CLOCK COUNTRY
Freiburg to Schluchsee

HIGHLIGHTS

Sun-soaked city
Bask in the sunshine in Freiburg, one of the most
attractive and sunny towns in Germany

Cuckoo clocks
Learn the history of the traditional Black Forest clock
at the Deutsches Uhrenmuseum at Furtwangen,
then choose a clock in Triberg

Serene lakes
Relax by boating or swimming in the
tranquil Titisee or Schluchsee

International vistas
Climb Feldberg, the highest mountain of the southern
Black Forest, for spectacular views of France
and Switzerland

Winter landscape in the pine-fringed Black Forest

CUCKOO CLOCK COUNTRY

Starting in the historic city of Freiburg, this trip leaves the broad Rhine Valley region and climbs up to the dense Black Forest on roads that twist through tiny villages and pass large, half-timbered farmsteads. The Black Forest is known as the land of cuckoo clocks and is famous for its Black Forest cherry gâteau. This tour takes drivers to the excellent clock museum in Furtwangen and to Triberg, where these timepieces can be bought as souvenirs. The wilder region to the southeast of Freiburg comes next and gathers around the Feldberg, which offers good hiking and, in winter, skiing. Neighbouring valleys contain the tranquil lakes of Titisee and Schluchsee and the spa town of St Blasien with its Baroque church.

KEY

Drive route

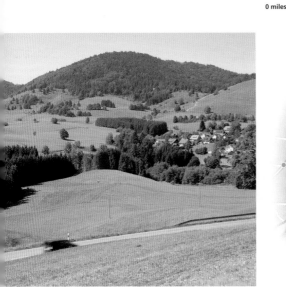

Above Rolling hills en route from Todtnau to St Blasien, *see p223*

ACTIVITIES

Trek to the Schlossberg or Rosskopf, near Freiburg, for spectacular views over the city as well as France

Pick a cuckoo clock as a souvenir from a selection of thousands in Triberg

Gorge on homemade Black Forest cherry gâteau in Triberg

Swim or go boating on the serene lakes of Titisee or Schluchsee

Take a chairlift or hike to the top of the Feldberg for wonderful views

Whizz down a summer toboggan run at Todtnau

Above Cuckoo-clock shop in Titisee, Black Forest, *see p222*

Left Traditional cottage, Titisee region, *see p222*

PLAN YOUR DRIVE

Start/finish: Freiburg to Schluchsee.

Number of days: 2–3 days, allowing half a day to explore Freiburg.

Distance: 173 km (108 miles).

Road conditions: Roads are well paved but often steep and winding, though driving is not particularly difficult. In winter, snow can cover the higher portions of the drive; winter tyres are recommended.

When to go: This drive is best avoided in the winter months (December–March), when the top of the Feldberg is snowbound.

Opening times: Most attractions are open daily. Shops are usually open from 9am to 5pm from Monday to Friday, and close early on Saturdays. Many shops and services are closed on Sundays. Restaurants generally close around 10pm.

Main market days: Freiburg: daily.

Shopping: Cuckoo clocks and woodcarvings can be bought from Uhren-Park in Triberg.

Major festivals: Freiburg: Fasnet (pre-Lenten carnival), Fri–Tue before Ash Wed; Frühlingsfest (spring festival), Apr/May; Zelt-Musik Festival (international tent music festival), late Jun/early Jul; Weinfest (wine festival), Jul; Freiburger Mess' (funfair), Oct; **Triberg:** Maifest (raising the Maypole), 1 May; Triberger Weihnachtszauber (fire and light show around Christmas), Dec; **Titisee:** Nacht in Weiss am Titisee (night in white), Jul; **Feldberg:** Sonnwendfeier (midsummer celebrations), 21 Jun.

DAY TRIP OPTIONS

Those interested in **history** can view the chronicles of the cuckoo clock by first visiting the **Deutsches Uhrmuseum** in Furtwangen and then the cuckoo-clock capital of Triberg. **Adventure lovers** will enjoy exploring the **high mountains**, **waterfalls** and **lakes** south of Freiburg, including Germany's highest waterfalls in Triberg and the region's highest point, Feldberg. For full details, *see p223*.

Above Flowers displayed at the local market in Münsterplatz, Freiburg

VISITING FREIBURG

Parking
Of the half-dozen car parks in central Freiburg, the multi-storey one on Schlossbergring is the most central and convenient.

Tourist Information
Rathausplatz 2-4, 79098; 0761 388 18 80; www.freiburg.de; open daily

WHERE TO STAY

FREIBURG

Zum Roten Bären *moderate*
Operating since 1120, this is the oldest hotel in Germany. It has scattered antiques to provide a historic atmosphere, but offers all modern amenities.
Oberlinden 12, 79098; 0761 38 78 70; www.roter-baeren.de

Colombi *expensive*
The local *grande dame* of hotels, Colombi combines tradition with luxury and modern facilities such as a pool, steam baths, sauna and a gourmet restaurant.
Rotteckring 16, 79098; 0761 210 60; www.colombi.de

TRIBERG

Parkhotel Wehrle *expensive*
The most prestigious lodging in Triberg, this 17th-century house exudes old-fashioned charm in its individually decorated rooms with rustic frills, while the health centre with a pool and garden provides fine areas in which to relax.
Gartenstrasse 24, 78098; 07722 860 20; www.parkhotel-wehrle.de

● FREIBURG

Baden-Württemberg; 79098
Blessed with the sunniest climate in Germany and wooded hills that rise above a picture-postcard old town, the Altstadt, Freiburg, or Freiburg im Breisgau, was founded in 1091. The old town fans out around a magnificent cathedral and has a series of quaint and historic squares with many tempting cafés and restaurants.

A 90-minute walking tour

From the Schlossbergring car park, turn left into Schoferstrasse, briefly right down Herrenstrasse and then left to reach the Gothic cathedral, the **Münster** ①. Rising above this is a tower *(open daily)* with an openwork spire. On leaving the Münster by its main west entrance, enter the heart of a bustling daily market. To the left lies the bright-red **Historisches Kaufhaus** ② built in 1530 when Freiburg was ruled by the Habsburg Empire. The 1761 Baroque town house to its left is the **Wentzingerhaus** ③, once the residence of sculptor Christian Wentzinger (1710–97) and now the Museum für Stadtgeschichte *(closed Mon)*, which offers an interesting insight into local history. To the right of the Wentzingerhaus is Buttergasse, which leads to **Schusterstrasse** ④, one of Freiburg's best-preserved medieval streets. Turn left into this street and right into **Herrenstrasse** ⑤, where pavement mosaics announce tradesmen and shops as they have done for centuries.

Wicker baskets, Freiburg market

Further down this street, turn right into Salzstrasse, looking out for the bronze tiles, **Stolpersteine** ⑥, laid into the cobbled pavement outside No. 7 Salzstrasse. Literally translated as "stumbling blocks", these tiles commemorate the victims of Nazi persecution and are among 75,000 laid around Germany. Further down the street, a left turn down Annengässle and another left into Grünwälderstrasse leads to Augustinerplatz, where the **Augustinermuseum** ⑦ *(closed Mon)* contains the extensive medieval art collection from a former monastery. A walk diagonally across the square leads down to the old tannery street, Gerberau. Continue to Kaiser-Joseph-Strasse, a main thoroughfare that leads to **Martinstor** ⑧, a town gate from 1202 that marks the beginning of the university quarter. Beyond, a left turn down Niemensstrasse leads to Universitätstrasse, where pavement cafés encourage lingering. A right turn down this street leads to **Rathausplatz**

Bächle

A curious feature of Freiburg is its *Bächle*, little streams that flow in pavement troughs through most streets. These streams originally provided water for animals, washing and for putting out fires, but today are largely decorative, though plenty of people use them to cool their feet on hot summer days.

⑨, where the Renaissance Neues Rathaus houses the tourist office. Towering beside this is the mid-14th-century **Martinskirche** ⑩ *(open daily)*, a former Franciscan monastery church that was battered during World War II, but has since been rebuilt. Bear right out of Rathausplatz and follow Rathausgasse to cross Kaiser-Joseph-Strasse and follow the length of Schusterstrasse across the street. Turn left down Herrenstrasse, right down Schoferstrasse and right along Schlossbergring to reach the car park.
🚗 *Turn right on to Schlossbergring and left at Wallstrasse, which becomes Kartäuserstrasse. Follow signs to the town of St Peter, then St Märgen and at Neuhäusle turn left for Glashütte. Drive past Neukirch and turn left on to the B500 to Furtwangen. Turn right into Lindenstrasse to park.*

❷ Deutsches Uhrenmuseum

Baden-Württemberg; 78120
Furtwangen's comprehensive Deutsches Uhrenmuseum *(closed Mon)* has a fascinating collection of 8,000 timepieces in myriad styles from almost every era. The display ranges from sundials and cuckoo clocks to mass-produced watches and clocks.
🚗 *Continue down Lindenstrasse, turn left on Gerwigstrasse, left at Marktplatz and then right on to the B500 to Triberg, and park in the market square.*

The Cuckoo Clock

It was in the 1730s that cuckoo clocks began to be made in the Black Forest area, with Triberg housing most of the early workshops. The quality of the craftsmanship quickly captured the imagination of the European market, as did the quirky designs, which included rooster clocks and moving automata of angry wives beating lazy husbands, as well as the traditional cuckoo popping out of a trapdoor.

❸ Triberg

Baden-Württemberg; 78098
The capital of cuckoo clocks, Triberg is also known for air so pure that it is now a health resort. The town centre, Marktplatz, is flanked by the Baroque **Wallfahrtskirche**. Uphill from here are a series of seven waterfalls and the **Schwarzwaldmuseum** *(Oct–Mar: closed Mon; Apr–Sep: open daily)*, with a collection of clock-making apparatus. South of town is the **Eble Uhren-Park** *(Schonachbach 27; open daily)*, a shop that claims to have the largest cuckoo clock in the world.
🚗 *Take the B500 to Furtwangen and further to Hinterzarten for the Titisee exit. Take Neustädter Strasse; park by the station.*

Above left Painting on the exterior of a clock shop, Triberg **Above** World's largest cuckoo clock, Triberg **Below** Forested slopes on the way to Titisee

HIKING AROUND FREIBURG

Freiburg is an excellent hub for hiking. An easy walk is the one up the Schlossberg or Castle Hill to the east of the old town, which links up with a good selection of further signposted trails. Recommended is the trail to the Rosskopf, the highest point in this cluster of hills, where a huge viewing tower provides superb views over the entire region. For hiking information and maps, contact the tourist information office in Freiburg.

EAT AND DRINK

FREIBURG

Hausbrauerei Feierling *moderate*
This microbrewery, with its wood-and-copper interior decor and lively beer garden, serves good pub food, including delicious giant *Schnitzel* (pork fillet). *Gerberau 46, 79098; 0761 24 34 80; www.feierling.de*

Oberkirchs Weinstube *moderate*
An excellent traditional restaurant with outdoor seating that serves large portions of regional food. *Münsterplatz 22, 79098; 0761 202 68 68; www.hotel-oberkirch.de; closed Sun*

Other options
The **Colombi** *expensive (Rotteckring 16, 79098; 0761 210 60; www.colombi. de; closed Sun & Mon)* has two restaurants – the rustic Hans-Thoma-Stube, with its veal and venison dishes, and the elegant Zirbelstube, which is rated among the best restaurants in Germany for its gourmet fare.

TRIBERG

Adler *inexpensive*
This is a café and hotel with some of the best cakes in the region – including a perfect *Schwarzwälder Kirschtorte* (Black Forest cherry gâteau). *Hauptstrasse 52, 78098; 07722 45 74; www.hotel-cafe-adler.de; closed Mon*

Right Rowing boats on Lake Schluchsee
Below left Church in the mountain town of
Todtnau **Below right** Visitors enjoying a day
out on Lake Schluchsee

BOATING AND CRUISING ON THE TITISEE

Bootsbetrieb Schweizer
Seestrasse 33, 79822; 07651 82 14;
www.bootsbetrieb-schweizer-titisee.de

WHERE TO STAY

TITISEE
Parkhotel Waldeck *moderate*
A traditional guesthouse with small,
simple rooms and spacious suites.
Parkstrasse 4–6, 79822; 07651 80 90;
www.parkhotelwaldeck.de

Treschers *moderate*
This hotel has superb facilities,
including a pool and sauna.
Seestrasse 10, 79822; 07651 80 50;
www.treschers.de

FELDBERG
Haus Waldvogel *moderate*
This large Black Forest house near the
Feldbergpass has plush modern rooms.
Köpfleweg 25, 79868; 07676 480;
www.cafe-waldvogel.de

ST BLASIEN
Dom-Hotel *inexpensive*
This modest but pleasant family-run
hotel is directly opposite the Dom.
Hauptstrasse 4, 79837; 07627 92 46 90;
www.dom-hotel-st-blasien.de

SCHLUCHSEE
Parkhotel Flora *expensive*
This charming four-star hotel offers
lake views along with a pool and sauna.
Sonnhalde 22, 79859; 07656 974 20;
www.parkhotel-flora.de

④ Titisee
Baden-Württemberg; 79822
The lake resort of Titisee offers an
extensive network of well-marked
hiking trails, including an easy 6-km
(4-mile) loop around the lake past
several good swimming spots. A
strenuous alternative is climbing
the 1,200-m (4,000-ft) Hochfirst
Mountain. Maps are available at the
tourist office *(Strandbadstrasse 4, 79822;
07652 120 60)*. Several companies also
offer short lake cruises or rent out
rowing boats, both available on the
lakefront near the town centre.

🚗 *Turn right outside the car park to
follow Neustädter Strasse, then turn
right on to the B500 to join the B317.
Turn right following signs to Haus der
Natur to the large car park beside it.*

⑤ Feldberg
Baden-Württemberg; 79868
At 1,493 m (4,898 ft), Feldberg is the
highest point in the Black Forest. It
has a broad, well-rounded summit,
which rises above the tree line to offer
wonderful views of the region. With
much of the upper mountain being
a nature reserve, wild flowers flourish
here. The scattered presence of Black
Forest farmhouses and the occasional
Alpine hut add to the charm. There are
good hiking options available here.
The 12-km (8-mile) long Feldberg-
Steig is an excellent hiking loop
between five Alpine huts around the
upper reaches of the mountain for
experienced hikers, while others can
reach the summit on the Feldberg
chairlift *(May–Oct: open daily)*.

🚗 *Return to the B317 and continue
on it southwestward toward Todtnau.
Turn left into Lindenstrasse to park at
the Hasenhorn chairlift car park.*

⑥ Todtnau
Baden-Württemberg; 79674
The quiet mountain town of
Todtnau bustles in winter as a gateway to the network of ski lifts around
Feldberg. In summer, most visitors
travel up using the Hasenhorn
chairlift *(May–Nov: open daily)* for the
summer toboggan run. This happens
on a thrilling 3-km (2-mile) long track
suitable for both children and adults.
Alternatively, explore a network
of hiking and mountain bike trails.
Maps are available at the tourist
office *(Meinard-Thoma-Strasse 21;
07652 120 60; closed Sat & Sun)*.

🚗 *Continue on the B317 and turn left
at Geschwend, following signs to St
Blasien. Take the signposted left turning
into the town. Continue on this till the
Hauptstrasse. Park on Hauptstrasse
across the river from the monastery.*

Left Scenic road between Todtnau and St Blasien **Below** Feldberg chairlift, which runs daily to the summit

BOAT TRIPS AROUND SCHLUCHSEE

Thomas Toth
Freiburger Strasse 16, 79859; 07656 92 30; www.seerundfahrten.de; tours from May–mid-Oct

EAT AND DRINK

TITISEE

Treschers *expensive*
An outstanding restaurant, particularly for fans of trout; the venison with wild mushrooms and juniper sauce is also exceptional.
Seestrasse 10, 79822; 07651 80 50; www.treschers.de

FELDBERG

Haus Sommerberg *moderate*
A hotel and restaurant serving light, seasonal gourmet food. Try the crispy roast pike perch with saffron sauce, glazed peas and Bamberger potatoes.
Am Sommerberg 14, 79868; 07655 14 11; www.sommerberg.com; closed Mon

TODTNAU

Zum Hirschen *moderate*
This small guesthouse's restaurant serves seasonal regional cuisine – asparagus in spring, chantarelle mushrooms in late summer and game in late autumn. All dishes are prepared by the chef-owner.
Kapellenstrasse 1, 79674; 07671 18 44; www.hirschen-brandenberg.de; closed Mon & Tue

SCHLUCHSEE

Seehotel Hubertus *moderate*
Located in a conservatory that offers views of Feldberg and the lake, this restaurant serves market-fresh produce and specializes in meat and game dishes.
Seebrugg 9, 79859; 07656 524; www.seehotel-hubertus-schluchsee.de; closed Mon–Wed

7 St Blasien
Baden-Württemberg; 79837

Nestled in a heavily forested valley, **Dom St Blasien** *(open daily)* dominates the skyline of St Blasien. This spa town can trace its roots to its 9th-century foundation as a Benedictine monastery. The Dom itself appeared almost a 1,000 years later. Commissioned by the powerful Prince-Abbot Martin Gerbert, this monastery was designed by French architect Michel d'Ixnard (1723–95), who used St Peter's Basilica in Rome as his model. Completed in 1783, it initiated a wave of monumental Neo-Classical architecture, which swept through Germany. The church has superb acoustics, which are best appreciated during the free classical music concerts *(Jun–early-Sep: held Tue & Sat)*.

🚗 *Return to the outskirts of the town and turn left on to the main road. At Häusern turn left on to the B500 to Schluchsee. On entering Schluchsee, park in the car park on the right.*

8 Schluchsee
Baden-Württemberg; 79859

A larger body of water than Titisee, and further off the beaten track,

Schluchsee is a calm and clean reservoir lake. There are many settlements on its eastern shore, the largest of which is also called Schluchsee. This town has a popular beach and a waterpark that is managed as Aqua Fun *(late-May–mid-Sep: open daily)*. Boat rides are possible with **Thomas Toth** *(May–late-Oct: open daily)*, which conducts trips around the lake with stops at various points. Since 1984, the Schluchseelauf, an 18-km (11-mile) run around the lake, has been held here every May.

DAY TRIP OPTIONS
To break up the drive into day trips, it is best to stay overnight in Freiburg, which is easily accessed from the B31.

On the trail of the cuckoo clock
After viewing the timepieces in Deutsches Uhrenmuseum 2, the clock museum in Furtwangen, head to Triberg 3. Here, visitors can see the cuckoo-clock shops,

as well as explore the town's church, regional museum and waterfalls.

Follow the tour to Furtwangen, take the B500 to Triberg and then follow signs on the B500 and B31 to Freiburg.

Lakes and mountains
Nature lovers will enjoy the scenery around the Titisee 4. From here, it is possible to climb the Feldberg 5

and then visit Lake Schluchsee 8. Adventure enthusiasts can also visit the mountain town of Todtnau 6 and then head to St Blasien 7.

Follow the route to Titisee. Then follow signs on the B500 and B317 to Feldberg. Get onto the B317 to Todtnau. Pass Todtnau and come off the B317 at Geschwend and follow signs to St Blasien and then to Schluchsee.

TRIP 22

CASTLES AND CAVES
Tübingen to Burg Hohenzollern

HIGHLIGHTS

Fairy-tale castles
Explore Schloss Lichtenstein and Burg Hohenzollern
in their stunning cliff-top settings

Limestone caverns
Clamber down into the depths of limestone
caves at Laichingen Tiefenhöhle

Sky-high spire
Marvel at Ulm's Münster, which has the
tallest church spire in the world

Gregorian chanting
Relax at the Baroque Kloster Beuron,
famous for its monastic singing

Schloss Lichtenstein perched on a cliff, Baden-Württemberg

CASTLES AND CAVES

A vast plateau that stretches from Bavaria to the Black Forest, the Swabian Jura (Schwäbische Alb) has always been sparsely populated. Beech woods dominate the landscape, whose system of interconnected stalagmitic caves was carved from sedimentary limestone rocks. The dramatically steep escarpments and craggy outcrops offer ideal perches for an array of romantic castles. The limestone scenery also offers interesting hikes, particularly along the southeastern edge of the Jura, where the Danube begins its trans-European journey along a gorge lined with huge jagged cliffs. This stretch is particularly colourful in spring, when wild flowers bloom, and in autumn, when it glows in a magnificent blanket of golden foliage. The gateway cities of Tübingen and Ulm are both lively and atmospheric, with historic centres.

ACTIVITIES

Descend into the fascinating limestone caves at Laichingen

Take a hike to the many lovely viewpoints around the town of Blaubeuren

Climb the highest church spire in Ulm for views as far back as the Black Forest and the Alps

Hear the dulcet sounds of Gregorian chanting at Kloster Beuron

Explore a 1st-century Roman estate at Hechingen

KEY

Drive route

PLAN YOUR DRIVE

Start/finish: Tübingen to Burg Hohenzollern.

Number of days: 4–5 days, allowing half a day to explore Ulm.

Distance: 370 km (230 miles).

Road conditions: Though narrow and winding in places, all major and minor roads are well paved.

When to go: This route is generally accessible year-round, though the Jura is sometimes snowbound in winter. Summer is the most enjoyable time to visit, particularly during one of Ulm's many festivals.

Opening times: Most attractions are open daily. Shops are open 9am to 6pm Monday to Friday and close early on Saturdays. Most shops and services are closed on Sundays. Restaurants generally close around 10pm.

Main market days: Tübingen: Mon, Wed & Fri; Ulm: Wed & Sat.

Shopping: Look out for delicious chocolates shaped like sparrows in the cafés in Ulm.

Major festivals: Ulm: Stadtfest (city festival), Jun; Bindertanz (coopers' dance), every four years in Jul, next in 2023; Donaufest (music and art festival), every two years in Jul, next in 2024; Schwörwoche (oath week), late Jul; Donaueschingen: Musiktage (music days), Oct.

Above Rural landscape between Beuron and Donaueschingen
Below Blautopf, the source of the Blau river, Blaubeuren, *see p229*

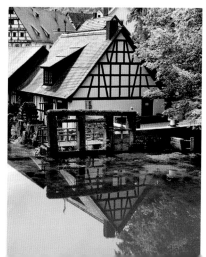

DAY TRIP OPTIONS

Families should visit the **majestic castle** of Schloss Lichtenstein before exploring the **caves** at Laichingen and rounding the day off with an ascent of Ulm's Münster spire. **History enthusiasts** should make the Münster the highlight of a **walking tour in Ulm**, followed by a visit to the local galleries. Those interested in **castles** can combine sightseeing at Lichtenstein with tours of Sigmaringen and Burg Hohenzollern. For a more **scenic journey**, a walk around Blaubeuren is rewarding before following the Danube down to Beuron to hear **Gregorian chanting**. For full details, *see p233*.

Above Punting on the idyllic Neckar river, Tübingen **Below** Town houses along the Neckar river, Tübingen

VISITING TÜBINGEN

Parking
The multi-storey Neckar-Parkhaus car park on Wöhrdstrasse is close to the tourist information office and only a short walk from the city centre.

Tourist Information
An der Neckarbrücke 1, 72072; 07071 913 60; www.tuebingen.de

WHERE TO STAY

TÜBINGEN

Hotel am Bad *moderate*
Located 1.5 km (1 mile) west of the city centre, this good mid-range hotel beside the Neckar offers clean, simple rooms with facilities such as Wi-Fi.
Freibad 2, 72072; 07071 797 40; www.hotel-am-bad.de

Hotel am Schloss *moderate*
This half-timbered hotel with traditional charm, close to the Schloss, offers fine views over the city.
Burgsteige 18, 72070; 07071 929 40; www.hotelamschloss.de

Hotel Krone *moderate*
A traditional-style riverside hotel by the Eberhardsbrücke with pleasant rooms that are furnished with the occasional antique.
Uhlandstrasse 1, 72072; 07071 133 10; www.krone-tuebingen.de

BLAUBEUREN

Ochsen *moderate*
This traditional, half-timbered three-star guesthouse in the heart of the town has comfortable airy rooms and free wireless internet.
Marktstrasse 4, 89143; 07344 96 98 90; www.ochsen-blaubeuren.de

① Tübingen
Baden-Württemberg; 72070
A medieval city, Tübingen first appeared in historical records in 1078 but only grew in status 400 years later, when one of Germany's finest universities was established here. The **Eberhardsbrücke** over the Neckar river is a useful orientation point and the location of the tourist information office. The bridge overlooks the **Platanenallee**, a leafy boulevard on a narrow artificial island alongside which punts pass in front of rows of colourful houses. Crossing the bridge, a left turn on Neue Strasse leads to Holzmarkt, a square dominated by the late 15th- century Gothic **Stiftskirche St Georg** *(open daily)*. Inside, magnificent star vaulting spreads across the nave and aisle roofs and the choir is dappled with beautiful stained-glass windows. A climb up the church tower reveals fine views over the old town. On the opposite side of the Holzmarkt, Kirchgasse leads to Tübingen's **Markt**, whose fountain, Neptunbrunnen, has jolly cherubs depicting the seasons. Behind the fountain, the Gothic **Rathaus** is decorated with Neo-Renaissance frescoes of local heroes, painted to celebrate the university's 400th birthday. On the lower side of the marketplace, Marktgasse runs into a network of old streets of the former wine-growing neighbourhood. Back at the Markt, a walk uphill leads to Burgsteige, where antique shops encourage lingering on the way to **Schloss Hohentübingen**. Expanded in the early 17th century, this 11th-century castle now serves various university departments and houses a scientific museum *(open Wed–Sun)*.

🚗 *From the multi-storey car park on Wöhrdstrasse, turn left and left again at Friedrichstrasse. Head south on B27, then turn left for Gomaringen and follow Lichtensteinstrasse until signs for Genkingen. Here, look out for brown signs to Schloss Lichtenstein car park.*

Tübingen's Scholars
Tübingen has attracted many fine scholars over the years, including theologian Philipp Melanchthon, philosopher Georg Wilhelm Friedrich Hegel, astronomer Johannes Keppler and psychiatrist Alois Alzheimer. The Romantic poet Friedrich Hölder spent the latter part of his life in the city, while Johann Wolfgang von Goethe published his first works here. More recently, Hermann Hesse worked as a bookbinder here before achieving literary fame.

② Schloss Lichtenstein

Baden-Württemberg; 72805

Perched at the top of a cliff on the edge of the Swabian Jura, the photogenic Schloss Lichtenstein *(Mar–Dec: open daily)* overlooks the plains around Tübingen, conveying a sense of being at the very periphery of a mountain range. The gabled and turreted castle dates back to the 1840s, when it was built according to the exaggerated literary descriptions of fairy-tale writer Wilhelm Hauff about an earlier castle that occu-pied this site. Bristling with horrific-looking weapons, the castle's most impressive feature, its armoury, is as vivid as any fairy tale.

🚗 *Return downhill from car park, then turn left toward Riedlingen/ Reutlingen, then Münsingen. From here, follow B465 through the town and on towards Laichingen until signs for Tiefenhöhle.*

③ Laichingen Tiefenhöhle

Baden-Württemberg; 89150

This cave network *(Easter–early Nov: open daily)* was discovered in 1892 by local sand-digger Johann Georg Mack, who wondered where all his piles of sand were disappearing until he found a crack in the ground into which he lowered his son. The local community developed Laichingen Tiefenhöhle into an attraction in the 1930s, building walkways and fitting ladders. It is now possible to descend 55 m (180 ft) into the caves without any special equipment. Visitors can wander the caverns at their own pace, which provides a sense of exploration. Warm clothing is required as the caves are at a constant temperature of 8° C (46° F).

🚗 *From Tiefenhöhle, turn left and follow signs for Blaubeuren via B28. Turn left at Marktstrasse, right at Bergstrasse, straight on to Weilerstrasse and then into Auf dem Graben, where there is a car park.*

④ Blaubeuren

Baden-Württemberg; 89143

Blaubeuren is worth a stop simply to see the source of the Blau river, which joins the Danube in Ulm. The 20-m (65-ft) deep **Blautopf**, or "Blue Pot", is usually an incredible, clear, turquoise-coloured pool of water, although rain transforms this into green, then yellowy brown. Beside it lies the **Hammerschmiede**, a mid-18th-century mill and smithy, which is at the trailhead of a number of hikes. Over the road, but accessed by entrances to the right, are the town's half-timbered former monastery workshops. Dating from 1510, these only saw 25 years of use before the Reformation disbanded the monastery, which had been founded here in 1085.

🚗 *Follow signs from centre of Blaubeuren to Ulm via B28. At Ulm follow signs for Stadtmitte over the bridge on to Wengengasse and turn right on to Sedelhofgasse, then left on to Bahnhofsplatz. Follow Friedrich-Ebert-Strasse and Neue Strasse to the Parkhaus am Rathaus car park.*

Below Limpid, aqua-coloured waters of Blautopf, Blaubeuren

Above Schloss Lichtenstein, immortalized in a novel by Wilhelm Hauff

HIKING AROUND BLAUBEUREN

The Blautopf is the trailhead of a number of hikes, including a circuit of Blaubeuren. Marked by an "A" on the trailhead map, this 6-km (4-mile) long trail circuits the valley to provide good views and takes around 90 minutes to complete. *www.blaubeuren.de*

EAT AND DRINK

TÜBINGEN

Neckarmüller *inexpensive*
A convivial riverside beer garden, attached to a microbrewery, with a fine selection of beers. The restaurant also serves good basic dishes, such as *Maultaschen* (Swabian ravioli). *Gartenstrasse 4, 72074; 07071 278 48; www.neckarmueller.de*

Tübinger Wurstküche *moderate*
Looking back on a 200-year history, Tübinger Wurstküche serves traditional fare. Try the "Swabian Aperitives" – house specialities – from the wine list,. *Am Lustnauer Tor 8, 72074; 07071 927 50; www.wurstkueche.com*

Weinstube Forelle *expensive*
This traditional, old-world wine bar offers good food such as trout in almond butter and a range of game dishes. An excellent selection of local wines is also available. *Kronenstrasse 8, 72070; 07071 566 89 80; www.weinstube-forelle.de*

BLAUBEUREN

Ochsen *moderate*
This restaurant has a reputation for fine regional cuisine. The oxtail ragout is a speciality, as is the seasonal asparagus. *Marktstrasse 4, 89143; 07344 96 98 90; www.ochsen-blaubeuren.de; closed Sun*

Above Weekly market on Münsterplatz, Ulm

VISITING ULM

Parking
The Parkhaus am Rathaus car park on Neue Strasse is very near the Münster.

Tourist Information
Münsterplatz 50, 89073; 0731 161 28 30; www.tourismus.ulm.de; Apr–Dec: open daily; Jan–Mar: open Mon–Sat

WHERE TO STAY

ULM

Hotel Bäumle *moderate*
A renovated building from 1413 with standard hotel rooms and free Internet.
Kohlgasse 6, 89073; 0731 622 87; www.hotel-baeumle.de

Münster Hotel *moderate*
The Münster Hotel provides en-suite rooms with pretty views of the Münster.
Münsterplatz 14, 89073; 07315 521 86 74; www.ulmermuensterhotel.de

Hotel Schiefes Haus *expensive*
This famously crooked half-timbered house from 1443 has uneven floors and beds with legs of different lengths.
Schwörhausgasse 6, 89073; 07319 679 30; www.hotelschiefeshausulm.de

Maritim Hotel *expensive*
With modern rooms, this is Ulm's best hotel. Facilities include bike hire.
Basteistrasse 40, 89073; 07319 230; www.maritim.de

AROUND KLOSTER BEURON

Burg Wildenstein *inexpensive*
This 11th-century stronghold on a cliff is now a youth hostel. The accommodation is ideal for family stays.
Jugendherberge Burg Wildenstein, 88637 Leibertingen (7 km/4 miles east of Kloster Beuron); 07466 411; www.jugendherberge.de

⑤ ULM

Baden-Württemberg; 89073
Lying on the Danube river, Ulm grew prosperous in the Middle Ages. Over time, corruption, wars and epidemics undermined the city's wealth. In 1944, its glorious historic core was destroyed during bombing raids. Fortunately, its giant Münster came out relatively unscathed. Today, a great deal of the city has been replaced by modern buildings.

A two-hour walking tour

From the Parkhaus am Rathaus car park, it is a very short walk up the Kramgasse to reach the vast sweep of **Münsterplatz** ①, which gives Ulm its focal point. The dimensions of the square are matched by the gigantic Gothic Münster *(open daily)*, which was begun in 1377. Designed for a standing congregation of 20,000, its plans included the world's tallest spire. However, it wasn't until 1890 that the spire reached its full height of 161 m (530 ft). The climb up its 768 steps offers fine views of the Black Forest and, on clearer days, the Alps. Inside, the eye is drawn upwards by the 42-m (138-ft) high nave and the pulpit. The elegant 26-m (85-ft) tabernacle is eye-catching, as is the vast 1471 fresco that covers the chancel arch. Turning left out of the Münster, cross Neue Strasse and turn right along Sattlergasse to arrive at Weinhof Square. The **Schwörhaus** ②, or oath house, is where Ulm residents gather

Flower market, outside the Münster

on *Schwörmontag* in the annual tradition of hearing their mayor pledge the 1397 city oath.

Back on Sattlergasse, a left turn leads to Weinhofberg and down to the start of Fischergasse and the heart of the old fisherman's quarter, **Fischerviertel** ③, once home to medieval artisans. Look out for the pretzel carved in the door frame of a baker at Fischergasse 22, and the symbol of a boatman at Fischergasse 18. An alley at the end of Fischergasse turns left to the quirky medieval **Schiefes Haus** ④, or crooked house, which leans precariously over a stream. Return to ischergasse and turn left to a small square where stairs climb onto the 1480 riverside defence wall.

A walk further along reveals another crooked building: the 14th-century defensive tower of the **Metzgerturm** ⑤. Walking uphill beneath the Metzgerturm leads to the marketplace, where the glassy central library, Zentralbibliothek, by architect Gottfried Böhm, lies opposite the Fischkastenbrunnen, or Fish Crate Fountain. Between the two, the 16th-century **Rathaus** ⑥ is decorated with lavish frescoes on its façade celebrating Ulm's medieval heyday. To the right of the Rathaus, the Kunsthalle Weishaupt *(closed Mon)*, a striking modern building over the square, displays Modern and Pop Art by various artists including Andy Warhol, Paul Klee, Wassily Kandinsky and Pablo Picasso. The gallery is joined to the **Ulmer Museum** ⑦ *(closed Mon)*, the city's history museum, which is interesting for paintings of medieval Ulm. Walk back to the corner of Neue Strasse and Kramgasse to the Parkhaus am Rathaus car park.

🚗 *Take the B19 and turn left on to B311. After 60 km (37 miles) crossing Ehingen turn right at Herbertingen on to B32 and left in Sigmaringen on to Fürst-Wilhelm-Strasse to the car park.*

The Tailor of Ulm
Dangling inside Ulm's Rathaus is a replica of the hang-glider of local tailor Albrecht Berblinger, who crash-landed this design into the Danube in 1811. Worn down by ceaseless jibes, with his business in tatters, he died bankrupt in 1825. His design has since proven to be the world's first workable aircraft.

⑥ Schloss Sigmaringen
Baden-Württemberg; 72488
The stately Schloss Sigmaringen *(Mar–Dec: open daily)* dominates the skyline of the small royal town of Sigmaringen. First mentioned in 1077, the castle was brutally ransacked by Swedes in 1632 during the Thirty Years' War and destroyed by a huge domestic fire in 1893, leaving only two towers standing. Substantially redesigned in the eclectic style from 1899, the castle is still owned by a branch of the Hohenzollern family, who unified Germany in the 19th century; a process helped by having this powerbase in the south. Its impressive armoury is a highlight of the castle tours.

🚗 *Return to B32, cross the bridge and turn left following signs to Beuron. At Beuron, turn left at signpost for Kloster Beuron for the car park.*

⑦ Kloster Beuron
Baden-Württemberg; 88631
Some of the most dramatic sections of the Upper Danube Valley lie around the village of Beuron. An enormous Baroque monastery, Kloster Beuron, was founded here in 1077 by Augustinians. Most of the buildings date from the late 17th century, and its church is relatively restrained by regional Baroque standards, though lively frescoes of the patron saints and legends of the foundation of the monastery decorate the naves. Of greatest interest is the glorious Gregorian chanting that accompanies some services, especially on holidays. Beuron is also a good base for hiking trips, and a map at the car park details well-marked local options.

🚗 *Return to Beuron and turn left to Tuttlingen on to B311, which becomes B31. Turn left on to B27 signposted "Donaueschingen", then right for Donaueschingen-Mitte, following signs for the Schloss.*

Above Aerial view of Kloster Beuron in the Danube Valley **Below** Schloss Sigmaringen towering over town buildings

EAT AND DRINK

ULM

Allgäuer Hof *moderate*
Fine old-fashioned inn where almost everything is served on a sweet or savoury *Pfannkuchen* (crêpe).
Fischergasse 12, 89073; 07316 74 08; www.erstes-ulmer-pfannkuchen haus.de; closed Mon

Zur Forelle *moderate*
This snug 1626 Fischerviertel house, with a Napoleonic cannonball lodged in the wall, serves good regional food. Try the *Gaisburger Marsch* (a hearty beef, potato and *Spätzle* stew), or the house speciality, *Forelle* (trout). Physicist Albert Einstein and conductor Herbert von Karajan both dined here. Booking is required.
Fischergasse 25, 89073; 07316 39 24; www.zurforelle.com; closed Sun

Bi:Braud *expensive*
A gourmet restaurant with a young team serving innovative regional cuisine. Try the charolais beef with artichokes or the smoked char.
Büchsengasse 20, 89073; 07311 53 75 12; www.bebrout.com; closed Sun & Mon

Panorama *expensive*
The best of three restaurants in the Maritim hotel serves high-quality international and regional cuisine with lovely views over Ulm from the 16th floor.
Basteistrasse 40, 89073; 0731 923 17 39; www.maritim.de

AROUND SCHLOSS SIGMARINGEN

Gasthaus Bären *moderate*
This hotel-restaurant serves traditional German food, game and, in the winter, fine Prague roast goose.
Burgstrasse 2, 72488 Sigmaringen (west of Schloss Sigmaringen); 07571 73 09 99; closed Mon

Above Lovely view of the town from castle grounds, Haigerloch **Below left** Orchestra fountain, Donaueschingen **Below right** Gateway to Schloss Haigerloch

WHERE TO STAY

DONAUESCHINGEN

Hotel Linde *moderate*
Traditional, central guesthouse above a good restaurant with standard rooms and free Wi-Fi.
Karlstrasse 18, 78166; 0771 831 80; www.hotel-linde-ds.de

Zum Hirschen *moderate*
Family-run guesthouse whose spacious rooms have a contemporary elegance. All have access to Wi-Fi.
Herdstrasse 5, 78166; 0771 898 55 80; www.hotel-zum-hirschen.de

Öschberghof *expensive*
This health and golf resort-hotel with boutique-style rooms offers a range of saunas and a large pool. The golf course is one of the best in the region.
Golfplatz 1, 78166; 0771 840; www.oeschberghof.com

HAIGERLOCH

Schloss Haigerloch *expensive*
Housed in a 16th-century castle, this lovely hotel offers brightly coloured rooms with all modern comforts.
Schlossstrasse 3, 72401; 07474 69 30; www.schloss-haigerloch.de

⑧ Donaueschingen
Baden-Württemberg; 78166

The longest river in Western Europe, the Danube begins in Donaueschingen, where its source is marked by a stone basin, Donauquelle. This lies on the fringes of the palace gardens of **Schloss Donaueschingen** *(Apr–Oct: open daily, guided tours only; 07712 296 775 63)*, an 18th-century Baroque palace that was extensively renovated in *belle époque* style at the end of the 19th century. Tours visit the luxurious rooms of the Fürstenberg family, who once resided here. In 1283, this family also started the **Fürstenberg Brewery**, which can be visited on pre-booked tours *(Jun–Sep: Mon–Fri, Oct–May: Tue–Fri; 0771 862 06)*. To get there from the car park, turn right and then take the first right down Postplatz before walking left along Haldenstrasse to the brewery complex.

🚗 *Return to the B27 following signs to Villingen-Schwenningen, then to Schwenningen Ost. At the first roundabout follow brown signs to Internationale Luftfahrtmuseum for the car park.*

⑨ Internationales Luftfahrtmuseum
Baden-Württemberg; 78056

The private collection of an avid pilot, Villingen-Schwenningen's **Internationales Luftfahrtmuseum** *(closed Mon)* is the fruit of a lifetime spent collecting and reconstructing aeronautical memorabilia. Among the collection are rebuilt versions of early World War I planes of the kind that the Red Baron, the German flying ace, once flew. But most of the aircraft are Cold War-era oddities, bought upon their decommissioning and flown here from around Europe. Every September there's a festival with flight demonstrations and parachute jumps.

Logo, Fürstenberg beer

🚗 *Return to B27 continue further passing Rottweil. Then turn left to B463 after crossing Balingen town. Continue northward, following signs for Haigerloch. Turn right to park in small multi-storey park in lower town centre.*

⑩ Haigerloch
Baden-Württemberg; 72401

Pretty Haigerloch is draped around a ridge and surrounded by lush greenery where lilacs blossom in spring. It is a quiet town, and very remote, which is why, during World War II, an old beer cellar at the base of a cliff here became a secret atomic research laboratory. Today, the **Atomkeller-Museum** *(May–Sep: open daily; Mar, Apr, Oct & Nov: open Sat & Sun)* commemorates this research. At the time, nuclear science was still in its infancy and the race was on to beat the Soviets and French to any research the Germans may have done, so the Americans sent scientists and troops to methodically dismantle and ship everything to the US. The whole cellar complex was to be blown up afterwards, but luckily, the priest from the 16th-century Gothic **Schlosskirche** *(open daily)*, perched on the cliff above, convinced the Americans to use small controlled explosions only after showing them the church's ornate Rococo decor and the impressive 1609 altar. The Renaissance **Schloss Haigerloch** (1580) beside the church is now an attractive hotel, restaurant and arts venue. On the opposite side of its courtyard, a short path leads along a cliff to a lookout with great views of the town. The steps up to the church and castle are found by turning right out of the Atomkeller and following the base of the cliff.

🚗 *From the car park turn left in the direction of Rangendingen and continue toward the signposted Freilichtmuseum car park.*

⑪ Freilichtmuseum Hechingen-Stein

Baden-Württemberg; 72379
A fascinating open-air museum, **Freilichtmuseum Hechingen-Stein** *(Apr–Oct: closed Mon)* preserves the ruins of a sizable Roman country estate, the result of a chance discovery during road construction. Between AD 1 and 3 this estate was of regional importance and a vital staging post for travellers passing through the area. Some key buildings have been reconstructed, while an ongoing archaeological excavation uncovers more foundations beyond the estate compound. Little is known about the estate – even its name is a mystery – but it was certainly destroyed by Germanic tribes as they pushed the Romans out of southern Germany.

🚗 *Exit the car park and take the first right down Römerstrasse. Continue toward the B27 junction and drive south until brown signs for Burg Hohenzollern lead to the castle. Turn right to car park at shuttle bus stop below Burg Hohenzollern.*

⑫ Burg Hohenzollern

Baden-Württemberg; 72379
Sitting on an isolated crag in a broad valley, Burg Hohenzollern *(open daily)* is one of Germany's finest fairy-tale castles. Yet its medieval-looking battlements and towers are deceptive, since they were built between 1846 and 1867, albeit using the foundations of castles that have stood here since the 11th century. Only **St-Michael-Kapelle**, a chapel with ornate stained glass, survives in its original state. The castle still belongs to the Hohenzollern family, who reigned over a united Germany between 1871 and 1918, and the crown of German Emperor Wilhelm II is the pride of the castle treasury. Also among the family artifacts are several snuff boxes from the collection of Frederick the Great.

Above Soaring towers of the majestic Neo-Gothic Burg Hohenzollern

EAT AND DRINK

DONAUESCHINGEN

Osteria Veneta *moderate*
The Hotel Linde restaurant serves excellent Italian food.
Karlstrasse 18, 78166; 07718 31 80; www.hotel-linde-ds.de

Other options
For pub food and beers, try **Bräustüble** *(Postplatz 1-4; 07713 669; www.braeu stueble-ds.de)*. The **Ösch Noir** *(Golfplatz 1, 78166; 0771 840; closed Mon & Tue)* is the best restaurant in the region.

HAIGERLOCH

Schloss Haigerloch *expensive*
Dine while listening to live piano music on Saturday nights.
Schlossstrasse 3, 72401; 07474 69 30; closed Mon–Wed & Sun dinner

Other options
Traditional fare vegan options at **Hotel Restaurant Krone** *(Oberstadtstrasse 47, 07474 954 40; www.krone-haigerloch. de; closed Wed & Thu)*.

DAY TRIP OPTIONS

With its pleasant atmosphere, Tübingen makes the best base along this drive. Local motorways, particularly the A81, help speed up the return part of day trips to the southern portion of the route.

Caves and historic Ulm

Visit Schloss Lichtenstein ❷ before exploring the caves at Laichingen ❸. To tour Ulm ❺, ascend the Münster spire; then visit the art museum, Kunsthalle Weishaupt, as well as the Ulmer Museum.

Follow the tour to Ulm, but skip stop at Blaubeuren. Follow the B28 to A8, then to Ulm. Return via the A8 and B28.

Castle hopping

Treat yourself to three of Germany's finest castles – Schloss Lichtenstein ❷, Schloss Sigmaringen ❻ and Burg Hohenzollern ⑫ – in a day and enjoy scenic drives on minor roads across the Swabian Alb.

Follow the route to Schloss Lichtenstein and beyond to the B313, turn left to Gammertingen on to the B32. Turn left to Sigmaringen. Retrace

the route, follow the B32 to turn left on to the B463, and then left again to Burg Hohenzollern.

Scenic trail along the Danube

The walk around picturesque Blaubeuren ❹ is a relaxed and scenic option. Next, follow the Danube to reach the imposing Benedictine monastery of Kloster Beuron ❼.

Follow the tour to Blaubeuren, take the B492, turn right at the B311 and right again on to the B32 via Sigmaringen to Beuron.

TRIP 23

GERMANY'S RIVIERA
Konstanz to Friedrichshafen

HIGHLIGHTS

Tranquil islands
Take a day trip to the Bodensee Islands of Reichenau
and Mainau, rich in history and flora

Prehistoric homes
Visit the Pfahlbauten, an open-air museum that has a
reconstruction of how Bodensee man is believed
to have lived 3,000 years ago

Zeppelins
Stop by the Zeppelin Museum in Friedrichshafen, which
commemorates an important aeronautical achievement
and is a hub for modern Zeppelin trips

Wines and vineyards
Sample local vintages from Germany's sunniest region
at the wine bars and vineyards along the route

GERMANY'S RIVIERA

The giant Lake Constance (Bodensee) forms much of Germany's southwest border with Switzerland, which provides a spectacular Alpine backdrop. The lake's balmy, dry climate makes it perfect for lounging on beaches and for outdoor activities such as hiking, cycling on lakeside trails, swimming and boating. The cosmopolitan hub of Konstanz has boat services to many points on the lake. Rich soils and a near-tropical climate have enabled Mainau to maintain one of Germany's most elaborate landscaped gardens, while Reichenau has specialized in market gardening. The towns that line Bodensee's northern shore include the attractive, medieval Meersburg, which has the oldest castle in Germany. To the east, Friedrichshafen, once the hub for Zeppelin flights around the world, has a fine museum devoted to the airships.

Below Arched gateway out of the old town, Konstanz, *see pp238–9*

ACTIVITIES

Spend the day at a beach near Konstanz

Take a boat trip to the gardens of Mainau or the ancient monasteries of Reichenau

Sample local wines while enjoying splendid views of the Alps at Weingut Aufricht, near Meersburg

Tour reconstructions of ancient Bodensee at Unteruhldingen's Pfahlbauten Museum

Take a trip in a modern Zeppelin over Friedrichshafen

Above Tree-lined road to Reichenau, *see p239*

KEY

▓▓ Drive route

0 kilometres   5

0 miles   5

PLAN YOUR DRIVE

Start/finish: Konstanz to Lindau Island.

Number of days: 2–3 days, allowing a day to explore the Bodensee Islands.

Distance: 90 km (56 miles).

Road conditions: Well-paved roads.

When to go: This trip is good year-round, though in summer (June, July & August) traffic along the coastal roads can be heavy. Spring (April & May), when fruit trees are in bloom, is particularly attractive. Wine lovers should try to visit during autumn (September & October), when many festivals are held.

Opening times: Most attractions open daily. Shops are open from 9am to 5pm, Monday to Friday, and close early on Saturdays. Most shops and services are closed on Sundays. Restaurants generally close around 10pm.

Main market days: Konstanz: Wed & Sat; Friedrichshafen: Tue, Fri & Sat.

Shopping: The Saturday market on Adenauerplatz in Konstanz sells fresh regional specialities, including homemade sausages and cheese.

Major festivals: Konstanz: Bodenseefestival (Bodensee festival), Apr/May; Konstanzer Musikfestival (Konstanz Music Days), mid-Jun & mid-Jul; Seenachtsfest (late night festival), Aug; **Mainau:** Orchideenschau (orchid show) Mar–May; Gräfliches Inselfest (count's island festival), May; **Meersburg:** Winzerfest (winegrowers' festival), Jul; Bodensee Weinfest (wine festival), Sep.

DAY TRIP OPTIONS

Despite the need for a ferry to access the northern shore, Konstanz is the best Bodensee base. A day can be spent exploring **historic** Konstanz and the nearby **garden island** of Mainau, with the option of **swimming** before heading back to Konstanz. The highlights of the north shore can be covered in a day and include **prehistoric dwellings**, a **Baroque church**, the **fairy-tale town** of Meersburg and the intriguing **Zeppelin Museum** in Friedrichshafen. For full details, *see p241*.

Above A scene from the *Chronicle of the Council of Konstanz* on the façade of a house, Konstanz

VISITING KONSTANZ

Parking
The most convenient car park is just off the Fischmarkt on Münzgasse.

Tourist Information
Bahnhofplatz 43, 78462; 07531 133 030; www.konstanz.de/tourismus; Nov–Apr: closed Sat & Sun

WALKING AROUND KONSTANZ

The Rhine promenade begins at the Archäologisches Landesmuseum in Konstanz and joins a lakeside path that leads to the ferry terminal at Staad, and beyond to Mainau, from where boats return to Konstanz. This enables a one-way hike of around two hours, with a string of beaches to stop and swim along the way. Take bus No. 1 from the ferry terminal to get back to Konstanz.

WHERE TO STAY IN KONSTANZ

Barbarossa *moderate*
A central, mid-range guesthouse with several elegantly furnished rooms.
Obermarkt 8–12, 78462; 07531 12 89 90; www.hotelbarbarossa.de

Hotel Halm *moderate*
A grand old hotel opposite the train station with modern rooms. The restaurant serves Moroccan dishes.
Bahnhofplatz 6, 78462; 07531 12 10; www.hotel-halm.de

Hotel Schiff *moderate*
A good waterfront option, close to the car ferry, this hotel has a fine restaurant.
William-Graf-Platz 2, 78464; 07531 310 41; www.hotel-schiff-konstanz.de

Steigenberger Inselhotel *expensive*
This five-star hotel is housed in a former 13th-century Dominican monastery.
Auf der Insel 1, 78462; 07531 12 50; www.steigenberger.com

❶ KONSTANZ

Baden-Württemberg; 78462

The largest settlement on the Bodensee, Konstanz (Constance) avoided being bombed during World War II as it straddled the border of neutral Switzerland. As a result, its old town remains intact and is a reminder of the time when the town thrived as an imperial Free City. It became famous between 1414 and 1418, when the Council of Konstanz met here to restructure the Catholic Church. The town's picturesque lakefront is dotted with promenades and statues.

A two-hour walking tour

From the car park turn left down Fischmarkt and cross the main road, Konzilstrasse, to arrive at the lakefront. Here stands the **Konzilgebäude** (council building) ①, a conference and concert hall that began life as a granary and warehouse. Its name suggests that it probably served as a venue for the Council of Konstanz. Also linked to that era is the Imperia, a 9-m (30-ft) rotating statue of a woman at the end of the pier. It represents a courtesan in an Honoré de Balzac novel, who used her charms to manipulate the Catholic clergy during the Council. Back near the beginning of the pier, another statue commemorates Count Graf Ferdinand von Zeppelin (1838–1917), a pioneer of airships who was born in Konstanz. From here the lakefront promenade passes a series of **old warehouses** ②,

which have been converted into a restaurant district beside a yacht harbour. At the end of the promenade lies the aquarium complex of **Sea Life** ③ *(open daily)*. Walk back and continue to the opposite end of the promenade, cross the Stadtgarten to the Insel, an island which was long occupied by a Dominican priory that is today the Steigenberger Inselhotel. Cross the Konzilstrasse and turn right to a pedestrian underpass that resurfaces on the banks of the Rhine beside the **Rheintorturm** ④, a 15th-century defensive tower with a conical roof. The bridge over the Rhine leads to the **Archäologisches Landesmuseum** ⑤ or State Archaeology Museum *(closed Mon)*, which is housed in a former convent. Many of its finds are Roman, including 2nd-century bronzes of lion heads and sea leopards. Returning over the Rhine bridge and along the pedestrian underpass, follow Konzilstrasse before turning right down **Münsterplatz** ⑥, which is surrounded by old town houses from as far back as the 15th century. The nearby Münster *(open daily)* commands attention – built of local sandstone, the church has oak doors that are known for their carvings of New Testament scenes. Later additions include the Baroque high altar and the Neo-Gothic spires, which can be climbed for views. From here turn left down Wessenbergstrasse,

Jan Hus (1370–1415)
A Bohemian religious reformer, Jan Hus attacked ecclesiastical abuses and started the Hussite religious movement, which demanded a set of reforms that anticipated the Protestant Reformation. Hus was excommunicated in 1411, then invited to the Council of Konstanz in 1415 to explain his position. Instead he was incarcerated and placed on trial. He is believed to have stood in the central aisle of the Münster to hear the judgement, which was that he should be burned at the stake for heresy. Later, he became a figurehead for the Czechs.

which becomes Hussenstrasse, where the **Hus-Museum** ⑦ *(closed Mon)* occupies the house where the reformer Jan Hus stayed prior to his imprisonment. This museum documents his life and ideologies through displays. Turn left from here, then right down Neugasse and left along Rosengartenstrasse, which leads to the **Rosgartenmuseum** ⑧ *(closed Mon)*, the town's history museum. Its collection helps bring medieval Konstanz to life and includes the *Chronicle of the Council of Konstanz*, a richly illustrated book by Ulrich Richental, a local landowner. Turn right to Markstätte, the commercial hub of the town. Walk to the right along this and left down Brotlaube to return to the Fischmarkt car park.
🚗 *From the car park, turn left and left again on to Konzilstrasse. Follow signs for Reichenau/B33, turning left to cross causeway to the island. The museum is signposted with facilities for car park.*

② Reichenau
Baden-Württemberg; 78479
Even though the causeway to the island of Reichenau is only 2 km (1 mile) long, the island's sense of remoteness, together with a perfect climate, encouraged Benedictines to found a monastery here in AD 724. One of Europe's centres of learning in the 10th century, it was famous for its library and scriptorium, where monks would produce manuscripts. Copies can be purchased in the **Museum Reichenau** *(Apr–Oct: open daily, Nov–Mar: open Sat & Sun)*, which provides an introduction to the island's three surviving churches.

Pretty flowers in Reichenau

🚗 *Return to the B33, turn left then right on to Radolfzeller Strasse. Turn right on to Unterer Riedhaldeweg, then left on to Hauptweg to park.*

③ Mainau
Baden-Württemberg; 78465
The thriving palm groves and flower gardens *(open daily)* of the island of Mainau are reminiscent of the Mediterranean, but against an Alpine backdrop. The formal gardens here were planted in 1853 on the initiative of Grand Duke Friedrich I of Baden and his current descendant, the German-Swedish Countess Bernadotte, continues the tradition. In summer, the Italian Rose Garden blooms, as do dahlias in autumn.
🚗 *Return to Unterer Riedhaldeweg and turn left on to it. In Staad, turn left on to the B33 to the dock for the Staad-Meersburg ferry.*

Above Vineyard with Bodensee in the background, Reichenau **Below** Cycling past the Benedictine monastery, Reichenau

EAT AND DRINK

KONSTANZ
Hafenhalle *moderate*
The largest of the harbourside restaurants, with a lively adjacent beer garden, Hafenhalle offers good local fish and game. During summer, stop here for Sunday brunch and enjoy bands playing Dixieland jazz.
Hafenstrasse 10, 78462; 07531 211 26; www.hafenhalle.com

Staader Fährhaus *moderate*
This stylish restaurant with a pleasant outdoor terrace beside the ferry terminal in Staad serves creative local fish dishes as well as a good selection of vegetarian food.
Fischerstrasse 30, 78464; 07531 361 67 63; www.staaderfaehrhaus.de; closed Tue dinner, Wed & Thu

Other options
Among the many cosy places to enjoy a drink in Konstanz are the **Brauhaus Johann Albrecht** *inexpensive (Konradigasse 2, 78462; 07531 250 45; www.brauhaus-joh-albrecht.de)*, a microbrewery with an array of beers and pub food. The **Weinhandlung Franz Fritz** *inexpensive (Niederburggasse 7, 78462; 07531 213 67; www.weinhandlung-fritz.de; closed Thu & Fri lunch)*, a rustic backstreet wine bar, serves regional wines until midnight.

MAINAU
Schwedenschenke *moderate*
A Swedish countryside restaurant in a romantic setting. It's renowned for its Swedish meatballs but also offers excellent fresh local perch and trout. .
Insel Mainau, 78465; 07531 303 156; www.mainau.de; closed Mon & Tue

WHERE TO STAY

MEERSBURG

Gasthof zum Bären *moderate*
A romantic 13th-century inn, with small rooms, enjoying a perfect location in the heart of the old town.
Marktplatz 11, 88709; 07532 432 20; www.baeren-meersburg.de

Seehof *moderate*
Overlooking the harbour, the Seehof has modern rooms, some with balcony and lake views. There's a shuttle service to the town car park beside the ferry landing.
Unterstadtstrasse 36, 88709; 07532 808 17 33; www.meersburg-seehof.de

FRIEDRICHSHAFEN

Buchhorner Hof *moderate*
This traditional hotel provides bright rooms with Bodensee views and modern facilities.
Friedrichstrasse 33, 88045; 07541 20 50; www.buchhorn.de

Gasthof Rebstock *moderate*
Located a short walk northwest of the centre, this family-run guesthouse has clean and comfortable rooms. It has a beer garden and offers e-bike rentals.
Werastrasse 35, 88045; 07541 950 16 40; www.gasthof-rebstock-fn.de

Hotel Maier *moderate*
The elegant Hotel Maier is 5 km (3 miles) west of central Friedrichshafen. Rooms are of the bold boutique variety and have a satellite TV and other facilities.
Poststrasse 1–3, 88048; 07541 40 40; www.hotel-maier.de

④ Meersburg
Baden-Württemberg; 88709

Nestled between vineyards and with an atmospheric castle looming over its half-timbered pedestrian centre, Meersburg is fairy-tale Germany come to life. From its main street, Unterstadtstrasse, which runs parallel to the lakefront, Steigstrasse leads to the gates of the austere Burg Meersburg, or **Alte Burg** *(open daily)*. With foundations laid by Merovingian King Dagobert I in AD 628, this is Germany's oldest castle. The Prince-Bishops of Konstanz, who used it as a

---

Annette von Droste-Hülshoff (1797–1848)

Perhaps the greatest ever German female poet, Annette von Droste-Hülshoff spent her later years in the Altes Schloss in Meersburg. The dank castle was the perfect muse for her tortured Romantic verses, but it was probably the cause of her death too, for she died of pneumonia here in 1848. Her flowery Biedermeier quarters have been well preserved and remain intact.

---

summer residence from 1268, were inspired to build a cheerful-looking palace in the 18th century. Baroque architect Balthasar Neumann built the pastel-pink **Neues Schloss**, but this could only be enjoyed until secularization in 1802. It provides great views of the Bodensee.

🚗 *Turn left on to B31/Unteruhldingen, then on to Meersburger Strasse. In Unteruhldingen, turn right on to main car park. Follow signs to the museum.*

⑤ The Pfahlbauten Museum
Unteruhldingen; 88690

A reconstructed prehistoric hamlet, the Pfahlbauten Museum *(closed Dec–Mar)* features open-air re-creations of Stone and Iron Age dwellings based on archaeological remains found here. These suggest that structures were built by driving huge stakes into the ground. The interiors provide a glimpse of what life was like here between 4000 and 850 BC.

🚗 *Turn right out of the car park toward Oberuhldingen and turn left for Birnau; park in Basilika's car park.*

⑥ Basilika Birnau
Uhldingen-Mühlhofen; 88690

The Rococo **Basilika Birnau** *(open daily)* was built between 1747 and 1750 by a celebrity cast of designers, including architect Peter Thumb, sculptor Josef Anton Feuchtmayer, who crafted the altar, and fresco painter Gottfried Bernhard Göz. To the right of the main altar is a side altar dedicated to St Bernard of Clairvaux, whose words were said to be sweet as honey, as depicted by the statue of a cherub who sucks a finger he has dipped in a beehive.

🚗 *Return to the B31 and turn right towards Friedrichshafen, taking the first exit into Uhldingen, and a left onto Tüfinger Strasse and then right on the L200a to Kloster Salem.*

⑦ Kloster Salem

Baden-Württemberg; 88682

Founded in 1136, the **Cistercian monastery** *(Apr–Oct: open daily; Nov–Mar: church closed, museum: open Sat & Sun; monastery tours: Sun at 2pm; 07553 916 53 36; www.salem.de)* at Salem became wealthy and powerful, until a fire in 1697 burnt down much of the complex. Rebuilt in Baroque style, the abbey buildings were used as a palace for the grand dukes of Baden after secularization in 1803; today it is partially still used as an elite school (Prince Philip attended in the 1930s). The large **Minster monastery church** dates back to 1285 and survived the fire. It features alabaster statues, rose windows and a four-piece organ with 7,690 pipes, which was the largest of its time in 1774, and can be heard during services and concerts.

🚗 *Drive back to Uhldingen and take the B31 east to Friedrichshafen. Exit at B30/Paulinenstrasse, turn left on to Eckenerstrasse and park at the Seeparkplatz car park, beside Seestrasse.*

⑧ Friedrichshafen

Baden-Württemberg; 88045

Although an industrial Bodensee town, Friedrichshafen also has a lakeside promenade. At its eastern end is the 22-m (72-ft) high Moleturm tower. To the west, the **Zeppelindenkmal**, an obelisk, and the **Zeppelinbrunnen** fountain, commemorate an aeronautical event. It was here on 2 July 1900 that Count Graf Ferdinand von Zeppelin launched his airships; within three decades, scheduled services began. A **Zeppelin Museum** *(May–Oct: open daily; Nov–Apr: closed Mon)* celebrates this achievement. Although the Zeppelin's popularity declined after the 1937 Hindenburg disaster, safer models have now been created. Trips on the Bodensee are run by the Deutsche-Zeppelin Reederei *(www.zeppelinflug.de).*

🚗 *Turn right on to Eckenerstrasse, then get on to the B31 toward Lindau. Follow signs to Langenargen, then past Wasserburg to Lindau. Turn right on to Langenweg, then cross the roundabout onto Chelles-Allee to take the causeway to the island.*

Left Elaborately arched pier, Friedrichshafen
Below Exhibits on display at at the Zeppelin Museum

WINE TASTING

The region around Meersburg produces some fine wines. Taste wines at a vineyard such as the **Weingut Aufricht** *(Höhenweg 8, 88719; 07532 24 27; www.aufricht.de; closed Sun)*. Also visit the **Staatsweingut Meersburg** *(Seminarstrasse 6, 88719; 07532 446 744; www.staatsweingut-meersburg.de; closed Sun)* to the left of the Neues Schloss.

EAT AND DRINK

MEERSBURG

Wilde Heimat *moderate*
This restaurant serves modern German cuisine, grilled fish and steaks. *Seepromenade 14, 88709; 07532 49 57 57; www.hotel-seepromenade.de; closed Mon*

Winzerstube zum Becher *moderate*
A cosy regional wine bar serving the finest regional food in town. *Höllgasse 4, 88709; 07532 90 09; closed Mon; www.zumbecher.de*

Other options
The **Café Gross** *(Unterstadtstrasse 22, 88709; 07532 60 55)* is worth seeking out for wonderful homemade cakes.

FRIEDRICHSHAFEN

Lammgarten *inexpensive*
Come here to taste Bodensee *Felchen* (whitefish). *Uferstrasse 27, 88045; 07541 603 39 30; www.zehrer-gastronomie.de; closed Sat & Sun*

Ferdinand *expensive*
Bodensee views accompany excellent international dishes at this restaurant. *Graf-Zeppelin-Haus, Olgastrasse 20, 88045; 07541 320 33*

Glückler *moderate*
A good place to enjoy *Zander*, Bodensee *Felchen* and trout. *Olgastrasse 23, 88045; 07541 221 64; www.weinstube-glueckler.de; closed Wed*

DAY TRIP OPTIONS

From Konstanz, all destinations on the northern shore of the Bodensee are best accessed using the ferry to Meersburg.

Coastal fun
Follow the walk around Konstanz ❶, then hop on a passenger ferry from its harbour to the gardens of Mainau ❸. Pack swimming gear, as several beaches dot the way.

Frequent passenger ferries travel to Mainau from the dock at the southern end of the promenade in Konstanz.

Scenic north shore
Explore the prehistoric dwellings in the Pfahlbauten Museum ❺ before heading to the Basilika Birnau ❻ and the attractive castle in Meersburg ❹. Finally, visit the interesting Zeppelin Museum in Friedrichshafen ❽.

Turn right on to the B33 and then take the Staad-Meersburg ferry to Meersburg. Then follow the tour from there on.

TRIP 24

THE GERMAN ALPS
Lindau to Schönau am Königsee

HIGHLIGHTS

"Mad" King Ludwig's vision
Visit the extravagant palaces of "Mad" King Ludwig, from fabulous Schloss Linderhof to Herrenchiemsee's extraordinary tribute to the Sun King

Faith and inspiration
Admire the remarkable works of art inspired by Bavaria's Catholicism, such as the beautiful Wieskirche

Natural splendour
Experience the region's scenic thrills, from crystal-clear mountain lakes to Germany's highest peak, the Zugspitze

Winter wonderland
Discover the Alps, the country's greatest winter sports playground

THE GERMAN ALPS

From the balmy shores of Lake Constance (Bodensee) in the west to the gates of Salzburg in the east, the German Alps (Bayerische Alpen) offer some of the country's most thrilling landscapes. Through high-altitude passes and along Alpine lakeshores, this consistently beautiful route meanders deep into the mountains. The stunning scenery it passes is just one of its attractions. Regarded as Germany's winter playground, the region offers a wealth of activities, from high-altitude skiing at Garmisch-Partenkirchen to the more usual winter sports at Bayrischzell or Reit im Winkl; in summer, it is a paradise for walkers and cyclists. There are cultural highlights, too, such as the charming optical illusions of the *Lüftlmalerei* paintings, the giddy excesses of "Mad" King Ludwig's palaces and the sumptuous interiors of Baroque and Rococo churches. Food lovers will enjoy the simple, hearty food, from Allgäu cheese and Swabian noodles to fresh fish and game in season.

Left Pretty geraniums outside a guesthouse in Reit im Winkl, *see p252*

ACTIVITIES

Enjoy skiing on the Zugspitze's high-altitude pistes at Garmisch-Partenkirchen, with superb views as far as Italy and Switzerland

Ascend a mountain in a summer cable car at Walchensee to enjoy the fresh air, exhilarating walks and breathtaking views

Admire the falconry displays at Aschau im Chiemgau's Schloss Hohenaschau

Take a yachting course on the beautiful blue Chiemsee

Slide down into Berchtesgaden's salt mine

KEY

 Drive route

0 kilometres 15
0 miles 15

Above Beautiful scenery near Garmisch, the best-known resort town in the Bavarian Alps, *see p250*
Below Bavaria's largest lake, Chiemsee, a paradise for watersports enthusiasts, *see p252*

PLAN YOUR DRIVE

Start/finish: Lindau to Schönau am Königsee.

Number of days: 5 days, allowing half a day to explore Lindau.

Distance: 461 km (286 miles).

Road conditions: Roads are well surfaced, but at times are steep and twisting. Ice and snow may be a problem in winter. There are occasional signposted roads with brown "Deutsche Alpenstrasse" signs.

When to go: The best weather is from May to October, while December to Easter is ideal for winter sports.

Opening times: Museums often close on Mondays, while shops remain closed on Sundays.

Major festivals: Immenstadt: Viehscheid (the return of the cows), Sep; Oberammergau: Oberammergauer Passionsspiele (passion play), May–Oct, every ten years, next in 2022.

DAY TRIP OPTIONS

The German Alps can be explored in a series of day trips. Lindau or Bad Hindelang are the best bases to explore the Allgäu, while Füssen and Oberammergau are ideal for experiencing the richest concentration of **churches** and **palaces**. For **stunning lake** and **mountain scenery**, Tegernsee or Bad Tölz are excellent bases, while the **salt-mining history** and **Nazi associations** of Berchtesgadener Land are easily explored from Berchtesgaden or Bad Reichenhall. For full details, *see p253*.

Above Cobbled street lined with houses in the town of Lindau

VISITING LINDAU

Parking
There is a paid car park Seeparkplatz P5 on the island across the railway from the tourist office and Altstadt. Cross the causeway and follow signs to reach it.

Tourist Information
Alfred Nobel Platz 1, 88131; 08382 889 99 00; www.lindau.de; Apr–Oct: open daily; Nov–Mar: open Mon–Fri

WHERE TO STAY

LINDAU

YachtHotel Helvetia *moderate*
This harbour-side hotel has suites on land as well as rooms on board its yacht and motorboat.
Inselgraben 3, 88131; 08382 91 30; www.hotel-helvetia.com

Hotel Bad Schachen *expensive*
This classic, grand old hotel with lovely views offers an outdoor pool by the lake and a spa with an indoor pool.
Bad Schachen 1, 88131; 08382 29 80; www.badschachen.de; open Apr–Oct

IMMENSTADT

Gasthof Drei König *moderate*
A 200-year-old *gasthof* (guesthouse) in the centre of Immenstadt offering double rooms with en-suite showers.
Marienplatz 11, 87509; 08323 86 28; www.drei-koenig.de

BAD HINDELANG

Gästehaus Wineberger *moderate*
This welcoming family-run hotel features cosy rooms and several saunas. It offers great views over the valley.
Gailenbergstrasse 15, 87541; 08324 330; www.haus-wineberger.de

① LINDAU

Bavaria; 88131
Occupying an island off the north shore of Lake Constance, the lake resort of Lindau prospered in the Middle Ages owing to its trade links with Italy across the Alps. The town's architectural legacy is a reminder of its early prosperity, and with its café-lined waterfront and breathtaking backdrop of the snow-capped Alps, Lindau is a delight to visit.

A two-hour walking tour

Park in the car park and cross the footbridge over the railway tracks to the main railway station. Continue past the station to the **Hafen** ①, or harbour, which is dominated by a mid-19th-century lighthouse and the statue of the Bavarian Lion, the symbol of Lindau. Pause here for cake or ice cream or simply to admire the lovely panorama of the Austrian and Swiss Alps. On the landward side of the harbour is the 13th-century **Mangturm** ②, a former lighthouse whose campanile-like architecture is a reminder of the town's Italian links. Continue along the waterfront, bearing left into Reichsplatz, which features the Lindavia Fountain and the step-gabled old town hall, the **Altes Rathaus** ③. Built between 1422 and 1436, it served as the venue of an imperial Diet or Reichstag in 1496. Turn right along Ludwigstrasse, at the

Epitaph of Andreas Bertsch, Stadtmuseum

end of which lies the town's **Theater** ④, housed in a 700-year-old former church of the Minorite Order. Continue past it into Fischergasse, where a half-timbered passageway between No. 19 and No. 21 leads to the **Gerberschanze** ⑤, a fragment of the old town wall. Return to Fischergasse, turn right to reach the **Heidenmauer** ⑥, another surviving part of the town wall. Turn left into Schmiedgasse to the Marktplatz, which is dominated by two churches – the Protestant parish **Kirche St Stephan** ⑦, with an interior dating from 1783, and the Catholic church of **Unserer Lieben Frau** ⑧, whose interior is designed in a florid southern German style. Facing the two churches across the square is the **Haus zum Cavazzen** ⑨, a Baroque mansion dating from 1730. Its interior houses the Stadtmuseum *(Apr–Oct: closed Mon)*. From the Marktplatz,

0 metres 100
0 yards 100

Left Bavarian Lion and lighthouse, the port of Lindau **Below** Rolling countryside around Immenstadt **Below left** Pretty town centre, Immenstadt **Bottom** The scenic Oberjoch-Passstrasse in Allgäu, Bavaria

bear left along Cramergasse to **Maximilianstrasse** ⑩, Lindau's main street, lined with old patrician houses. Turn right into Schafgasse and left to the **Peterskirche** ⑪, an ancient church which now serves as the town's war memorial today. The interior contains the only known frescoes by Hans Holbein the Elder (c. 1460–1524). Next to it is the **Diebsturm** ⑫, or Thief's Tower, whose fairy-tale appearance belies its historical role as a jail. Take Zeppelinstrasse, turn right to return to the car park.

🚗 *Return to the mainland across the causeway. At the landward end, bear right. Follow signs for A96, leave the roundabout and get on to the B12. After Lindau, turn right on to the B31, which becomes the B308 to continue to Immenstadt. Park in the signposted P2 Zentrum or P4 Bahnhof.*

② Immenstadt
Bavaria; 87509
To the east of Immenstadt town lies the **Grosse Alpsee**, the Allgäu's largest natural lake. Popular in summer for watersports, visitors can hire pedal boats, rowing boats, sailing dinghies or try windsurfing *(www.immenstadt.de)* here. To the west lies Germany's longest summer toboggan run, the **Alpsee Bergwelt Sommerrodelbahn** *(May–Nov: open*

> **The Viehscheid**
> Immenstadt's famous cheese is made with the milk produced by cows that graze the Alpine meadows above the town in summer. At the end of the season, in September, some 1,000 cows are brought down during the festival known as the Viehscheid. The herdsmen wear traditional folk dress, including *Lederhosen*.

daily; Dec–Apr: open Sat & Sun; www.alpsee-bergwelt.de).

🚗 *Continue along Sonthofener Strasse. Follow the B19/B308 to Sonthofen, where the B308 leads to Bad Hindelang. Stay on the B308 to Reute. Park on the left next to the B308.*

③ Bad Hindelang
Bavaria; 87541
This Alpine paradise by the Austrian border is made up of scattered settlements. The meadows here are among the richest in Germany for wild flowers, and include some 40 species of orchid.

Logo of an Allgäu cheese factory, Immenstadt

The town provides opportunities in summer for hiking and rock climbing. More than 60 hiking trails *(tourist office; Unterer Buigenweg 2; 08324 89 20)* are available here. Visitors can try the challenging, cable-secured Salewa Klettersteig climbing course, which ascends the 1,876-m (6,155-ft) Iseler peak. In winter, the ski resort **Oberjoch**, which lies to the east, has a reliable snow record.

🚗 *Continue on the B308/Jochstrasse to Oberjoch, follow the B310 and turn right on to the B309 to Nesselwang.*

EAT AND DRINK

LINDAU
Ratsstuben *moderate*
Fresh seasonal produce, from Allgäu cheese to fish from the lake, paired with excellent Italian wine, is served at this simple but stylish hotel restaurant.
Ludwigstrasse 7, 88131; 08382 66 26; www.ratsstuben.li; closed Sun, Mon & Jan–Feb

Bayerischer Hof *expensive*
Local produce is cooked with an Italian flair at this plush hotel's dining room, which offers dishes such as carpaccio of Allgäu veal.
Bahnhofsplatz 2, 88131; 08382 91 50; www.bayerischerhof-lindau.de

IMMENSTADT
Gasthof Drei König *moderate*
There is a strong regional feel to the menu at this restaurant in the centre of Immenstadt, serving *Maultaschen* (Swabian ravioli) and *Kässpatzen* (noodles with Allgäu mountain cheese) alongside meat and fish options.
Marienplatz 11, 87509; 08323 86 28; www.drei-koenig.de

BAD HINDELANG
Schlosskeller *moderate*
The vaults of the elegant Rathaus (town hall), which used to serve as a hunting lodge, now house a restaurant that offers traditional dishes. There's a lovely garden terrace too.
Marktstrasse 9, 87541; 08324 973 84 81; www.schlosskeller-hindelang.de; closed Sun & Mon

Right Idyllic pastures along the way to Füssen **Below** *Lüftlmalerei*, traditional Bavarian wall paintings, Oberammergau **Below right** Gilded statues and pool in the gardens in front of Schloss Linderhof

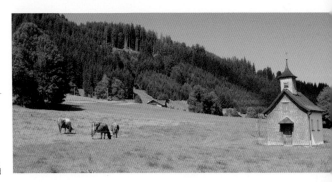

WHERE TO STAY

NESSELWANG

Brauerei-Gasthof Hotel Post
moderate
This family-run hotel opposite Nesselwang's parish church has 23 rooms with en-suite baths or showers. It also has an attractive wood-panelled restaurant and its own brewery.
Hauptstrasse 25, 87484; 08361 309 10; www.hotel-post-nesselwang.de

FÜSSEN

Hotel Schlosskrone *expensive*
This established hotel in the centre of Füssen offers well-equipped doubles and deluxe rooms with marble bathrooms and air conditioning. There is also a spa, a café and restaurant.
Prinzregentenplatz, 87629; 08362 93 01 80; www.schlosskrone.de

OBERAMMERGAU

Alte Post *moderate*
A lovely old inn dating back to 1612. Rooms have en-suite baths or showers, LCD TV and internet.
Dorfstrasse 19, 82487; 08822 91 00; www.altepost.com

ETTAL

Klosterhotel Ludwig der Bayer
moderate
Located opposite Ettal's magnificent abbey, this hotel is named after the abbey's founder. Rooms, suites and apartments are tastefully decorated; some have balconies. Facilities include an indoor pool and a bowling alley.
Kaiser-Ludwig-Platz 10-12, 82488; 08822 91 50; www.ludwig-der-bayer.de

④ Nesselwang
Bavaria; 87484

Set amid meadows at the foot of the 1,575-m (5,167-ft) Alpspitze, the village of Nesselwang is a centre for activity holidays, such as mountain biking and canyoning in summer and skiing in winter *(tourist office; Hauptstrasse 20, 08361 92 30 40; www.nesselwang.de)*. In 2003, Nesselwang opened Bavaria's first **Nordic Walking Park**, which is part of a 420-km (261-mile) network stretching into neighbouring districts. In winter, the **Alpspitzbahn** gondola serves the Alpspitze's mostly blue ski runs, which are generally for beginners. There's even floodlit evening skiing on the lower slopes. The village clusters around the imposing church of **St Andreas**, which was rebuilt in a Neo-Baroque style between 1904 and 1906 after falling into disrepair.

🚗 *Continue along the B309/Füssener Strasse, which becomes the B310/Pfronter Strasse just before Pfronten. Continue on the B310 to Füssen. Park in one of the signposted underground car parks close to the tourist office and the old town.*

⑤ Füssen
Bavaria; 87629

The main urban centre for southeastern Allgäu, Füssen is surrounded by lakes and mountains. The old town, or Altstadt, is dominated by the **Hohes Schloss**, a former summer palace of Augsburg's bishops, which houses two **art galleries** *(Apr–Oct: closed Mon; Nov–Mar: open Fri–Sun)*. Also worth visiting are the former Benedictine monastery of **Kloster St Mang** and the **Heilig Geist Spitalkirche**, or the Church of the Holy Ghost.

🚗 *Continue along Sebastianstrasse, then take the B17 to Steingaden. In*

Schloss Neuschwanstein

A visit to "Mad" King Ludwig II's *(see p207)* castle of Neuschwanstein *(open daily)* is worth a detour off the Alpenstrasse route. Perched on a crag above Hohenschwangau, the castle was inspired by Wagner's operas and only completed in 1884. To reach Hohenschwangau, look out for the brown "Königsschlösser" signs along the B17.

Left House decorated with *Lüftlmalerei*, Oberammergau **Below** Exterior of the Kloster Ettal monastery

EAT AND DRINK

NESSELWANG

Brauerei-Gasthof Hotel Post *moderate*
With its traditional tiled oven and wood-panelled ceiling, the Hotel Post's dining room is an attractive setting for hearty meals. Begin with pork with onions and caraway followed by beer goulash or *Schnitzel* (pork fillet) in brewer's malt and breadcrumbs.
Hauptstrasse 25, 87484; 08361 309 10; www.hotel-post-nesselwang.de

FÜSSEN

Gasthof zum Schwanen *moderate*
This restaurant serves specialities from Swabia and the Allgäu, including *Maultaschen* (Swabian ravioli) with Emmenthal, as well as Croatian dishes such as *čevapčići* (grilled minced meat) and pork cutlet stuffed with ham and cheese.
Brotmarkt 4, 87629; 08362 61 74; closed Tue

OBERAMMERGAU

Benedikt's *expensive*
Oberammergau's most elegant hotel, Maximilian, is the setting for Benedikt's, an acclaimed gourmet restaurant with excellent Mediterranean cuisine. The hotel also has its own microbrewery, Maxbräu, which serves classic Bavarian food.
Hotel Maximilian, Ettaler Strasse 5, 82487; 08822 94 87 40; www. maximilian-oberammergau.de; closed Sun & Mon

Steingaden turn right and at the next junction turn right again to Wies/ Wieskirche. There is paid parking close to the church.

⑥ Wieskirche
Bavaria; 86989
About 5 km (3 miles) from Steingaden, in the district of Pfaffenwinkel (priest's corner), lies the Rococo Wieskirche, a UNESCO World Heritage Site. Completed in 1754 by German architect Dominikus Zimmermann, this church is a masterpiece of 18th-century southern German architecture.
🚗 *Return to last junction, head east and pass Schwaig. Turn right on to the B23 for Oberammergau. There is free parking near the tourist office.*

Oberammergau's Passion Play
Performed every 10 years – the next is due in 2022 – the Passion Play has its origins in a promise made by the villagers in 1633 during the Thirty Years' War. They pledged to perform a play about the life of Christ if God would spare them from the plague that was ravaging the surrounding district. The play is performed all summer long by locals on an open-air stage. During the years when the play is not being performed, it is still possible to tour the Passionstheater.

⑦ Oberammergau
Bavaria; 82487
Renowned worldwide for its Passion Play, Oberammergau is also worth a visit for its lovely setting in the Ammergau Alps, its strong tradition of handicrafts and woodcarving, and its southern German charm. The town's houses are decorated with some of the best *Lüftlmalerei* work

in Bavaria, most notably on the 18th-century **Pilatushaus**, whose astonishing frescoes are the work of Franz Seraph Zwink (1748–92).
🚗 *Continue on the B23 to Ettal. There is free parking in front of Kloster Ettal.*

⑧ Ettal
Bavaria; 82488
Ettal, about 4 km (3 miles) from Oberammergau, was founded by Ludwig IV of Bavaria. It is best known for the Benedictine monastery of **Kloster Ettal**, one of the most grand of Bavaria's Baroque abbeys. The domed abbey church *(open daily)* assumed its present form between 1744 and 1753, when architect Joseph Schmuzer was commissioned to complete the fire-damaged church. The interior is decorated with Rococo stuccowork.
🚗 *Turn left from the western end of Ettal. Get on to Linderhof Strasse to Linderhof. Follow signs to the car park.*

⑨ Schloss Linderhof
Bavaria; 82488
In the early 1850s, Linderhof was bought by the Bavarian King Maximilian II. This mountain district appealed to his young heir, who later went on to become "Mad" King Ludwig and was responsible for Schloss Linderhof *(open daily)*. Set in terraced gardens, between Ettal and the Austrian border, Schloss Linderhof was originally built by Ludwig II as a hunting lodge for his father. It was transformed into its current Neo-Rococo appearance by Georg Dollmann between 1870 and 1872.
🚗 *Return to Ettal, turn right along the B23, then right at Oberau to get on the B2 for Garmisch-Partenkirchen. Look out for signposted car parks in Garmisch and in Partenkirchen.*

Right Yacht sailing on the Walchensee
Far right Isar river, Bad Tölz **Below right**
Bad Tölz's Marktstrasse, lined with houses
with painted façades

ACTIVITIES AROUND TEGERNSEE

Mountain biking is a popular activity in Tegernsee *(www.tegernsee.com)*. Every summer the town has a mountain biking festival *(www.mtb-festival.de)*. The Gleitschirmschule Tegernsee offers tandem jumps and paragliding courses *(Tegernseerstrasse 88, 83700 Reitrain; 08022 25 56; www.paragliding-tegernsee.de)*.

VISITING GARMISCH-PARTENKIRCHEN

Parking
The paid car park at the Kongresshaus is the most central in Garmisch.

Tourist Information
Richard-Strauss-Platz 2, 82467; 08821 18 07 00; www.gapa.de; mid-May–late Oct, mid-Dec–mid-Jan: open daily

WHERE TO STAY

GARMISCH-PARTENKIRCHEN

Atlas Grand Hotel *moderate*
Partenkirchen's oldest hotel is located on its main street. Rooms have en-suite baths or showers.
Ludwigstrasse 49, 82467; 08821 936 30; www.atlas-grandhotel.com

Reindl's Partenkirchner Hof *expensive*
This five-star, traditional hotel has a welcoming rustic ambience.
Bahnhofstrasse 15, 82467; 08821 94 38 70; www.reindls.de

WALCHENSEE

Gästehaus Seehof *moderate*
Set between the lake and the mountains, this family-run guesthouse offers lovely views and has a café.
Seestrasse 44, 82432; 08858 222; www.seehof-walchensee.de

BAD TÖLZ

Posthotel Kolberbräu *moderate*
This family-run former coaching inn has 32 tastefully decorated rooms.
Marktstrasse 29, 83646; 08041 768 80; www.kolberbraeu.de

TEGERNSEE

Hotel Das Tegernsee *expensive*
The sleek and elegant rooms in this hotel range in size and style. There is also an on-site spa.
Neureuthstrasse 23, 83684; 08022 18 20; www.dastegernsee.de

⑩ Garmisch-Partenkirchen
Bavaria; 82467

Facing each other across the narrow Partnach stream in the shadow of Germany's highest mountain, the 2,962-m (9,718-ft) **Zugspitze**, the twin towns of Garmisch and Partenkirchen feature Germany's best-known ski resort. The towns were amalgamated at the time of the 1936 Winter Olympics but still have quite distinct characters: Garmisch is cosmopolitan, while Partenkirchen preserves its old-fashioned Alpine charm. In Partenkirchen, composer **Richard Strauss's villa** *(closed Sat & Sun)* is now a small museum.

🚗 *Continue along the B2 to Krün, turn left on to the B11 for Walchensee. Park at signposted car parks along the route.*

Winter Sports

The towering Zugspitze provides a spectacular backdrop for Garmisch-Partenkirchen's pistes, which include Germany's only glacier skiing and the fearsome Kandahar Run, used for World Championship downhill races. The Zugspitze offers 22 km (14 miles) of high-altitude skiing at a height of almost 3,000 m (9,843 ft); for beginners, runs are graded blue *(www.zugspitze.de)*. Due to the altitude of its pistes, the ski season here is a long one, beginning in November and continuing through to May.

---

⑪ Walchensee
Bavaria; 82432

Surrounded by impressive mountains, Walchensee lies 802 m (2,631 ft) above sea level and is among Bavaria's most beautiful lakes. Despite its scenic grandeur, it remains relatively undiscovered. In summer the lake offers everything from angling and swimming to windsurfing and sailing. Enjoy an excursion in the Herzogstandbahn cable car *(Am Tanneneck 6, 82432; open daily)*, which goes from the north end of Walchensee village to the top of the 1,731-m (5,679-ft) **Herzogstand**, offering breathtaking panoramas of the surrounding landscape.

🚗 *Take the B11 to Kochel am See. Park on signposted car parks at the lake, city or museum.*

⑫ Kochel am See
Bavaria; 82431

To the north of Walchensee lies Kochel am See. The town is closely associated with artist Franz Marc (1880–1916), who, in the years before World War I, was a leading member of the Munich-based Blauer Reiter group of Expressionist painters. A villa overlooking the lake now houses the **Franz Marc Museum** *(closed Mon)*, which displays about 200 of the artist's works.

🚗 *Continue along the B11 to Benediktbeuern. The abbey is well signposted and provides parking space.*

⑬ Benediktbeuern
Bavaria; 83671

Visible from a distance, the Bavarian onion-domed towers of the basilica of Benediktbeuern rise above an abbey complex of considerable size and splendour. Founded around AD 725, the Benedictine abbey was rebuilt in Baroque style after 1669 and secularized in 1803; it is now home to the Salesians Don Boscos, a Roman Catholic order.

🚗 *Continue along the B11, bypassing Brichl and turn right on to the B472 for Bad Tölz. Park in one of the riverside car parks or on street in the spa quarter (Kurzone) close to the tourist office.*

14 Bad Tölz

Bavaria; 83646

The town of Bad Tölz straddles the Isar river, with a leafy spa quarter on the west bank facing an attractive, hilly old town. The main street, **Marktstrasse**, owes its present appearance to the Munich architect Gabriel von Seidl, who in the early 20th century re-emphasized the street's Alpine character. To the south of Marktstrasse is the **Gries**, a quaint artisans' quarter.

🚗 *Take the B13/Lenggrieser Strasse. At Sylvensteinsee reservoir turn left on to the B307 and continue to Tegernsee. Park at signposted car park in Strandbad and Ortsmitte.*

15 Tegernsee

Bavaria; 83684

Crystal-clear Tegernsee is framed by wooded hills and mountains rising from its southern shore toward the Austrian border. It is among the most chic of Bavaria's mountain lakes, with a sprinkling of resorts along its shores, and has a reputation as an upmarket destination. The lake acts as a scenic backdrop to a range of activities, from mountain biking to paragliding.

🚗 *Take the B307/ Münchner Strasse. At Am See, turn right to Hausham, then right again to the level crossing. Turn right on to the B307 for Schliersee. Park along the route on signposted car parks.*

16 Schliersee

Bavaria; 83727

Modest in size and appearance in comparison to Tegernsee, Schliersee shares the same lovely mountain backdrop. The lakefront is home to a modern spa complex, **Monte Mare** *(open daily)*, complete with a pool, sauna and whirlpool. Hourly cruises *(May–Sep: open daily)*, depart from the jetty in front of the spa complex for the island of Wörth in the centre of the lake.

🚗 *Continue along the B307 to Bayrischzell. For parking, follow signs to Ortsmitte.*

17 Bayrischzell

Bavaria; 83735

Nestled at the foot of the 1,838-m (6,030-ft) **Wendelstein** is the rustic village of Bayrischzell. Wendelstein can be ascended by cable car *(open daily; departures hourly; www.wendel steinbahn.de)* from Osterhofen just west of the village, or by old-fashioned cog railway from Brannenburg in the northeast. To the east of the village lies the **Sudelfeld**, Germany's largest contiguous ski complex. It has 21 lifts and 31 km (19 miles) of red (intermediate) and blue (easy) pistes, though there are some black (advanced) runs too *(www.sudelfeld.de).*

🚗 *Continue on the B307/Alpenstrasse and pass Oberaudorf to Niederaudorf. Turn left to Brannenburg along Rosenheimer Strasse. At Brannenburg turn right on to Nussdorfer Strasse to Neubeuern. Turn right to Frasdorf and get on to the Rosenheimer Strasse to reach Aschau im Chiemgau. Park at the car park near the tourist office.*

Above Diners at a monastery-café in Tegernsee **Below left** Boating on the Tegernsee **Below right** Lush pasture land in Bayrischzell

VISITING BAD TÖLZ

Parking
Park in one of the car parks on the riverside or on street in the area around the tourist information office.

Tourist Information
Max-Höfler-Platz 1, 8346; 08041 786 70; www.bad-toelz.de; open Mon–Sat

EAT AND DRINK

BENEDIKTBEUERN

Kloster Bräustüberl *moderate*
This monastery restaurant serves excellent Bavarian fare along with beer brewed by the monks. In summer there's a large Biergarten. *Zeile Weg 2, 83671; 08857 94 07; www.klosterwirt.de; closed mid-Oct–Mar: Mon & Tue*

BAD TÖLZ

Wirtshaus zum Starnbräu *moderate*
Beers from Munich's Hofbräuhaus brewery accompany the traditional Bavarian fare at the Starnbräu. *Marktstrasse 4, 83646; 08041 440 00 30*

Right Twin-towered church in Aschau
im Chiemgau **Below** Picturesque view
of Ruhpolding

WHERE TO STAY

ASCHAU IM CHIEMGAU

Residenz Heinz Winkler *expensive*
This five-star hotel occupies a historic
inn; the main building dates back to
1405. Rooms and suites are furnished
in traditional style, while the hotel's
restaurant is one of Germany's best-
known gourmet restaurants. There
are spa facilities.
Kirchplatz 1, 83229; 08052 179 90;
www.residenz-heinz-winkler.de

REIT IM WINKL

Unterwirt *moderate*
An old family-run hotel, Unterwirt
exudes Alpine character, from its
wooden ceilings to the traditional tiled
ovens and country-style furnishings.
There's a garden with an outdoor pool,
a spa and a sauna. The menu of the
hotel's restaurant offers *Leberkäse* (a
form of meatloaf) and speciality meat
served from its own butchery.
Kirchplatz 2, 83242; 08640 80 10;
www.unterwirt.de

RUHPOLDING

Steinberger Hof *moderate*
Nestled into the hillside, this
traditional Alpine hotel has balconies
with lovely views over the town.
Some of the suites come equipped
with a kitchen. The host family offers
free skiing lessons in winter.
Steinberg 2, 83324; 08663 59 24;
www.steinbergerhof.de

BERCHTESGADEN

Vier Jahreszeiten *moderate*
This family-run three-star hotel with
mountain panoramas sits on the
hillside close to the centre of town.
Rooms are decorated in traditional
style and have en-suite bath or
shower; many have balconies or
mountain views.
Maximilianstrasse 20, 83471; 08652
95 20; www.hotel-vierjahreszeiten-
berchtesgaden.de

18 Aschau im Chiemgau
Bavaria; 83229
This village is dominated by **Schloss
Hohenaschau** *(guided tours: May–Oct:
Tue–Fri & Sun)*, an 800 year-old fortress
remodelled during the Renaissance.
It now houses the **Priental Museum**,
which explores the history of the iron
industry in the Prien Valley and is the
venue for falconry displays *(open Tue–
Fri)*. Nearby, the **Kampenwandbahn**
gondola ascends the 1,669-m
(5,476-ft) mountain, giving access
to ski runs in winter and hiking
trails in summer *(tourist office;
Kampenwandstrasse 38; 08052 904 90)*.

🚗 *Take Bernauer Strasse. At Bernau,
turn left for the B305. Cross the A8 and
take Priener Strasse to the nearest
town, Prien. Park at signposted car
park in the town or at the harbour.*

19 Chiemsee
Bavaria; 83209
The blue waters of Bavaria's largest
lake, the Chiemsee, are a paradise for
yachtsmen in the summer months
*(Chiemsee Yachtschule; 08051 17 40;
www.dhh.de)*. Take a ferry to the
lake's islands, **Herreninsel** and
Fraueninsel. The former is the site
of the **Schloss Herrenchiemsee**
(open daily), which was King Ludwig
II's attempt to re-create Versailles.
The castle is modelled after the
original palace and is devoted
to the life of Ludwig II.

🚗 *From Prien, return to Bernau.
Continue on the B305 to Reit im Winkl.
Follow signs to a car park.*

20 Reit im Winkl
Bavaria; 83242
Situated in a broad valley surrounded
by mountains, Reit im Winkl is a
charming Alpine town with chalet-
style architecture and one of the

best snow records of any German
ski resort. Skiing was introduced
to the area in the 19th century by
foresters and Norwegian students;
the **Skimuseum** *(open Tue & Thu)*
documents the story in detail.

🚗 *Take the B305/Weitseestrasse to
Waich, turn left on to Seehauserstrasse
for Ruhpolding. In Ruhpolding, follow
the car park routing system.*

21 Ruhpolding
Bavaria; 83324
Ruhpolding is the perfect spot to
ascend in a cable car to the 1,672-m
(5,485-ft) **Rauschberg**, which offers
a panorama of 600 Alpine peaks. The
town has 160 km (99 miles) of cross-
country ski runs. South of the town is
the **Holzknechtmuseum** *(May–Oct:
closed Mon; Jan–Mar: open Wed)* with
exhibits relating to the area's
woodwork tradition.

🚗 *Return to the B305, turn left to
Schneitzlreuth, then left again on
to the B21 for Bad Reichenhall. Park
at signposted car parks in the town
or at Alte Saline.*

22 Bad Reichenhall
Bavaria; 83435
A conservative German spa town,
Bad Reichenhall is somewhat
medicinal. The main focus of the
town is the Kurpark, fringed by
buildings such as the **Gradierhaus**,
an outdoor saline inhaler originally
intended to reproduce the health
benefits of sea air. On the south side
of the town is the former royal salt
works, the **Alte Saline** *(Apr–Oct:
open daily; Nov–Mar: closed Mon;*

www.alte-saline.de), with brine springs and a tunnel system.
🚗 *Return on the B21 to Unterjettenberg, turn left on to the B305 for Berchtesgaden. Park in the car park at Kur- und Kongresshaus.*

㉓ Berchtesgaden
Bavaria; 83471
Berchtesgaden was once an independent Prince-Bishopric living off the proceeds of the **Salzbergwerk**, or salt mine *(Bergwerkstrasse 83, 83471; open daily; www.salzbergwerk.de)*. The village has the atmosphere of a miniature capital city, notably on **Schlossplatz**, which is dominated by the Stiftskirche and the façade of the **Königliches Schloss** *(open Mon–Fri; guided tours only)*, a former bishops' palace that now belongs to the Bavarian royal family, the Wittelsbachs.
🚗 *Continue on the Salzbergstrasse, up the steep ascent to Obersalzberg. Park at the Dokumentation Obersalzberg.*

㉔ Obersalzberg
Bavaria; 83471
A favourite holiday retreat of high-ranking Nazis, the mountain village of Obersalzberg is home to the **Dokumentation Obersalzberg** *(Apr–Oct: open daily; Nov–Mar: closed Mon)*. This museum occupies the site of Adolf Hitler's former mountain home

and documents the rise, fall and crimes of the Nazis. It ends with a visit to the warren of tunnels in which the Nazis planned to make their last stand. In summer, buses depart from the adjacent terminal for the ascent to the **Kehlsteinhaus**, or Eagle's Nest, the dictator's mountain-top tearoom.
🚗 *Return to Berchtesgaden. Turn left on to the B305, then left at the round-about on to the B20 to Schönau am Königsee. Park away from the lake and complete the journey on foot.*

㉕ Schönau am Königsee
Bavaria; 83471
Around 4 km (2 miles) south of Berchtesgaden lies Schönau am Königsee, which is home to the 8-km (5-mile) long fjord-like lake, **Königsee**. The lake lies in the shadow of the 2,713-m (8,901-ft) **Watzmann** at the eastern limit of the Deutsche Alpenstrasse. The chapel of **St Bartholomä**, which stands at the foot of the mountain, can only be reached by boat. Tour boats *(daily)* depart from the village of Schönau for the chapel.

Above left Berchtesgaden, with the Alps in the background **Top** Chalet and signposts in Ruhpolding **Above** Passenger ship on Bavaria's largest lake, the Chiemsee **Centre left** Kehlsteinhaus or Eagle's Nest, Obersalzberg

EAT AND DRINK

AROUND CHIEMSEE
Schlosswirtschaft Herrenchiemsee *moderate*
Try local fish from the Chiemsee while enjoying the view of the lake from here.
Schlosshotel 5, 83209 Herrenchiemsee; 08051 962 76 70; www.schloss wirtschaft-herrenchiemsee.de; closed Nov–Jan; Mar: closed Mon & Tue

BAD REICHENHALL
Axelstüberl *moderate*
This restaurant features a refined take on the cooking of the region.
Hotel Axelmannstein, Salzburger Strasse 2–6, 83435; 08651 77 70; www. precisehotels.com

BERCHTESGADEN
Hubertusstuben *moderate*
Enjoy venison with creamed mushrooms, and *Spätzle* (Swabian noodles).
Maximilianstrasse 20, 83471; 08652 95 20; www.hubstuben.com

DAY TRIP OPTIONS
The region can be explored in a series of day trips.

Architectural haven
Visit the church of Wieskirche ❻, then head to Oberammergau ❼ to admire the façade paintings. Stop at Ettal ❽ to see the Baroque abbey.

From Wieskirche, follow directions to Oberammergau; take the B23 to Ettal.

Lakes and mountains
Head to lake Walchensee ⓫, then stop by Kochel am See ⓬. Next, visit the Tegernsee ⓯ and Schliersee ⓰.

Follow the B11 to Kochel am See. Go past Benediktbeuern to the B472 to Bad Tölz. Take the B13

and B307 to Tegernsee. Follow directions to Schliersee.

Historical associations
Learn about Berchtesgaden's ㉓ salt-mining history, then visit the Nazis' holiday retreat at Obersalzberg ㉔.

Follow Salzbergstrasse from Berchtesgaden to the Dokumentation Obersalzberg.

INDEX

Page numbers in **bold** refer to main entries

ACKNOWLEDGMENTS

Dorling Kindersley would like to thank the many people whose help and assistance contributed to the preparation of this book.

Photography
Alex Havret, Lynn McPeake, James Tye

Additional Photography
Sheeba Bhatnagar, Witold Danilkiewicz, Geoff Dann, Adam Hajder, Michael Jackson, Diana Jarvis, Dorota and Mariusz Jarymowicz, Jamie Marshall, Wojciech Medrzak, Tomasz Mysluk, Ian O'Leary, Pawel Wojcik.

Maps
Cartographic Production Lovell Johns Ltd, www. lovelljohns.com

Source Data
Base mapping supplied by Kartographie Huber, www.kartographie.de

Elevation Data
SRTM data courtesy of ESRI

Picture Credits
Every effort has been made to trace the copyright holders of images, and we apologize in advance for any unintentional omissions. We would be pleased to insert the appropriate acknowledgments in any subsequent edition of this publication.

The Publishers would like to thank the following individuals, companies and picture libraries for their kind permission to reproduce their photographs:

Key: t= top; c= centre; l= left; r= right; b= bottom.

123RF.com: jakobradlgruber 190, Bernd Juergens 180.
4Corners: Frank Lukasseck 30.
Alamy Images: Westend61 GmbH / Patrice von Collani 102; imagebroker 22bl, 129tl; Interfoto 56br; Robertharding / Markus Lange 40; Kvitka Nastroyu 74; Werner Otto 134tr; Bildagentur-online / Schoening 11bc; sculpies 224; Jochen Tack 20br; mauritius images GmbH / Andreas Vitting 48; Peter Widmann 55bl.
Auf Schönburg. Burghotel und

Restaurant : Volker Linger 23tl.
Dorling Kindersley: Michael Jackson 26tr; Schloss (Burg) Lichtenstein 229tr. **Dreamstime.com:** Artzzz 13tc. Boarding1now 10tr, 11bl; Cbechinie 13bl; Michel Dreher 215tr; SimonDannhauer 208; Editor77 10bl; Franz1212 21tr; Susanne Fritzsche 162tr; Larisa Irimeeva 199tc; Conny Pokorny 231tr; Rosshelen 112; Björn Wylezich 14bc; Xbrchx 198cr.
iStockphoto.com: bluejayphoto 88; bpperry 66; DieterMeyrl 200; DR pics24 58; E+ / DieterMeyrl 28-29; ewg3D 80; fokkebok 94; Matthias Lindner 156; chris-mueller 124; Rocky89 242; romrodinka 2-3; rusm 136; saiko3p 144; TommL 118tr.
Masterfile: 175br; Robert Harding Images 248br. **Photolibrary:** Bahnmueller Bahnmueller 27br; Barbara Boensch 133br; DEA Picture Library 179tl; euroluftbild 98tl ; Stefan Kiefer 189tl; Werner Otto 39c, 52br, 134br; Chris Seba 37tr; Siepmann 177bl; Konrad Wothe 21tl; Ernst Wrba 100tl. **Richard Neville Walker:** 164br.
Shutterstock.com: LaMantarraya 216; Sergej Razvodovskij 234; Boris Stroujko 168. **Tourist Information Creglingen:** 195cl, 195br. **Wikipedia, The Free Encyclopedia:** Wolfgang Manousek - http://en.wikipedia.org/wiki/File:Building_in_germany.jpg 253cl; Public Domain 167c.

Sheet map
Getty Images: Fabian Vogl.

Jacket
Front & Spine: **Getty Images:** Fabian Vogl. Back: **AWL Images:** Marco Bottigelli tl, ClickAlps cla; **Getty Images:** Moment / Marco Bottigelli crb, Fabian Vogl b; **Shutterstock.com:** Boris Stroujko tr

All other images © Dorling Kindersley For further information see: www.dkimages.com

Illustrator
Arun Pottirayil

DK | Penguin Random House

THIS EDITION UPDATED BY
CONTRIBUTOR Jeroen van Marle
SENIOR EDITOR Alison McGill
SENIOR DESIGNER Stuti Tiwari Bhatia
PROJECT EDITOR Dipika Dasgupta
PROJECT ART EDITOR Ankita Sharma
EDITOR Anuroop Sanwalia
ASSISTANT PICTURE RESEARCH ADMINISTRATOR Vagisha Pushp
PICTURE RESEARCH MANAGER Taiyaba Khatoon
JACKET COORDINATOR Bella Talbot
JACKET DESIGNERS Ben Hinks, Jordan Lambley
SENIOR CARTOGRAPHER Subhashree Bharati
CARTOGRAPHY MANAGER Suresh Kumar
SENIOR DTP DESIGNER Tanveer Abbas Zaidi
SENIOR PRODUCTION EDITOR Jason Little
SENIOR PRODUCTION CONTROLLER Samantha Cross
DEPUTY MANAGING EDITOR Beverly Smart
MANAGING EDITORS Shikha Kulkarni, Hollie Teague
SENIOR MANAGING ART EDITOR Priyanka Thakur
ART DIRECTOR Maxine Pedliham
PUBLISHING DIRECTOR Georgina Dee

First edition 2011
Published in Great Britain by
Dorling Kindersley Limited, DK, One Embassy Gardens, 8 Viaduct Gardens, London SW11 7BW
The authorised representative in the EEA is Dorling Kindersley Verlag GmbH. Arnulfstr. 124, 80636 Munich, Germany
Published in the United States by DK Publishing, 1745 Broadway, 20th Floor, New York, NY 10019
Copyright © 2011, 2022 Dorling Kindersley Limited
A Penguin Random House Company
23 24 25 10 9 8 7 6 5 4 3 2
Reprinted with revisions 2014, 2017, 2022
All rights reserved.

A CIP catalogue record for this book is available from the British Library.
A catalogue record for this book is available from the Library of Congress.
ISSN 1542 1554
ISBN 9780 2414 6150 1
Printed and bound in China
www.dk.com

MIX
Paper | Supporting responsible forestry
FSC www.fsc.org FSC™ C018179

This book was made with Forest Stewardship Council™ certified paper – one small step in DK's commitment to a sustainable future.
For more information go to www.dk.com/our-green-pledge

PHRASE BOOK

In an Emergency

Where is the telephone?	Wo ist das Telefon?	voh ist duss tel-e-fone?
Help!	Hilfe!	hilf-uh
Please call a doctor	Bitte rufen Sie einen Arzt	bitt-uh roof'n zee ine-en artst
Please call the police	Bitte rufen Sie die Polizei	bitt-uh roof'n zee dee poli-tsy
Please call the fire brigade	Bitte rufen Sie die Feuerwehr	bitt-uh roof'n zee dee foyer-vayr
Stop!	Halt!	hult

Communication Essentials

Yes	Ja	yah
No	Nein	nine
Please	Bitte	bitt-uh
Thank you	Danke	dunk-uh
Excuse me	Verzeihung	fair-tsy-hoong
Hello (good day)	Guten Tag	goot-en tahk
Goodbye	Auf Wiedersehen	owf-veed-er-zay-ern
Good evening	Guten Abend	goot'n ahb'nt
Good night	Gute Nacht	goot-uh nukht
Until tomorrow	Bis morgen	biss morg'n
See you	Tschüss	chooss
What is that?	Was ist das?	voss ist duss
Why?	Warum?	var-room
Where?	Wo?	voh
When?	Wann?	vunn
Today	heute	hoyt-uh
Tomorrow	morgen	morg'n
Month	Monat	mohn-aht
Night	Nacht	nukht
Afternoon	Nachmittag	nahkh-mit-tahk.
Morning	Morgen	morg'n
Year	Jahr	yar
There	dort	dort
Here	hier	hear
Week	Woche	vokh-uh
Yesterday	gestern	gest'n
Evening	Abend	ahb'nt

Useful Phrases

How are you? (informal)	Wie geht's?	vee gayts
Fine, thanks	Danke, es geht mir gut	dunk-uh, es gayt meer goot
Until later	Bis später	biss shpay-ter
Where is/are…?	Wo ist/sind…?	voh ist/sind
How far is it to…?	Wie weit ist es…?	vee vite ist ess
Do you speak English?	Sprechen Sie Englisch?	shpresh'n zee eng-glish
I don't understand	Ich verstehe nicht	ish fair-shtay-uh nisht
Could you speak more slowly?	Könnten Sie langsamer sprechen?	kurnt-en zee lung-zam-er shpresh'n

Useful Words

large	gross	grohss
small	klein	kline
hot	heiss	hyce
cold	kalt	kult
good	gut	goot
bad	schlecht	shlesht
open	geöffnet	g'urff-nett
closed	geschlossen	g'shloss'n
left	links	links
right	rechts	reshts
straight ahead	geradeaus	g'rah-der-owss

Making a Telephone Call

I would like to make a phone call	Ich möchte telefonieren	ish mer-shtuh tel-e-fon-eer'n
I'll try again later	Ich versuche es später noch einmal	ish fair-zookh-uh es shpay-ter nokh ine-mull
Can I leave a message?	Kann ich eine Nachricht hinterlassen?	kan ish ine-uh nakh-risht hint-er-lahss-en
answer phone	Anrufbeantworter	an-roof-be-ahnt vort-er

telephone card	Telefonkarte	tel-e-fone-kart-uh
receiver	Hörer	hur-er
mobile	Handy	han-dee
engaged (busy)	besetzt	b'zetst
wrong number	falsche Verbindung	falsh-uh fair-bin-doong

Sightseeing

library	Bibliothek	bib-leo-tek
entrance ticket	Eintrittskarte	ine-tritz-kart-uh
cemetery	Friedhof	freed-hofe
train station	Bahnhof	barn-hofe
gallery	Galerie	gall-er-ree
information	Auskunft	owss-koonft
church	Kirche	keersh-uh
garden	Garten	gart'n
palace/castle	Palast/Schloss	pallast/shloss
place (square)	Platz	plats
bus stop	Haltestelle	hal-te-shtel-uh
national holiday	Nationalfeiertag	nats-yon-ahl-fire tahk
theatre	Theater	tay-aht-er
free admission	Eintritt frei	ine-tritt fry

Shopping

Do you have/ Is there…?	Gibt es…?	geept ess
How much does it cost?	Was kostet das?	voss kost't duss?
When do you open/	Wann öffnen Sie?	vunn off'n zee
close?	schliessen Sie?	shlees'n zee
this	das	duss
expensive	teuer	toy-er
cheap	preiswert	price-vurt
size	Grösse	gruhs-uh
number	Nummer	noom-er
colour	Farbe	farb-uh
brown	braun	brown
black	schwarz	shvarts
red	rot	roht
blue	blau	blau
green	grün	groon
yellow	gelb	gelp

Types of Shops

antique shop	Antikladen	ahn-teak-lard'n
pharmacy	Apotheke	appo-tay-kuh
bank	Bank	bunk
bakery	Bäckerei	beck-er-eye
bookshop	Buchhandlung	bookh-hant-loong
clothes shop	Kleiderladen,	klyder-lard'n
boutique	Boutique	boo-teek-uh
department store	Warenhaus	vahr'n-hows
drugstore	Drogerie	droog-er-ree
food shop	Lebensmittel- geschäft	lay-bens-mittel- gush-eft
glass, porcelain	Glas, Porzellan	glars, Port-sellahn
hairdresser	Friseur	freezz-er
market	Markt	markt
travel agency	Reisebüro	rye-zer-boo-roe
newspaper kiosk	Zeitungskiosk	tsytoongs-kee-osk
post office	Post	posst
shop/store	Geschäft/Laden	gush-eft/lard'n
shoe shop	Schuhladen	shoo-lard'n
supermarket	Supermarkt	super-mahrkt

Staying in a Hotel

Do you have any vacancies?	Haben Sie noch Zimmer frei?	harb'n zee nokh tsimm-er-fry
with twin beds?	mit zwei Betten?	mitt tsvy bett'n
with a double bed?	mit einem Doppelbett?	mitt ine'm dopp'l-bet
with a bath?	mit Bad?	mitt bart
with a shower?	mit Dusche?	mitt doosh-uh
Wi-Fi?	WLAN?	way-lahn
I have a reservation	Ich habe eine Reservierung	ish harb-uh ine-uh rez-er-veer-oong
key	Schlüssel	shlooss'l
porter	Pförtner	pfert-ner

Eating Out

Do you have a table for…?	Haben sie einen Tisch für…?	harb'n zee tish foor
I would like to reserve a table	Ich möchte eine Reservierung machen	ish mer-shtuh ine-uh rezer-veer-oong makh'n
I'm a vegetarian	Ich bin Vegetarier	ish bin vegg-er-tah-ree-er
Excuse me!	Verzeihung!	fair-tsy-hoong
The bill, please	Die Rechnung, bitte	dee resh-noong bitt-uh
breakfast	Frühstück	froo-shtock
lunch	Mittagessen	mit-targ-ess'n
dinner	Abendessen	arb'nt-ess'n
bottle	Flasche	flush-uh
dish of the day	Tagesgericht	tahg-es-gur-isht
main dish	Hauptgericht	howpt-gur-isht
dessert	Nachtisch	nakhh-tish
cup	Tasse	tass-uh
wine list	Weinkarte	vine-kart-uh
glass	Glas	glars
spoon	Löffel	lerff'l
teaspoon	Teelöffel	tay-lerff'l
tip	Trinkgeld	trink-gelt
knife	Messer	mess-er
starter (appetizer)	Vorspeise	for-shpize-uh
plate	Teller	tell-er
fork	Gabel	gahb'l

Menu Decoder

Aal	arl	eel
Apfel	upf'l	apple
Apfelschorle	upf'l-shoorl-uh	apple juice with sparkling mineral water
Apfelsine	upf'l-seen-uh	orange
Aprikose	upri-kawz-uh	apricot
Artischocke	arti-shokh-uh-	artichoke
Aubergine	or-ber-jeen-uh	aubergine (eggplant)
Banane	bar-narn-uh	banana
Beefsteak	beef-stayk	steak
Bier	beer	beer
Bockwurst	bokh-voorst	a type of sausage
Bohnensuppe	burn-en-zoop-uh	bean soup
Branntwein	brant-vine	spirits
Bratkartoffeln	brat-kar-toff'ln	fried potatoes
Bratwurst	brat-voorst	fried sausage
Brötchen	bret-tchen	bread roll
Brot	brot	bread
Brühe	bruh-uh	broth
Butter	boot-ter	butter
Champignon	shum-pin-yong	mushroom
Currywurst	kha-ree-voorst	sausage with curry sauce
Dill	dill	dill
Ei	eye	egg
Eis	ice	ice/ice cream
Ente	ent-uh	duck
Erdbeeren	ayrt-beer'n	strawberries
Fisch	fish	fish
Forelle	for-ell-uh	trout
Frikadelle	frika-dayl-uh	rissole/hamburger
Garnele	gar-nayl-uh	prawn/shrimp
gebraten	g'braat'n	fried
gegrillt	g'grilt	grilled
gekocht	g'kokht	boiled
geräuchert	g'rowk-ert	smoked
Geflügel	g'floog'l	poultry
Gemüse	g'mooz-uh	vegetables
Gulasch	goo-lush	goulash
Gurke	goork-uh	gherkin
Hammelbraten	hamm'l-braat'n	roast mutton
Hähnchen	haynsh'n	chicken
Hering	hair-ing	herring
Honig	hoe-nikh	honey
Kaffee	kaf-fay	coffee
Kalbfleisch	kalp-flysh	veal
Kaninchen	ka-neensh'n	rabbit
Karpfen	karpf'n	carp
Kartoffelpüree	kar-toff'l-poor-ay	mashed potatoes
Käse	kayz-uh	cheese
Kaviar	kar-vee-ar	caviar
Knödel	k'nerd'l	noodle
Kopfsalat	kopf-zal-aat	lettuce
Krebs	krayps	crab
Kuchen	kookh'n	cake
Lachs	lahkhs	salmon
Leber	lay-ber	liver
mariniert	mari-neert	marinated

Marmelade	marmer-lard-uh	marmalade/jam
Milch	milsh	milk
Mineralwasser	minn-er-arl-vuss-er	mineral water
Olive	o-leev-uh	olive
Petersilie	payt-er-zee-li-uh	parsley
Pfeffer	pfeff-er	pepper
Pfirsich	pfir-zish	peach
Pflaumen	pflow-men	plum
Pommes frites	pomm-fritt	chips/French fries
Quark	kvark	soft cheese
Rindfleisch	rint-flysh	beef
Rippchen	rip-sh'n	cured pork rib
Rührei	rhoo-er-eye	scrambled eggs
Saft	zuft	juice
Salat	zal-aat	salad
Salz	zults	salt
Salzkartoffeln	zults-kar-toff'l	boiled potatoes
Sauerkirschen	zow-er-keersh'n	cherries
Sauerkraut	zow-er-krowt	sauerkraut
Sekt	zekt	sparkling wine
scharf	sharf	spicy
Schaschlik	shash-lik	kebab
Schlagsahne	shlahgg-zarn-uh	whipped cream
Schnittlauch	shnit-lowhkh	chives
Schnitzel	shnitz'l	veal or pork cutlet
Schweinefleisch	shvine-flysh	pork
Spargel	shparg'l	asparagus
Spiegelei	shpeeg'l-eye	fried egg
Spinat	shpin-art	spinach
Tee	tay	tea
Tomate	tom-art-uh	tomato
Wassermelone	vuss-er-me-lohn-uh	watermelon
Wein	vine	wine
Weintrauben	vine-trowb'n	grapes
Wiener Würstchen	veen-er voorst-sh'n	frankfurter
Zander	tsan-der	pike-perch
Zitrone	tsi-trohn-uh	lemon
Zucker	tsook-er	sugar
Zwiebel	tsveeb'l	onion

Numbers

0	null	nool
1	eins	eye'ns
2	zwei	tsvy
3	drei	dry
4	vier	feer
5	fünf	foonf
6	sechs	zex
7	sieben	zeeb'n
8	acht	uhkht
9	neun	noyn
10	zehn	tsayn
11	elf	elf
12	zwölf	tserlf
13	dreizehn	dry-tsayn
14	vierzehn	feer-tsayn
15	fünfzehn	foonf-tsayn
16	sechzehn	zex-tsayn
17	siebzehn	zeep-tsayn
18	achtzehn	uhkht-tsayn
19	neunzehn	noyn-tsayn
20	zwanzig	tsvunn-tsig
21	einundzwanzig	ine-oont-tsvunn-tsig
30	dreißig	dry-sig
40	vierzig	feer-sig
50	fünfzig	foonf-tsig
60	sechzig	zex-tsig
70	siebzig	zeep-tsig
80	achtzig	uhkht-tsig
90	neunzig	noyn-tsig
100	hundert	hoond't
1,000	tausend	towz'nt
1,000,000	eine Million	ine-uh mill-yon

Time

one minute	eine Minute	ine-uh min-oot-uh
one hour	eine Stunde	ine-uh shtoond-uh
half an hour	eine halbe Stunde	ine-uh hullb-uh shtoond-uh
Monday	Montag	mohn-targ
Tuesday	Dienstag	deens-targ
Wednesday	Mittwoch	mitt-vokh
Thursday	Donnerstag	donn-ers-targ
Friday	Freitag	fry-targ
Saturday	Samstag/ Sonnabend	zums-targ zonn-ah-bent
Sunday	Sonntag	zon-targ

DRIVER'S PHRASE BOOK

SOME COMMON ROAD SIGNS

Achtung	watch out
Anlieger frei	residents only
Autobahn	motorway
Autobahndreieck	motorway junction
Autobahnkreuz	motorway intersection
Bahnübergang	level crossing
Baustelle	roadworks
bei Frost Glatteisgefahr	icy in cold weather
bitte einordnen	get in lane
Bundesautobahn	federal motorway
Bundesstrasse	A-road/trunk road
Durchgangsverkehr	through traffic
Einbahnstrasse	one-way street
eingeschränktes Halteverbot	restricted parking
Fahrradweg	cycle path
Frostschäden	frost damage
Fussgänger	pedestrians
Fussgängerzone	pedestrianized precinct
Gefahr	danger
gefährliche Kreuzung	dangerous junction
gefährliche Kurve	dangerous bend
Gegenverkehr hat Vorfahrt	oncoming traffic has right of way
gesperrt für Fahrzeuge aller Art	closed to all vehicles
Halteverbot	no stopping
Höchstgeschwindigkeit	maximum speed
keine Zufahrt	no entry
Kreuzung	crossroads
Kriechspur	crawler lane
kurvenreiche Strecke	bends
Landstrasse	A-road/B-road
langsam fahren	drive slowly
Nebel	fog
nur für Busse	buses only
parken nur mit Parkscheibe	parking with parking disc only
Parkverbot	no parking
Radweg kreuzt	cycle track crossing
Raststätte	services area
rechts fahren	keep to the right
Sackgasse	no through road
schlechte Fahrbahn	bad surface
Schule	school
Schwerlastverkehr	heavy vehicles
Seitenstreifen nicht befahrbar	soft verges
Stadtmitte	town centre
starkes Gefälle	steep gradient
Stau	tailback/traffic jam
Steinschlag	beware of stone-chips
Strassenbahn	tram
Überholen verboten	no overtaking
Umgehungsstrasse	bypass
Umleitung	diversion
Unebenheiten	uneven surface
verengte Fahrbahn	road narrows
Vorfahrt gewähren	give way
Vorfahrtsstrasse	drivers on this road have priority
Zoll	customs

DIRECTIONS YOU MAY BE GIVEN

an der nächsten Ausfahrt	at the next junction
an der nächsten Kreuzung	at the next crossroads
erste Strasse rechts	first on the right
geradeaus	straight on
ladestation	charging station
links	on the left
links abbiegen	turn left
rechts	on the right
rechts abbiegen	turn right
vorbei an…	past the…
zweite Strasse links	second on the left

THINGS YOU'LL SEE

Ausfahrt	exit
Autowäsche	car wash
Benzin	petrol
bleifrei	lead free
Bremsflüssigkeit	brake fluid
Einfahrt	entrance/way in
Geschwindigkeits-beschränkung	speed limit
Luftdruck	air pressure
Münztank	coin-operated pump
Öl	oil
Parkhaus	multi-storey car park
Parkplatz	car park
Parkschein entnehmen	take a ticket
PKW	private car
Reifendruck	tyre pressure
Reparaturwerkstatt	garage/repairs
unverbleit	unleaded
verbleit	leaded
Waschstrasse	car wash
Wasser	water
Zapfsäule	petrol pump

USEFUL PHRASES

I need some petrol/diesel/oil/water
Ich brauche Benzin/Diesel/Öl/Wasser
ish browkhuh bentseen/deesul/url/Vasser

Fill it up, please!
Volltanken, bitte!
folltanken bittuh

20 litres of 4-star unleaded, please
Zwanzig Liter Super Bleifrei, bitte
tsvantsish leeter zooper bly-fry bittuh

Would you check the tyres, please?
Könnten Sie bitte die Reifen überprüfen?
kurnten zee bittuh dee rife-enooberproofen

Do you do repairs?
Machen sie Reparaturen?
makhen zee reparatooren

Can you repair the clutch?
Können sie die Kupplung reparieren?
kurnen zee dee kooploong repareeren

There is something wrong with the engine
Mit dem Motor stimmt etwas nicht
mit daym mohtor shtimmt etvuss nisht

The engine is overheating
Der Motor ist heissgelaufen
dair mohtor ist hice-gulowfen

I need a new tyre
Ich brauche einen neuen Reifen
ish browkhuh ine-en noyen rife-en

Can you replace this?
Haben Sie dafür einen Ersatz?
hahben zee dafoor ine-en airsats

The indicator is not working
Der Blinker funktioniert nicht
dair blinker foonkts-yoneert nisht

How long will it take?
Wie lange wird das dauern?
vee lang-uh veert dass dowern

Where can I park?
Wo kann ich parken?
vo kan ish parken

Can I park here?
Kann ich hier parken?
kan ish heer parken

I'd like to hire a car
Ich möchte ein Auto mieten
ish murshtuh ine owto meeten

I'd like an automatic/a manual
Ich möchte ein Auto mit Automatik/mit Handschaltung
ish murshtuh ine owto mit owtomahtik/mit hantshaltoong

Can we hire a baby/child seat?
Können wir einen Baby/Kindersitz mieten?
kurnnen veer ine-nen Baibee/Kindairzits meeten

How much is it for one day?
Was kostet es pro Tag?
Vuss kostet ess pro tahk

Where is the nearest petrol station?
Wo ist die nächste Tankstelle?
vo ist dee naykstuh tankshtelluh

How do I get to…?
Wie komme ich nach…?
vee komma ish nahkh

Is this the road to…?
Ist das die Strasse nach…?
ist dass dee shtrahssuh nahkh

Which is the quickest way to…?
Was ist der schnellste Weg zum…?
vuss ist dair shnelstuh vayk tsoo

USEFUL WORDS

bonnet	**die Motorhaube**	*mohtorhowbuh*
boot	**der Kofferraum**	*kofferrowm*
brake	**die Bremse**	*bremzuh*
breakdown	**die Panne**	*pannuh*
car	**das Auto**	*owto*
car park	**der Parkplatz**	*parkplats*
(multi-storey)	**das Parkhaus**	*parkhowss*
caravan	**der Wohnwagen**	*vohn-vahgen*
clutch	**die Kupplung**	*kooploong*
crossroads	**die Kreuzung**	*kroytsoong*
drive (verb)	**fahren**	*faren*
engine	**der Motor**	*mohtor*
exhaust	**der Auspuff**	*owss-poof*
fan belt	**der Keilriemen**	*kile-reemen*
garage (for repairs)	**die Werkstatt**	*vairkshtat*
(for petrol)	**die Tankstelle**	*tankshtelluh*
gear	**der Gang**	*gang*
gears/gear box	**das Getriebe**	*gutreebuh*
headlights	**die Scheinwerfer**	*shine-vairfer*
indicator	**der Blinker**	*blinker*
junction	**die Kreuzung**	*kroytsoong*
(motorway entry)	**die Auffahrt**	*owf-fart*
(motorway exit)	**die Ausfahrt**	*owss-fart*
licence	**der Führerschein**	*fⱽrer-shine*
lorry	**der Lastwagen**	*last-vahgen*
motorbike	**das Motorrad**	*motor-raht*
motorway	**die Autobahn**	*owtoh-bahn*
number plate	**das Nummernschild**	*noom mern-shilt*
parking meter	**die Parkuhr**	*park-oor*
parking ticket	**der Strafzettel**	*shtrahf-tsettel*
petrol	**das Benzin**	*bentseen*
petrol station	**die Tankstelle**	*tankshtelluh*
rear lights	**das Rücklicht**	*rooklisht*
road	**die Strasse**	*shtrahssuh*
spark plug	**die Zündkerze**	*tsⱽnt-kairtsuh*
speed	**die Geschwindigkeit**	*gush vindish-kite*
speedometer	**der Tacho(meter)**	*takho(mayter)*
steering wheel	**das Lenkrad**	*lenkraht*
tow	**abschleppen**	*apshleppen*
traffic lights	**die Ampel**	*ampel*
trailer	**der Anhänger**	*anheng-er*
tyre	**der Reifen**	*rife-en*
van	**der Lieferwagen**	*leefer-vahgen*
wheel	**das Rad**	*raht*
windscreen	**die Windschutz- scheibe**	*vint-shoots- shybuh*
windscreen wiper	**der Scheibenwischer**	*shyben- visher*